UNMENTIONABLES

WORLDING THE MIDDLE EAST

Unmentionables

TEXTILES, GARMENT WORK,
AND THE SYRIAN AMERICAN
WORKING CLASS

Stacy D. Fahrenthold

STANFORD UNIVERSITY PRESS
STANFORD, CALIFORNIA

Stanford University Press
Stanford, California

© 2025 by Stacy Diane Fahrenthold. All rights reserved.

No part of this book may be reproduced or transmitted in any form or by any means, electronic or mechanical, including photocopying and recording, or in any information storage or retrieval system, without the prior written permission of Stanford University Press.

This book has been partially underwritten by the Susan Groag Bell Publication Fund in Women's History. For more information on the fund, please see www.sup.org/bellfund.

Printed in the United States of America on acid-free, archival-quality paper.

Library of Congress Cataloging-in-Publication Data
Names: Fahrenthold, Stacy D., author.
Title: Unmentionables : textiles, garment work, and the Syrian American working class / Stacy D. Fahrenthold.
Other titles: Worlding the Middle East.
Description: Stanford, California : Stanford University Press, [2025] | Series: Worlding the Middle East | Includes bibliographical references and index.
Identifiers: LCCN 2024029433 (print) | LCCN 2024029434 (ebook) | ISBN 9781503638082 (cloth) | ISBN 9781503641303 (paperback) | ISBN 9781503641310 (ebook)
Subjects: LCSH: Syrian Americans—History. | Immigrants—United States—History. | Working class—United States—History. | Textile workers—United States—History. | Textile industry—United States—History. | United States—Emigration and immigration—History. | Syria—Emigration and immigration—History.
Classification: LCC E184.S98 F35 2025 (print) | LCC E184.S98 (ebook)
LC record available at https://lccn.loc.gov/2024029433
LC ebook record available at https://lccn.loc.gov/2024029434

Cover design: Gabriele Wilson
Cover photograph: Room of women at sewing machines, ca. 1930 (photographer unknown), Faris and Yamna Naff Arab American Collection, Archives Center, National Museum of American History, Smithsonian Institution

For Dwight Allen Fahrenthold

CONTENTS

Acknowledgments	ix
INTRODUCTION Looking for Work	1
1 Snowballs and Bayonets *The Syrian Strikers of Lawrence*	24
2 Mutual Aid *Syrian Societies in Industrial Massachusetts*	58
3 The Syrian Shop *Garment Manufacturing in New York City*	88
4 Laboring for Empire *Madeira Island's* Fase Síria	125
5 Logistics *Selling Textiles in the US-Mexico Borderlands*	156
CONCLUSION Syrian Shops for the Syrians	187
Notes	201
Bibliography	263
Index	283

ACKNOWLEDGMENTS

AS USUAL, I OWE AN enormous debt of gratitude to the thinkers in whose company I have learned, thought about, and discussed work and labor, race, and diaspora capitalism over the last several years. First, I would like to thank colleagues, mentors, and friends who generously read and critiqued early iterations of this work, affording me opportunities to improve it, including Reem Bailony, Lily Balloffet, Lauren Banko, Tylor Brand, Ryan Cartwright, Annia Ciezadlo, Corrie Decker, Edward Dickinson, Jaimey Fisher, Liza Grandia, Milmon Harrison, Ashley Johnson Bavery, Ilham Khuri-Makdisi, Lisa Materson, Devi Mays, José Juan Pérez Meléndez, Chris Rominger, Marian Schlotterbeck, Archana Venkatesan, and Gina Werfel. As I completed this project, I benefited from crucial mentorship by Sarah M. A. Gualtieri and Elizabeth Thompson, and from innumerable reading recommendations, gestures of support, and conversations with scholars like Ziad Abu-Rish, Adey Almohsen, Andrew Arsan, Diogo Bercito, Isa Blumi, Claude Boustany, Lâle Can, Lori Clune, Omnia El Shakry, Vladimir Hamed-Troyansky, Marya Hannun, Pauline Homsi Vinson, Donna Gabaccia, Julie Greene, David Gutman, Haakon Ikonomou, Suad Joseph, Charlotte Karem Albrecht, Akram Khater, Janet Klein, Owain Lawson, Devin Naar, Jacob Norris, Benjamin Nobbs-Thiessen, Ramazan Hakkı Öztan, Uğur Peçe, Mezna Qato, Nicole Ranganath, Elizabeth Saylor, Nadya Sbaiti, Sudipta Sen, Charles Sills, Matthew Stiffler, Kathy Stuart, Nefertiti Takla, Randa Tawil, Baki Tezcan, Benjamin Thomas White, and Kenyon Zimmer.

Then there are the people with whom I cowrote in our writing group, whose solidarity and energy has spilled into these pages, including Adam Anderson, Ayşe Baltacıoğlu-Brammer, Jazmine Contreras, Mehdi Faraji, Jennifer Foray, Maddalena Marinari, Johanna Mellis, Laurie Pearce, Nisrine Rahal, and Emmanuelle Salgues.

I would like to thank the archivists and librarians who have helped me make sense of this history. At the Lawrence History Center, I learned from conversations with Kathy Flynn, Amita Kiley, and Susan Grabsky, and I am grateful for their preservation of life histories in the Immigrant City (in an unexpected twist, Kathy reintroduced me to my great-great-grandfather, James, who worked alongside some of this book's characters a century ago). Librarians at the Arthur and Elizabeth Schlesinger Library on the History of Women in America facilitated this work in its earliest stages in 2008 by assisting me with the records of the Syrian Ladies' Aid Society of Boston. Archivists and staff at the Arab American National Museum, Immigration History Research Center Archives, Jafet Memorial Library at the American University of Beirut, the National Museum of American History Archives Center, the Immigration History Research Center Archives at University of Minnesota, the Direção Regional do Arquivo e Biblioteca da Madeira, and Widener Library's Middle Eastern Division at Harvard University were also crucial interlocutors as I hemmed this work together. Special thanks go to Matthew Stiffler (at AANM), Samar Mikati Kaissi and Hiba Farhat (at AUB), Daniel Necas (at IHRCA), and Regina Isabel Oliveira (at DRABM) for assistance with their collections. I am also deeply appreciative of individuals who trusted this work by corresponding with me or by sharing life histories, photos, or family papers including George Ellenbogen, Nolan Kane and Hazel Elmendorf, Bob Goodhouse, and Charles Samaha. I am also grateful to several individuals who reached out to me privately to share stories about their mothers, aunts, great-uncles, and grandfathers; your family histories and apocryphal lore enriched this research with a powerful reminder about how pasts (remembered or forgotten) shape presence. Historical writing is never a solo endeavor, and all of you have been my favorite community.

Workshop presentations at the Massachusetts Historical Society, the Newberry Library Latino/a and Borderlands History Seminar, the Center for Arab American Studies at the University of Michigan, Dearborn, the University of Neuchatel, Universität Bern, the UC Davis Humanities Institute, and the UC Davis Women's and Gender History Program gave me space to sound out ideas as well as the push to work through them. A fellowship from the National Endowment for the Humanities and further support from the University of California Davis Humanities Institute generated precious space and time for putting pen to paper. I would like to acknowledge research assistance by Bruna Lauermann as well as three student research assistants at the University of California Davis and California State University, Fresno. And at Stanford University Press, I have relied upon and benefited from the labors of Kate Wahl, Cat Ng Pavel, Thane Hale, Catherine Mallon, Gabriele Wilson, Chris Peterson, and three anonymous peer reviewers who helped me fathom the global frame of Syrian work and Syrian workers. My thanks are due to Molly Reed for her thoughtful editorial work as I completed the manuscript, and Tim DeBold for indexing. Finally, I am deeply grateful to David Schultz, whose belief in my work has never wavered. Thank you.

Dedicated to my brother, Dwight, who took pride in his labor and for whom the right to move formed the basis of human dignity. This one's for you.

INTRODUCTION

LOOKING FOR WORK

There are three men. One of them likes to be in the shade all the time.
Answer: snow and ice.
The second is an old man, but as soon as he reaches
    old age he becomes young again.
Answer: the moon.
The third man is a dead man, and yet he speaks to live men all the time.
Answer: writing in a book.

RIDDLE RECORDED IN BOSTON'S SYRIAN QUARTER, 1903.[1]

JANUARY 29, 1912—THE MOON WAS nearly full the night before John Ramey died. The snow was several days old now, hardened with daily melt into a thick sheet of ice that refracted the moonlight surrounding the checkpoint. A makeshift garrison protected state guardsmen who had come to Lawrence, Massachusetts, to stop rioters from tossing the ice through mill windows. This billet was at the corner of Elm Street, a throughfare in Lawrence's Syrian Quarter. "That's where they found the dynamite," one militiaman said to another, tipping back a bottle of local *araq* to kill the cold. Behind them, a cluster of boys assembled unnoticed in preparation for an ambush. The boys crept closer, gathering snow to build an arsenal of projectiles. One of them yelled, and they started chucking snowballs at the men occupying their neighborhood. Startled, the militia broke formation and, in the ensuing chaos, guardsmen began frantically chasing their assailants through the Syrian tenements. They captured two Syrian boys, so-called child operatives employed by the American Woolen Company (AWC) then on strike with the Industrial Workers of the World (IWW). Najib Kalil, age fifteen, and Abdallah Najjum, age sixteen, were detained at the mill building overnight, guarded by armed men deployed by the state. The rest of the Syrian boys fled into the night, but within an hour Kalil's and Najjum's fathers—also AWC strikers—joined an angry crowd that descended on the garrison. Surrounding the checkpoint and banging pots and pans, they woke up the city and demanded the boys' release. A standoff resulted. And John Ramey was observed there, holding at the front.

In later sworn testimony, police and state officials squabbled over whether John Ramey was sixteen, eighteen, or twenty years old.[2] Some said he was among those boys who had thrown ice at the garrison and that he returned with a seething mob after his friends were detained. Others claimed he was never there. What is certain is that the next day—January 30, at noon—John marched at the head of a strike demonstration through the mill zone, carrying the cornet he played with the city's Syrian Drum Corps. Ramey led hundreds of Syrians to the canal separating the AWC factories from the tenements known as the Syrian Quarter. As demonstrators pushed the armed militiamen across the canal bridge, Ramey was bayoneted twice: in the shoulder and back. He fled home to his parents, who brought him to a hospital where he died from his injuries. Fearing a retaliatory insurrection, officials banned public assembly and locked down the city. But that night, the moon reached fullness as the Syrian Drum Corps marched on the streets, men playing their drums and women at the flanks, banging pots and pans. Midnight marches came every night that followed, as grieving Syrian strikers reminded Lawrence about their slain cornet player. John Ramey's body was interred at St. Anthony's Maronite Church. The garrisons stayed. Neighborhood boys continued to pelt soldiers with snowballs.

This is what we know about John Ramey. He was born in Falougha, in Ottoman Mount Lebanon, and he died by bayonet in Lawrence, one of three people killed during the Bread and Roses Strike of 1912. Ramey's story is repeated everywhere one reads about the Syrian immigrant working class, inflected a little differently each time. There's a version where John is marching at the militias at the head of an IWW contingent; another where he is an innocent bystander, not a striker at all. In one account, John witnesses a police officer brutalizing a Syrian woman and is stabbed in the back as he defends her. John Ramey, an anarchist villain engaging in deportable offenses; John Ramey, a factory boy murdered for tossing snowballs at police.[3] In each of these stories, Ramey's ghost speaks for the living, put to work in the memorialization of the strike credited with making the American working class. John Ramey offers a glimpse into Syrian proletarian life in the *mahjar* (diaspora); an entirely new history awaits behind him.[4]

This book explores the making of the global Syrian working class, situating Arab textile workers within the fields of labor history, migration studies, and critical studies of capitalism.[5] It also traces the development of the Syrian textile industries in the mahjar. As weavers, stitchers, garment workers, or peddlers, Syrian migrants fed a transnational textile trade directed by Syrian merchants. These workers had a vastly different experience of the mahjar from that celebrated by cultural elites of the time. This is revealed in Syrian American print culture and the numerous serials, novels, and books that champion titans of Syrian commerce: the chiefs (*zuʿama*) of émigré politics, the intellectual luminaries of the Pen League (*al-Rabita al-Qalamiyya*), or the nostalgic, pioneering figure of the pack peddler. Each of these figures told a specific history of the mahjar, portraying emigrants as shrewd and entrepreneurial, upwardly mobile, racially respectable, hardworking, and devoted to living in two worlds, both Syrian and American. Early histories of this diaspora call Syrians "incurable emigrants and traders," connecting their arrival in America to "an age-long movement, a chapter in a long series of migrations" dating back to the Phoenicians.[6] Syrians "did not usually take up factory employment" and are remembered for their commercial ventures instead.[7] "Profiting by the special aptitudes of their race and prompted by wanderlust and the desire for profitable trade," historian Philip Khuri Hitti wrote in 1924, "business is their lodestar . . . no nook of the world escapes them."[8] Hitti published *The Syrians in America* the same year that the 1924 Immigration Act imposed quota restrictions on new arrivals, necessitating a migration story staked on racial respectability and Arab contributions to America.[9]

Yet, the well-known arc of mahjari historical writing and its fixation with commerce as its central driver is discordant with evidence that factory labor formed both the bones and sinews of the mahjar's economy. Syrian factory operatives struck and shut down factories in Lawrence in 1912, 1919,

1921, and 1924; in Paterson in 1913, 1919, and 1924; and in New York City in 1913, 1916, 1919, and through the 1930s. In New England mill towns, Syrians formed a crucial part of woolens, leather, silk, and cotton broadcloth industries, a unit capable of organizing across multiple mills and taking a strike general. Many labor unions saw Syrians as a key constituency, and Syrian workers joined the Industrial Workers of the World (IWW), the International Ladies' Garment Workers' Union, and the Amalgamated Clothing Workers of America. However, the conservative wings of the American labor movement, including the United Textile Workers (UTW, an American Federation of Labor affiliate) viewed them as a racial threat to native labor. The AFL's craft unionism sought to protect skilled white industrial workers from immigrant labor, a strategy that was "exclusionary by nature" and led the union to endorse instruments like hiring controls, immigration restrictions, and deportations. Xenophobic organizers joined employers in stereotyping Syrians as irredeemable radicals.[10] During a 1919 silk strike in Paterson, New Jersey, UTW vice president Thomas McMahon condemned Syrian weavers linked to the IWW, calling them "traitors in the industrial movement" who "through their un-American organizations . . . and every underhanded method seek to arouse class hatreds and racial animosities."[11] These weavers stopped work to protest McMahon's refusal to discuss their demands for a forty-four-hour work week. Two thousand of them walked off the job, undermining UTW's bargaining power with Paterson's silk manufacturers. Trade unions were not only aware of the numbers of Syrian workers in woolens, cotton, and silks but appreciated that Syrian organizers could quickly mobilize 3,000 workers in Lawrence, or 5,000 in New York, Brooklyn, or Paterson.

In addition to working for U.S. firms, Syrian immigrants, particularly young women in garment work, were employed in factories established by other Syrians. The so-called "Syrian shops" (as unions called them) appeared in New York, New Jersey, and Massachusetts, established by émigré merchants who had followed Syrian textile workers abroad. New factories emerged as the Syrian merchant-manufacturer class scaled up, employing anywhere from a few dozen to a thousand people. Most of these factories produced white goods: undergarments, lingerie, pajamas, and household linens with lace or hand embroidery. Of all these goods, the Syrian kimono was most iconic, a collarless long robe that opened in the front, adapted to American tastes from its Syrian skandarani silk counterpart. The kimono

FIGURE 1. Portrait of an Unidentified Syrian Operative, Ayer Mill, American Woolen Company, Lawrence, MA, circa 1914–1922. Source: Lawrence History Center Photography Collection.

created a new émigré industrial elite, the so-called kimono kings of New York: Mikha'il Arida, Abdalla Barsa, and Elias Mouakad, among others.[12] Popular writings on the mahjar often begin here, with a Carlylean fascination with émigré merchant-manufacturers, great men with rags-to-riches stories, who achieved immense wealth, status, and power. The workers who stitched these pieces are effaced from these narratives; the presence of Syrian women workers in the garment factories was as "unmentionable" as the lingerie they produced. Once finished, the Syrian American kimono joined the abundance of white goods in the suitcases of Syrian pack peddlers.

The Syrian peddler is the next hero of the celebratory mahjar story: he is a humble protagonist, an appealing narrator, and a symbol for the migrant community's upward social mobility. The peddler's hegemony similarly originated in the laudatory journalism of the early twentieth century, establishing a cultural heritage which has informed successive generations of scholarship. Writing of Syrian peddlers in 1921, Syrian American journalist Sallum Mukarzil described him as a "pioneer of Syrian trade and the chief factor in its development." Working with Syrian merchant-manufacturers across the United States and Latin America, peddlers discovered and expanded markets; if the mahjar was a human body, Mukarzil reasoned, peddlers "are like the eyes with which to see what is around it, to notice the markets, and to move its feet forward."[13] In subsequent historical writing, the peddler became a romantic figure; his appeal derived from the perception that he was untethered to the struggles of industrial wage labor.[14] He was a symbol of success as well as a representation of an alternative destiny, a totem to economic freedom in a mahjar where many actually experienced wage precarity. Notably, these representations were invariably male, though peddling was also women's work.[15] Meanwhile, new scholarship contests the peddler's hegemony as *the* diaspora story that matters, proposing plural Arab American histories in place of Mayflowerist reductions.[16] Though once thought of as merchants in miniature, peddlers were also textile workers, the final link in a supply chain upon which the rest of the industry depended.

A history of the mahjar's textile industries and the people who forged them, this book examines how Syrians working in textiles navigated processes of class formation, racialization, immigration restriction, and labor contestation. The mahjar's textile industry both originated in and depended on a hemispheric labor economy which doubled as its primary commodity market. Syrian merchant-manufacturers directed the influx of new Syrian migrants, who picked up either factory work or peddling to feed the industry. The continuous, circular migration of these workers enabled the expansion of Syrian manufacturing across the hemisphere, reaching global scale by the early 1920s. Syrians working in all facets of the textile industries navigated the politics of class, race, and gender—politics which defined the Syrian community's right to belong in America. Émigré merchant-manufacturers cultivated claims to mainstream American whiteness; prominent Syrian Americans petitioned U.S. courts "to prove their status as 'white persons,'" most memorably by supporting the 1915 appellate case of George Dow.[17] In New York City, Syrian American manufacturers moved capably among chambers of commerce, trade commissions, and regulatory bodies to defend their commercial interests. Meanwhile, Syrian factory workers found themselves marked as racially other, perceived by U.S. employers as an insular minority to be leveraged against native-born workers, and by unions as a threat. This position led them in two directions: into union-resistant Syrian shops, or, alternatively, into the radical wings of the labor movement. Syrian peddlers navigated the liminalities of situational whiteness, maintaining their legibility through multiple passports and letters of marque signed by merchant elites, or by cultivating relationships with consular staff and plugging their trade into American narratives about expansion and free trade. Syrian American class formation was also deeply gendered: while the majority of Syrian textile and garment workers were women, the industry's celebrated heroes are all men. This book illustrates how Syrian women's work in textiles, their management of labor and mutual aid networks, and their strike activities sustained Syrian textiles in the mahjar. It also addresses the politics of these workers' erasure, questioning the class politics that rendered them unmentionable.

While historians have long understood the significance of textiles to the early Syrian diaspora, both structural theories of class and the contours of available archives have shaped how Syrian textile workers are remembered. A focus on class as a structural location rather than a set of social relations influenced classic economic histories of the Middle East and its diasporas, starting with a definition of class as a direct economic relationship to the means of production. Immigrant workers were defined as working class if they traded labor power for wages in a factory setting; this structural relationship presumes workplaces as central to class belonging at the expense of all other spheres of activity that uphold, maintain, and facilitate waged work: households, religious institutions, mutual aid networks, welfare organizations, or other sites of unpaid labor.[18] Put another way, in Syrian American working communities, spaces beyond the factory floor were most generative of class identity and consciousness. This was especially true for women workers as they took on economic roles in their communities in addition to waged factory work. Their labors were both waged and unwaged. These spaces of class identity and organizing cannot be reconstructed in major institutional archives like employer records or the files of trade unions.[19]

Available archival collections can also only partly explain the elision of workers from the mahjar's historiography. The mahjar's vast print cultural footprint, featuring dozens of serials, newspapers, literary works, and small-run publishing houses, expanded across multiple continents yet narrowly recorded the perspectives of metropolitan elites and their politics.[20] From the Ottoman period through interwar European Mandates, Syrians in the Americas campaigned for development, national liberation, and anticolonialism from abroad.[21] This politics relied on the networks and technologies of a transnational professional class that was, at best, uneasy about groups who contested racial respectability tropes and at worst, hostile to them.[22] Syrian workers shutting down factories, factory women contesting paternalistic nationalisms, and child operatives throwing snowballs at the cops challenged the image of a mahjar cooperating with capital in a hemispheric project of racial uplift. The sources that make up this book, therefore, come from the records of Syrian American workers' societies, individual life histories, union records, employment files, business ledgers, and consular correspondence, in addition to print culture. What results is a new history of Syrian transnationalism centered on the textile industry, its contours across the Arab Atlantic, and the workers who sustained it.

This book takes its shape by tracing the movement of people and textile goods through one interconnected route across the Arab Atlantic, shaped by the passenger steamship routes running from Beirut to Marseille, and onward to New York City and Veracruz. This was never the only route that shaped the hemispheric mahjar; others brought Syrian, Lebanese, and Palestinian migrants to the Caribbean, to Central and South America, or to West Africa. But to make sense of the mahjar's textile industries, one must build on the geography set forth by the recognizable imprints of its economic activity: the movement of silk weavers and lace makers; the routes of peddlers; the couriering of raw linen, cotton yarns, silk cocoons, and fabrics; Syrian merchant-manufacturers pursuing global supply chains; and the Syrian jobbers who directed the flow of all of them.

A transatlantic journey from Beirut took between twenty-eight and thirty-two days by steamship, making stops at Mediterranean and Atlantic ports which became important nodes in the mahjar's textile economy. For Syrian immigrants traveling in third class, the experience of passage was almost never linear.[23] There were disruptions and setbacks. There were prolonged quarantines, denied entries, and deportations. There was fraud, perpetrated sometimes by malicious smugglers but also by marginalized people, motivated by self-preservation. Though the moment of arrival often symbolized the telos of immigration in popular accounts, a substantial historiography demonstrates that passage was a process that transformed the people who endured it.[24] A steamship ticket could turn into weeks or months of delay, of negotiating contradictory migration regimes, of running out of money or luck along the way. The trip required a routinized, high-stakes performance of identity at each waystation.[25] At waypoints, entry ports, or land borders, officials responsible for vetting new immigrants demonstrated preferences for the right documents or witness letters. Savvy travelers consulted mahjari whisper networks or advice literature, committing the correct answers to memory.[26]

Beirut was the departure port for most Syrian emigrants before 1914. An Ottoman seaport moving both commerce and passenger traffic, the imperial government wavered between a liberal stance on emigration control and concerns about the increasing numbers of Arab departures.[27] After departing Beirut, the next stop for emigrants was usually Marseille. The French port city had a "virtual monopoly on the transit of Syrians" to the Americas; 2,000 to 4,000 emigrants moved through annually in the 1890s, rising to 10,000 per year by 1913.[28] Using port records, Céline Regnard reveals, "Syrian emigrants were a majority among the transient populations in Marseille," and boardinghouses, migration agents, and textile merchants proliferated there to serve them as they awaited their transfer to America.[29] Recollecting his family history from Boston, Charles (Khalil) Shagoury described how his father, Joseph, arrived in Marseille from Damascus in 1906 with wife, Wadia, and two small children.[30] French officials detained Joseph on suspicion of trachoma, a suspicion Charles's sister, Laurice Shagoury Maloley, attributed not to actual illness but to a "scam" perpetrated against Syrians "perceived to have some money."[31] His wife and children proceeded to the United States, leaving Joseph behind in France. After several weeks, Joseph made an agreement with a Syrian merchant from Boston, who paid his passage in exchange for his work as a textile peddler.[32] Though such arrangements felt improvised and were remembered as such, they were becoming institutional: by 1920, several Syrian textile merchants had opened stores in Marseille to recruit potential workers before their arrival in America.[33]

Leaving Europe, Syrian migrants proceeded to America, usually arriving in New York to be processed at Ellis Island. Upon arrival, they could expect invasive medical testing and interviews about their family status or financial circumstances. The Shagoury family was no exception. Arriving without her husband, Wadia Shagoury knew she was at risk of rejection. On the ship, she handed one of her two infant children off to another family, changing that child's surname to Homsy as a result.[34] Wadia and her remaining infant were held at Ellis Island for eighteen hours, where they "underwent extensive physical examination, and endless questioning and filling out forms."[35] Her daughter, Laurice Maloley, recalls in a family history that Wadia was cleared only when a relative from Boston came to her rescue.[36] Once in Massachusetts, Wadia worked at a Boston dress factory; her husband, Joseph, arrived several weeks later and peddled table linens, underwear, and children's apparel.[37]

Each step of the Shagoury family's passage meant walking a categorical tightrope: to avoid being deemed "likely to become a public charge" and deported, immigrants needed to demonstrate a connection to a job, or a relative, and prove their medical and racial fitness. Joseph's delay in France, Wadia's concern about arriving with two children and no husband, and the role of New England Syrians in vouching for them amounted to a performance of identity beyond the Ottoman passports they carried. That the Shagourys understood how to navigate these performances illustrates how circuits of knowledge also moved along this corridor via networks of kith and kin.[38] Despite their successes, the threat of removal loomed for years: Wadia resisted her children's suggestions that she apply for U.S. citizenship for decades because her immigration papers erroneously "listed her as a widow with one child."[39] Deportation was a very real risk. In an oral history taken in Lawrence, Massachusetts, the grandson of Shehadi Batal describes how Shehadi was jailed for eleven days and then deported to Marseille because he had been "evasive" during his interview at Ellis Island. "He was stuck in France with no money" to either proceed to America or return home to Mashghara, Lebanon. Shehadi took odd jobs in town, saving for another ticket and living in a spare room at the docks. He got lucky when he met "a man from Worcester called Forsley," who connected him to another relative in Massachusetts who sponsored his visa under an assumed name.[40] Shehadi worked sweeping floors in a Worcester textile mill before again encountering trouble with his immigration status; he quit the factory and began selling "holy pictures" and trinkets as a peddler.[41] With disruptions, setbacks, and guile, the Shagoury and Batal families navigated the Marseille–New York line. For others, the route from Marseille turned to the south.

Arriving at the Mexican port of Veracruz in the 1890s, Syrian merchants and their peddling networks became an increasingly visible community in Mexico's textile trades. Syrian merchants in Veracruz, Yucatán, Mexico City, and the northern borderlands states managed one branch of a hemispheric textile trade remarked on by historians of Argentina, Brazil, Chile, Central America, and the United States.[42] They imported textile goods from Europe and the Middle East and later from Syrian-owned factories in the United States or Latin America. This trade extended into the U.S.-Mexico borderlands, a distinct commercial zone where peddlers organized to supply Mexican retailers with goods sourced from around the mahjar.

Whether headed for New York City, Veracruz, or another port on the Atlantic, hundreds of thousands of Syrians, Lebanese, and Palestinians moved through this migration corridor.[43] While most passengers stayed aboard when ships stopped at Madeira or the Azores, a few disembarked at these ports as well. In 1924, Anthony Ramey was one of them. Anthony grew up in Lawrence, Massachusetts, until his parents caught him with a local girl and decided to send him home to Falougha. Anthony spent a year in Lebanon; he married there, sold off some family properties, and returned to Massachusetts with his bride to open a butcher shop. In an oral history interview, Anthony described his shore leave on the island of Terceira, where he bumped into an Azorean teenager also from Massachusetts: "He's looking at me, and I'm looking at him. And I says, 'I should know this fellow.' He tells me 'I'm from Lowell but I used to go to Lawrence [for work] and used to hang around Valley Street.' And I says 'wait a minute, I used to meet you up at Merrimack Park at the dance hall!'"[44] The pair spent the day together near São Miguel, where Anthony learned his companion was fleeing a felony charge; this was the reason his parents sent him to Terceira. As the pair returned to the port that evening, they passed right by the storefronts of Mallouk Bros. and K. W. Saydah and Co.: Syrian embroidery firms whose factories appeared on the islands and whose goods sat below deck on Anthony's ship, bound for Beirut.

Such points of connection recur in the archives of Syrian migration. Each instance feels spontaneous, but the total sum reveals a mahjar linked by specific patterns of migration, work, capitalist accumulation, and debt. In addition to the route explored in this book—Beirut, Marseille, Funchal, New York, Boston, Veracruz—Syrian merchants conducted similar patterns of migration and trade between Mediterranean Europe and French

West Africa, as well as in the Philippines, China, and Australia.[45] Furthermore, these routes did not end with seaports but joined railway networks leading Syrians across continents: into the U.S. Midwest, the U.S.-Mexico borderlands, or Argentina's interior.[46] But as this work seeks to make sense of *this* route across the Arab Atlantic through its industrial patterns, one turns now to the specific labor economies that confronted Syrian workers upon arrival.

TATREEZ, KIMONO, KASHEH:
THE MAHJAR'S TEXTILE LABOR ECONOMY

This book explores diverse forms of labor in mahjari textile production, and its chapters are organized by global labor and material supply chains. This diaspora's economy was arranged around the movement of raw silk, cotton, and linen, handworked laces and other textile components, finished undergarments or ready-wear clothing, and workers, all circulating the Arab Atlantic. Syrian merchant-manufacturers, notably in New York City's Garment District, directed this movement, managing supply chains and shifting sites of production in pursuit of favorable trade conditions.

A global labor history approach allows for deeper study of Syrian labor and the networks which developed, sustained, and channeled it. As Marcel Van der Linden describes: "The working class consists of all carriers of labor power whose labor power is sold or hired out to employers... whether under economic or noneconomic compulsion, regardless of whether these carriers of labor power are themselves selling or hiring out their labor power and also regardless of whether these carriers themselves own means of production."[47] Considering the relations between employers and laborers at the point of production, alongside circuits of recruitment, migration, credit, and mutual aid, reveals the complex dynamics between the factory floor and the world beyond it. This approach also creates room to examine the emergence of the mahjar's merchant elites and to consider forms of labor often treated as anomalies in labor history, specifically, women and girls engaged in home work.

Just as this book is about the development of a global Syrian working class, it is also a history of Syrian merchant-manufacturers, a capitalist class that assumed control over critical textile supply chains after 1910. Merchant capitalism, defined here as direct merchant control over supply chains, allowed Syrian firms to squeeze vendors producing commodities and to relocate sites of production as needed. Building on Wallerstein's theory of the commodity chain as "a network of labor and production processes whose end result is a finished commodity," Nelson Lichtenstein terms this direct merchant control "supply-chain power."[48] Supply-chain power was a central organizing principle for the Syrian textile industry: merchant-manufacturers increasingly dominated the diaspora's textile labor market, manufacturing sector, and retail networks. This section briefly examines each stage of this process: labor economy, manufacturing, and retail networks in the mahjar.

Upon arrival in the Americas, Syrian labor migrants typically entered one of two sectors in the textile industry: manufacturing or retail. Many Syrians employed in spinning, weaving, and garment sectors had performed similar work in the Middle East prior to emigration, and scholars describe how foreknowledge of silk processing, weaving, or needlework may have made some Syrians more mobile than their counterparts who lacked this expertise.[49] However, first-time proletarians (both women and men) were also prevalent across the industry, especially in woolens, shoe leathers, piecework, or the needlework sectors. Most Arab workers came abroad in pursuit of better wages and steady work, encouraged further by Beirut's growing passenger steamship traffic, a global shift in favor of international labor migration and, increasingly, the presence of Syrian ethnic communities abroad.[50] According to a 1911 industry conditions survey by the U.S. Immigration Commission, nearly half (46.7 percent) of Syrian men working in U.S. textiles had prior experience in Syrian factories. The rate among Syrian women workers was 19 percent; most of the rest listed as "no occupation" prior to emigration. Most Syrian women who joined American textile firms performed "unskilled" tasks like garment stitching, which were considered heritage crafts in the Middle East.[51] In essence, the textile work carried out by Syrian women in America in the early twentieth century represented a new form of labor commoditization, transforming work that was once done within households into standardized, industrial production.

Textile labor in the mahjar did not solely occur in factory settings. Syrian women continued to do various sorts of home textile production, including seamstressing, hemming, lacemaking, and hand embroidery (*tatreez*). The latter underwent a transformation in Syria, Mount Lebanon, and Palestine in the decades before mass emigration: the arrival of imported machine yarns led to the commoditization of Syrian lace and embroideries, and Syrian women who once hand spun thread for household use began to accept piecework contracts with metropolitan merchants.[52] This trend followed Syrian women to the mahjar, where their lace and needlework designs became marketable commodities alongside laces from Irish, Florentine, Philippine, or Madeiran textile goods. Needlework served as an economic lifeline for Syrian families in the mahjar; it was a hand skill that resisted full mechanization and could be performed at home, often amid other sorts of household economic production. In 1901, the U.S. Immigration Commission reported that "if the man goes peddling . . . his wife and children will find shelter with some poor family from their own village and . . . turn their attention to the manufacture and sale of lace which all Syrian women and girls can make."[53] Syrian merchant-manufacturers delivered yarns to these working households, where women worked them into cuffs and collars, appliques, or edging trim.[54] The laces would be added to garments in the Syrian shops and consigned to peddlers who distributed them to wholesale or retail markets across state lines or international borders. Charlotte Karem Albrecht articulates the gendered dimensions of this sector perfectly: "Peddling relied on Syrian women not only as peddlers but also as those who labored in multiple ways to make peddling a profitable occupation."[55] Their labor was rarely recorded in state archives. Writing of Syrian and Ottoman Sephardi immigrants, Devi Mays argues, "It is all too easy to overlook the migrant women . . . who appear as 'homemakers' on all official documents but who worked late into the night sewing the clothing their husbands, fathers, or they themselves peddled."[56]

Needlework often served as a supplementary income source for Syrian women alongside their factory employment. A 1915 report by the Immigration Commission noted this practice, claiming that it offered Syrian women economic flexibility: "The labor supply is fluid, because of the ease with which considerable proportions of immigrants can withdraw from the labor market by returning to their homes in times of industrial insecurity."[57] However, returning to the household did not signify a departure from the labor market. Women who did needlework at home sustained a household income. Their piecework also mitigated the risks associated with family peddling businesses and subsidized the commercial endeavors of husbands, father, uncles, or male cousins. In an oral history collected by her daughter, Hannah Sabbagh Shakir recounts how she and her friends worked with imported Aleppan laces for her brother's business, Sabbagh Bros. of Boston in the 1910s. Hannah performed this needlework in addition to shifts at the factory where she and her mother were employed: "We made the gingham, and I ran six big looms, just like a man. We worked twelve hours a day, from six in the morning till six at night, with half an hour for lunch, and Saturdays till twelve. I made $6 a week."[58] Hannah's father and brother all worked as weavers in Saco, Maine, and Boston before leaving industrial work to establish an importing business.[59]

The same qualities that made Syrian hand lace so popular in the mahjar also contributed to its obscurity in histories of this diaspora; Syrian women did this work in improvised spaces, creating a commodity lace which manufacturers blended with imports from abroad and branded as "Irish," "Florentine," or "Cluny." Produced behind the scenes, its origins were effaced as it moved through the supply chain. Syrian lace workers in homes across New England, New York, or elsewhere are thus remembered as purveyors of craft, rather than piece-rate laborers.

After picking up lace pieces, a runner carried them in a suitcase to the factory, where Syrian merchant-manufacturers employed women to stitch them onto garments. In addition to the thousands of Syrians who worked for American employers in vast textile mills, Syrian merchants cornered the whites and lingerie industries specifically, opening dozens of factories devoted to the supply, manufacture, and finishing of underwear, hosiery, household whites, and kimonos. The Syrian shops developed out of import businesses, managed directly by merchants who experimented with local textile production as a means to combat the uncertainties of the global commodities markets. The Syrian shops emerged following a global price shock and financial panic in 1907, which struck the textile and garment industries particularly hard, bankrupting several Syrian import merchants and jobbers and resulting in factory layoffs for garment workers. Merchants who weathered the panic branched into local textile manufacture, drawing on the labor of Syrian women and men in the migrant colonies.

Syrian garment factories appeared in industrial centers across Massachusetts, New Jersey, and New York, and, in the beginning, directly fed peddler networks. Often, they began as improvised workshops composed of a few dozen people employed by Syrian merchants: in east Boston, for example, Albert Homsy opened an apron factory and, employing a dozen Syrian women who had previously sewn aprons under mill conditions, produced a competing product within the community.⁶⁰ Homsy's operation remained small. Never employing more than a dozen women, many of them with direct ties with one another, the Homsy apron business illustrates how petty merchants moved into specialty products and could rely on personal networks as both a labor source and a market. Homsy's pattern—the recruitment of labor through "relatives or acquaintances from the Old Country" and the maintenance of "small shops [that] demanded little expensive technology . . . had low labor costs [and] easily undercut older, larger factories"—replicated an industrial strategy embraced by various immigrant groups in garment work around the same time.⁶¹ These products expanded Syrian commercial networks: when Homsy aprons left Albert's factory they moved into suitcase trades to be sold by peddlers who also carried Syrian kimonos.

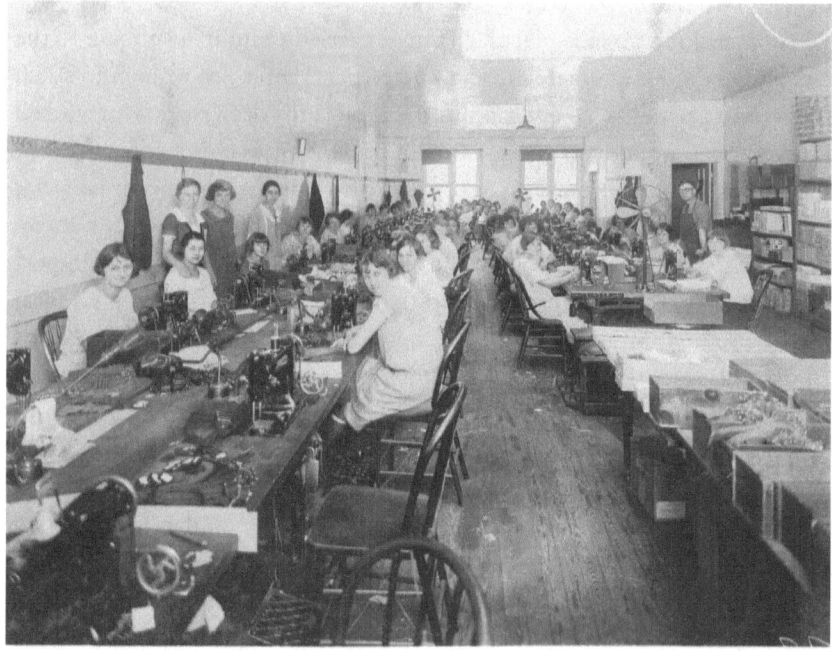

FIGURE 2. Women seated at Singer machines at one of New York City's "Syrian shops," garment firms manufacturing kimonos and other white goods under direct merchant control, circa 1930. Source: Faris and Yamna Naff Arab American Collection, Archives Center, National Museum of American History, Smithsonian Institution.

Large Syrian manufacturers began as improvised, semi-centralized piecework workshops attached to merchant businesses before graduating into full-fledged factories with mechanized production, branded products, contracts with department stores and national retailers, and a workforce ranging from dozens to thousands of people. The heart of this manufacturing was New York City's Garment District, where Syrian merchant-manufacturers produced garments for retail distribution, for the peddling market, and by the 1920s, for export to Latin America and the Middle East.[62] In these factories, women vastly outnumbered men, working on sex-segregated floors managed by (usually male) supervisors. Male operatives did large format work like broadcloth weaving, cutting, or machining, leaving the stitching and garment finishing portions to women. Segregation by sex in New York's "Syrian shops" followed global historical patterns. This wage segmentation strategy was widely practiced across the Americas, Europe, Asia, and the Middle East: women's wages were lower, and their work was classified as unskilled. In Ottoman Mount Lebanon, this practice also had cultural implications; Akram Khater illustrates how sex segregation served as a means of preserving patriarchal family honor.[63]

Just as Syrian workers relied on hometown networks as they moved abroad, the mahjar's merchant-manufacturers also operated in concert with one another. Circuits of textile production, finance, and commodities intertwined with merchants' personal networks as they cooperated to enter new markets, control supply chains, contest trade regulations and tariffs, or oust competitors.[64] As a class, mahjari men of capital achieved near monopolies over kimonos in New York, embroideries on Madeira Island, and undergarments in the Philippines. Being men of capital required more than economic success. Sherene Seikaly brilliantly illustrates how land holders, merchants, and industrialists in interwar Palestine held themselves responsible for "embodying a new kind of economic conduct," one that would benefit the nation and realize its independence through economic knowledge production, calculation, and management of economy, partnerships, and accumulation.[65] Headquartered in New York City, Syrian merchant-manufacturers placed a similar faith in "economic accumulation that would realize national independence," a stance that coded this elite's attitudes on unionization as well as its stewardship of the mahjar's respectability tropes.[66] Émigré merchant-manufacturers relied on transnational class alliances to combat labor uprisings and keep Syrian labor disputes out of the papers; they also invoked the need for race solidarity to quell strikes. These corporate actions were based in the merchant-manufacturers' class position but also reflected ideas about homeland national development, industrial patriotism, or diasporic noblesse oblige.

As the final vector in the mahjar's global supply chain, the peddler carried goods from the factories to retailers and consumers; logistics was his business. The carrying trades mirrored the same piece-rate system observed of Syrian needlework: merchant-manufacturers lent textile goods to peddlers at an agreed-upon piece price that once satisfied, allowed him to accrue his own profits. Peddlers operated at all scales, from small door-to-door operations where Syrian women and men forged personal relationships with their customers, to concerted operations with contiguous territories managed by bosses who subcontracted work to new immigrants.[67] Borderlands trading between the U.S. and Mexico was particularly lucrative, attracting both petty and established merchant networks. As both material and migrants moved through these networks, the peddling trades also became sites for labor migration, including clandestine migration and smuggling of people and illicit goods.

Textile workers, merchant-manufacturers, and peddlers. These are the main characters in this book, and their labor histories can only be understood together. Syrian peddlers represented a labor force and a market for merchant-manufacturers, as well as an outlet for surplus labor. Syrian women who crocheted lace or worked in garment factories paid the rent, enabling male relatives to pursue merchant businesses. Merchant-manufacturers employed thousands of Syrian garment workers and outsourced production abroad, as they faced off against the unions and women who staged pickets outside their factories. And pack peddlers expanded local markets as they moved across borders, establishing new commodity chains that attracted merchant capital and, in some cases, inspired the construction of new textile factories in Latin America. The political economy of this industry was thoroughly transnational, dependent on ties of ethnicity, race, and diaspora embedded within circuits of exchange. A history of work in the mahjar, therefore, must consider striking workers in Lawrence, Massachusetts, suitcase peddlers in northern Mexico, merchant capitalists on Madeira Island, and kimono factory bosses in New York City. And it must contemplate them together.

UNMENTIONABLES: LOOKING FOR WORK

Many of the garments associated with the Syrian American diaspora were undergarments: kimonos, underwear, stockings, and laces Americans colloquially referred to as "unmentionables." In many ways, the labor that went into producing these articles was similarly unmentionable: Syrian women and children in factory work went unmentioned, as did their contests against Syrian American capital, the use of race respectability to compel labor quiescence, and the immigrant community's labor politics at large. This book is arranged episodically along productions points in Syrian supply chains, "looking for work" across the mahjar from the turn of the twentieth century through the Great Depression. This period is defined by the emergence of Syrian labor emigration to the 1930s collapse of the American garment industries and consequent relocation of production abroad. Several important contexts shaped Syrian American labor during this period. The first was a global pattern of mass labor migration: millions of people moved for wage work during the age of steam and print, a pattern that reshaped labor along the coasts of the Atlantic, Pacific, and Mediterranean littorals in the late nineteenth century.[68] Across the Americas, this period was also one of mounting hostility to Asian, Middle Eastern, and southern European workers, as iterated in restrictive immigration laws, racist workplaces, discriminatory housing practices, and violent vigilantism against immigrant communities.[69] Receiving states embraced passport controls to restrict admittance during World War I.[70] And in the American textile industry, mill owners profited by underpaying immigrant laborers and stoking racial divisions to pit workers against one another.[71] Finally, this period witnessed the emergence and increasing militancy of radical trade unions, which organized successful interracial coalitions among textile workers.[72] It also saw the rise of a conservative countermovement in the form of unions which treated Syrian workers as a threat and a source of anti-American subversion.

Chapter 1 picks up in Lawrence, Massachusetts, where we left John Ramey's grave marker in the snow. It narrates the 1912 textile strike known as "Bread and Roses" from the perspectives of its Syrian participants. This strike reportedly made the American labor movement: in 1912, thousands of immigrant workers walked off the job at the mills of the American Woolen Company (AWC), demanding better pay, improved working conditions, and better sanitation in both the AWC factories and the company's tenement housing where most Syrian workers lived. Though the walkout was spontaneous, the Industrial Workers of the World (IWW) quickly organized pickets of Italian, Polish, Lithuanian, and Syrian workers and placed interracial cooperation at the forefront of strikers' demands. Syrian involvement in this strike has assumed primacy in Arab American historiography, but very little is known about how this strike fed broader patterns of labor contestation and class consciousness among Syrian textile workers across New England's many textile mills. The chapter pulls at this thread, unraveling how the oft-told story of John Ramey has shaped our understandings of the Syrian American working class and imagining what a counternarrative might look like along the way.

Chapter 2 digs into the networks of Syrian labor power emerging after the Bread and Roses Strike, examining the politics of mutual aid in industrial Massachusetts. Syrian mutual aid societies appeared in communities across the mahjar, providing myriad services to support the working class: unemployment insurance, healthcare benefits, housing and heating assistance, and food aid. Though often remembered as spaces for leisure, ethnic cultural preservation, or Americanization, mutual aid societies were also sites of labor history: they gave Arab workers a powerful transnational alternative to formal trade unionism in a racially hostile environment. In Massachusetts mill towns, Syrian societies pooled resources for workers' direct benefit and opened meeting halls where they organized strike committees, selected labor leaders to represent their nationality, and nurtured whisper networks capable of inspiring Syrian sympathy strikes out of town. The chapter illustrates that radical textile unions valued Syrian workers as an asset due to their numbers, but the extant historiography posits them as marginal participants in the labor movement owing to their relative silence in formal union records. I argue that there is a good reason for this omission: most Syrian American labor activism, solidarity building, and class consciousness happened within Syrian spaces. Building from the records of three Syrian mutual aid societies operating in Massachusetts, the chapter reveals that by the time Syrian leaders approached union leadership to join a strike, the ethnic infrastructure behind them was already sophisticated enough to take that strike general.

Chapter 3 moves from the mills of New England into New York City's Garment District, where three to five thousand Syrian women garment workers stitched kimonos adjacent to the Washington Street Little Syria ethnic colony. The Syrian shops emerged in response to a vibrant carrying trade in imported textiles, linking Syrian importers to peddling networks that stretched into the American interior. Syrian merchants established garment factories to supply peddling networks locally, starting with Syrian lace and underwear before landing on the signature open-front kimono. Dozens of Syrian shops opened after 1910, rising to national prominence by the 1920s, when Syrian kimonos were featured in *Vogue* magazine and sold in the city's department stores. The chapter also narrates a new labor history of the Syrian shops, where shop bosses resisted unionization, including an assertive campaign by the International Ladies' Garment Workers' Union (ILGWU) between 1913 and 1919. Syrian merchant-manufacturers achieved this by maintaining a segmented, primarily female Syrian labor force bound by a factory culture that centered racial respectability and a patriarchal obligation to find employment within the Syrian community, rather than beyond it.

Chapter 4 boards a steamship from the port of New York and arrives at Madeira Island, one among many islands that became sites for Syrian textile manufacturing in the 1910s. The source of the island's eponymous linen goods, Madeira embroideries came to America almost exclusively via German immigrants until World War I, when Syrian merchant-manufacturers purchased the German embroidery houses, seizing the supply lines linking Funchal to New York. They operated a virtual monopoly through the 1920s. Working within diasporan trade networks to crush competitors, Syrian American firms, led by naturalized citizens, lobbied Funchal's U.S. Consulate to protect their trade interests. The chapter tells the story of Madeira's Syrian merchants and the supply chain they guarded, situating it among similar Syrian supply chains operating in Italy, the Philippines, China, and Japan during this period.

Chapter 5 follows Syrian supply chains in the opposite direction, tracking embroidered linens, silk kimonos, and lace goods as they moved into the hands of peddlers who carried them into the U.S.-Mexico borderlands. Mexico was a primary market for Syrian American textiles, and for new immigrants arriving via Veracruz, peddling labor was a primary means of getting by. Though Syrian peddlers are frequently thought of as merchants in miniature—as capitalist entrepreneurs working at molecular scale—this chapter instead argues they represented a casualized workforce bringing Syrian goods through the "last mile" on behalf of large textile firms.

Brought into peddling through channels subsidized by the mahjar's textile merchant-manufacturers, the borderlands were both a migration corridor and a space for work. Syrian *comerciantes ambulantes* fanned out among competing cells of merchants, who managed both the traffic of migrants seeking to join families in the United States as well as the movement of textile goods into the stores and homes of Mexican buyers. Meanwhile, immigration officials on both sides of the border struggled to parse licit from illicit trades, following orders to facilitate cross-border commerce while prohibiting unauthorized immigration and smuggling of contraband.

Finally, this book's conclusion looks back at Syria and Lebanon, states which emerged under a colonial French Mandate during this period. As émigré merchant-manufacturers globalized their brands, some sought to revitalize the textile industries in their homeland. Raising money from the mahjar or leveraging assets in Asia, the Americas, or the North Atlantic, these manufacturers mounted campaigns to establish new, mechanized factories in the Middle East, deploying ideas about diasporic obligation, economic development, and hopes for independence. It examines two projects: an abortive 1920 attempt by 'Assy Shaheen and Sons to establish a "cocoon to garment" silk plant in Beirut and the 1930s establishment of the Arida plant in Tripoli. It considers the role that industrial developmentalism played in émigré elite politics, especially as Syrian American workers again went on strike in the early 1930s.

Syrian workers began arriving in textile towns around 1900, working first in the bottom rungs of the spinning, weaving, and woolens industries. As an ethnic group usually associated with itinerant commerce, Syrians working in industry were initially treated as oddities or anomalies. But their numbers grew. The U.S. Immigration Commission noted the presence of the "industrial Syrian" in New England and New York, concluding in 1901 that 15 to 20 percent of Syrian immigrant women were "dependent upon textile-mill work."[73] The same report remarked on the Syrian's "docility as a proletarian," a stereotype that led manufacturers to fill factories with Syrian immigrants as a buttress against "strike-ready" groups of Italian or Jewish workers. The perception that Syrians were born strikebreakers began in 1900, when Paterson, New Jersey, silk manufacturers weathered a ten-week strike by trucking in Syrian and Armenian silk workers. Unorganized, not local, and not conversant in English, these workers ran the plants with a skeleton crew; they were also encamped in the mill zone to avoid the shouts and projectiles hurtled at them by striking weavers picketing outside.[74] In another instance of strikebreaking in Camden, Maine, a 1910 strike turned violent when management trucked in Syrian adjuncts to run the machines. Discovering Syrian "scabs" in the company boardinghouse, strikers shot at them with pistols before a stick of dynamite was detonated, leveling the tenement, injuring eight, and causing the rest to flee. Undeterred, mill owners trucked in thirteen more Syrians the next day; they were beaten by strikers before they could be put to work.[75]

Manufacturers' use of Syrian out-of-towners became so predictable that local newspapers mentioned it as an expected benchmark in coverage of textile strikes. In 1907, a disturbance in Waterville, Maine, broke out when mill owners pitted Greek, Armenian, and Syrian workers against one another to stave off a strike over wages. As mill operatives sought to overcome ethnic divisions, management used distrust as a wedge, offering each group of immigrants the jobs of the others. A riot resulted. "Will Waterville have a race war?" the *Boston Globe* asked. Yet despite the conflict's clear material bases, the press attributed the violence to "tribal hatreds" and the mercenary "knownothingness of representatives of foreign lands."[76] Syrian workers experienced intense racial animus in textile towns, often distrusted by labor organizers who perceived them as strike-proof despite the poor living and working conditions they endured. "Other nationalities distrust him," a 1901 congressional report concludes about the Syrian worker, warning that though Syrians have "not been brought into any organization," the "recent unrestricted competition has so lowered the price of his labor that he is himself quite dissatisfied."[77] Mistreatment by manufacturers—especially during strikes—formed the first grievance Syrian workers launched at their employers, the first rallying cry that led them to organize mutual aid societies, join the unions, and oppose the politics of racial division that management had assigned to them. And they would leverage their networks across the mahjar to force the boss's hand.

ONE

SNOWBALLS AND BAYONETS
The Syrian Strikers of Lawrence

The Syrians are for the most part aggregations of traders . . . only in a few mill towns does the Syrian rank as a proletarian [because] the strong trading characteristic of the race militates against the acceptance of factory life as a finality.

U.S. IMMIGRATION COMMISSION REPORT, 1901[1]

JANUARY 19, 1912—AFTER A DAY of standing at the pickets, Joseph Assef returned to the Syrian Quarter to discover a package had been delivered to his home. Assef lived in a tenement he shared with three roommates: two Armenian woolens workers and a Syrian tailor called Farris Marad. The latter, like Assef, represented the Syrian community during the textile strike in Lawrence, Massachusetts, at the American Woolen Company (AWC). The strike was barely a week old. As the package was addressed to Marad, Assef brought it inside, and opened it, to discover it contained "sticks like sausages or candles." Maybe the sticks were "red fire," Assef reasoned to himself, handheld flares strikers carried with them as they marched down Essex Street each day. Recalling the red fire's warmth on his cheeks, Assef considered "touching a match to one of the things to see if it would light."[2] Instead, he decided to bring the package to the coffeehouse where he was scheduled to meet Marad after a strike committee meeting with the Industrial Workers of the World (IWW). Farris wasn't there yet. Assef was first to arrive and sat down with a cup of coffee. When a friend asked about the box, he opened it to reveal the six flares sitting within. His friend's face blanched. "That is dynamite, Joseph, get rid of it, who sent dynamite here?" Assef hurried home and buried the box deep at the bottom of his closet.[3]

The next day, three separate boxes of dynamite were discovered across the Syrian colony of Lawrence. In addition to the six sticks delivered to the Marad tenement, similar packages were discovered in a cobbler's shop and hidden among headstones at a nearby cemetery. Police arrested seven people in connection to the explosives: all but one of them were Syrian.[4] At the center of this dragnet was Farris Marad, a labor organizer "who has appeared at the head of parades and has figured as spokesman for the Syrian strikers" of AWC's mills.[5] Police told the public they believed the dynamite was stolen from a Pennsylvania mine and that there might be a conspiracy to detonate the AWC mills.[6] The news rattled the city; the mayor asked Massachusetts Governor Eugene Foss to dispatch state militias to Lawrence. Memories of Chicago's 1886 Haymarket bombing loomed, as did anxieties over recent bomb plots in mill towns like Camden, Waterville, Saco, and Lowell.[7] Responding to the arrests, IWW leaders Joseph Ettor and Arturo Giovannitti accused AWC of conspiring to plant the dynamite in the Syrian neighborhood to frame and villainize the strikers. Both Ettor and Giovannitti had recently arrived in Lawrence to organize the 20,000 women, men, and children picketing that week.[8] They were acutely aware that the dynamite's discovery could ignite a moral panic, undermining the strikers' bargaining position. Ettor urged "all strikers at this critical time to be cool and collected," reminding them that this was an AWC tactic to "raise dust to blur the issues" animating their strike.[9]

State militias arrived in late January, constructing garrisons around the mill complex, its canal bridge, and at both ends of the tenements that housed striking workers. From these installations, they surveilled strikers as they came and went and enforced a nightly curfew. Their leader, Colonel E. Leroy Sweetser, "established the nearest thing to Martial Law that is possible in Massachusetts without special legislation," as one militiaman recollected in his memoir.[10] Anyone moving through the Syrian neighborhood was monitored. Militiamen regularly detained passersby for questioning; workers accused them of harassing women and lashing out at children. Complaints mounted about their heavy-handed tactics, especially as evening curfews approached. Drunkenness was also a problem at the garrisons, exacerbated by the sale of bootlegged Syrian *araq* to the soldiers.[11] Militiamen whispered rumors that the Syrians plying them with drink were trying to poison them.[12] Nevertheless they tipped the bottles back, whether they were cold, resentful, or just bored. Their drunkenness fueled Syrian anger over their presence.[13] *Araq* played a role in the midnight standoff over Najib Kalil and Abdallah Najjum, the two Syrian boys detained for throwing snowballs in this book's opening pages. The boys were held by half-drunk militiamen as a Syrian crowd encircled them, clattering pots and pans; the following morning, John Ramey led the demonstration where he met his demise.

Famously called the Bread and Roses Strike, the 1912 Lawrence textile strike is often credited with making the American working class. The drama of this strike—a mass walkout spurred by shorted pay, the imprisonment of IWW leaders Joseph Ettor and Arturo Giovannitti, the arrests of children and mothers, and successive public revelations about AWC President William Wood leading to his legacy as villain—drew the nation's attention to the horrific conditions that prevailed in America's textile industry. This strike resulted in new federal legislation governing child labor, working hours, and sanitary conditions in heavy industries. Labor historians also point to Bread and Roses as the moment the IWW refined its methods and set the blueprint for the two decades of labor militancy which followed.[14] The strike forged new interracial solidarities among immigrants previously pitted against one another. Syrians joined Italian, Lithuanian, and Polish workers, and a dozen other nationality groups to protest racial discrimination by AWC.[15] This strategy allowed Syrian strikers to win major concessions and weather AWC attempts to sow racial discord.

At the same time, the history of this strike is often told from the perspectives of the IWW national leadership, relying on union records and the speeches of Ettor and Giovannitti or, after both men were jailed, William (Bill) Haywood and Elizabeth Gurley Flynn. Lawrence's Syrian strikers are assumed to be marginal to this labor history, credited for their numbers while strategically dodging the spotlight. Furthermore, all Syrians weathered the militia lockdown of their neighborhood following the dynamite plot. Their immigrant colony was the site of daily demonstrations, curfews, collisions with police, repression by armed militiamen, and coordinated business closures. Syrians elected a strike committee who met daily to liaise with union leadership, but crucially, most of the work Syrians did to sustain this strike occurred beyond IWW's eyes, among Syrian workers and their families within tenement spaces.

This chapter examines the emergence of Lawrence's Syrian colony, narrating the 1912 strike from the perspectives of Syrian textile workers. As shall be seen, Syrian activists managed their community's visibility and invisibility within IWW's multiracial coalition, protecting their most vulnerable strikers while contesting the politics of race division both in AWC factories and in the unions representing AWC workers.

THE SYRIAN COLONY OF LAWRENCE, MASSACHUSETTS

Syrian migration to New England mill towns began in the late 1890s, peaking the decade before World War I. Often arriving in extended family units, Syrian workers settled in urban tenements adjacent to large textile mills across the region: Saco and Waterville, Maine; Boston, Fall River, Lawrence, Lowell, Pittsfield, New Bedford, Worcester, and Pittsfield, Massachusetts; Dover and Manchester, New Hampshire; and Barre and Burlington, Vermont. Lawrence was the largest of these Syrian settlements.[16] In 1895, an estimated 3,000 Syrians lived in Massachusetts, "the greater part of [them] ... employed in the textile mills."[17] Ten years later, in 1905, the city of Lawrence alone hosted 2,700 Syrian workers, nearly all employed by AWC and over half of them under twenty-five years old.[18] By 1912, the Lawrence Syrian community numbered 5,000, making it the second-largest Arab immigrant community in America. Like other immigrants in Lawrence, Syrians were drawn by the textile mills.[19] American Woolen Company was the town's largest employer, recruiting Syrians alongside Italian, Armenian, and Lithuanian workers to operate three new factories constructed in the Merrimack canal zone by 1910: the Washington, Wood, and Ayer mills.[20]

Transnational networks of kin drew entire Syrian families across the Atlantic. Oral histories collected by the Lawrence History Center illustrate how newly arriving immigrants relied on relatives to secure housing and employment, creating a chain migration pattern broadly remarked on in studies of the mahjar.[21] For instance, in an interview with Juliet Bistany, Rosaline Beshara Habeeb relayed that both of her parents, George Beshara and Mary Bolis, arrived from Hammana, Mount Lebanon, between 1900 and 1905 after relatives in Lawrence sent for them. George worked as a mill section hand and met Mary on company grounds; they married and had daughter Rosaline in 1913, a year after Bread and Roses.[22] Similarly, Roger Aziz reported that his father, Aziz Aziz, came to Lawrence as a child with his mother, two brothers, and two sisters. Aziz Aziz's mother was a widow; the entire family left Lebanon after his maternal grandfather's death in 1900 because "my grandmother had some friends here . . . it was protection because they came where they knew people." This search for kin living abroad was strong, Roger remembered, "You know in the old country, if you're born in a town, even if you're not directly related—because you came from that town, you are considered a cousin, you know."[23]

In addition to kinship ties, more formal patterns of labor recruitment also shaped how Syrian workers traveled, where they landed, and what companies they worked for. Another of Juliet Bistany's oral history informants, Anthony Ramey, described how his father operated a boardinghouse to assist new arrivals. The Rameys were from Falougha; Philip had worked as a silk merchant before coming to Lawrence in 1899 or 1900, hoping to start over after a series of commercial misfortunes.[24] Philip never worked in the mills; instead, he opened a grocery store and established the boardinghouse, letting out rooms for $1 a week "as people drifted into the area . . . looking for a place to sleep." The Ramey house rented to textile workers specifically. Philip would go to Boston to meet them at South Station, picking them up at the railway platform after their arrival from Ellis Island. Once, Anthony remembered, his father was called to New York City to testify at the Immigration Commission because "they wanted to know how come he got so many relatives out here. Everybody . . . says well, Mr. Ramey is a cousin of ours or a brother of mine, and he has a lot of explaining to do up there."[25] Kin was kin, fictive or not. In addition to these sorts of sponsorships, Lawrence also hosted immigration agencies that paired Syrian arrivals with employers. A 1910 Syrian American directory illustrates this activity: Kalil Maaraowie, on Elm Street at the heart of the Syrian Quarter, advertised his services as an AWC employment agent.[26] Though AWC dominated Lawrence's industrial scene, a few Syrians also ran small workshops here. Ilyas Marun Hilu, for instance, bought a small factory where he employed his countrymen in manufacturing sweaters for the ready-wear market, most likely as a subcontractor.[27]

Lawrence's Syrian colony was primarily Christian; Greek Orthodox and Melkite immigrants outnumbered Maronites, a demographic trend mirrored across Massachusetts mill towns but which diverged from the older, more diverse Little Syria colony in New York City.[28] Particularities like this existed in every Syrian community in the mahjar; there was perhaps more variance among working-class mill towns, owing to the critical role of personal networks in immigration decisions.[29] The silk mills of Paterson, New Jersey, featured a concentration of Aleppans; by contrast, Boston's garment factories were dominated by Damascenes, and so forth. However, even with such distinctions, it would be a mistake to overdetermine the communal makeup of the Lawrence Syrian community: workers from Beirut, Damascus, Dayr al-Qamar, Mount Lebanon, Rashaya, and Zahle were all present, and four Syrian churches operated in town: St. Anthony's (Maronite), St. George's (Antiochian Orthodox), St. Joseph's (Melkite Greek Catholic), and the Syrian Protestant Church. Though nearby mill towns like Peabody hosted large numbers of Turkish-speaking Muslim immigrants, officials noted that "the Mohammadan from Syria [had] hardly begun to arrive" in Lawrence. Town officials assumed their arrival in town was spurred "by the well-known difficulties in which the Syrian is placed by the ascendency in his own land of an alien race and faith."[30]

Immigrants arriving in Lawrence discovered the second densest industrial city in the United States. Situated among rows of tenement housing next to the Merrimack River, a canal bridge separated company housing from a vast complex made up of half a dozen mill buildings. The Pacific Mill was the biggest (it was, in fact, one of the world's largest factories at the time), with over 15,000 operatives working 200,000 spindles as well as centralized wool sorting, grading, and weaving under one massive roof. Staffing its machines required the mass recruitment of new immigrants from Mediterranean Europe and Middle East, and the Portuguese Azores, groups who crowded into dense company tenements before spilling out into adjacent boardinghouses on Elm, Oak, and Essex Streets and Valley Avenue. "Their homes are congregated in one quarter of the city," a Labor Board report wrote of Syrians. "They maintain several of their own shops and cafés [and] exhibit considerable national solidarity."[31] On Elm Street, Joseph Mrad Khoury and Ghusn Ghusn established the colony's first newspaper in 1907, *al-Wafa'*.[32] On nearby White Street, Khalil Munayyir opened the Maktabat al-Sha'b (the People's Library), providing reading space in Arabic letters.

In the years before Bread and Roses in 1912, the United Syrian Society and other ethnic associations emerged to support workers. "There was no such thing as welfare in them days," Anthony Ramey recalls of his childhood, "in them days, nobody got nothing."[33] Syrians had to look out for their own interests, working within their own community.

In addition to being the town's largest employer, AWC also owned most of the tenement housing where Syrians lived. Rents were between $1.75 and $2.00 a week per occupant in 1912. This rent paid for a room within a shared apartment comprising two rooms and a kitchen. Each unit housed working families of two to four adults and as many as five or eight dependents; the units were stacked in three-story structures with forty to fifty occupants who shared a single bathroom facility (the units themselves lacked running water).[34] Overcrowding drew the concern of the state Department of Public Health, which cited AWC in 1908 for unsanitary conditions and "overcrowding in the tenement district occupied by Greeks, Armenians and Syrians." However, rather than fining AWC, the company was ordered to "post notice in all the rooms in these houses, restricting the number of persons allowed to sleep in any one room."[35] So in the years immediately preceding the 1912 strike, poor living conditions, deferred maintenance, and high rents all contributed to Syrian complaints. "Practically all of the textile mill employees in Lawrence, Mass., were found to be living in rented tenements," an Immigration Commission investigation revealed, adding that housing scarcity bolstered high rents and was a major cause of the 1912 strike.[36]

Crossing the canal bridge from the tenements to the mill complex, Syrian operatives confronted an intensely international workplace. Operatives with Anglo-American, French Canadian, Italian, Polish, Lithuanian, Portuguese, and Armenian origins all shared the shop floor, though they were often divided into ethnic units attributed to "skilled" or "unskilled" classes. Both Syrian women and men worked in the mills, though women vastly outnumbered men, and Syrian workers were disproportionately younger, less experienced, and limited to the bottom rungs of the industrial hierarchy. Adele Bistany "talked a lot about the girls at work who were not Lebanese," her daughter recollected in an oral history interview. "She was most fascinated by some French girls who were allowed to go out and dance and my mother would come home instead."[37] Mary Ead described working with "Italians, Polish, yeah, every kind" in the spinning room, and Anthony Ramey remembered his father, Philip, communicating between Syrian and

Italian picketers during strikes.[38] Most of the respondents interviewed by the Lawrence History Center described Syrian operatives navigating complex shop politics, seeking to blend with other immigrant groups in class solidarity. However, ethnic conflict was also present. Thomas Kattar recalled how, during his childhood, people called his parents "dagos." He also described how Syrian and Italian boys would engage in internecine street combat for supremacy of the tenements: "to see who's the champ of that street whatever it is, you know, at the time." Immigrant parents discouraged fistfights but also stressed the importance of not getting caught. "Before they would finish fighting," Kattar recounted, "the police would come along and everybody evaporates" into the neighborhood's dense network of alleyways.[39] Such rivalries had to be overcome at Bread and Roses, as AWC managers exploited them as a means of labor control.

The work in the AWC mill complex was physically demanding and dangerous. In an oral history interview, Thomas Kattar remembered how his father worked in a Pacific Mills factory making a weekly wage of $3.25 for a seventy-hour work week in 1911. His mother also took a job in the Ayer Mill after arriving in Lawrence in 1913; both of Thomas's parents stayed in the factory through the 1920s.[40] Syrian working families depended on the contributions of all who could manage the physical labor of the job, and they started work young. According to her daughter, Juliet, Adele Bistany began work at the Pacific Mill in 1912 at twelve years old. Adele's father had also been an AWC employee: he brought Adele to the mill and told the foreman that she was twenty-two years old; the foreman did not believe she was old enough but looked the other way. Juliet's mother "was a spinner all her life; I remember the smell she brought in with her [when returning from work] ... it was this oily gooky smell" from machine oil that coated her arms up to the shoulders. As a young woman, Adele worked two daily shifts to afford a flat outside of AWC tenements, five a.m. to ten a.m., and four p.m. to nine p.m. Once she became a mother, this schedule allowed Adele to watch her children while her husband clerked at a grocery store.[41]

Child labor was a central piece of AWC's industrial model. In 1904, the Massachusetts legislature introduced age restrictions limiting factory employment of children. Children between fourteen and sixteen years old were limited in both the hours and tasks they could perform; employing children under age fourteen was illegal.[42] Despite such efforts, it fell to the city police department to remove children from the mills. Reporting to the state labor board, a Lawrence police officer described Syrians "swearing falsely" to their children's ages to render them work-eligible. "I consider Syrians the most unreliable people coming to this country; they think it is no crime to take a false oath or use a different name in every place where they may be employed. Such people make conditions in our manufacturing cities very bad, especially for the manufacturers giving employment."[43] Progressive social reformers also expressed alarm over immigrant parents withdrawing their children from school to work. But in Lawrence, Syrian child operatives could earn up to $3 a week in combing or carding, wages that supplemented their parents' earnings.[44] While, in theory, Syrian child operatives were at least fourteen years old, oral histories confirm that they frequently started work younger than that. AWC hired Aziz Aziz at twelve years old and eventually both of his brothers too. "He never went too far to tell us about the hardships," Aziz's son Roger remembered of his father. "We should have asked him a lot more questions than we did."[45] These arrangements were so common that when the 1912 strike began, a third of the 25,000 operatives on strike were sixteen years old or younger and therefore legally minors.[46]

Meanwhile, in the mill complex, AWC managers reported to state regulators on labor relations among the company's nationality groups. Just months before the 1912 strike, AWC described mounting tensions between so-called old and new immigrants working at the mills. AWC expanded between 1905 and 1912, opening new factories and assertively recruiting Italians, Portuguese, Syrians, and Armenians. White operatives from Anglo, Scottish, and French-Canadian backgrounds, and the craft unions that represented them, blamed these workers for slumping wages. AWC recruited recent immigrants as a means of labor control, slotting them into the less skilled, poorly paid sectors of production. The increasing visibility of thousands of Italian and Syrian workers drove white resentment, particularly among the AWC shop foremen. Even as AWC recruited these workers, the company's leaders were anxious about their strike readiness. In a 1912 report, one mill superintendent complained of Italians and Syrians that "no sooner [do they] get a job than they want something better; they work in droves; discharge one and they all go."[47] Both groups had earned reputations for collective reprisal against employers who mistreated their compatriots; walkouts, absenteeism, slowdowns, and mass movement to one of AWC's competitors were all weapons at hand to disruptive labor. Spinner

FIGURE 3. A Syrian tenement in Lowell, Massachusetts, 1903. Lawrence's Syrian tenements were torn down in an urban renewal project in the 1960s but resembled the three-story row houses shown here. The housing in this photo was condemned for overcrowding and torn down. Source: Herbert Dearden Hope, *Housing, Conditions: United States. Massachusetts. Lowell: Tenements in French, Greek and Polish Districts: Environment after Immigration, Perpetuation of European Standards in America, Housing Conditions, Lowell, Mass.: Off Middlesex Street: Tenements Occupied by Syrians*, Harvard Art Museums/Fogg Museum, Transfer from the Carpenter Center for the Visual Arts, Social Museum Collection, Photo Copr. President and Fellows of Harvard College, 3.2002.46.3.

Mary Ead told her interviewers that whenever conditions got bad enough, "we could stop work in one mill . . . and change for another."[48] Originally from Deir-el-Kamar, Ead worked in both the Wood and Washington Mills as a girl. AWC was markedly more concerned about Italian workers than Syrians in 1912, however, because of that group's broad association with labor militancy. In comparisons to Italian workers, "the Syrians are somewhat less definitely placed in the estimation of employers," concluded a state labor board report. "Some speak well of them, and others are critical. Many are intelligent and possess considerable commercial ability; others apparently have a different reputation."[49]

AWC's president in 1912 was William M. Wood. The son of a Portuguese immigrant with an assumed surname, Wood rose from shop foreman to woolens magnate in one lifetime, crediting his success to a trade secret that allowed his mills to worst and weave woolens at a fraction of his competitors' costs. In 1912, Wood owned thirty-three mills in New England, employing tens of thousands of foreign-born workers. These shops were open (not unionized), but competing locals of the conservative United Textile Workers of America and the radical Industrial Workers of the World existed within them. Lawrence's IWW chapter was tiny, however, representing a scant 300 AWC operatives before 1912.

As Mediterranean workers became a visible majority among AWC's

FIGURE 4. Left: Joe (Yusuf) Hajjar and three workers at Ayer Mill. Right: Nimer Hajjar and unidentified Syrian worker at Ayer Mill. These undated photographs were likely taken between 1918 and 1921, when Hajjar served as Ayer Mill's arbiter. Source: Lawrence History Center Photography Collection.

workforce, white workers accused William Wood of practicing illegal labor contracting to undermine Lawrence's craft unions. They pointed to numerous instances where mill managers trucked in Syrian workers to break strikes. Such complaints merged into broader xenophobic narratives about racial unfitness and prevailing discourses on Mediterranean and Asian labor then circulating in the United States and other settler states.[50] White workers expected labor organizations to privilege their material standing through labor policy and immigration restrictions. In Lawrence, union complaints prompted the U.S. Immigration Commission to investigate whether large firms like AWC imported contract labor in violation of an 1894 law prohibiting indenture. One such investigation into "instances in which silk mill-owners have used Syrian help in attempts to break strikes" led the Immigration Commission to note a clear pattern of racial segmentation in the industry. However, the commission dismissed accusations that textile manufacturers were actively engaged in illegal labor contracting, concluding instead that "mill owners ... have been the victims of cajolery" by labor organizations seeking to preserve the privilege of white workers.[51]

These tensions were present in Lawrence, where the United Textile Workers (UTW) investigated claims about AWC's acquisition of Syrian, Italian, and Portuguese immigrant labor. The union found no evidence that the company had engaged in illegal contracting but maintained a hostile stance toward Lawrence's Syrian workers. The UTW repeatedly called on state legislators to impose restrictions on new immigration to protect white American workers. When asked in congressional testimony about the demographic shifts he had observed in Lawrence mills, UTW President John Golden asserted, "It began to show itself about ten years ago [and] has become more pronounced on account of the construction of these large mills in the last six years." Golden was then asked whether Syrian and Italian workers came "of their own volition" or were "brought here by connivance of their ultimate employers?" He answered unambiguously: "I believe that proof can be submitted that many thousands of people were brought over by agents that went over there to secure help."[52] UTW never submitted this proof to Congress, but the narrative was powerful enough to generate its own gravity. For UTW, American workers merited protection from both unscrupulous factory owners and the rabble of non-white immigrants. Though framed through the prism of immigration, it was the racial difference that made these new workers so threatening.[53] Similarly, public conflation of Italian and Syrian workers with "Turks" or "Africans" strategically denied these groups the benefits of whiteness during an era when whiteness was a prerequisite to American citizenship.[54]

Racial animosity was central to the Syrian workers' experience of the Lawrence textile industries. "The only nationalities more hated by the trade-unionist [than the Poles] are the political rough-scuff of Europe now coming over in increasing numbers: the Armenians, Greeks, and Syrians," a woolens industry magazine described. "These are all lumped as strike breakers in a class by themselves."[55] Racial resentments informed how city officials, AWC management, and some workers responded to the 1912 strike. Though the strike was immediately taken up by Italian, Syrian, and Polish workers, workers of Anglo-American, Scottish, and French-Canadian origin opposed the action and even called for strikers to be deported.[56] Nevertheless, something new occurred in January 1912. Resisting AWC's efforts to exploit racial divisions to maintain industrial peace, an interethnic coalition of workers locked arms and collectively rejected the stereotype of "strikebreaker."

SHORT PAY! ALL OUT!

The Bread and Roses Strike began in January 1912, spurred by a dispute over working hours. The previous year, the Massachusetts legislature mandated a 3.5 percent reduction in operating hours for the woolens industry, from fifty-six to fifty-four hours per week. The legislation was designed to improve working conditions by imposing a ceiling on the work week; a similar reduction had been mandated in 1909.[57] AWC President William Wood opposed this legislation, responding with an announcement that effective January 1, 1912, his employees could expect a 4 percent wage cut to compensate for the reduction in hours. For most of AWC's workers, this meant a $0.32 weekly decrease starting with the first paycheck of the new year.[58] Ahead of the paycheck, the Industrial Workers of the World local met on January 3 to discuss the possibilities for a strike. However, in a workforce of 40,000 people that had recently weathered two failed strikes, the local's 300-person membership assessed themselves "as replaceable as bobbins" and decided against a fight.[59] Efforts at bargaining with AWC also failed. Union members approached mill supervisors who "told them to go back to their machines," recalled IWW organizer Samuel Lipson; they were "absolutely turned down," and a union letter to William Wood was ignored.⁶⁰ Rather than declaring a strike from the top, then, AWC workers resorted to coordinating their moves within their respective nationality groups. On the factory floor, these operatives eyed management uneasily for two weeks; all anticipated a clash as the first pay period of the year ended. Midday on January 12, the walkout came when Italian, Polish, and Syrian operatives marched through the mills shouting, "Short pay! All out! All out!"⁶¹ Women went from room to room, agitating the workers into a mass outside the mill building. Brandishing knives, men pushed through the mob, slashing the leather bands that ran the machines on their way out, proceeding from Washington Mill into Pacific Mill, the largest in the complex. Lawrence police arrived at the scene but were overwhelmed by the crowd as strikers threw ice and rocks at them. The *Boston Globe* recorded this eviction: "400 rioters . . . Italian and Syrian workers . . . stormed four mills today" forcing 13,000 workers to "forsake the works, most of them under compulsion."⁶² The IWW's serial, *Industrial Worker*, accused Lawrence police of beating people gratuitously: "Dozens of women were knocked about and trampled . . . several men were cut and bruised, [and] three policemen were hurt."⁶³

This dramatic walkout emboldened thousands of AWC operatives, producing an eight-week strike of between 20,000 and 30,000 workers. Seventeen nationality groups participated, cooperating across racial and linguistic lines. Initially forged by horizontal cooperation, strikers coalesced into the IWW "Committee of Ten," a bargaining team of organizers representing seven of Lawrence's largest ethnic communities.⁶⁴ The Committee of Ten held meetings in the town square daily, negotiating demands, planning strategy, and giving strikers a platform to speak with simultaneous translation to the crowd. Three men represented Syrian interests to the Committee of Ten: Iskandar Hajjar, Farris Marad, and James Brox. Crucially, these men were not employed by AWC at the time, making them invulnerable to retaliation. They were also U.S. citizens, which protected them from deportation. They each commanded civic legibility in Lawrence, could bargain in English, and were elected on those bases by Syrian AWC operatives who met regularly at the Syrian National Club (SNC). Their selection allowed workers on strike—most of them Syrian women and girls—to maintain a strategic invisibility while also having their demands heard.

Dr. Iskandar Abdalla Hajjar, a dentist, was a respected man of radical politics who navigated between the immigrants and IWW national leadership as they arrived in town. Born in Mashghara in 1864 and educated at Beirut College, Hajjar came to Massachusetts in 1890, was naturalized in 1898, and came to Lawrence in 1903 to open his dental practice.[65] A Protestant Congregationalist, Hajjar was also a preacher who evangelized among Syrian immigrants in Lawrence, Lowell, and Worcester. He delivered Arabic interpretations of the services at Lowell's First Trinitarian Church and (after 1907) gathered Lawrence's small Syrian Protestant community for Sunday study.[66] He joined the local Tuscan Freemasons Lodge of Lawrence in 1910.[67] Iskandar Hajjar had numerous relatives working in AWC mills, most notably Joe and Asʿad Hajjar, who assumed arbiter roles with AWC after 1919.[68] Hajjar figured among Lawrence's local elite, his credentials bolstered by his standing within the Syrian community as a member of one of the colony's first families. As a freemason, preacher, and most importantly, a Syrian beyond AWC's reach, Hajjar served as interlocutor and interpreter at strike meetings.

A former AWC dyer and self-employed tailor, Farris Marad also commanded local respectability. Before the strike, he had worked as an interpreter for the local courts, assisting Syrians in immigration matters and taking beat shifts as a police deputy.[69] When AWC workers went on strike, Marad led the parades through town and was observed de-escalating violent confrontations between militiamen and demonstrators. James Brox was a greengrocer originally from Zahle, where he was born in 1879. Arriving in Boston in 1892, James worked as a "mill hand" and became a U.S. citizen in 1900.[70] James came to Lawrence around 1910 to open his grocery shop, living with brother William Brox (Brux), who was employed by AWC. Like Hajjar, Brox was a freemason. Before the strike, James was most well known as the president of the city's Young Men of Zahle Order, a fraternal society devoted to enhancing the material conditions of youth from the town. James's fluency in English and his status as a former factory worker—therefore as someone who understood the strikers' grievances while remaining invulnerable to AWC retaliation—was crucial to his election to the IWW Strike Committee.[71] James and William were also founding members of the Syrian National Club.[72]

In addition to the three Syrian representatives on the Committee of Ten, local merchants Joseph Shaheen and Mike Saliba also liaised between the IWW and the Syrian societies in town.[73] Informally, but with significant effect, the ministers of all three of the city's Syrian churches also supported the strikers, despite their unease about the IWW.[74] Striker Justus Ebert recorded that early strike meetings between Syrian and Italian leaders took place at one of the town's Syrian churches; Ebert also recorded a speech given at this church in Italian by Arturo Giovannitti, likely to an interethnic audience, addressing common grievances: "Capitalism is the same in the Fatherland as it is here. Nobody cares for you; nobody is interested in you. You are considered nothing but machines . . . *if any effort is made to improve your conditions and raise you to the dignity of manhood and womanhood, that must come from yourselves alone.* It is only by your own power, your own determined will, your own solidarity, that you can rise to better things."[75] James Brox also recalled this support in a 1952 interview with historian Edwin Fenton: Syrian priests were "closer to the problems of the poorer unskilled workers" than were their white counterparts.[76] Brox believed this proximity drove their sympathies with the strikers "despite philosophical opposition to syndicalism."[77] The 1912 strike thus relied upon existing institutions within the Syrian community to build interracial solidarity. These networks were defined by multiple points of connection, leading from Syrian spaces into IWW spaces; action was coordinated in Arabic from the bottom up. This pattern presided in most of Lawrence's ethnic communities. As Ardis Cameron brilliantly encapsulates, "At the level of daily life, neighbors and kin converted the familiar and the routine into powerful weapons of protest and resistance."[78]

With this context in mind, the Committee of Ten operated as an umbrella organization, a mediating space that preserved the autonomy of each nationality and left them free to operate independently, while also creating a multiracial bargaining team to liaise with AWC and state officials. Most of the strike's Syrian demonstrations were planned within the ethnic community, including daily marches and drum parades, mass defiance of curfew, and a relief kitchen to sustain hungry picketers.[79] Working within nationality groups allowed Syrian strikers to engage in direct action while benefiting from relative anonymity. Marad, Hajjar, and Brox all ended up in the papers but did so as ethnic advocates who were present at mass actions but never singled out as orchestrating them. This strategic approach created a powerful advantage as city officials targeted picketers with law enforcement.

Pickets formed at the AWC canal zone daily, with thousands lining up to shame operatives who crossed the picket line. Labor historians credit

Joseph Ettor for teaching "inexperienced immigrants the nature of industrial warfare," particularly in nonviolent coercive tactics like the picket line.[80] Similarly, the IWW sought to maintain nonviolence as AWC and city police provoked picketers by turning water hoses on them in freezing weather. Petty arrests for charges of rioting and tossing stones through mill windows were common, as were arrests following scuffles as AWC tried to install out-of-town "scabs" at the complex.[81] City police arrested dozens of strikers on riot charges each day, booking them into the Essex County Jail. The jail quickly reached capacity, forcing police to adopt a new strategy of arresting and detaining strikers for hours or days before releasing them without charges.

In principle, riot charges were a serious matter; the standard sentence was one year imprisonment, doubled to two years if the defendant also carried a weapon. However, in practice, only strikers whose rioting was deemed violent were tried and convicted; even then, they appealed their sentences (usually successfully). An Armenian spinner, for instance, was charged with rioting, but her charge was dropped to disturbing the peace, and her sentence was commuted after thirty days on appeal.[82] Syrian operative A. Yazza's riot charge was reduced to intimidation, requiring him to pay a $10 fine rather than suffering imprisonment.[83] Another Armenian operative was convicted of a lesser malicious mischief charge after vandalizing an AWC building; he paid restitution and spent a few days in jail.[84] Even those convicted of rioting regained their freedom after the strike concluded: an Italian woolens operative was sentenced to two years for felony riot and weapons charges, but was released early after publicly attesting that "the IWW made a fool" of him.[85]

Aside from the six arrested in the January dynamite case, Syrians were rarely booked into the county jail, congregating at the picket lines instead. Reporters walked the lines and collected the stories of Syrian strikers. "An American couldn't, and probably wouldn't do [this job]," one told the *Boston Globe*, adding that his wage left him only 80 cents per week after paying rent. Telling their stories, picketers won the press over quickly: "The courage, determination, and persistence [of the immigrant worker] is a contribution to America which does not belong to the debased and degraded of the earth."[86] This reporter was convinced these immigrants "have shown the stuff they are made of which can be molded to the purpose of the Nation"; the real tragedy was the intransigence of AWC management.[87] As the contours of the standoff emerged, thousands of picketers went to the canal zone each morning, and police were given orders to encircle them.

Both Syrian women and men were at the pickets in force. Precise numbers are hard to come by, but Ardis Cameron determines Syrian women composed 11 percent of the city's female strikers, a visible minority.[88] These women played on American respectability politics as a strategy to garner greater attention to their cause: they donned their best clothing before arriving at the pickets, drawing the attention of reporters covering the strike. "The Syrians are especially gentle," remarked a female reporter from the *Boston Globe*. "Most of the mothers seem as carefree as children ... attractively dressed, some of the women with shawls upon their heads, but they sure looked more comfortable than those who wore the top-jeavu, bird-laden hats of their sisters."[89] Then, rather than remaining in the canal zone, the Syrian women marched down on Essex Street, the thoroughfare running along the Syrian Quarter.[90] Reporters followed, gathering more quotes declaring the women's resolve to withstand a long strike: "Are we going back to work for that money? No, indeed, we don't have to."[91] Marching down Essex in their finest garments—silk shawls, linen or cotton aprons, pretty dresses, leather boots—women strikers simultaneously overturned class stereotypes about mill workers and racial and Orientalist stereotypes about Syrian women as passive homemakers. Though the Syrians elected to join the IWW strike committee were all men, Syrian women assertively led the strike from its center. They picketed, marched, planned direct action, and attended daily rallies. They organized mutual aid campaigns to provide rent relief and ran a Syrian relief kitchen.[92] Funded by Syrian church groups, the relief kitchen served up daily rice, lamb *kibbeh*, and yogurt to hungry strikers of all nationalities as well as the children of the Syrian community at large.[93]

American onlookers were intrigued and shocked by the central roles immigrant women played in the textile strike. But in doing strike work, these women often referred to protest traditions that began in their homelands.[94] At the same time, in America it was important for them to perform a feminine respectability not usually ascribed to immigrant women of their class. By dressing up and going out, performing tasks coded as feminine on city sidewalks, the strikers visually undermined AWC claims that the walkout was nothing more than an anarchist mob.

In addition to picketing in the canal zone, Syrians led daily strike pa-

FIGURE 5. A Syrian couple poses in the Lawrence tenement neighborhood known as the Syrian Quarter, circa 1910. Source: Lawrence History Center Photography Collection.

rades through the city, usually at noon. Demonstrations of 1,500 or 2,000 people led by "a bunch of Syrians with drums and red fire" made their way through downtown, "parading through the streets rather aimlessly collecting adherents as they go and making a rather pretty red glow on the snow."[95] The Syrian Drum Corps accompanied the marchers, with John Ramey playing the cornet. The band's drums and brass kept spirits high and lent the strike an air of carnival. These daily parades filled the streets, disrupting traffic as neighborhood Syrians, hearing the drums, grabbed their pots, wooden spoons, and improvised instruments of all kinds to march along. They chanted IWW slogans, welcomed townspeople to join them, and jeered at opponents. At the City Mission, Reverend Clark Carter watched these parades daily. Though he worked in immigrant welfare, Carter opposed the strike and made several public statements against the IWW; the union responded by calling him "a paid tool of the Wool mills."[96] Carter believed the IWW took advantage of new immigrants for ideological ends, and this view fueled his frustration with the parades that passed his office each day. In congressional testimony given later, he described the "mobs" of Syrian demonstrators this way:

> Their arms are all raised in the air and waved excitedly, and the marchers are all shouting and screaming and applying epithets to the people they see in the windows that they do not like, and cheering some whom they do . . . I saw this occur directly in front of my office: a band of young men, who are in one company, locked arms . . . making a solid mass of humanity, and undertook to make it reach from curb to curb . . . there was not only a crowd of people between the curbstones, but there were many people lined up on the sidewalks, all moving in the same direction.

He added that "they had not learned how to keep step exactly, and they began to reel and break a little; it made me smile." As he watched Syrian men line up, reaching "their arms over each other's shoulders," kicking up their heels before spinning back into the mass, dropping, disbanding, Carter supposed they were struggling to march on icy cobbles before realizing the men were dancing.[97] They swayed in city intersections, arms linked in a *dabke*, before parading up Essex Street toward Broadway.

After a week of pickets and parades, the Committee of Ten congregated 2,000 people into the city commons and presented the IWW's demands: a 15 percent pay increase on the fifty-four-hour work week, double pay for overtime, elimination of the premium system (bonus payments based on sped up production), and amnesty for all strikers.[98] AWC President William Wood had agreed to meet with Joseph Ettor in principle, but vehemently opposed any discussion of a wage increase.

SUCH THAT LIFE AND PROPERTY ARE IN DANGER

The City of Lawrence responded to rowdy parade activity with an intense police presence, deploying patrols to the canal zone to discourage vandalism and scuffles. A series of such incidents led officials to call for state militia support to keep order in Lawrence, beginning with a riot at the mill complex on the same day dynamite was discovered in the Syrian Quarter. On

January 20, 14,000 operatives were on strike, thousands of them in the canal zone halting AWC's production.[99] AWC attempted to bring in replacement workers, who were repelled by picketers who threw ice and rocks at them before clashing with police. The subsequent discovery of explosives gave Massachusetts Governor Eugene Foss his pretext for sending in militias. Foss was a longtime industry ally, a Republican who embraced anti-union politics. Responding to reports that a "collision between the strikers and the police" had injured dozens, he deployed "a number of companies of militia" to impose order by armed force.[100] Foss's order was to preserve life and property, but under Massachusetts Colonel Leroy Sweetser, this order led to the construction of garrisons, a nightly curfew, expansive use of force against civilians, and a culture of impunity among guardsmen. The arrival of militiamen escalated the conflict considerably, stiffening strikers' resolve and intensifying the possibilities for violent confrontation. At the same time, it became clear that AWC was explicitly targeting Syrian workers to undermine the strike.

The discovery of explosives in the Syrian tenements, including in Committee of Ten member Farris Marad's closet, was the first escalatory incident, soon termed the "dynamite conspiracy." Police arrested six Syrians that day. From the start, Farris Marad, Joseph Assef, and the others maintained their innocence. Speaking on Marad's behalf, IWW leader Joseph Ettor accused AWC of planting the dynamite in a frame job: "Our situation is satisfactory, and the bosses are losing. They are desperate, and that accounts for the dynamite. If any bombs or dynamite sticks are found it will be found by those who planted them."[101] Supporting these attestations of innocence, the Lawrence police expressed serious doubts about the case almost immediately, even as state guardsmen arrived and occupied the Syrian Quarter. On the same day Marad was arrested, a woman came forward to tell police a white man had attempted to deliver a mysterious package to her home. The man falsely claimed the bundle "had been sent by the bootblack place of Shakara Samya," her brother-in-law. She "began yelling and made so much noise the man ran away."[102] City police told the press their case against the Syrians did not "look good," and there "was much to indicate that some of these persons may have been dupes" framed by a third party. Marad and his fellow strikers were held in the city jail for two weeks as police investigated whether the dynamite's appearance was an Arab conspiracy or a frame job targeting Syrian labor leaders.[103] Police released the detained Syrians on February 3 and subsequently arrested the city undertaker, a white man called John Breen.[104] Marad returned to the Committee of Ten to a chorus of applause and "fiery speeches of denunciation" against AWC actions toward strikers.[105]

John Breen's arrest puzzled Syrians in town. He was known by many Syrians and had attended the picket lines. He was even quoted in the press calling Syrians "a gentle people." He went on to say, "They never had a hand in that dynamite scheme, I am sure . . . as for Marad, a man who leads parades the way he did, really at the risk of his life . . . that man never had any desire to use dynamite. He's a good man, I know him."[106] Whether Breen made these statements out of a guilty conscience or in an alibi attempt, his arrest ultimately unraveled a conspiracy linking him to Dennis Collins and Ernest Pitman of Boston, men who procured stolen dynamite on behalf of AWC's president, William Wood. At trial, Collins admitted to handing the dynamite to Breen and instructing him to plant it in the Syrian Quarter. His co-conspirator, Ernest Pitman, was arrested but fatally shot himself to avoid prosecution.[107] Ultimately, Breen was convicted and forced to pay restitution to the seven people wrongfully arrested in the case. William Wood was also arrested and tried for orchestrating the bomb plot; he was ultimately acquitted in 1913.[108]

At his trial, John Breen admitted the dynamite plot was intended to delegitimize and "settle the strike" in AWC's favor. He testified that he had been instructed to deliver the explosives to the Marad and Samya tenements; he had also tried to enter a Syrian printing house and the meeting hall of the United Syrian Society on Oak Street, where strikers were gathering nightly.[109] "I tried the Syrian hall, but the door was locked," Breen testified. Then panicking, he dumped the last of the explosives in the St. Mary's Cemetery instead.[110] The goal was to stoke racial tensions and isolate Syrians from the Italian and Polish workers organizing with the IWW. Had Breen been more a competent conspirator, the discovery of explosives would have cast Syrian labor leaders as terrorist radicals, reigniting the specter of violent labor confrontations like Chicago's Haymarket Affair of 1886, when a demonstrator threw dynamite at police, killing one and injuring dozens. The dynamite in Farris Marad's closet was not meant to be detonated: it was representational, designed to fit him (a tailor, an interpreter, a police deputy) into the Mediterranean anarchist archetype and bolster voices calling for deportation of Syrians. This was a near miss, one that shaped the organizational strategies Syrian workers adopted during textile strikes for decades after 1912.

Despite the Lawrence Police Department's acknowledgment that the dynamite case was suspicious, the discovery of explosives prompted Governor Foss to order additional militias to town. Colonel Sweetser installed the troops in the Syrian Quarter, where their heavy-handed tactics fueled Syrian resentment, particularly during enforcement of nightly curfews. At first nightfall after the garrisons were installed, 1,500 Syrian and Italian workers gathered for a night march, in open defiance of Sweetser's curfew. They marched from the tenements to the city center, "led by an Italian woman carrying a big American flag" to the beat of the Syrian Drum Corps "crashing out the weird airs of their nation, parading the streets."[111] Arriving at Essex Street, this group met another 5,000 protesters and the IWW leadership awaiting them. Together, the crowd then proceeded to the canal zone, where they met soldiers with rifles and bayonets, positioned on the canal bridge between town and the AWC mill complex. The night marchers "jeered at the soldiers as they passed them."[112] Militiamen beat protesters with the butts of their rifles, and police made a dozen arrests, but the demonstrators made clear that their numbers could still overwhelm the militia presence.

The danger increased over the next several days, as more militiamen arrived and confrontations like this multiplied. Daytime pickets remained mostly peaceful, but evening demonstrations led to violence instigated by militiamen pushing demonstrators away from the canal zone and enforcing the Syrian Quarter's nightly curfew. On January 29, the shooting death of an Italian women, Anna LoPizzo, at an IWW event led police to arrest Joseph Ettor and Arturo Giovannitti as accessories to murder.[113] LoPizzo's death was the result of a stray gunfire, but officials held Ettor and Giovannitti for months, hoping to sap strikers' energies by depriving them of their leaders. The militias again maintained a lockdown of AWC tenements and were ordered to hold a firm perimeter. LoPizzo was killed on the night of the snowball incident in the Syrian Quarter. A group of Syrian boys ambushed a garrison and pelted militiamen with snowballs, leading them to chase and detain two AWC child operatives. By midnight, 200 Syrians, having learned of the detained children, had encircled the garrison "carrying tin pans and other household effects that were suitable for making a noise." The guardsmen stood "with fixed bayonets" and threatened to advance, throwing the neighborhood into a dangerous uproar "and a menacing attitude was assumed toward the soldiers."[114] This standoff ended when Colonel Sweetser dispatched another company from the canal zone to disperse the protesters. But Syrian rage continued the next day when a new confrontation resulted in John Ramey's death.

The son of Michael Ramey and Merta Habib, John Ramey worked at AWC's Arlington Mill. A cornet player for the Syrian Drum Corps, he led several strike parades and was observed marching alongside Farris Marad in the days before Marad's arrest on January 20. Following Marad's arrest, the drum corps had been skirting the city in careful routes that avoided direct clashes with armed militiamen. By contrast, the procession that took Ramey into the canal zone on January 30 was bold and confrontational. Coming immediately on the heels of the midnight standoff in the Syrian Quarter, this procession was a direct refusal of militia occupation. Unlike preceding marches, this procession attempted to cross the canal bridge separating the city from the mill complex.

Meanwhile, on the morning of January 30, officials at City Hall issued a total prohibition on political assembly. "Conditions are such in the city," Commissioner of Public Safety C. F. Lynch announced, "that life and property are in danger."[115] From militia headquarters in the canal zone, Colonel Sweetser contacted the IWW strike committee and ordered them to cancel planned demonstrations. Many of the day's actions were called off, but with Farris Marad in jail, Syrians congregating to march against militia impunity may not have learned of the new public safety order or they may have intentionally defied it. At noon, the Syrian Drum Corps led a procession of several hundred protesters to the canal zone. Observing them from one of the AWC mill buildings across the canal bridge, Sweetser ordered sixteen infantry companies and two troops of calvary to intercept the demonstrators at the bridge and disperse them. The two sides met on the canal's southern bank, a melee erupting as Syrian protesters tried to force their way onto the narrow canal bridge. Militiamen leveled bayonets, pushing them into the crowd. John Ramey was holding this front line, his cornet still in hand when, according to a witness, "he tried to grab the gun of one soldier and a second one stabbed him."[116] Ramey fled home with deep bayonet lacerations to his shoulder, arm, and back.[117] His mother rushed him to the hospital, where he died from his injuries.[118] Lawrence seethed with anger as Sweetser's men imposed a complete citywide lockdown and forced residents into their homes.[119]

The days that followed brought hostile recriminations by Italian and Syrian strikers, aimed at Colonel Sweetser, Lawrence police, and AWC. Committee of Ten leaders Iskandar Hajjar and James Brox "blamed the city government for calling the militias here" and causing John Ramey's death.[120] Reeling, strikers met at the Syrian National Club to plan a response to the killing. Officials blamed Ramey's death on the demonstrators; Commissioner C. F. Lynch went even further, suggesting that "having the Anarchistic elements among the textile workers deported" would produce a "lessening of tension in the city." Meeting a press scrum at City Hall, Lynch told them he was working with the federal Immigration Service to pursue whether "laws regarding undesirable citizens can be invoked to end this intolerable situation." Such threats were growing common against immigrant workers.[121] Among Syrians, rumors circulated that the private who bayoneted Ramey was drunk; such accusations would never be substantiated because Sweetser insisted that the incident must be investigated by the state militia, not the Police Department. Ramey was interred on the grounds of St. Anthony's Maronite Church. A private funeral was held, but "no parade was allowed," and in the IWW's words, "the militia continued to look for trouble" as the Ramey family grieved in the Syrian Quarter.[122]

Meanwhile, the arrests of Joseph Ettor and Arturo Giovannitti initiated a new phase of the strike. IWW leaders Bill Haywood and Elizabeth Gurley Flynn came to Lawrence to assume leadership over the Committee of Ten, and the national IWW made a concerted escalatory push for sympathy strikes, expressions of solidarity, and fundraising across and beyond New England.[123] The Committee of Ten circulated a public appeal calling on workers across the region to "help your fellow workers." In part, the circular read:

> Twenty-five thousand men, women, and children, employed in the textile mills of Lawrence ... are out on strike [and] have dared to rebel against conditions that are unbearable. Because they have dared to assert their manhood and womanhood and determinedly insisted for an opportunity to live by their labor hired, military hessians have been sent to terrorize the workers into going back to work.
> We workers, who have done our utmost share to clothe the world, are now

asking the world of labor and all those who sympathize with the cause of the workers for bread. Contribute liberally. It is our fight today, who knows it may be you tomorrow who will need support.[124]

The arrival of socialist leaders brought national attention to the Lawrence strike, and the IWW coordinated a series of campaigns to hold that attention. In February, when Polish, Lithuanian, and Jewish AWC operatives sought to send their children away to safely await the strike's outcome, police arrived at the train station with wooden batons and arrested several women on the platform.[125] A series of violent confrontations followed as police and militiamen sought to forcibly remove children from train cars in repeated actions, collectively called the "children's exodus." The spectacle of sending Lawrence's children away signaled the strikers' resolve for a long-haul strike; the working mothers arrested each day on the train platform won public sympathy.[126] Speaking to strikers about arrest, Haywood assured them to keep faith because after all, "the food and accommodation in the worst jails are better than the wages that the mills provide."[127]

Syrian families were noticeably absent from the children's exodus. After John Ramey's killing, it was unthinkable to send more Syrian boys into a confrontation with police, and the community had no reason to believe its boys would be cast with the same sympathetic light as white immigrant children. Syrian women continued to picket, protest, and march, but after Ramey's death they faced heightened police intimidation. On February 19, twenty Syrian women met on the grounds of St Anthony's Maronite Church to picket. "Counting on the fact that neither soldiers nor policemen would harm women," they prepared to march to Essex Street but were surrounded by a squadron of cavalry and twenty-six policemen who kettled them as they moved across the Syrian Quarter for several hours before arresting three for "molesting and intimidating" armed soldiers.[128] At strike committee headquarters, Hajjar and Brox continued negotiating with the IWW.[129] They also liaised with ethnic associations across Massachusetts mill towns, inviting Syrians from Worcester, Fall River, Boston, and Lowell to leave their machines and join the marches in Lawrence.[130] At this point the strike reached its apogee: 30,000 workers halted work, and AWC was unable to open its factories. The strikers had achieved two core goals: securing sympathetic national attention and imposing steep financial losses on

AWC. As the strike hurtled to its final weeks, a new line of inquiry opened: Had John Ramey been a boy or a man? What did it mean for America if the Syrian killed in Lawrence was a child striker?

INVESTIGATING JOHN RAMEY

Two narratives of John Ramey's death emerged during the Lawrence textile strike. The first of these narratives was articulated by the IWW and the Syrian strikers themselves. "Had the militias never been called to the scene," Bill Haywood told supporters, "John Ramey never would have been brutally murdered by as foul a hessian band as ever disgraced darkest Russia."[131] However, another narrative was emerging among policymakers in Washington D.C., where the U.S. House of Representatives Rules Committee opened an inquiry into the strike in March 1912. Acting in response to public outrage, Congress called union leaders, strikers, child operatives, and police representatives to testify in hearings centered primarily on the question of AWC's use of child labor. In these hearings, the death of the Syrian teenager took primacy. "You have not told us anything about the wounding of a Syrian," Republican congressman John Dalzell pressed John Sullivan, Lawrence City Marshall and Chief of Police.[132] "I did not see it myself," Sullivan testified. "That morning, after parades were forbidden, word was sent to the police and militia that a crowd was forming in the Syrian district to have a parade ... a section of militia was sent to disperse those musicians. The young man who was bayoneted was one of those musicians. Just how it occurred I do not know."[133]

Depositions by police and state guard officials regarding Ramey's death were filtered through new anxieties in the national consciousness about industrial labor by children.[134] Testimonies brought "to light the deplorable status of affairs among thousands of foreign born workers," but the accounts of AWC's mistreatment of child operatives, violations of labor law, and the militias' rough handling of child strikers shifted national sympathies in the IWW's favor.[135] Child operatives narrated their experiences in open session, with details repeated in the national press.[136] Fifteen-year-old Samuel Goldberg, for instance, testified that AWC paid him between $1.64 and $5.10 per week but docked his pay for drinking water or taking breaks. Samuel had a seventh-grade education; his parents pulled him from school shortly after his fourteenth birthday. State law required that AWC furnish their operatives with water, but the "drinking water" Samuel drank was polluted, pulled up from the canal; AWC docked 5 cents per week for this amenity "whether we drank it or not." Being five minutes late resulted in a fine of one hour's pay; multiple infractions meant losing the whole week's wage.[137] All in all, testimony like Goldberg's revealed a shocking pattern of AWC taxing their workers for compliance with the barest labor laws. Goldberg described casual police brutality, including a police officer who "grabbed a woman by the throat and hit her ... with a club. A good club, too." In subsequent witness testimony, it was discovered that police, militias, and men paid by AWC had used batons manufactured at a nearby wheel factory against striking women and children.[138] It was against testimony like this that anyone speaking about the benefits of children's labor was situated. Police Chief John J. Sullivan was questioned about his decision to arrest twenty-five children at the train station that February, separating them from their mothers as the latter were booked into the county jail.[139] To counter testimony sympathetic to strikers, others spoke to the benefits of children's labor. "The work the children do in the mill is perfectly proper for children to do," Reverend Clark Carter opined in his testimony.[140]

The House Rules Committee was tasked with making recommendations for new laws governing child labor, and so a partisan contest over the definition of childhood arose. Was a sixteen-year-old mill operative a child or a man? Had the militiaman who bayoneted John Ramey murdered a child, or had he acted appropriately against a criminal rioter? For strikers and union representatives, Ramey's death was evidence of militia impunity and disregard for the lives of child workers. City officials, by contrast, described a young man whose death was the tragic result of a Syrian riot he helped incite. To fit Ramey's story into one of these competing narratives, congressmen and witnesses traded hostile exchanges over Ramey's actual age. When Representative Thomas Hardwick (R-Georgia) questioned striker Samuel Lipson, for instance, Lipson described how the strike was the first time that many in IWW's interracial coalition worked together: "There are sixteen nationalities represented in the Lawrence mills but they never commingled before, owing to the difference in tongues. *But the stomach language speaks to all.*"[141] After Lipson mentioned "a Syrian boy had been stabbed" in January, Hardwick asked:

> HARDWICK: Is that boy here?
> LIPSON: He's stabbed—dead—to death. He was running away when the soldier stabbed him.
> HARDWICK: How old was he?
> LIPSON: He was 16 to 20 years old.
> HARDWICK: Then he wasn't a child?
> LIPSON: Well, he was pretty young to be stabbed. The soldier was exonerated.[142]

As Hardwick continued to question Lipson's perception of Ramey, he analogized between young men dying in battle and young men dying on picket lines, asking, "He was old enough for military service, was he not?" Lipson responded, "Do you think a boy of 16 or 17 years is old enough for military service?" and Rep. Hardwick demurred, "Of course, it varies in different countries."[143] Lipson also described John Ramey's injuries and corpse for the assembled members.

Congressional lawyers also focused on the authorities' shoddy investigation into Ramey's death. Lawrence police never investigated the incident because the state guard claimed jurisdiction over the case and resisted police attempts to intercede. Police Chief Sullivan told Congress that "the parents of this boy went to military headquarters and asked for an investigation." They were told "this boy had a musical instrument, that a procession was about to be formed on Oak Street, near White Street and a parade was intended," and that in scattering the crowd, "this boy was bayoneted." Sullivan also testified that "no complaint was ever made to the police or to the civil authorities . . . by the boy's relatives or friends." The deposing lawyer, Mr. Stanley, asked Sullivan, "Do you wait in this country, when a man is killed, for some complaint from his relatives or friends before you inquire into the nature of the killing?" Sullivan replied, "These were extraordinary circumstances."[144]

> STANLEY: In what respect?
> SULLIVAN: In the respect—
> STANLEY: A man with a horn has a bayonet run through him, through the back. That is an extraordinary circumstance, the only thing extraordinary I see about it.

Sullivan replied, "He was killed by a soldier who was in the performance of his duty put upon him by his superiors. It was a matter for the military authorities." In multiple depositions, Sullivan maintained that the guardsmen handled the incident report without his involvement. He described John Ramey's parents as satisfied: "After the circumstances were explained to them and they learned them, while they regretted the circumstances, they were satisfied that the boy was to blame."[145] Neither of John's parents appeared before Congress. Asked where Ramey's parents were, Samuel Lipson said he had last seen them the week of the funeral and did not know if they were still in Lawrence or not.

During the hearings, partisan disagreements over John Ramey's story fed a broader discourse about the Syrian presence in Lawrence, their IWW involvement, and potential ties to subversive political ideologies. Both police and strikers told stories about Farris Marad, James Brox, and Dr. Iskandar Hajjar. Sullivan described remarks made by Hajjar the night of Ramey's death; in an unguarded moment of grief and rage, Hajjar called an emergency meeting and allegedly "asked for twenty five men to go with him to throw themselves on the bayonets of the soldiers as a sacrifice to the cause—and that by doing that, it would bring the attention of the world to the strikers."[146] A Syrian merchant present at that meeting informed the police. However, all follow-up questions into Syrian radicalism fell apart: officials could not tell Congress anything more damning, and the strikers who testified directly contradicted the police informants. Even Reverend Clark Carter was unable to say more. When asked, "Do you know a Syrian by the name of Brooks [sic, likely Brox], a doctor?" he responded, "No, I think you have got the name wrong." "The one who wanted to jump on the bayonets?" "There was a Dr. Hajjia [sic, likely Hajjar]." "No, this is another one," to which Rev. Carter replied, "I know no Dr. Brooks in Lawrence."[147] In his testimony, AWC weaver and IWW partisan Samuel Lipson denied that Marad, Hajjar, and Brox were even strikers at all, because none of them were employed by AWC.[148]

After eight weeks of picketing, the strike ended in victory: workers won a 20 percent wage increase and assurances about protection of work hours.[149] At a final mass meeting in the town common on March 14, Bill Haywood mounted a platform and asked each of the nationalities assembled to vote in favor of going back to work. "Syrians," Haywood called, and then Dr. Hajjar "squeezed to the rail and told the crowd below" to vote, and a resounding "aye" sent them back to work.[150] The IWW was widely seen as the strike's victors, and its Lawrence local went from 300 members to 10,000 in a year (though nearly all these memberships lapsed with the outbreak of World War I).[151] Local operatives carried the strike's strategic lessons forward, embracing direct action as well as interracial cooperation in textile strikes across the industry. In Lawrence and beyond, Syrians continued to organize within the ethnic community, and in cooperation with the radical wings of the American labor movement. They joined the IWW again in Paterson, New Jersey, participating in major textile strikes in 1912, 1913, and 1924.[152] In Massachusetts, they also struck with the Amalgamated Clothing Workers of America (ACWA), most notably in Boston during the 1910s and 1920s.[153] By contrast, conservative unions like the United Textile Workers

FIGURE 6. Bill Haywood and Elizabeth Gurley Flynn stand with Syrian and Italian strike leaders during the vote to return to work in Lawrence, March 14, 1912. Source: *Boston Globe*, March 15, 1912, 2.

(UTW) continued to marginalize Syrian workers, its leadership representing them as a dangerous racial outgroup whose exclusion from immigration would protect American labor.

Though Syrians strategically joined unions in strikes, union leadership tended to underacknowledge them as a mobilizable force outside of stoppages. As a group, they so numerically dominated sectors of the New England and Atlantic textile industries that their presence at pickets was a major factor, but they were simultaneously reticent union members. Nearly all Syrian organizing happened within the diaspora's own ethnic clubs which remained inaccessible to national union leadership. Part of this approach was paternalistic: during a strike when most of the strikers were immigrant women, it is notable that men represented their demands publicly. Notably, too, the Syrians who liaised with the IWW were not textile workers themselves; these men could represent Syrian demands while shielding the strikers from AWC as well as police. Syrians were acutely aware that they walked a delicate line between their own readiness to walk off the job and their bosses' readiness to associate them with anarchism. Deportation was the risk of falling to the wrong side of that line.

That caveat aside, interethnic solidarity remained a central feature in textile labor organizing through the 1920s. In another strike in Lawrence in 1922, Syrian workers organized a "parade of all races" (*li-l-jaliyyat*) through the city throughfare to illustrate interethnic solidarity as the key to social betterment.[154] In 1924, Syrian participation in a Boston garment factory strike led by ACWA was pivotal in securing concessions from management; in that strike, Syrian stitchers convinced their union to place race discrimination at the foreground of strikers' grievances.[155] Millowners' attempts to divide immigrants continued apace; in a 1925 strike in Fall River, factory owners attempted to import Syrian workers from Lawrence to replace striking Portuguese workers.[156] Once the Lawrence Syrians arrived, they learned that the bosses were "offering the jobs of striking Syrians to Portuguese and the jobs of striking Portuguese to Syrians." They joined the Portuguese strikers in solidarity, stopping all work in both Fall River and Lawrence to wrest concessions from management.[157]

Interracial cooperation was a core facet of the Bread and Roses Strike, but this cooperation and solidarity was not built overnight. The Syrian strikers organized primarily *within* their own community rather than beyond it, predominantly within Syrian clubs, women's homes, or the church sanctuary. A weekly town hall at an Oak Street building rented by a mutual aid society called the United Syrian Society gave Syrian workers opportunities to liaise with IWW leadership as well as a pulpit for broader discussions about labor, life, and community needs. After 1912, workers institutionalized their strike work into a new Syrian club that met monthly: the Syrian National Club (Jama'iyyat al-Muntada al-Suri al-'Umumiyya).[158] The Syrian National Club organized from 1912 until at least the late 1920s, sharing its Oak Street meeting space with the United Syrian Society and operating under a charter in "service to the Syrian people regardless of differences in sect and background [*ala ikhtilaf al-tawa'if wa-l-musharib*]" in New England. The club's president was Farid Ghusn, a printer who got his start working with his father for *al-Wafa'* before establishing his own paper, *al-Fajr* (the Dawn) after World War I.[159] For Ghusn, the Syrian National Club represented "the renaissance of national brotherhood."[160] Together with *al-Wafa'* and *al-Rawda* newspapers and the Maktabat al-Sha'b (People's Library) operated by Khalil Munayyir (Monayer),[161] the Syrian National Club represented the locus of a new kind of Syrian fraternalism devoted to workingmen's betterment.

Rather than homeland nationalism, the club's mandate was to care for Syrian textile workers and institutionalize class solidarity through mutual aid and emergency relief for the unemployed, the disabled, and the poor. In Lawrence, the Syrian National Club redistributed $1,200 (on average) in member dues within Lawrence annually.[162] A second chapter opened in Boston's Syrian Quarter during World War I, aligned with Wadi' Shakir and his paper, *Fatat Boston*; it similarly focused on relief provision until its dissolution in 1926.[163] Across the industrial mill towns, mutual aid societies provided Syrians with a material safety net and a social setting beyond the factory floor. These were spaces for the discussion of social improvement, shared grievances, and strategies for collective action that could then be animated by the call to strike. The historiography of the mahjar regularly examines these institutions as ethnic spaces, but, crucially, they were simultaneously sites for cultivating labor politics.

FIGURE 7. Induction of officers at the Syrian National Club of Lawrence, 1917. Source: Lawrence History Center Photography Collection.

TWO

MUTUAL AID
Syrian Societies in Industrial Massachusetts

STRIKES RESPOND TO MATERIAL GRIEVANCES; they also rely on systems of material support. To issue a credible call to strike, a community must first create and sustain such systems. And when union leaders guide strikers toward a successful confrontation with management, they depend on groundswells of support that make headlines but are far from spontaneous. Bread and Roses captured national attention because of its spectacular contours: a dramatic walkout and daily pickets; police brutality and the trials of Joseph Ettor, Arturo Giovannitti, and William Wood; public displays of interracial solidarity; massive parades and civil disobedience. Strikers were undeterred by the politics of race division, threats of retaliatory deportation, and even a bomb plot. Syrians joined forces with Italian, Polish, and Jewish workers in the strike of 1912. At the same time, interracial strike coordination depended on the operations of autonomous institutions within multiple ethnic communities. In the Syrian community, permanent networks of mutual aid directly supported Syrian workers. Responding to their immediate material, social, and representational needs, local mutual aid societies mitigated the economic precarity, social isolation, and legal jeopardy Syrians experienced in Massachusetts mill towns. This chapter examines the history of Syrian mutual aid societies as the setting for labor history. It argues that mutual aid politics emerged in the context of dual economic and social precarity, leading Syrian organizers to create autonomous spaces in the absence of larger labor outreach.

Associationism has been the focus of a substantial literature in both Middle Eastern and American immigration histories. In the Syrian mahjar, mutual aid represented one facet of a broader culture of associational activity; between the 1890s and 1930s, hundreds of ethnic societies incorporated across the Americas, most of them responding to the welfare needs of the Syrian, Lebanese, and Palestinian poor at home or abroad.[1] Much of the literature that examines mahjari associational culture explores the role these clubs played in homeland political activism, particularly in the politics of anticolonial nationalisms. The strengths of established archives shape this focus. The mahjar's print culture and numerous interwar petitioning campaigns highlighted homeland nationalist politics, literally "papering the mahjar," in a bid to represent the community in an internationalist context.[2] This kind of paper politics was also a class project, closely associated with the diaspora's emergent transnational middle class rather than with workers. By contrast, the goals established by Syrian mutual aid societies to benefit workers and their families were utilitarian, local, and aimed at the community's preservation. These societies were often ephemeral, forming around immediate perceived needs in the ethnic community, faltering if disputes over priorities or social politics sapped members' energies, and disbanding if workers (or the industries that employed them) moved away. These societies avoided the public spotlight by design and maintained themselves behind the scenes. Though highly effective, this strategy remains difficult to trace via formal archival repositories.

Nevertheless, the records of a few Syrian American mutual aid societies have survived, preserved initially in private family collections and subsequently through counterarchival efforts. Responding to a recognition that government archives are not "sites of knowledge retrieval" but of knowledge production,[3] counterarchives seek to recover the perspectives of communities marginalized by the bureaucratic imperatives of state records.[4] Counterarchival collections are often sites for the preservation of diasporic identity; they preserve and disseminate private papers as a means of celebrating ethnic pride, to combat the white supremacy in dominant narratives of American history, or to make "a radical intervention in the production of historiographic knowledge."[5] These collections are often arranged according to a topical logic, rather than one based on the institutional provenance of individual records.[6] This replicates how users access information and has shaped the cultural-historical trajectory of mahjar studies. But counterarchival collections demand the same questions about curation that historians ask of state archives: Which diasporic stories are selected for preservation? Whose histories are told, whose are marginalized, and why?[7] Historians working on the Syrian American mahjar, for instance, now challenge the "model minority" narratives present in some of the field's extant counterarchival collections, which center examples of commercial success, upward social mobility, and political quiescence at the expense of examples of collective action.[8]

This chapter examines the records of three Syrian mutual aid societies in Massachusetts: the United Syrian Society of Lawrence, the Young Men of Deir-el-Kamar of Lawrence, and the Syrian Ladies' Aid Society of Boston. These records were preserved by counterarchival projects by Alixa Naff, Evelyn Shakir, Evelyn Abdala Menconi, Juliet Bistany, and Elizabeth Boosahda and through community-based conservation efforts by the Immigrant City Archive (and its successor, the Lawrence History Center). Notably, these archival projects were themselves women's work; contributors established a praxis of narration through personal stories, family portraiture, and oral histories that reflected a desire to build on, in Sarah Gualtieri's words, "an Arab feminist tradition in which one woman passes her story—and her voice—to another who makes that voice the basis of her own writing and creation."[9] Animated by an ethic of recovering lost voices and a desire to speak back to the assimilationist narratives, scholars also situated Syrian associationism as representing authentic ethnic spaces, sites of literary or artistic celebration and hyphenated Arab Americanism.[10] In addition to being *cultural* projects, this chapter considers the explicit role mutual aid societies played in *material* custodianship of the Syrian community by alleviating suffering and economic precarity, serving the working class, and facilitating Arab American participation in the labor movement.

SERVING WHOM? THE LABOR POLITICS OF MUTUAL AID

Syrian communities across the mahjar organized in ethnic mutual aid societies which offered support for social, legal, or charitable needs. In Massachusetts, Syrian clubs opened meeting halls, offering a public forum for the discussion of issues of mutual concern or (as seen in chapter 1) a staging ground for labor organizers. Syrian clubs also organized beneficence work, philanthropy, and private welfare, often working across the diaspora.[11] Though these organizations universally espoused a desire to "raise the Syrian name" through good works and community stewardship, they also imagined different migrant publics, served distinct local communities, and defined "good works" in diverse ways. In the absence of public welfare programs, immigrant mutual aid societies offered direct redistribution of resources: rent relief, food or medical aid, burial services, or legal services. This work required a low profile and a bottom-up approach.[12] Organizers walked a tightrope as they projected a public image of the ethnic community as responsible, self-reliant, industrious, and patriotic while also demanding racial equity, protesting discrimination, and quietly providing a safety net for the unemployed. Because these clubs engaged in redistributive work to soften poverty's edges, they have been described as instruments of social reproduction and a means of preventing social protest, even staving off labor contests.[13] However, this view does not account for the ways mutual aid societies organized Syrian workers, enabling them to prolong strikes and facilitating their partnerships with trade unions. The same public image that mutual aid societies projected outward—as respectable stewards of "the Syrian name"—includes abundant negative space.

The distinction between immigrant mutual aid and immigrant philanthropy is relevant here. Whereas philanthropy served the immigrant needy from above, it also reinforced what Daniel Soyer calls "a class and power hierarchy between donors and recipients, even when both sides were members of the same ethnic group." By contrast, mutual aid "flowed back and forth among equals who had pooled their resources" operating on an "ethos of egalitarianism, democracy, and independence."[14] In Massachusetts, Syrian workers' societies had three goals: to meet immediate survival needs, to build a shared understanding about why people did not have what they needed, and to support community members as they fought to improve their material conditions. To achieve these goals, mutual aid societies engaged in direct welfare relief, fellowship work to strengthen ethnic solidarities among Syrian workers, and interethnic coalition building between Syrians and other immigrant groups.

Mutual aid societies served a variegated working class. Syrian immigrants worked in all facets of the Massachusetts textile industries. Depending on whether they worked in the manufacture of silks, cotton (weaving or garment work), woolens, or leatherwork, workers encountered different levels of risk, incommensurate wages, and uneven job security. Internal hierarchies emerged, based on wage scales and perceptions of prestige. Silk work, for instance, paid the highest wages because the job demanded a specific set of skills sought by U.S. employers; fully two-thirds of Arab Americans who worked in silk came to America after working in Syrian or Lebanese silk factories.[15] In comparison, cotton weaving, garment work, and woolens employed a wider cross-section of the Syrian American working classes, most of them coming from peasant or agricultural backgrounds in Mount Lebanon, Syria, or Palestine. In 1911, barely 6 percent of these workers had any prior industrial experience before arrival in America, according to a U.S. Immigration Commission Report.[16] At the bottom of this hierarchy were Ottoman leatherworkers (Turks as well as Syrians dominated this sector), who performed the dangerous work of cutting and perforating uppers for boots and shoes in factories that experienced frequent accidents and closures. They were nearly all first-time proletarians: 90.9 percent of Ottoman leatherworkers had been landless tenant farmers prior to emigration.[17]

In all types of factory labor, Syrians joined other Ottoman workers as well as the Italian, Greek, and Portuguese immigrants whose neighborhoods they shared.[18] Relative to Turkish workers, Syrian textile workers were comparatively privileged, earning an average of $400–$500 a year, mostly in the silk, cotton, or woolens industries (Turkish annual wages averaged around $260, mostly because this group was disproportionately employed in leather).[19] However, rates of trade unionism also played a role: even in leatherworking, Syrians commanded higher wages because of union membership rates of 59 percent, compared to 10 percent of Turkish workers.[20] Access to legal naturalization also deepened this disparity over time. In 1913, 20.3 percent of Syrian men in the industry were either declarant or naturalized U.S. citizens, categories of status that remained out of reach for nearly all Ottoman Turkish immigrants through World War I.[21]

Gender also shaped how Syrian immigrants approached textile work. "Boston, that is where women came to work," Bahieh Kappaz recalled in her oral history interview with Alixa Naff. "The men work in the shoe factory, the women, most of them, in sewing."[22] Arriving from Damascus in 1912, Kappaz was fourteen when she started work at the Salim Ayoub kimono factory, "I come [to America] on a Thursday, and Monday I went to work."

Bahieh and her older sister both performed piece work: "I had a hard time [at first], the whole week, $3, rip and sewing, rip and sewing, and the next week I make $11. Because I'm hungry [for] money."[23] The Kappaz sisters sent their wages to Syria to bring the rest of the family abroad in 1920. Bahieh illustrates that access to wage work was deeply gendered in Boston: she and her sister worked in housedress and apron shops owned by Syrian merchants, while Syrian men were limited to the city's leather factory. When Bahieh's brothers came over in 1920, the family relocated to Detroit, where better paid factory jobs could be found for the men. Zahdi Fallaha Barsa reported comparable working conditions in a Boston apron factory in 1914. "Syrians did factory work: shoe shop factory, apron factory, dresses factory . . . you see those aprons with the piping on them? I worked on those aprons, I used to put the piping." Zahdi reported that her factory was "all Syrian. The owner was Syrian, the workers Syrian, all Syrian! My first week I made $6, and I thought I'd made a million dollars!"[24] She lived with her grandparents, who also worked in factories; both of her brothers attended school instead.

Though working conditions varied considerably across the industry, Syrian workers shared a common experience of economic precarity, structured by the labor practices of their employers. America's textile industries were shaped by seasonality, making intermittent unemployment a central challenge.[25] Both large U.S. factories and Syrian American contractor workshops laid Syrians off during slack periods, creating vulnerabilities that disproportionately affected the ethnic community. Rates of full employment (defined as working twelve months a year) swung wildly between 37 and 85 percent year-to-year among Syrian workers.[26] In 1913, the U.S. Immigration Commission reported Syrians were almost twice as likely to apply for state agency support than their French, Canadian, or European peers; 75.4 percent of Syrians seeking state support reported lack of employment, rather than disability, as the cause of their poverty. These figures reflect an industry-wide practice of casualizing "new" immigrant labor, creating Syrian working neighborhoods that were shaped by cycles of industrial boom-and-bust and which housed a permanent unemployed underclass.[27]

Even if formal employment was intermittent, everybody in Syrian textile households worked. Whether married or unmarried, young or old, Syrian women and men worked, as did children fourteen and older, particularly girls. A common configuration involved young women performing factory work to subsidize the shops or peddling businesses of male relatives, a pattern also repeated in Ottoman Lebanon.[28] In Massachusetts mill towns, Syrian women's wages were so important that social reformers suggested that "the fathers of mill families were but little more important as breadwinners than the mothers and children." Drawing on reform discourses, a 1915 Immigration Commission report concluded that "the mothers contributed more to the family income" than did their husbands.[29] Despite these reports, rates of Syrian employment in Massachusetts textiles suggest that Syrian men assumed industrial employment at comparable rates to Syrian women.[30] In addition to formal factory work, the Syrian household was itself a site of economic production: women worked as seamstresses, performed piecework, or made laces at home, often in conjunction with factory shifts.

Syrian American working households also expanded because of labor migration, illustrating how notions of kinship flexed to economic realities. In contrast to the nuclear households that typified this diaspora's emerging middle classes, Arab American workers maintained larger households defined by employment networks and the shared sense of proletarian precarity.[31] "We lived in an extended family neighborhood," Laurice Shagoury Maloley reports of her childhood. "There were no strangers in the community, and the residents cared for each other, all of which served to mollify our economic condition."[32] The Shagourys lived next door to the Homsys; they were kin who emigrated from Syria together and resided on Tyler Street in Boston's Syrian Quarter. This pattern was typical: distant relatives cohabited in new ways, and Syrians from like villages banded together in households focused around work rhythms.[33] Working households also took on boarders who paid a share of the rent.[34] Across Massachusetts, half of Syrian households rented rooms out to men recently arrived from the Middle East.[35] Male heads of household also secured employment for their boarders, resulting in entire households employed by one firm. Syrian women managed these complex household systems as landladies, blending rental income with intervals of factory labor, in-home textile production, or childcare.[36]

Most Syrian textile families depended on weekly wages between $2.60 and $6.50 per person, a rate that offered basic subsistence without accounting for disruptions, illnesses, injuries, marriage, death, or layoffs. Debt was common, but there was little relief. The court system offered one unappealing way out: if a husband failed to provide for his dependents, a wife could seek relief in municipal court by accusing her husband of "neglect of family," a charge which produced judgment on his wages at the cost of his honor and potential imprisonment. In Lawrence in 1912, for instance, Pacific Mills employee G. Hassoud*, age twenty-two, was arrested for neglect of family, bailed the same day, and assessed a judgment of $50, to be paid in $3 weekly increments to his wife.[37] This debtors charge was a back end settlement of family disputes over money; the fine was consistently awarded to a man's wife and, at $2 to $3 per week, was presumably for rent. Usually, these judgments did not escalate; however, if a man could not pay his fine, he could be imprisoned. This is what happened to E. Saab, twenty-eight, arrested in 1913 for neglect of family, and assessed a $50 fine to be paid in $2 weekly increments to his wife for rent.[38] When Saab failed to pay his fine, he was sentenced to ninety days in the county jail. The logic behind this punitive system was that holding debtors would incentivize them to liquidate hidden assets. However, mill operatives had few assets to begin with. In Saab's case, the jail released him a month early after concluding that as "a poor prisoner," imprisoning him only robbed him of earning capacity and deepened his family's crisis.[39] Making a complaint of neglect was a painful decision with social consequences for wives who were facing eviction. Despite the risks of social shame and stigma of criminality, Syrian families ended up in neglect proceedings as a last resort because they lacked access to unemployment insurance or public welfare.

Syrian mutual aid societies emerged to respond to these challenges, pooling resources for matters of life, death, illness, or injury; they provided for dependents, paid out for medical costs, and offered burial services. Amid conditions of grinding poverty, private direct aid mitigated the risk of crimes of neglect and maintained the community's reputation as law-abiding. Societies also compensated workers during strikes and maintained bail funds to keep Syrian workers out of the county jail. During the 1912 strike, for instance, dozens of Syrians arrested on charges like "rioting," illegal assembly, or defiance of curfew were bailed out before they were booked into the county jail. Together, these clubs alleviated poverty, but they also built Syrian understandings about the sources of poverty, mobilizing their members around ethnic solidarity and collective action. Membership was an important source of practical protection for Syrian workers.

THE UNITED SYRIAN SOCIETY OF LAWRENCE, MASSACHUSETTS

As Syrians arrived in Lawrence, Massachusetts, to work in the woolens industry, practical questions surfaced about meeting community needs. Foremost among these needs were matters of death and dying. Contrary to stereotypes about early immigrants being young, unattached men, Syrians usually came to Lawrence as multigenerational family units. Many of these households arrived with a female head: widowed women with children, unmarried sisters, or cousins of working families took factory jobs at AWC to support families which usually included elders. Such family configurations made providing for aging dependents and planning for funerary expenses a significant community focus. Burial in Massachusetts was expensive: the average cost of a modest plot, casket, and service ranged between $45 and $90 in 1915, the latter sum representing nearly six months of an operative's wages. Deaths in the Syrian colony also precipitated new questions about the community's ethnic identity: Where could Syrians be buried? Who would absorb funeral costs, and what happened if costs were insurmountable? How would a deceased relative be grieved, in whose presence, and what significance would communal differences play in this multi-confessional ethnic community? Each time new obituaries appeared in *al-Wafa'* newspaper, questions about identity recurred. In 1907, a society called the United Syrian Society (Jama'iyyat al-Ittihad al-Suri, hereafter USS) emerged to serve as Lawrence's first nondenominational burial society. The USS began with a campaign to establish a new Syrian cemetery, but it expanded into a deliberately multi-confessional fraternal order devoted to mutual aid, social insurance, and a spirit of service to the Syrian ethnic community.

Funeral assistance had been a feature of Syrian life in Lawrence before 1907, but funds were channeled through—and burial plots restricted to—the city's Syrian churches. Lawrence also hosted several homeland associations serving the needs of immigrants from, for instance, Qab Ilyas, Machghara, Hammana, or Falougha. However, critics pointed to their role in maintaining confessional particularisms at the expense of wider ethnic solidarity. "Every [Syrian] town had its own club here," explained Roger Aziz in an oral history interview. "This is something that my father didn't like." Roger's father, Aziz Aziz, founded the USS because "he didn't like each individual town to have its own club because, you see, Lebanon is a small—a very small place. And the people—rather than have them split up, he thought they would be better if they were united." The USS's founders were mill workers who shared a desire for Syrian solidarity in the context of a racial order which placed them at the margins. Aziz and his brothers, Abdo and Abdalla, had come to Massachusetts with their mother in 1900 after his father's death. Sponsored by another relative in Lawrence, Aziz, his brothers, and his mother all worked for AWC, at the Acadia, Ayer, and Pacific Mills.[40]

The death of a fellow Syrian who could not be buried in the church graveyard prompted Aziz and his co-activists to act. Roger explained: "It was because of the death of a man . . . they had no place to bury him. Because the people didn't realize that the Lebanese were Christians regardless of whether they were Orthodox or Melkites or Maronites."[41] Three Syrian churches then operated in town: St. Anthony's (Maronite), St. Joseph's (Melkite), and St. George's (Greek Orthodox), though many also attended the St. Mary's Catholic Church. Of the three, only St. Anthony's had a small cemetery on its grounds, but the decedent could not be buried there because of his confession. Most working families interred their dead in the city's public Bellevue Cemetery, but this site was considered undesirable to Syrians who wished to be among kin. "So, they had a hard time burying this man," concluded Roger Aziz. His body sat at the undertaker's office for weeks as a serious debate emerged over the church's refusal to bury a man from beyond its congregation. "That is when my father said, 'We will start our own organization. We will buy our own land. We will make our own cemetery. *And there will be no churches involved.*'"[42] Aziz Aziz and his co-activists placed an advertisement in *al-Wafa*' announcing their intention to build a nondenominational Syrian cemetery.[43]

From its origins as a burial society, the USS developed into a network of mill operatives who rejected confessionalism and embraced the notion of an obligation of care rooted in Syrian identity. The society met monthly, first in the Elm Street tenements and later in a rented meeting hall on Oak Street, a commons the USS later shared with the Syrian National Club. The USS charter welcomed all ethnic Syrians and Lebanese, regardless of confession or hometown, and expressly prohibited the clergy's involvement.[44] They collected modest dues to seed a burial insurance fund and accepted donations from the community. As they campaigned, Aziz Aziz and Lutfullah Jarjoura led town hall meetings in Lawrence; they also approached wealthy Syrian merchants in Boston and New York City and accepted gifts from workers and from the churches, resulting in the purchase of a five-acre cemetery plot in 1909.[45]

The United Syrian Cemetery (now also called the United Lebanese Cemetery) was America's first Syrian nondenominational cemetery. Clergy were allowed to perform funerary rites on its grounds but were otherwise absent from the space. At $15 per plot, burial in the cemetery was inexpensive compared to local alternatives. Syrian families worked with the city undertaker, John Breen, until the Hajjar family opened an undertaking business to see to the washing, embalming, and interment of the dead.[46] One reason funerals remained inexpensive was because the cemetery ran on volunteer labor: "They would go up and dig a grave by hand for free," Roger Aziz recalled later. "Nobody got paid." The work was then assigned to a USS cemetery committee.[47] The cemetery contains nearly 600 burial sites dating from at least 1912 through 2021.[48] Though the USS was the first, other nondenominational Syrian burial societies emerged across the region during this period: Boston's Syrian Burial Society formed in 1910, and two more Syrian cemeteries opened in Burlington and Barre, Vermont, by 1930.[49]

In the meantime, the USS expanded its fraternal goals to provide services for the living, applying the same ethic of nonsectarian, open membership to Syrians interested in "meritorious service" to the ethnic community.[50] No formal membership roster has been preserved, but the group boasted hundreds of members who each paid $5 annually (or $0.10 per week) to remain in good standing.[51] These funds were allocated to three pools: the funeral fund; welfare relief for ill, impoverished, or unemployed workers; and stipendiary payments for striking workers. After the 1912 Bread and Roses Strike, the USS incorporated and received its charter from the Commonwealth of Massachusetts, renaming itself the United Syrian Charitable Society of Lawrence. Roger Aziz noted that this was an important legitimating move, one he credited to his father's connections to friends in the Italian community: "They [the Syrian founders] had a lot of help from some of the people who had been here before them . . . these people helped them get organized [and] told them what to do."[52] Though the tenements were uniformly Syrian, Aziz Aziz and his co-founders relied on the organizational expertise of Italian immigrants with sophisticated traditions of ethnic mutual aid.

The society's daily operations focused on improvement of material conditions. "There was no such thing as welfare in the old days," according to Roger Aziz, and "people would rather starve than go down to the town hall and beg for a few little things." City programs were limited. Applicants could receive grants of $2 for food or emergency expenses, but municipal authorities would "come and investigate" if Syrians accepted them; anyone who did so was seen as bringing shame to the community. Providing direct relief through private channels, the USS enhanced the immigrants' autonomy while protecting their reputation. The club organized a relief committee to identify local needs and consider applications for rent relief, heating assistance, coverage of medical or legal expenses, and food aid. Roger Aziz emphasized the confidentiality of these interactions: "God help you if you ever mentioned the name of somebody you helped. If you were a member and you said, 'Oh, we helped them,' you know, that was a no-no." This concern for privacy was such that even USS officers did not know who received aid; that knowledge belonged only to the committee.[53]

The USS's relief ledgers are not archived, but the society applied the ethics of nonsectarian, private assistance to its work. "If they found a family that was in need, they did not care who they were or what parish they belonged to," recollected Roger Aziz. "It didn't matter because we had members of all of the parishes that belonged to our society." Society membership was not obligatory, and relief in the form of cash grants was allocated based on urgency of need.[54] Once the USS gained its own meeting hall, the society also hosted dances, creating a respectable social setting for young, second-generation Syrian men and women that was more easily monitored than Lawrence's taverns and dance halls.

Occasionally, the USS responded to local emergencies. When a fire destroyed the Tanyus Khalil and Sons dry goods shop in 1922, USS President Kalil Moraway called a meeting at the club's hall and raised $477 to aid families affected by the tragedy.[55] Like his co-activists, Moraway was a factory worker: he came to Lawrence in 1904 to work for AWC and lived in the Valley Street boardinghouse, a common landing spot for Syrian workers.[56]

The society's Oak Street meeting hall was primarily a men's club, where Syrians gathered to discuss the day's news, read serials, play backgammon, or seek employment or assistance. However, a Ladies Auxiliary also formed in 1916 and was given a dedicated meeting room, separate from the men's leisure spaces. The women of the USS auxiliary were known as particularly effective fundraisers. One much-anticipated event at the USS hall was their

FIGURE 8. The United Syrian Charitable Society hosts its fortieth anniversary banquet at the Hibernian Hall in Lawrence, Massachusetts, 1947. Source: Lawrence History Center Photography Collection.

monthly *sahra*, which Roger Aziz recalled as "a little supper (where) men would come, eat, and contribute some money" to the society. These dinners netted the USS $150–$200 a month, making it a powerful revenue source; for comparison, the average two-week grocery bill for a family was $5 at the time. The *sahrat* were especially popular among young, unmarried men: "there were a lot of bachelors around," men who appreciated a homecooked Syrian meal and whose donations sustained families with significant economic burdens. Finally, and fitting with USS's origins as a burial society, the hall served as a funeral space. Anthony Ramey held a wake there for his father Philip Ramey in 1930; Philip had previously served as the society's president.[57]

The USS, later known as the United Syrian Charitable Society, was an important institution to the immigrant generation. Among second-generation Arab Americans born in Massachusetts, the club was a space for their fathers.[58] As the immigrant generation aged, the society experienced challenges. Membership attenuated in the 1940s and 1950s, but the club continued to operate. By the time of Roger Aziz's oral history interview in 1985, the club claimed 250 members but had sold its Oak Street meeting hall to the Young Syrian Men's Association.[59]

THE YOUNG MEN OF DEIR-EL-KAMAR OF LAWRENCE, MASSACHUSETTS

In addition to meeting specific material needs, Syrian mutual aid societies also reimagined the ethnic community's contours and began to shift shared understandings of a diasporic common good. In addition to ethnic clubs like the USS, numerous hometown associations emerged in Massachusetts mill towns, focusing not only on the local projects typical of immigrant mutual aid but also on improving conditions in the homeland through remittances, return travel, or transnational institution building.[60] In Lawrence, these societies reflected the diverse origins of the Syrian community: some were named for villages (the Becharre Welfare Society, the Young Men of Zahle, Young Men's Hammana Society, Mashgara Society), regions (Grand Sons of Mount Lebanon, the Cedar Club), or kinship groups (the Bistany Women's Club). The Young Men of Deir-el-Kamar (Jama'iyyat Shaban Dayr al-Qamar, hereafter YMDK) was one of Lawrence's largest hometown clubs, its records partially preserved by the Lawrence History Center.

Established in 1914 by 300 "young and old men from Deir-el-Kamar and its suburbs (who) emigrated to the New World and settled down at Lawrence," the society institutionalized the personal networks of men from this part of Lebanon. Meeting local needs was top-of-mind: in an autobiographical society ledger, founder James (Najib) Shebaby recalls that new immigrants in Lawrence "had no unity of any sort to make them recognizable by other peoples."[61] The politics of organizing village networks in the mahjar were both local and transnational. The YMDK raised relief for their home village: the society sent relief to Lebanon during the 1925–27 revolt, to restore a church in 1928, and to build a new schoolhouse in 1929, for instance.[62] The organization also linked itself with Deirani societies organizing elsewhere in the diaspora: after 1920, sister chapters of the YMDK emerged in nearby Danbury, Connecticut, as well as in Mexico.[63] The club also welcomed new arrivals from Lebanon, helped young men find employment, and offered fellowship. The club worked to raise the immigrant community's profile in town, putting on plays and dinners to invite residents into the YMDK club space. Ranging between 60 and 300 members, the club maintained a meeting space adjacent to the Syrian Quarter. The club hosted monthly meeting to discuss matters of concern and plan relief work; dues were accessible, between 15 and 25 cents weekly.[64] Like the USS, the YMDK began as a men's club. Its members were predominantly mill workers, many of them kin: fathers and sons, cousins, brothers, and uncles. The convergence of these two ties—work and kinship—informed the club's mutual aid ethic.

The YMDK focused substantially on social insurance, and payment of medical benefits represented its largest expenditure. Usually, payments were designed to cover lost wages while members convalesced from serious illness or injury. Like the USS, the YMDK had a permanent relief committee which assessed claims and distributed funds, and all current members were eligible. The typical "sick aid" benefit amounted to the average wage replacement: $7 per week in the club's first years, and $10–$15 per week by the late 1920s and early 1930s. Recipients initially received two weeks of assistance but could reapply in the event of prolonged illness or disability. Importantly, the YMDK's relief ethic was mutual: the club pooled resources and risk, established equity in benefits, and encouraged regular usage by members. The campaign can therefore be more accurately understood as a form of social insurance than as a philanthropic effort. The YMDK's Sick Aid policy was widely subscribed to: a comparison of membership records with distribution receipts illustrates that about half (47 percent) of society members received benefits at least once between 1917 and 1939, and about a quarter of members received payments more than once for chronic conditions or end-of-life care. Club ledgers also record one-time payments to members for surgeries performed after workplace injuries or automobile accidents. In a community where a single injury, illness, or disability could bring a working family to ruin, the YMDK provided a crucial safety net.

In addition to medical aid, the society purchased heating coal for distribution to Syrian households, focusing on the tenements near the mill zone. Heating Syrian homes was expensive: within each of the three-story tenement structures, multigenerational families with as many as fifty members depended on a single coal stove for building heat, cooking, and hot water. Club ledgers show coal was distributed primarily to elders, to the fathers and uncles of club members who could not work or whose younger relatives were unable to cover heating costs on mill operative wages. Applications for heating coal rose and fell with general economic conditions in the woolens mills: when the industry experienced slowdowns between 1927 and 1933, for instance, the YMDK heated dozens of households, delivering the $10–$15 supply of anthracite coal needed to heat each tenement building through the winter.[65]

After medical aid and cash grants, death benefits constituted the YMDK's third major expenditure, particularly in the 1930s and 1940s as the immigrant generation aged. Membership included entitlement to a death benefit paid to surviving family to offset funeral costs or settle debts. Unlike the Sick Aid program, which had a strictly equal benefit system, death benefit payouts varied depending on the financial circumstances of the deceased and the surviving family in Lawrence and Lebanon. The society offered death benefits to parents grieving the loss of children, covering burial costs to spare families the indignity of interment in an unmarked city grave. These death benefits were also remitted transnationally. When a young member died tragically in a 1917 accident, the club sent a $50 check to his mother in Lebanon. Because of the naval embargo during World War I, the payment (and news of her son's death) only reached her months after the war's cessation.[66]

By pooling resources for direct redistribution, the YMDK mitigated the economic risks Syrian men assumed if they worked in Massachusetts mill towns. The club similarly supported Syrian American labor activism, exempting striking workers from dues payments and offering them strike pay as they picketed. Though poorly recorded in Syrian American archival sources generally, the Lawrence textile strikes of 1919 and 1922 feature prominently in the YMDK's relief ledgers. In early 1919, the American Federation of Labor (AFL) affiliate, the United Textile Workers of America (UTW), bargained with the American Woolen Company for a reduction in weekly working hours from fifty-four to forty-eight hours. AWC agreed to this reduction on the condition that UTW accept a compensatory wage cut, a Faustian bargain that reminded workers of the pay cut which precipitated the Bread and Roses Strike seven years earlier. The rank and file were deeply divided on this issue: English-speaking operatives accepted the wage cut, but Italian and Syrian immigrant workers opposed it.[67] UTW exacerbated these tensions by excluding Syrian workers from its bargaining. The International Workers of the World (IWW) had championed Italian and Syrian demands in 1912, but the union's local had disintegrated during World War I following repressive government tactics and a wave of arrests. Only the ethnic mutual aid societies represented workers in the Syrian and Italian neighborhoods.[68] Emboldened by a recent strike wave in Paterson and Passaic and enraged by UTW's contract, Italian and Syrian workers walked out of the AWC mills in a February 1919 wildcat strike.[69] In addition to wages, the strikers were driven by "resentments engendered by the maltreatment that the 'new immigrants' received at the hands of 'American' workers and bosses alike."[70]

U.S. intelligence officers watched the 1919 Lawrence strike closely. "The workers will merely work eight hours daily, refusing to work longer and then resisting any attempt by mill owners to pay them a reduced wage," officer John O'Neill reported to his bureau chief. "It is believed that effective speakers in the native tongues of the different nationalities . . . might succeed in whipping up a large part of the population into a strong Bolshevist movement."[71] Represented by the Syrian National Club, Syrian workers joined the strike, protesting the wage cut and their exclusion from UTW. Over eight weeks, the strike grew from 17,000 to 30,000 as more operatives stopped work and police struggled to push picketers out of the canal zone. An interracial "Committee of Fifteen" demanded direct bargaining with the manufacturers. The Committee of Fifteen aligned itself with the Amalgamated Clothing Workers of America (ACWA), a radical union that emerged in Boston in 1914 after a rift with AFL locals in that city's garment sector.[72] In both Lawrence and Boston, Syrian workers found the tactics they favored in ACWA: the union embraced direct action, protested racial labor market segmentation, and championed recent immigrant workers and their concerns about race discrimination.[73] The Committee of Fifteen met at the Syrian National Club (SNC) meeting house on Oak Street, where Syrian workers coordinated with Italian, Lithuanian, and Polish leadership.[74] YMDK members joined them, but the club simultaneously preserved its autonomy; the club was a mutual aid body, not a labor organization. However, it offered stipends to striking members and subsidized Committee of Fifteen leaders who went daily to SNC to plan strategy.[75]

In its grievances, tactics (e.g., daily parades), and a shared spirit of interracial solidarity, the 1919 strike readily recalled the Bread and Roses Strike. AWC and city police responded with familiar repressive moves. Violence at picket lines was common, and city officials called in the state guard to maintain order. Strikers, in turn, imposed boycotts on local businesses and called a general strike to protest police repression. Strikers and their sympathizers tossed rocks through the windows of any shops that remained open in the Syrian Quarter and harassed proprietors into locking up.[76] When state guardsmen learned that strikers had snuck Italian American anarchist Carlo Tresca into town by cover of darkness for a speech at the Working-man's Club, they responded by "mounting a machine gun at the heart of the Syrian neighborhood." This was an open provocation to violence that strike leaders only narrowly averted by prevailing on their own countrymen.[77] Meanwhile, AWC trucked in adjunct labor to maintain partial productive capacity, housing strikebreakers in guarded tenements. When strikers discovered them, Syrians assembled outside, threw rocks, and taunted the strikebreakers as they came and went. On April 9, several Syrians were arrested after a "riotous disturbance" outside one such tenement. As police tried to break up the demonstrators, a fistfight broke out; a striker seized an officer's billy club and beat him with it. Six men were arrested and fined for incitement; the man who brandished the billy club was sentenced for assault.[78]

As violence mounted, Syrian strikers imposed joint pressure on AWC and UTW demanding a seat at the bargaining table. Though direct bargaining was denied to them, after Massachusetts Governor Calvin Coolidge called on AWC to enter arbitration with the striking workers, UTW renegotiated its deal with AWC to add terms imposed by the Syrian strikers: a forty-eight-hour week and 15 percent pay increase in May 1919. Their material demands satisfied, Syrians went back to work, though their achievements were never directly acknowledged by UTW. The Syrian community's own associations, autonomous from the town's dominant labor union, remained workers' principal resource in labor disputes. Similarly, their ability to wrest concessions was the result of ethnic coalition building with other marginalized immigrants outside of official bargaining channels, which remained closed to them.

Lawrence's next strike year was 1922. A proposed 20 percent wage cut prompted mill operatives across several Massachusetts mill towns to side with one of the now-familiar camps: the AFL's United Textile Workers or the radical leadership of the One Big Union.[79] The 1922 strike shuttered half of the city's plants; an estimated 18,000 operatives went on strike for weeks before AWC and Pacific Mills canceled the wage reduction and conceded to worker demands.[80] Syrian workers again met in the Syrian National Club hall; as in 1919, the YMDK suspended dues collection and instead "aided nearly all members" with strike pay, covering their bills so they could fill daily picket lines.[81] Aid was similarly dispersed to members who participated in strike actions in 1924 and 1931.[82] YMDK's ledgers record this labor history in the barest of terms, dispassionately registering strike pay and acknowledging their cooperation with the Syrian National Club, the United Syrian Society, and other associations in town.

Remaining autonomous from union politics was strategically important for ethnic societies like the YMDK, because their ability to do redistributive work depended on maintaining the guise of political neutrality. Syrian clubs that too overtly embraced labor politics could lose their associational rights: the Syrian National Club, for instance, had its charter revoked in 1913. That year, the Commonwealth of Massachusetts investigated SNC after an anonymous complaint that its members "were members of the I.W.W." whose work was not "conducting an athletic, literary, and benevolent club" as described by their charter, but "Bolshevist political agitation." Finding that SNC members "have been arrested for rioting" and that "one of them was taken for planting dynamite during the strike [of 1912]," investigators recommended the club's charter be revoked.[83] It did not matter that the SNC members in question (Farris Marad, Joseph Assef, and others) were proven to have been framed in the 1912 dynamite conspiracy. The SNC lost its charter—and its ability to legally pool and redistribute resources—because of its purported radicalism. The club continued to meet on Oak Street but depended on links to the United Syrian Society and the Young Men of Deir-el-Kamar to accord space for its meetings.

Considered in this light, the YMDK's ability to sustain its members materially depended on careful management of its public reputation. The society balanced its front-facing activities with its quieter redistributive projects; as its members planned strike tactics at SNC in 1922, the society simultaneously participated in the City of Lawrence's "Parade for All Races," a civic procession celebrating ethnic culture, clothing, and cuisine in the public square.[84] The society's dinners, theatrical productions, and general spirit of ethnic fraternalism illustrate a similar attention to the relationship between public representation and private mutual aid. Events were open to all and raised relief for the needy. At the same time, that relief laid down the material foundations for Syrian labor politics during the strike wave of 1912–1924.

THE SYRIAN LADIES' AID SOCIETY OF BOSTON, MASSACHUSETTS

Like the Young Men of Deir-el-Kamar, the founders of the Syrian Ladies' Aid Society of Boston faced concerns about the role of Syrian mutual aid in supporting the city's working-class labor movements.[85] Boston's Syrian colony was home to an estimated 3,500 Arabic-speaking immigrants residing in the South End on Tyler, Hudson, and Kneeland Streets.[86] Though Boston's Syrian colony was a bit smaller than Lawrence's, the neighborhood enjoyed what Alixa Naff termed "mother colony" status: as an immigration port and railway center, new Syrian immigrants arrived in Boston before moving to mill towns like Fall River, Lowell, New Bedford, Pittsfield, Springfield, Worcester, or southern Maine or Vermont.[87] Boston Syrians worked mostly in garment work, though the city's leather and rubber factories also employed Syrian men. In the garment factories, Syrian women worked alongside Italians, Greeks, Armenians, Turks, Azoreans, and Cape Verdeans.[88] Others worked for Syrian American contractor shops, filling orders for large firms among a homogeneous Syrian workforce. By 1910, Boston had two Syrian banks owned by prominent émigré merchants; immigrants could seek small loans there or remit funds to family in the Middle East.[89]

In Boston, Syrian families lived in tenement-style houses like those found in Lawrence: three-story multifamily row houses lacking central heating, plumbing, or electricity. Rents were high and Syrian families usually took on boarders.[90] Immigrant boardinghouses also served Syrian workers: in an oral history interview with Alixa Naff, Charles Teebagy recalls paying $1.50 a week to stay in a shared Kneeland Street bedroom in 1902. His room had no furniture or utilities; Charles slept on the floor and showered at the public facilities stationed at the neighborhood's corners.[91] Intense poverty and precarity characterized Syrian livelihood in Boston. In her memoir, Laurice Maloley describes how her father, Joseph Shagoury, came to Boston to peddle but soon developed pneumonia. He was unable to work for two years. Laurice's mother, Wadia, became the head of household and the sole income earner for her three children at nineteen years old. Wadia attempted peddling, carrying "exclusively night clothing and fancy women's underwear, which she made by hand" door-to-door in Boston's wealthier neighborhoods.[92] When it became clear she could not provide for her children by this means, Wadia was forced to place her three daughters in foster care. Daughters Rose and Mary thrived with their foster family for the two years that Wadia and Joseph struggled to get back on their feet, but Wadia's youngest daughter, Nora, died in state custody.[93] Joseph eventually recovered from his illness and resumed peddling in 1910, and Wadia began a new job in a Hudson Street dress factory. Rose and Mary returned to their mother's home, but Nora's loss haunted Wadia: "My mother was never able to find out where or how that little one died, or where she was buried," Laurice Maloley recalled in 2002. "I have looked up her name in the state files of youngsters who passed away as wards of the state and she isn't listed anywhere. I am still trying to solve that mystery."[94]

The desperate situation the Shagourys found themselves in threatened many Syrian immigrant families; households were one illness or accident away from serious jeopardy. Such dire conditions motivated the volunteers of the Syrian Ladies' Aid Society of Boston (SLAS), founded in 1917 to serve the needs of Syrian working communities. SLAS members were intimately aware of the emergencies Syrian women faced; 60 percent of the society's early volunteers worked in the garment industry, many of them also doing hemming, garment piecework, lacemaking, or hand embroidery at home after shifts in the factory.[95] The SLAS's central goal was to provide for Syrian working women and their families, and, through this gendered politics of care, to reach needy Syrians across the state. Like the other societies explored in this chapter, the SLAS's work was centered on private distribution of pooled social resources. This commitment set the SLAS apart from other poverty relief work conducted by Boston's Syrian churches. St. George Antiochian Church, established in 1900, the Syrian Orthodox Association of Spiritual Union (est. 1913), and the Society of St. John of Damascus (est. 1914) all engaged in welfare relief.[96] But as Boston's first nondenominational society staffed entirely by women, the SLAS's direct aid moved through female channels to the working poor according to the principles of reciprocity and ethnic solidarity.

Despite the SLAS's proletarian preoccupations, what is usually remembered about this society is not the practical parts of its relief work, but its public-facing galas, ribbon drives, plays, and other social gatherings where the club fundraised for Syrians both locally and abroad.[97] Though women's mutual aid societies were common in the mahjar, the records of these clubs were rarely preserved owing to the dual marginalization their leaders faced as immigrant women. The Boston SLAS is a remarkable exception, its records preserved by Arab American studies scholar Evelyn Shakir. Shakir's mother, Hannah Sabbagh Shakir, was among the SLAS's founders and kept the club's records, relief ledgers, and event ephemera in a private family collection which is now jointly maintained by the Harvard University Schlesinger Library in the History of American Women and the Arab American National Museum.

Born in the Ain al-Rummaneh in 1895, Hannah Sabbagh came to Massachusetts in 1907 with her mother, joining five brothers and an uncle who had all come abroad to work in the textile sector.[98] Hannah took her first job as a child operative in a Fall River cotton factory at fourteen years old.[99] In 1910, virtually every unwed Syrian woman in Fall River worked in this factory.[100] Relocating to Boston a couple of years later, Hannah acquired some machines and opened a specialized apron firm, employing "the neighbors, six or seven women; we taught them how to sew."[101] Her brothers, meanwhile, established the Sabbagh Brothers business, a wholesale importing outfit that expanded and contracted with the chaotic rhythms of the global markets, necessitating Hannah's income to balance the books. "I went to work in the factory. All my life I worked," she explained in a 1983 oral history interview. "[My older brother] Alexander learned to weave, but he didn't work much. So, I had to make money for us to live on."[102] As she grew older, marrying in 1931, she continued to work in textiles. In 1944, she opened Parkway Manufacturing, employing fifteen women to produce women's skirts, suiting, and blazers.[103] Biographers often claim Hannah Sabbagh Shakir as an example of the class mobility that Arab Americans enjoyed in metropolitan New England. This was a vision rooted in the affluence her generation experienced from the perspective of the radically different economic conditions of the postwar era. In the 1920s and 1930s, by contrast, Sabbagh's activism reflected the cooperative strategies of the class she was a part of: immigrant textile workers in industrial Massachusetts. She worked because her wages were steadier than those of her brothers, and those wages belonged to her family, providing them with an economic cushion.[104]

Sabbagh's early experiences of work convinced her that technical training provided Syrian immigrants with a meaningful source of income in what was an otherwise unpredictable commercial economy. This was the animating spirit behind her organizing with the SLAS. However, women in Syrian American textile towns also had to contend with the reputational gender politics of welfare work. The SLAS described its work as operating outside of national or class politics, a self-presentation which protected the society during years of rising public animus against Middle Eastern immigrants. Forming its first committee in 1917, the SLAS confronted competing demands on their philanthropic labor during the war. The U.S. government subjected Syrian Americans to heightened scrutiny and pressure to perform political loyalty through humanitarian campaigns, purchase of Liberty Bonds, or enlistment.[105] Employers imposed similar pressures, for instance, requiring immigrant workers to purchase Liberty Bonds via direct payroll deductions on pain of retaliation.[106] At the same time, as fraternal organizations rushed to raise relief for Syria and Mount Lebanon, men's clubs also exerted pressure on the SLAS (and women's groups like it) to prioritize homeland rescue over local mutual aid.

FIGURE 9. Portrait of Hannah Sabbagh taken in Boston, circa 1920s. Working in textile factories from the age of fourteen, Hannah devoted herself to the material benefit of the Syrian working poor. Photo courtesy of George Ellenbogen.

Early SLAS meeting minutes illustrate these tensions. Upon learning that a new women's organization had recently formed, the Syria Mount Lebanon Liberation League of New York sent delegates to liaise with SLAS officers in March 1918. A diaspora nationalist organization leading a campaign for Syrian war relief, the league's delegate, Yusuf Touma, requested the SLAS work exclusively for the homeland. As club secretary Hannah Sabbagh recorded protesting to Touma, "This is not a political party; it is a philanthropic organization with pious aims," to which Touma shot back, "And what is your society's purpose if not Syria and Lebanon?"[107] A debate ensued (its precise contours are unrecorded) but by that meeting's end, Hannah's perturbed hand scribbled that a majority of the women assembled had agreed to raise relief for Syria until the war's end. The SLAS spent the war years knitting blankets, coats, and garments to be sold to benefit Syria.[108] In the fall of 1919, the society revisited the issue when younger members protested the ongoing poverty faced by Syrians in Boston. Members resolved that "we will help any Syrian who requests our assistance, without discrimination, in Syria and in America."[109] The SLAS issued a statement declaring that its aid programs benefit "those daughters of Syria, especially those far away from their families and who know no one in this place."[110] Maintaining financial autonomy was a concern for all mutual aid societies, but as a women's organization the SLAS also grappled with the patriarchal expectations that "ladies aid" be subsidiary to the patriotic projects of Syrian men's clubs.

By organizing among women workers in women's spaces, the SLAS maintained its autonomy and became a central institution in Boston's Syrian colony. The society incorporated in 1920 and rented a meeting house on Tyler Street. Chartered to "help Syrian needy families in Massachusetts," the Tyler Street house gave every Syrian immigrant a place to call their own.[111] The SLAS held weekly meetings there, organized fundraisers, and rented the hall to fraternal organizations for supplemental income. In addition to meeting space, boarding rooms, and a kitchen, the hall welcomed visitors with a modest library of books in Arabic and English.[112] Volunteers maintained the grounds and offered after-school programming for children, and night classes for Syrian workers: needleworking, spinning, and language training were the most popular.[113] The SLAS also offered a weekly *sahra*, a supper club open to residents each Thursday. Those who could afford to paid $1 for a hearty Syrian meal, and those who could not pay ate for free.[114] Providing sustenance to the city's Syrian working poor allowed the SLAS to observe the community's socioeconomic needs, especially those of its children, who the Relief Committee specifically looked out for. One of the SLAS's most ardent child welfare advocates was Rose Shagoury Homsy, daughter of Wadia and Joseph Shagoury, who spent part of her childhood as a ward of the state. Rose's brother, Charles (Khalil) Shagoury, described how her SLAS volunteerism in the 1920s was driven by desires to keep Syrian children out of state foster care.[115] Rose also managed the SLAS's milk and grocery relief campaigns, distributing food to Syrian homes across Massachusetts.

SLAS meetings were held in the evenings when members could join after their shifts in the garment factories. Members held varied positions in textile production: Hannah Sabbagh, for instance, worked in both weaving and garment work in her youth, trading this work for her own dressmaking contractor operation in the early 1930s.[116] Rose Shagoury Homsy and sister Mary Shagoury worked in the East Boston apron factory owned by Rose's husband, Albert, in 1921 before moving on to a dress factory where they stitched along with their mother, Wadia, through the 1930s.[117] Factory work was common, but even Syrian women who did not work in industrial settings did hand embroidery at home. The Tyler Street house itself became a site of production: ledgers record that members "engaged in handiwork during the day" and were paid at piece rate by local contractors.[118] The presence of pieceworkers in the Tyler Street house eventually led the SLAS to form a volunteer "Work Committee" who would donate a portion of their pieces to relief campaigns: Hannah Sabbagh coordinated the sale of embroidered linens, handmade laces, and garments to create a permanent fund for private welfare through the 1920s.[119] The Work Committee's fundraising capacity could be substantial. In February 1921, for instance, Sabbagh recorded that twenty-seven women were engaged in regular SLAS needlework; these workers had finished 148 pieces for sale that month.[120] Though the work began as a volunteer operation and a night course for local Syrian women, the Work Committee eventually turned into a redistributive body of its own, offering needlework pieces to unemployed women as a form of poverty alleviation. The pieces were typically consigned to Syrian merchants in Boston or New York. Hannah's brother, Elias Sabbagh, sold much of the club's handiwork to peddlers through his business, Sabbagh Bros.[121] By the early 1930s, Hannah Sabbagh was consigning one hundred yards of Syrian lace trimming for stitching by the Work Committee per month.¹²² The society also ran craft bazaars at the Tyler Street house as well as at nearby social settlements like the Denison House.¹²³ The sale of Work Committee Goods, ad hoc donations, member dues, and rental income for the Tyler Street meeting hall generated between $2,000 and $3,100 in annual redistribution through the 1920s and early 1930s.¹²⁴

The society elected a special Relief Committee to assess applications for assistance by Syrian families across New England. Meeting monthly, the Relief Committee looked at the SLAS's founding charter as it weighed the needs of Syrian working families. As with the other societies in this chapter, the SLAS favored direct aid, usually cash grants given to families experiencing sudden unemployment or emergency expenses that put their well-being at risk. Very often, relief recipients were textile operatives laid off during times of recession. In February 1921, for instance, the committee reviewed the application of Ibrahim,* widower and father of seven who was laid off during a mill slowdown the previous month.¹²⁵ Slowdowns were routine in

FIGURE 10. Syrian Ladies' Aid Society founders participate in the City of Boston's Armistice Day Parade, 1925. Hannah Sabbagh appears in white, at right next to the float's Gold Star Mother honoree. Photo courtesy of George Ellenbogen.

1920s Massachusetts; at the bottom of the labor hierarchy, Middle Eastern workers were acutely vulnerable to dismissal. They were also the least likely to have savings to rely upon. The SLAS sent Ibrahim $10 a week for rent, groceries, and milk deliveries as well as a half-ton of heating coal from the society's reserves.[126] The SLAS subsidy would relieve household expenses while Ibrahim sought work; a representative of the Relief Committee was assigned to check in on Ibrahim and his children regularly to ensure the funds were spent appropriately.

The Relief Committee offered aid to Syrian families across Massachusetts, with attention to housing: $25 a month to families in Lawrence and North Adams after mill closures in 1925,[127] or $20 monthly to a Fall River family threatened with unemployment.[128] The significance of these payments swells when one considers the economics of Syrian working households: entire households tended to be employed by one company in a mill town, leading to a total loss of income during recessions. A 1926 application from Lawrence is illustrative: nine people lived in the Bustani* household: three men, four female dependents, and two unrelated male boarders. All five men were laid off when the AWC mill they worked for closed.[129] Unable to make rent, the boarders moved out, and the Bustanis would have been evicted without assistance from the SLAS. A SLAS delegation went to Lawrence to meet the family and assess their desperate situation. They granted the family rent relief and found two of the men temporary work out of town.[130] The 1926–27 contraction affected most of the Massachusetts textile industries; in Lawrence, the Young Men of Deir-el-Kamar ledgers recorded that "most of [its] members have disbanded" as the mills failed; "some went to Danbury and others to different places" in search of work.[131] In Boston, the SLAS's Relief Committee fielded a jump in applications from mill operatives seeking rental assistance or help in relocating out of the state or to return to the Middle East, or assistance with foster placements for Syrian children facing homelessness.[132] The SLAS's broad focus on poverty alleviation among Syrian working families set it apart from its partner societies in the region. While many Syrian mutual aid clubs managed private insurance schemes and offered emergency relief to their members, the SLAS of Boston was engaged in maintaining Syrian working classes across the region and in mitigating the economic ills they experienced as a result of industry swings.

The SLAS was never directly involved in trade unionism or other forms of labor militancy, though individual SLAS members may have been engaged in this work. Gender expectations played an important role here, as did the SLAS's approach of offering piecework to unemployed young women outside the factory setting. Whereas the United Syrian Society or the Young Men of Deir-el-Kamar paid direct relief to striking workers in order to sustain the pickets, the SLAS tried to make work available to women who were deprived of a formal wage. This same strategy of income generation is evident in SLAS relief ledgers: payment for piecework or janitorial assistance, free board at the Tyler Street house, and job training or placement was common, but strike pay was not. The SLAS also worked with other Syrian societies and more selectively, with U.S. social welfare agencies. It regularly co-organized with the Syrian American Club of Boston, a fraternal organization with ties to the United Syrian Society of Lawrence. Syrian American Club officers were also closely connected with SLAS officers: Elias Sabbagh, Rasheed Abdelnour, Wadi' Shakir, and Ibrahim al-Khuri were each related to SLAS members, and the Syrian American Club rented the SLAS hall on Tyler Street for its own meetings and functions. Several other ethnic clubs also rented the Tyler Street meeting hall, demonstrating its centrality: the Syrian Cultural Union, the St. John of Damascus Society, the Free Sons of Lebanon, the Brothers of Beirut, and the Women of Douma Philanthropic Society appear in early SLAS ledgers. The society made its hall available to homeland associations, lay organizations, and even political clubs, but it strictly prohibited discrimination and sectarianism, and declined to cooperate with groups that limited membership on the bases of sect, class, or creed.[133]

Among American agencies, the SLAS was most closely associated with the Denison House, a social settlement house engaged in relief among Syrian and Chinese immigrants in the South End.[134] SLAS officers carefully ensured that all partnership work directly aligned with the society's practices of direct aid, self-service, and Syrian financial autonomy. The SLAS held suppers at the Denison House at which wealthy Bostonians ventured into the immigrant neighborhood for "a real Syrian meal"; the proceeds were explicitly earmarked for "needy Syrian families in the district" identified by the SLAS's Relief Committee.[135] The SLAS also offered educational programming and childcare for Syrian children together with the Denison House, initiatives that are often remembered as part of the effort to Americanize Syrian immigrants.[136] Some local Syrians objected to the Denison House's involvement in the Syrian colony. Laurice Shagoury Maloley remembers how both her grandmother, Wadia Shagoury and her aunt Rose Homsy learned English at the Denison House; Wadia even taught sewing courses there in the 1930s. But "while many immigrant women enrolled" in these programs, "very few of the men in the community would register" because they "resented the Denison House . . . they had the notion that the women and children were being taught customs and mores contrary to Arabic culture."[137] Denison House social workers certainly described their efforts as Americanization; however, the SLAS's club records reveal a general Syrian indifference to such overtures. The society's volunteers were focused on Syrian economic betterment and giving women workers meaningful skills to advance in industry.

By drawing directly on the skills and experiences of young women working in textiles, the SLAS turned the community's prime vulnerability—its unpredictable labor market—into a strength. The system was flexible and plugged easily into existing Arab American cloth economies. When cash donations to the SLAS flagged in lean times, the club relied on in-kind donations. The society's ability to pivot toward paying for piece work insured Syrian families against the insecurities of factory work, while releasing Syrian women from dependence on mill managers and manufacturers' associations. As the club's relief economy turned inward, fitting seamlessly into the mahjar's merchant peddler networks, the SLAS was able to reinforce the community's ethnic autonomy while softening the pains of poverty.

Dedicated to meeting the needs of workers within ethnic networks of service, care, and financial support, Syrian mutual aid societies represented the locus of Syrian working-class communities across Massachusetts. Whether they were digging graves in Lawrence, offering meeting space to strikers, serving meals, or employing Syrian women in embroidery, mutual aid activists mitigated the structural precarities they faced as a marginalized working-class community. On one hand, these associations facilitated the emergence of Syrian American labor leaders who bargained for better working conditions on the community's behalf. On the other hand, mutual aid ameliorated working poverty by feeding the hungry, educating the young, sustaining the sick, and grieving the lost in the absence of robust public welfare programs. This work was not charitable; it was mutual. Operated by workers and for their own direct benefit, these societies were concerned with social reproduction and maintenance of Syrian communities rather than with the themes of Americanization, assimilation, or racial uplift that animated the social settlement movement sitting adjacent to their movement.

Meanwhile, more Syrians arrived in various sectors of the textile industry, in New England, New York, and across the hemispheric mahjar. When the famous Little Syria colony emerged on Washington Street in New York City, its workers similarly engaged in mutual aid work and community service. New York also had a Syrian Ladies' Aid Society, headquartered in Brooklyn. Its immigration assistance began at Ellis Island. Sending a representative to the immigration center to "to meet the immigrants, act as their interpreter, their guide in the maze of legalistic red tape, and their counsel in trouble," the New York SLAS took special charge of unaccompanied young women, sponsoring their arrival, and setting them up with employment.[138] Overwhelmingly, Syrian women and girls in New York found work in garment factories owned by other Syrian Americans, as contractor shops of this emergent merchant-manufacturer class spread through the city's Garment District. But being a Syrian garment worker in a Syrian-owned shop presented specific new challenges: what did contests between labor and capital look like, for instance, within a factory where management espoused Syrian racial solidarity as a means of labor control? It is to those factories we now turn.

THREE

THE SYRIAN SHOP
Garment Manufacturing in New York City

Seeking female workers for machine sewing;
good wages, comfortable treatment.

R. TAHAN AND BROS., 1917[1]

Seeking female workers for sewing shirts and silk underwear. We pay $1–2 more than our competitors, half days on Saturdays!

KIAMIE BROS., 1918[2]

We need 50 female machine sewers! $6 a week to start.

EDDY CURY AND BROS., 1916[3]

CRATES OF SYRIAN LACE WERE stored at the U.S. Customs House at the Port of New York, each marked with a tag proving its point of origin. As the appraiser carefully weighed each crate, grading its contents to assess its tariff value, the contours of the Syrian lace trade appeared in these origin tags: Florence, Dublin, or Venice; Funchal or Angra; Zahle, Tripoli, or Damascus; Manila, Shanghai, or Yokohama. The goods were consigned to Syrian merchant-manufacturers of New York, who would claim the materials, pay duties, and transport them to Syrian factories in lower Manhattan, Brooklyn, or New Jersey. In those factories, cuff-and-collar sets were sewn onto white goods. Lace trim was stitched onto pillow shams or table linens in preparation for the peddling markets. Thousands of garment workers stitched specialty silk adornments into lingerie, underwear, pajamas and most famously, the Syrian-style kimonos sold on Fifth Avenue.

In New York City, the department stores displayed these kimonos, which became a sought-after fashion in the early 1920s, with Syrian brands like Mouakad, Bardwil, and Macksoud appearing in the pages of *Vogue* magazine. But the kimono trade was simultaneously sustained in the "old" way, by brands loaning out merchandise to Syrian peddlers, men and women who carried the goods in their *kashehs* (large trunks and suitcases) along the railways, by car, or by drawn carriage into the American interior and to the doorsteps of American consumers. According to Alixa Naff, pack peddling was "the most fundamental factor in the assimilation of Syrians in America," a trade that most Syrians "preferred ... to the drudgery of factory life."[4] However, the goods that Syrian peddlers carried came from somewhere. Most of them were sewn by Syrian workers in the garment factories of New York City.

This chapter examines the emergence of Syrian American garment manufacturing in New York City after the Panic of 1907, specifically the development of the so-called Syrian shops. Established by Syrian merchants to mitigate the impacts of price fluctuations and supply chain issues in global importing, the Syrian shops produced lingerie, household white goods, and kimono wrappers to feed the mahjar's wholesale market. Of these goods, the Syrian kimono placed New York's Little Syria at the center of American fashion between World War I and the early 1920s. Producing kimonos at scale depended on the Syrian shops' ability to command and retain its workforce of young Syrian women who stitched, adorned, and finished the garments at minimum wage rates. Syrian merchant-manufacturers met their labor needs by recruiting recent Syrian immigrant women and leveraging these workers' understandings of ethnic obligation, patriotic duty, and the prevailing gender norms that governed women's labor power. Merchant-manufacturers also built their businesses by maintaining distinct—yet connected—labor economies in garment work, textile peddling, and Syrian immigration through Ellis Island. All the while, the Syrian shops weathered strikes and resisted the unionization efforts that otherwise animated the industry between 1909 and the mid-1920s.

Before the arrival of the Syrian factory, there was the Syrian importer. Starting in the 1880s, Syrian merchants brought in a variety of goods from the Ottoman Mediterranean through the Port of New York: rugs and silks, tobacco, white goods, and devotional objects to be sold in remembrance of the Holy Land.[5] The first of these businesses was opened in 1883 by Jurj Melhame, an importer of devotional objects from Beirut. According to a 1920 interview with Sallum Mukarzil, Melhame sold his items directly to Syrian peddlers; he also assisted newly arrived Syrians through the immigration process before outfitting them for the peddling business.[6] Others soon followed: the Hamati Brothers of Batroun (est. 1896), Mahal Rahim Faris (est. 1900), Mahal Mansour Hilu (est. 1905), Mahal Zurayk and Brothers (est. 1912), and dozens of similar import firms opened shop adjacent to the Syrian colony. The importers were concentrated on Carlisle Street, a tiny 200-meter alleyway hosting a Syrian boardinghouse which lodged many peddlers upon their arrival. By 1900, the U.S. Immigration Commission had noticed the flow of Syrian peddlers from Ellis Island to 5 Carlisle Street, where they stayed overnight before being dispatched with their goods to the railways, holding tickets to the Midwest, Texas, or the American South.[7]

As the importing business grew in scale, new institutions appeared to direct the movement of goods and labor through the ports. Dry goods importers Daniel, Doumit, and Yusuf Faour, for instance, moved into lending and credit, opening the colony's first Syrian American bank in 1891.[8] The Faour Bros. Bank institutionalized networks of informal credit and lending that enabled Syrian immigrants arriving in New York to join the peddling business. The Faour brothers plugged themselves into Carlisle Street, making petty loans to Syrian peddlers through their storefront, Mahal Faour. Leasing a Washington Street building in 1891, the Faour Brothers Bank was more than simply a credit institution. The building offered an array of commercial activities and was more *khan* than bank: Faour rented storehouses to merchants; insured their transactions; organized remittance campaigns; and established a Syrian American Chamber of Commerce (al-Ghurfa al-Tijariyya al-Suriyya al-Amrikiyya fi-Niyu Yurk) there in 1911.[9]

As a class, Syrian importers generally supplied the peddling trades, forming a dense network of immigration agents, lenders, and wholesalers who worked jointly to protect their share of the industry.[10] As these businesses grew, they became more specialized; a growing number of merchants focused on the import of "Turkish lace" after 1900, competing with Anglo, Irish, and German immigrant importers bringing European laces through the port. Syrian merchants were upstarts in the whites business, manufacturing everyday underclothes and household textiles. They succeeded due to two factors: their exclusive access to Ottoman, Levantine, and Egyptian goods, and their command of a ready labor force of Syrian American foot peddlers to carry these items to consumers across the hemispheric mahjar. And so Syrian merchants in New York focused first on procuring white goods from Beirut, Damascus, and Istanbul, forming partnerships with merchants among their nationality in the Ottoman Empire and Egypt.[11] Sallum Mukarzil said of the trade in 1921, "The merchants succeeded [in the beginning] thanks to the presence of Syrian businesses and traders among the Syrian emigres." For the traders who supplied these merchants, bonds of fealty were often simultaneously commercial, ethnic, and familial.[12] Eventually, these firms expanded into European and Asian supply zones, establishing partnerships with Syrian merchants living in cities like Marseille, Manchester, Florence, Manila, Yokohama, and Shanghai, or opening their own branches there.[13] As supply chains lengthened, so did the retail pipeline, as Syrian peddling businesses expanded to bring import goods from New York to American consumers. Syrian merchants in New York, meanwhile, established partnerships with their diasporic counterparts in Atlantic port cities, particularly in Mexico, Cuba, Brazil, and Argentina.

Lace and hand embroideries became big business in particular: in 1911, the New York Customs House estimated the trade was worth $500,000 annually, a figure that doubled to $1,000,000 by 1920.[14] For generations, women and girls had completed hand embroideries and lace mostly for household use in Syria, Mount Lebanon, and Palestine. A traditional handicraft, hand embroideries were not considered a commercial item before the nineteenth century, but their commoditization in the Syrian American diaspora transformed them into a meaningful avenue to make a living. Leading merchants in Syria and Mount Lebanon commissioned village women and girls to make cuff/collar sets, trims, and other lace and crocheted goods destined for export. Apparently, orders from abroad were valuable enough to reshape local production: in 1911, the U.S. Consul General in Beirut W. Stanley Hollis, noted that "the Syrians are imitating Irish lace" to meet the demands of New York wholesalers.[15] He added that Syrian women increasingly relied on imported European threads for their tatting. These were provided by Beiruti merchants to better mimic the transatlantic lace sets sold by their foreign competitors.

Though most émigré importers worked through merchants in Beirut to procure laces, others went further. In 1907, for instance, the Hamrah Bros.

Company of New York opened its own factory in Zahle to secure a steady supply of Syrian export lace.[16] Brothers Alexander and Peter Hamrah came to the United States in 1896, working as wholesalers in Chicago before opening their New York lace business in 1905. The Zahle factory was Peter's idea: repatriating to Mount Lebanon in 1907, he imported European threads and linens to Zahle to be worked into Abu Hamrah brand lace cuffs and collars, table linens and bedding, and other embroidered goods for export to Alexander Hamrah's showroom on Rector Street. The Hamrah luxury lace brand became so popular that Alexander began supplying New York City department stores. During the Balkan Wars of 1911 and 1913, export shipping became more difficult, and Peter Hamrah's Zahle factory struggled to keep up with orders, prompting Alexander to open new factories in New York, Florence, and eventually in Shanghai, Funchal, and the Azores.[17]

Local factory production of Syrian lace and white goods in New York City developed as part of this same transition. The uncertainties of the global shipping market left Syrian importers struggling to meet increasing demand, so they hired Syrian immigrant women and girls to create laces and embroideries at home or in improvised workshops in the back of their stores. These locally manufactured Syrian laces supplemented imported items, where they fetched less on the retail market but still supplied the peddling trades. The women who did the stitching went unnoticed by U.S. commentators at first, as the work was improvised and conducted entirely behind the scenes. One needleworker, Nabeha Merhige, describes this informal, invisible work in her memoir. An orphan from Homs, Nabeha arrived in New York in 1898 and lived in the Watts Orphanage, where she crocheted lace for a store owned by her uncle. Upon reaching adulthood, Nabeha basted lace edging to patterned linen, leaving her uncle's workshop when she married in 1908 and moved to Worcester, Massachusetts.[18] Nabeha's uncle was Amin Merhige, one of New York City's most established importers of Istanbul silks. Responding to disruptions in the silk market in 1907, Amin pivoted toward local Syrian lace and embroideries, establishing a garment factory first and subsequently, a Brooklyn silk ribbon plant to supply it in 1913.[19] Merhige's factories made him enormously wealthy; by the end of World War I, his firm was worth a million dollars. A single garment accounted for that rise to wealth: the Syrian kimono.

KIMONOS AND THE EMERGENCE OF THE SYRIAN SHOP

The emergence of Syrian-owned textile factories in New York City was an outgrowth of two factors: the accumulation of émigré merchant capital in the lace, embroideries, and white goods industries, and the accumulation of unorganized Syrian immigrant labor in the city's Washington Street colony. This mix of labor and capital paired with the intrinsically labor-intensive nature of garment work. "The cutting and stitching of soft materials used in clothing do not lend themselves to technological rationalization" that could otherwise "displace the one worker, one machine ratio," as Elizabeth McLean Petras puts it.[20] In his 1904 survey, Lucius Miller concluded that Manhattan's Syrian-owned garment factories employed 26.8 percent of the state's Syrian immigrants aged fourteen or older. Miller estimated that Syrian men represented 58 percent of the industrial workforce on average, and Syrian women 42 percent; men tended to concentrate in weaving, and women in sewing. Garment factories also depended on piece rate workers, a substantial labor force that was 98 percent female.[21] Syrian women and girls predominated in kimono shops: the International Ladies' Garment Workers' Union estimated there were 2,000 Syrian women and girls working inside Syrian-owned kimono factories in lower Manhattan by 1914 (an estimate which does not include home pieceworkers). Thus, in an immigrant colony of 7,500 people, the garment industry was the largest single economic sector.[22] While a few Syrian shops also hired Armenian, Sephardi, Spanish, and Italian workers, most of these factories employed an entirely Syrian labor force.[23] Such figures lend credence to testimony given to the U.S. Immigration Commission about Syrian workers: "none but Syrians are employed by Syrians."[24]

Syrian women and girls performed all facets of garment work, from lace piecework to cutting, stitching, embroidering, and finishing garments in a factory setting. As was common across the industry, immigrants began this work as children: girls as young as twelve made laces, supplementing their parents' wages. At fourteen, they worked in the factories that sprang up in the Washington Street neighborhood and later, in Brooklyn. In these factories, they apprenticed and learned how to operate sewing machines; children also worked as janitors, in packaging, or other unskilled parts of the production process. Syrian women cut and basted, sewed, stitched, and hemmed new garments in the main rooms of these factories. Despite stereotypes that garment work was for the young, women of all ages performed this labor. Whether unmarried, married, or widowed, girls and women of all walks of life could be found in the Syrian factories.

Though small numbers of Syrians joined Jewish, Italian, or Polish workers in garment factories across the city, most of the Syrian women who worked within the "Syrian shops" were inaccessible to the trade unions before 1913. Most garment workers were recent immigrants who had not yet gained U.S. citizenship. This element of recency was by design: Syrian American manufacturers integrated themselves into transnational labor pipelines to ensure a steady source of workers for their factories, relying on the same means that brought them peddlers. A 1913 study of immigrant textile workers found that only 20.3 percent of Syrian men had declared their intention to be naturalized in the United States, and even fewer Syrian women had done so.[25]

Whether performed in a factory or at home, Syrian women's garment work complemented the economic pursuits of husbands, uncles, brothers, or male cousins by maintaining the household or by subsidizing the commercial pursuits of men who absented themselves on the peddling trail.[26] Sensitive to the gender implications of a largely female industrial workforce, Syrian American kimono manufacturers maintained policies of strict sex segregation in their factories, mirroring the layout that Akram Khater describes of silk factories in Ottoman Mount Lebanon.[27] Three additional practices defined the shape of the New York City "Syrian shop:" direct merchant ownership, an ethnically homogeneous workforce, and efforts to maintain a "Syrian" industrial culture on the shop floor. Syrian merchant-manufacturers espoused these practices as a form of industrial patriotism, in the expectation that these factories would channel the mahjar's economic production toward a national ideal.

Little Syria's first kimono firm appeared in 1905, with Mahal Mikha'il Arida. Widely credited as the originator of the Syrian kimono, Mikha'il Arida arrived in New York in 1902, the eighteen-year-old son of a successful silk merchant family which moved goods from Homs and Damascus through Beirut for export abroad.[28] As he scouted factory locations within the immigrant community to expand his family's business empire, Arida's story already diverged from the "rags to riches" pathos that accompanies memories of immigrant businessman of his generation.[29] Arida chose locations on or near Washington Street to capitalize on the dense networks of

Syrian American immigration officials, wholesalers, peddlers, and textile workers already living there. In 1904, Arida opened his first shop: Mahal Arida, on Carlisle Street, next door to the Syrian boardinghouse at 5 Carlisle, the well-known landing site for many Syrians arriving from Ellis Island. Arida worked jointly with Najib Arbeely, the Syrian American immigration inspector at Ellis Island; after Arbeely steered arriving immigrants to Arida's shop, he sold wares to peddlers headed west on the railways.[30] Arbeely would then retrieve these men, accompany them to the railways, and secure tickets for them to Sherman, Texas, the gateway to the borderlands trade, or to the Midwest, or to California.[31]

Mahal Arida sold several items imported from Syria and Istanbul, but the kimono quickly became a runaway favorite. A sleek collarless robe that opened in the front and was made of skandarani silk, the Arida kimono was imported from Mikha'il's brother, Kemal Arida, in Damascus. Arida kimonos were a unique lingerie item that Carlisle Street peddlers preferred because they sold well despite their high price point. Peddlers brought them to American homes, and as the kimono caught on, American shoppers ventured to Carlisle Street to buy them. As demand for kimonos multiplied, supply remained limited. These constraints simultaneously drove prices up while creating markets for a new, locally produced version of the kimono, made from less expensive silk-cotton blends and lace appliques then popular in the Garment District. Arida experimented with local materials, hiring a dozen Syrian immigrant women to produce inexpensive kimonos in the back of his store. The first Arida "factory" was improvised: women basted the robes at home before bringing them to Carlisle Street to finish them on Arida's sole sewing machine. In 1906, Arida leased a factory building at 93 Washington Street to centralize kimono production, hiring several dozen full-time garment workers. Within a year he expanded again, establishing a second factory on West 22nd Street in the city's Garment District; that factory employed seventy-five Syrian women in garment work, and fifteen Syrian men in sales.[32] Arida kimonos exploded from a cult item to a mainstream fashion piece. By World War I, Arida kimonos were sold in major department stores, and by 1920, the Arida Corporation mass produced them in factories in New York City and Union Hill, New Jersey.[33]

Like most of the Syrian shops, a transnational merchant family managed Mahal Arida. Mikha'il oversaw operations in New York but depended on his older brother for goods, silk components, and capitalization in Damascus.

Kamel Arida traveled between New York and Syria several times, ultimately resettling there when Mikha'il tragically died in a 1913 boating accident.[34] Younger brother Rufa'il Arida also joined the business after coming to the United States to study at Columbia University in 1909. After graduation, Rufa'il managed the new Arida plant on West 22nd Street. Other relatives also worked with the firm at intervals. Though he is better-known for his literary work, Pen League (al-Rabita al-Qalamiyya) founder Nasib Arida assumed management of an independent Arida Corporation branch in 1919, lending the brand additional cultural cache among Syrian émigrés and American elites.[35]

As the Arida kimono took off, competitors emerged. The 1908 Mokarzel-Otash Syrian American Business Directory records twenty-four kimono manufacturers in the city, concentrated in the Lower West Side.[36] By 1930 this number had grown to fifty-five.[37] Established Syrian American textile firms introduced their own kimono lines, as Abdalla Barsa and Bros. did in 1913, leasing a factory on West 23rd Street. Like Arida, Abdalla Barsa was a merchant from Damascus, arriving in New York in 1896 where he worked in rug imports.[38] Abdalla's interest in textiles was limited until 1906, when his brother Simon arrived in New York via Mexico.[39] Simon pushed the Barsa firm toward undergarments, manufacturing petticoats before crossing over into kimonos.[40]

The Barsa factory grew from a single-story plant with a workforce of 130 (100 women, 30 men) into a staggering six-story factory by 1919. This was one of three production centers Abdalla and Simon managed jointly.[41] "If you enter the main Barsa and Bros. factory . . . and explore their various floors," reported Sallum Mukarzil after touring the plant, "you would be amazed at the enormity of scale as well as the careful arrangement" of both machinery and labor.[42] At 44,000 square feet, the Barsa factory featured four manufacturing floors, business offices, and a factory showroom and store. Walking Mukarzil through the buildings works, the Barsa Company foreman explained the modern machinery: on one floor, Syrian silk weavers ran power looms, and on the rest, Syrian women worked to piece, edge, and adorn kimonos and undergarments at sewing machines. Mukarzil marveled at how each floor of the factory was devoted to a specific task, a distinct class of labor arranged vertically as fibers transformed into garments. He reported with pleasure how the factory processed silk cloth and produced garments simultaneously; stages of production usually reserved

FIGURE 11. Above: Syrian women working in the Arida kimono factory, 1920. Below: Mikha'il Arida (r) and brother Rufa'il Arida (l) in 1911. Source: Mukarzil, *Tarikh al-Tijara*, 46; James Ansara Papers, IHRC208, Immigration History Research Center Archives, University of Minnesota.

for different sectors were now spatially represented by floors at the Barsa Co. This vision of the modern factory replicated the spatial logic of massive plants like the famous American Woolen Company in Massachusetts, but it was a first for the Syrian garment industry, which up to that point was defined by smaller firms working in conjunction and moving goods among themselves. Observing this in-house approach to production at scale, Mukarzil wrote, "You would say to yourself, 'It is true! Syrian work in America has reached such a level of advancement!' especially if you are aware of how simple Syrian commerce was in the beginning."[43]

Mukarzil applauded the Barsa factory's modern, centralized production process as well as its spatial segmentation into distinct floors, appreciating

FIGURE 12. The Abdalla Barsa factory in 1920. The year before, the shop was the setting for the start of a citywide kimono strike when workers walked off the floor in a dispute over working conditions. Source: Mukarzil, *Tarikh al-Tijara*, 49; James Ansara Papers, IHRC208, Immigration History Research Center Archives, University of Minnesota.

that this approach afforded limitless opportunities for vertical integration. By contrast, he was silent on the impact of this layout on labor. Syrian workers were at once concentrated in one space but segmented into functions that were inaccessible to one another, allowing for greater labor control by management. Raw materials moved into the plant, and they were woven, stamped, cut, and stitched by Syrian workers who, though working together, barely interacted. Centralized shop conditions set the tone for massive labor actions across the U.S. textile industry, most notably in the New York garment worker strikes of 1909, 1912, and 1913. The spatial segmentation of the Syrian shops may have contributed to the difficulties activists faced when trying to organize Syrian workers.

'Assy Shaheen and Sons embraced a similar shop culture of "cocoon to finished garment" manufacturing.[44] Arriving in New York from Arbaniye, Mount Lebanon, in 1887, Shaheen worked in lace importing until 1912, when he went into kimono manufacturing with sons George and Tawfiq.[45] The first Shaheen kimono shop opened in the Garment District on Broadway Avenue, supplied by the firm's silk processing plant in Cranford, New Jersey. Like the Barsa company, Shaheen and Sons expanded across the production process, from spinning and weaving to cutting and piecework, each plant owned and operated by one of the brothers. Collectively, the Shaheen plants were the "largest Syrian factories in the world," selling bulk silk fabric and ready-wear garments across the hemisphere by 1920, for 20 to 30 percent less than their competitors.[46] However, as the Shaheens expanded in New Jersey, they faced intense competition from established silk plants in Paterson. They met this challenge by moving into real estate, buying tract properties, and constructing small single-family homes in Cranford designed for Shaheen and Sons silk workers. The firm marketed these properties to the "young Syrian family," an enticement to Syrian silk workers from Paterson to relocate for a job at the Shaheen plant.[47] 'Assy Shaheen reinvested his real estate profits back into the silk business. In 1920, he even sought to build a silk plant in Lebanon identical to his Cranford factory to revitalize the country's battered silk industry, though the project faltered when the French Mandate emerged.

The largest manufacturer of Syrian kimonos in 1920 was Mahal Kiamie with a total workforce of 5,000 Syrian men, women, and girls.[48] Like the Merhiges, Aridas, Barsas, and Shaheens, the Kiamie brothers began as merchants; the family had been in the silk trade since the 1840s. Arriving from

Shweir, Mount Lebanon, Philip and Najib Kiamie first opened a wholesale store targeting the peddling market.[49] The Kiamie business in the mahjar was an extension of the firm's preexisting networks: they came to America to gain access to the itinerant textile trade, joining New York factories to consumers in the Midwest and the U.S.-Mexico borderlands. As seen above, the strategy was common among Syrian merchants and not limited to the United States: while Philip and Najib came to New York, a third Kiamie brother went to Latin America.[50]

Mahal Kiamie was primarily an import firm before World War I, relying on family ties to bring Syrian and Lebanese silks to the American market. When war broke out in 1914, the allied naval blockade on the Ottoman Mediterranean cut off the Kiamie supply chain, prompting Philip and Najib to invest in local manufacturing. The first Kiamie factory at 60 Washington Street was modest, employing a couple dozen Syrian women in stitching undergarments, moving into kimonos as demand for the silk wrappers took off.[51] Focused at first on supplying their peddling networks, the Kiamie brothers started by subcontracting kimono work to small workshops across the immigrant quarter, before leasing a factory on East 18th Street. They established an even larger 6,000 square foot factory in Brooklyn, on Atlantic Avenue as business expanded. It was this massive factory that Sallum Mukarzil toured in 1920. Mukarzil was led from floor to floor as silk threads were spun, woven, and processed into the Kiamie kimonos. Kimonos were big business for Kiamie Brothers after the war, the firm recording annual sales of $750,000.[52] By 1931, the firm opened retail showrooms on Madison Avenue in New York and in Chicago, expanding even as the Great Depression decimated much of the garment industry.[53]

American enthusiasm for the kimono fueled dozens of Syrian shops across New York City, where merchant-manufacturers scaled up production to meet orders from department stores while supplying mahjari commercial networks across the hemisphere. "Planted in American soil by the hands of the immigrant peddler," the kimono was a prized item universally associated with Syrian merchants, who Sallum Mukarzil credited for their enormous popularity.[54] A luxurious alternative to the common housedress, Syrian kimono sellers marketed the robes as prized romantic gifts, an item husbands gave to wives wrapped in perfumed tissue paper. As luxurious, romantic objects, Syrian kimonos were highly coveted, but they became a fashion phenomenon because the Syrian shops also made them affordable. Before 1914,

FIGURE 13. Above: The Shaheen and Sons showroom in New York City, with silk kimonos on display, 1920. Below: The Brooklyn Kiamie factory, 1920. Operatives look up from stitching, a piano sits at left. Source: Mukarzil, *Tarikh al-Tijara*, 54, 57; James Ansara Papers, IHRC208, Immigration History Research Center Archives, University of Minnesota.

the finest imported silk kimonos fetched prices of $125 or $150, far beyond the means of the average American consumer.[55] By mass producing them locally of silk or silk-cotton blends, the Syrian shops of New York offered kimonos at every price point, to be worn not only "by the lady who lives in a palace, but also the factory girl who rents a furnished room in the city, and also by village girls who take refuge in her rural hut."[56] The cheaper, more durable blends also offered brand opportunities: Mahal Amin Merhige, for instance, marketed its silk-cotton "Maltese blend" to middle-class Americans.[57] The finer silk kimonos were still popular among those who could afford them, but the kimono simultaneously became an aspirational item for upwardly mobile youth and a prized gift available on the mass market.

Mass production reshaped kimono fashions in significant ways.[58] In addition to the wider use of fabric blends, new silk printing technologies adorned the robes with colorful patterns, often in addition to hand lace appliques. During the war, kimonos featured landscape images, geometric patterns, and florals, and Syrian American manufacturers cultivated brand identities around their designs. The Arida Corporation, for instance, retained local designers to develop its apple blossom collection, a brand asset that brought the company to $1 million in annual sales in 1920.[59] The reopening of transatlantic shipping after the war's end brought high-flying optimism among Syrian merchant-manufacturers, who set about bringing the kimono and related Syrian white goods to the world. Some firms sought new export markets, sending garments to Syrian retailers in Latin America or Europe. Elias Mouakad, the so-called kimono king of Fourth Street, concentrated on the export market through the 1920s.[60]

The boom in Syrian kimonos favored large, highly capitalized merchant-manufacturers firms of New York, but dozens of smaller Syrian shops also shaped the industry. Modest Syrian factories adjacent to Washington Street filled orders, sometimes as subcontractors and more often for direct wholesale. Calef Brothers (26 employees, 20 of them women); Ganis Brothers (36 employees, 24 women); H. and J. Homsy (36 employees, 30 women); S. Khoury and Co. (37/28); Kassar Brothers (23/20); Lutfy and Macksoud (23/20); Shohfi Brothers (29/25); Naser, Katan and Nahass (38/33); and Nasrallah and Meena (61/55) were all more typical in size and scope for the industry.[61] Whereas the larger firms sourced and processed most of their materials, the small shops tended to focus primarily on piecework and stitching, buying wholesale ribbons, laces, and embroideries imported from abroad by Syrian merchants like the Mallouk Corporation, Bardwil Brothers, or Jabara, Lian, and Mabarak.[62] Regardless of whether the Syrian women who stitched these kimonos did so in vast factories or in small Syrian shops of a few dozen workers, they labored under direct merchant-manufacturer control, in conditions that isolated them from the broader currents of garment work trade unionism.

FIGURE 14. A 1921 Arida design. "A gay-colored sweetbriar negligee in an apple-blossom design. Neck and panel back edged with satin ribbon." Source: *Silk* 14, no. 8 (August 1921), 63.

As the New York garment industry experienced a wave of unionization following the Uprising of 20,000 in 1909 and the Triangle Shirtwaist Factory Fire in 1911, government regulators and trade unions commented on the difficulties they faced in improving working conditions in immigrant shops. Reporting to the U.S. Commission on Industrial Relations in 1915, economist Edgar Sydenstricker argued that small factories' tendency toward ethnic segregation "means nothing less than [workers'] disbarment from participation in the affairs of the community." An operative who "is unable to exercise and does not know how to exercise a voice in the matters that affect his own environment . . . is exploited not only by leaders of their own race, but by natives. [Such workers] are regarded as legitimate tools by which unscrupulous ward-healers despoil the public."[63] Trade unions confronted unique challenges when trying to organize Syrian workers, because their shop system was simultaneously diffuse (scattered across dozens of shops, many of them small) and under the firm control of a merchant class which vigilantly rooted out unionization.

THE INTERNATIONAL LADIES' GARMENT WORKERS' UNION CAMPAIGN

As the number of Syrian kimono shops in New York City multiplied between 1907 and 1920, they drew the attention of trade unions, particularly the International Ladies' Garment Workers' Union (ILGWU). Established in 1900, the ILGWU rose to prominence in New York during successful textile strikes in 1909 and 1910, organizing thousands of workers across the city's entire garment industry and marking a transition away from craft unionism.[64] The ILGWU originated in the activism of Eastern European Jewish immigrant garment workers, many of whom were sympathetic to socialism. As a union for and by immigrant workers, the ILGWU sought to champion the rights of the foreign-born working class to safe working conditions, a fair wage, and collective closed-shop bargaining citywide.[65] Campaigning from 1909 through World War I, the ILGWU enjoyed broad support among garment workers: 40 percent of the U.S. garment industry unionized during this period, marking an unprecedented development in American labor history.[66] It was in this context that the ILGWU targeted the Syrian shops in the Washington Street district. Seeking to organize immigrants working for kimono manufacturers, the union led thousands of

Syrian women to the pickets, but it also struggled to translate Syrian participation in strikes into a culture of collective bargaining in the Syrian shops.

In New York's kimono, wrapper, and housedress trades, the workforce was overwhelmingly female. The work was abundant but poorly paid: $2–$3 a week was the standard wage for unskilled immigrant garment workers, accruing to an average of $5–$12 a week as they gained experience.[67] The poor pay was worsened by unsafe working conditions: the ignition of flammable fabrics in the overcrowded Triangle Shirtwaist Company factory fed a devastating fire in 1911, killing 146 workers and shocking the nation's conscience.[68] The ILGWU pushed for greater regulation of sanitation in garment factories and argued that improvement of conditions was the manufacturers' responsibility. In the 1910s, the union brought this energy into "a strenuous effort to organize the wrapper and kimono workers trade." The kimono factories in the Syrian Quarter drew ILGWU's concern because of their insularity and the "extreme youth of the workers." Investigating the Syrian shops in 1913, the ILGWU described their conditions as "deplorable: the workers are being compelled to own their own machines, to furnish foot power, pay for electric power, pay for thread, needles, and machine oil."[69] Though the union had, by 1913, made some headway in organizing garment workers across the negligee, housedress, and wrapper industries, the Syrian kimono sector was a holdout. ILGWU Local 41, the Wrapper, Kimono and House Dress Makers Union of New York, began agitating to organize Syrian kimono workers under Fannia M. Cohn's leadership, starting with the Strike of 1913.[70]

At the root of this strike was a contest over working conditions. Responding to concessions recently won across U.S. textiles, the ILGWU demanded that the New York City white goods sector improve sanitary conditions in their factories, abolish child labor, and adhere to a fifty-hour work week at a $10 weekly minimum wage. The strike began with a walkout on January 8: 1,000 male cutters and 10,000 women and girls dramatically quit their machines before forming pickets outside. The ILGWU swiftly circulated a broadside calling for all 60,000 of the city's whites workers to join them.[71] The daily pickets caught national attention: socialist groups opened a soup kitchen to feed the assembly, Theodore Roosevelt wrote a sympathetic letter to congress after visiting the picket line, and Socialist congressman Victor Berger demanded an investigation into ILGWU allegations of wage theft.[72] The strike lasted six weeks. On February 13, ILGWU Local 41 signed a protocol ensuring industrial peace in exchange for a preferential shop system in the kimono and wrapper industries, ending the strike.[73]

Some Syrian women and girls answered the ILGWU's call for an industry walkout and joined the pickets, but their numbers were small. The Syrian kimono shops were surprisingly impervious to the effects of the strike, humming along as their workers were forbidden from expressing sympathy with union demands. Syrian American manufacturers represented 50 percent of the kimono and wrapper industry in 1913, and therefore, the ILGWU regarded these factories as a "dangerous competitive force to the American and Jewish elements in the trade."[74] Local 41 was even more worried, reporting that the Syrian workers' resistance had thwarted its efforts to impose a general strike: 35 percent of New York's kimono workers had joined Local 41, the remaining balance overwhelmingly employed by Syrian shops.[75] Studying the Syrian shop phenomenon after the strike's conclusion, the ILGWU estimated the factories employed 2,000 young Syrian women and girls in conditions of ethnic isolation.[76] In "Syrian-Turkish shops, men and women are working longer hours for lower wages," Local 41 explained in this report, adding "these people have to be organized; the sooner the better for all concerned."[77] To make matters worse, reports rolled into the ILGWU that the Syrian kimono firms began a retaliatory campaign of layoffs after the strike's conclusion, firing women who were seen as sympathetic to the union.[78] In December 1913, the ILGWU leadership lamented that the city "still swarmed with factories owned largely by Syrian-Turkish manufacturers who carried on a merciless competition against the unionized section of the trade and smothered them." Following this "campaign of reprisal" against Syrian garment workers, organizers worried that the entire immigrant community could "lose faith in the Union." Taking these threats under consideration, the ILGWU issued Resolution 107, which reorganized two ILGWU locals (Kimonos, Local 41 with House Dresses, Local 45) in order to boost their numbers relative to the Syrian manufacturers. They also ordered the ILGWU general executive board to organize "a general strike in the unorganized shops of the house garment industry in New York, *particularly among the Syrian manufacturers*, as the only means of putting the entire industry on an equal basis and building up a strong, permanent union."[79]

Local 41 endeavored to organize Syrian women beginning with the kimono factories on Washington Street, where "there are several thousands ... who are still to be organized."[80] The union had two goals: to identify and support Syrian women workers in organizing their units directly, but failing that, to force their employers' compliance with industry norms through targeted stoppages. The union's appeals to Syrian workers centered class unity and a rejection of racial division, as captured in a 1913 editorial by ILGWU organizer Pauline Newman: "All over this country working women are beginning to feel the great need of acting together in order to improve their economic conditions . . . [No matter one's] religion, politics, nationality or creed . . . in the shop or in the factory the interests of the workers are alike. You may be Jew, Gentile, Italian, Turk, or Syrian—if the conditions are bad, you ALL suffer from them, do you not? If, on the other hand, the conditions are better, you ALL enjoy them, do you not?"[81] Newman addressed Syrian women directly in her editorials, challenging the industrial culture that prevailed in the Syrian shops which situated kimono stitchers as Syrians first, women second, and finally as workers—a distant third. "You must remember that you belong to *one class*," Newman asserted, adding that individuals must eschew ethnic divides, nationalist politics, and sectarian grievances to embrace their responsibilities to their fellow workers.[82]

Local 41's campaign continued through the difficult war years, all the while swimming against the tide of diasporic long-distance nationalisms which soon dominated the Arab American press and political scene. Working with the Women's Trade Union League (WTUL, another ILGWU body), the local attempted to organize "Syrian girls working in the [kimono] trade," focusing on younger, unmarried women who were most numerous in these spaces. The union sent settlement house worker Gertrude Barnum to the Syrian Quarter in late 1913 to connect with women workers and distribute ILGWU literature. Barnum focused on raising microunits within the neighborhood's small subcontractor workshops. She worked there for several months, hoping to draw the small Syrian shops into a ILGWU general strike planned for 1914, but despite some initial gains "the agitation was interrupted" when several Syrian workers were summarily laid off after they were seen with Barnum.[83] Barnum's status as an American social worker from a wealthy background also undermined her credibility. Paired with Local 41's inability to protect Syrian women workers from retaliation, the campaign faltered and the union pulled Barnum.[84]

Local 41 requested funds to hire a Syrian organizer, a request granted under ILGWU Resolution No. 92, which granted a stipend for a Syrian organizer and translator to liaise between Local 41 and kimono workers for the 1916 season.[85] ILGWU records do not record the Syrian organizer's name but list him as male; he was hired from "among the thousands of Syrians employed [in] the kimono trade" and charged with developing a Syrian contingent for the next strike.[86] The organizer brought a delegation of Syrian kimono workers to a mass meeting at Cooper Union in December 1915, where Local 41 reported that "great enthusiasm was displayed for a general strike; we hope to establish a strong organization in these industries before the spring season is over."[87] The meeting authorized a strike in 1916; afterward, the Syrian organizer translated an ILGWU appeal letter to Syrian workers to join the union and honor the picket lines:

> Oh, Syrian workers, do not be late! The workers of the *kimuna* mills have united solidly and intend to strike to improve their wages and conditions. Thousands and thousands of ~~American and Jewish girls~~ kimono workers—men and women, Jews, Italians, and many others—have united with the Union [*ittahadu bi-l-union*] in the recent days. You Syrian workers are just like the Americans, Jews, and Italians in intelligence, rights, and are deserving of the same wages they are taking. So, you must join the Union and help your loved ones prepare for this strike.
>
> When the strike begins, not one person should begin their work in the shop. Instead, all will go out together and rage until the bullies are forced to submit to the Union's demands: better wages, better working conditions.[88]

As promised, 1916 was another significant strike year: Local 41 led a citywide industry stoppage in the white goods and kimono factories to force the city's manufacturers into arbitration. After reaching an impasse with manufacturers, "the kimono workers left their shops to a person" in February, including 2,000 Syrians, primarily young women, who vacated the shops on both Washington Street and Atlantic Avenue in Brooklyn.[89] By joining 3,600 members of Local 41, Syrian kimono workers nearly doubled the numbers of picketers stationed in the streets.[90] The walkout proved that the Syrian shops need not be closed in order for the ILGWU to demand industry change. The Syrian picketers were overwhelmingly not dues-paying members of Local 41, but that did not matter; they halted production citywide and were a visible lynchpin to union power.

Syrian women picketed outside thirty-five Syrian kimono factories across the city, led by the ILGWU's Syrian organizer, who liaised between them and union leadership.[91] In addition to an increase in wages to meet the industry standard, Syrian strikers demanded improved working conditions. "It is public knowledge that in the [kimono] trades girls have been receiving a wage as low as $4.00 a week," recounted the *Ladies' Garment Worker*. "The Syrian girls abounding in this trade, employed by their own compatriots, have to pay for the use of the machine and other accessories out of this miserable pittance."[92] The strikers demanded wage increases, a forty-nine-hour work week, and the adoption of the ILGWU's industry governance system, a project to establish structured arbitration boards to regulate wage scales, sanitation, and collective bargaining procedures. The Manufacturers Associations balked at these demands, and while picketers remained out of the factories, the ILGWU escalated its strike, closing additional factories in New York, New Jersey, Philadelphia, and Chicago through the spring of 1916. At the height of the movement, 40,000 garment workers were on strike nationwide.[93]

As the strike wore on, the city's kimono manufacturers resorted to repression, sending "hired thugs" who "beat up the pickets and assaulted strikers." Hired provocateurs initiated a string of violent confrontations, leading to the arrest of dozens of picketers. "While the police back up the employers and their hirelings by annoyance," strikers endured repeated cycles of arrests and court fines.[94] The violence yielded bad press, winning the public to the union's side, and leading manufacturers to bargain with Local 41 and grant workers a forty-nine-hour work week, sanitary and grievance arbitration, and a preferential union clause in select kimono shops.[95] In its annual report for 1916, Local 41 cited the Syrian picketers as pivotal to their victory.[96] That December, the local held another mass meeting where it "secured a resolve for Syrian and Spanish organizers [to] aid in efforts to organize the entire trade."[97]

However, just as swiftly as Syrian kimono workers organized with ILGWU in 1916, this cooperation fell apart when America entered World War I the following April. Wartime created challenging conditions for labor organizations, especially those representing foreign-born workers. Syrian immigrants faced intense pressure to perform American patriotism. As Ottoman nationals classified as "neutral allies of the enemy," Syrian workers, activists, and merchants experienced intensified state surveillance during the war. Achieving U.S. citizenship and registering for the draft became markers of patriotism. In industry, Syrian merchant-manufacturers declared their support for the U.S. war effort. They expected their employees to demonstrate love of country by avoiding work stoppages or through purchase of Liberty Bonds. The government subjected trade unions suspected of radicalism to scrutiny. Syrian mill workers in Paterson, New Jersey, and Lawrence, Massachusetts, were named in anti-Americanism investigations targeting the Industrial Workers of the World (IWW); the ILGWU escaped this fate, but all these pressures undermined the ILGWU's fragile cooperation with Syrian kimono workers in New York.

Just six weeks after America's entry into the war, Local 41 reported that "the results obtained from... the Syrian organizer [have] proved very negligible" following the strike.[98] A year later in 1918, Local 41 appears to have conceded the kimono industry totally, reporting to the ILGWU executive board that "few kimono shops are now under its control." The primary reason for this reversal, according to the local, was that the city's kimono factories "are in the hands of Syrian and Spanish or Portuguese workers... They are all relatives and countrymen" and this "stand(s) in the way of organizing them."[99] Subsequent union reports mentioned "language and nationality obstacles" as primary barriers "that lie in the way of organizing these Eastern workers."[100] The war years dampened Syrian labor activism. However, after the war's conclusion, Syrian kimono workers again appeared at picket lines in 1919.

The basic contours of the strike of 1919 were familiar: amid a nationwide background of industrial disruptions coming out of the war, contract negotiations between the ILGWU and garment industry manufacturers broke down in January, prompting garment workers to walk off the job. Though they were overwhelmingly not union shops, the Syrian kimono factories were affected: between 3,000 and 5,000 kimono workers participated in the walkout, including thousands of Syrians in Manhattan and Brooklyn. ILGWU Local 41 presented its demands to manufacturers: a forty-four-hour work week and wage increases across the board.[101] Again, the union focused on the presence of "the Assyrian and Spanish element" among the strikers. ILGWU President Benjamin Schlesinger joined Syrian picketers outside of their factories and accused the Syrian shops of racial discrimination. Because these shops "paid a much lower rate of wages than [is] given to other workers" across the industry, they were exploiting their own workers to gain competitive advantage. Schlesinger argued that improving wage rates at the Syrian shops was also necessary because "American manufacturers will be driven out of business unless the Assyrian and Spanish element are given the same rate," threading the needle between pro-worker solidarity and a broader current of American nativism.[102]

Local 41's pickets remained outside the Syrian shops for weeks, growing as more women workers joined the action. Two weeks in, fifteen Syrian kimono factories had been forced to halt production. Three thousand Syrian workers stood outside of the Abdalla Barsa plant, one of the largest kimono firms in the city.[103] Some manufacturers again responded with force, and local police abused picketers. Schlesinger anticipated these clashes and, staying with the strikers, he reported the abuses widely to the press.[104] Although the 1919 strike failed at shutting down all the Syrian kimono shops, it succeeded in bringing Syrian merchant-manufacturers to the bargaining table. In February 1919, a group of Syrian manufacturers requested an independent meeting with ILGWU leadership, attempting to avert an escalation. Local 41 denied the request, stating the union's position that "all kimono makers shall be brought into line before any agreements are made in the industry" and referring them to their peers in manufacturing.[105] Triangulating kimono manufacturers against one another was this strike's hallmark move: spurned by union representatives, Syrian factory owners had to bargain within their networks to help bring the industry to terms. Meanwhile, Syrian kimono workers joined daily mass meetings in significant numbers, even prompting the ILGWU to hold lectures in Arabic.[106] Ultimately, the strike ended in April 1919: the workers had won a forty-four-hour work week and a few oversight concessions, but no wage increase.[107] The Syrian shops resisted a preferential union clause, as they had in 1916, but the ILGWU's dominance across the industry nevertheless forced some concessions.

Despite their presence at ILGWU pickets in 1913, 1916, and 1919, Syrian kimono workers remained just beyond the union's reach: ready to strike but reticent to join. Taking stock after the strike of 1919, the ILGWU noted that 75 percent of New York City's ladies' garment workers were members of the union.[108] However, Syrians working in Syrian-owned kimono factories were conspicuously absent from this tally. For their part, the city's Syrian merchant-manufacturers resisted unionization, retaliating against union sympathizers with dismissals. The ethnic makeup of these shops—their reliance on Syrian labor and direct merchant control—contributed to the ILGWU's inability to reach Syrian women workers, a challenge compounded by the union's reliance on a male organizer in 1916. Structurally, the ILGWU's reliance on protocolism delivered mixed results in reshaping the prevailing labor economy in the ethnic garment factories. On one hand, the ILGWU protocols in 1913, 1916, and 1919 established standards to improve conditions industry-wide, regardless of union membership.[109] However, enforcement of these protocols was limited to closed (unionized) shops, leaving Syrian shops in a position to accede to some demands while rejecting others. As a result, in matters of working hours and, over time, prevailing wages, the Syrian shop conditions mirrored ILGWU closed shops after 1919; however, they did not allow oversight mechanisms and repeatedly resisted arbitration.

SHOP CULTURE: FACTORY WOMEN ON AND OFF THE FLOOR

"One secret to success in this business is to provide joy for the workers," Najib Kiamie explained to Sallum Mukarzil; "give them small amenities to excite their thoughts, lift their spirits, and renew their activities."[110] As he led Mukarzil on a tour of his kimono factory in 1920, Najib Kiamie emphasized delight. Here is where Syrian women workers manufactured bedclothes, underwear, and negligees; there, a state-of-the-art phonograph was stationed at the center of the floor. Kiamie kept a library of the best new recorded music of Syrian New York: records from A. J. Macksoud Records and Maloof Phonograph Company lightened the air.[111] Surveying the space during the lunch hour, Mukarzil described women workers dancing and laughing together as the record played. In another room, a piano sat conspicuously next to stitching tables, where Kiamie hired a regular player and workers could sing along as they worked their garments. Peeking into this room after the break's end, Mukarzil described "the singing of the female workers," which reminded him of "silk factories in the homeland, where they have fun sharing songs while plunging their fingers into boiling water to retrieve cocoons." Kiamie told him such enticements improved worker retention in a competitive industry and that his workers "come to work with great enthusiasm." Reporting on his visit in the press, Mukarzil concurs, "it did not occur to me that we would find such high-end theories of management employed in a Syrian factory."[112]

Preoccupations with shop floor culture circulated among manufacturers and Syrian American elites generally, starting during the strike wave of 1913–1919 and persisting until the Great Depression. In the press, prescriptive literature on how to run a business prevailed: editorials on double-entry bookkeeping, use of timecards, vertical integration, and reinvestment strategies found their audiences alongside monthly updates on global commodities prices, currency exchange rates, and tariff shifts.[113] Much of this discourse critiqued the "old ways" of doing things.[114] Writing in 1916, Khalil al-Aswad argued that the itinerant "mercenary trader" thrived only by arranging peddlers beneath him and ensnaring them in debt. "Both seller and merchant perish" because debt "brings the both of them into decline." According to Aswad, the Syrians in America had experienced good fortune by expanding into garment manufacturing. This luck would be squandered unless Syrians studied "the natural laws governing commercial affairs"; without close knowledge of trade principles, "I think the Syrian remains technically unprepared for commercial pursuits."[115] Newspaperman Sallum Mukarzil took it further, establishing a new serial in 1918, *al-Majalla al-Tijariyya al-Suriyya al-Amrikiyya (The Syrian American Commercial Magazine)*, devoted to "Syrian education in economic and commercial matters" as well as "the strengthening of trade relations among the sons of the Arabic language around the world."[116] Mukarzil saw this as a novel project, filling an important niche: "This magazine differs from others in serving merchants; the trader needs a serial like this one."[117]

Discussions in the diaspora press on economics, business ethics, and modern commerce strike a dissonant chord with its silence on labor issues. Syrian papers in New York gave virtually no coverage to textile strikes, either locally or across the mahjar (though they offered some coverage of labor contests in the Middle East). Any discussion of labor issues was limited to taciturn, between-the-lines remarks within editorials aimed squarely at the elite readers assumed as the audience: Syrian merchants, manufacturers, importers, and businessmen. In a 1920 article on the economic thought of Charles Eaton, for instance, Mukarzil described how savvy factory owners "promote, among their workers, a better understanding of their civic duties" and that this "civilizing factor" was a boss's responsibility, "especially because the relationship between owners and workers is no longer what it was in the past—it is now based in independence feeling."[118] Beyond this immigrant community, veiled references to a need for "cooperation" between labor and capital were common in the open shop debates of the early

1920s.[119] At the same time, in the Syrian American press the ongoing strikes, disputes, and stoppages were represented in distant, indeterminant shadows, limited to the negative space around explicit elite desires for industrial peace and civility.

Meanwhile, Syrian garment workers appeared almost entirely in two spaces in the Syrian newspapers: in classified advertisements and in the editorials of Arab American feminist writers like 'Afifa Karam and Victoria Tannous. In classified ads, Syrian manufacturers laid claim to Syrian women workers through appeals to race solidarity and the gendered expectation that Syrian women would favor all-Syrian workplaces. Garment workers grappled with this multiplying set of cultural expectations, while also navigating an open shop system that continued to prevail after the strikes of 1913–1919. At the same time, the resulting contradictions—that factory women should be workers but that they should also be happier, more pliant, more feminine—set the stage for a feminist critique in the mahjar. By the interwar period, the Syrian 'amila offered a powerful figure in critique of traditional gender norms, family configurations, and attitudes about marriage, love, and work.

"At this time when there is less work to be had, we need female workers ['amilat] to staff our kimono factory," wrote the Barsa Company in January 1917. The author was prompted by the recent strike to add, "It is our policy to satisfy our workers and give them their rights in return for their labor."[120] Both Syrian and non-Syrian firms placed notices in the Arab American newspapers, most of which sought female garment workers to work in stitching, piecing, and finishing. A subtle politics of identity emerged in these ads, marked first by a firm's choice to disclose the company name or not. "Workers needed! Female apprentices for shirtwaists, $4 a week," wrote an August 1917 ad in al-Sa'ih: only the factory's address is given, an American firm offering the minimum wage.[121] Syrian firms tended to include the company name and—competing for the same pool of female operatives—progressively added more details about the jobs they advertised. "We seek skilled female workers [shaggilat mahirat] for machine sewing shirtwaists and underwear... our workers leave at half one on Saturdays, and have a 45-minute lunch break daily," wrote the Kiamie Co.; "we also pay $1–2 better than our competitor's best wages, and we increase wages twice a year!"[122] Some firms indicated their desire to train young women and girls: "We need 50 female machine sewers! $6 a week to start, we will teach you if you're no good," the Eddy Cury and Bros. company confidently asserted in *al-Nasr* in 1916.[123] "Ask any woman who works in this shop," proclaimed a 1915 Arida Co. ad in *al-Sa'ih*. "She will tell you about good management, cleanliness, and our maintenance of workers' health and comfort, which we do our very best to provide."[124]

All classified ads included language about "good wages" and "steady work," generic promises that appeared without fail in every Syrian shop notice in *al-Nasr, al-Sa'ih*, and *al-Alam al-Jadid* between 1916 and 1921. Manufacturers presented such promises as safeguarding Syrian workers against the intermittency, layoffs, and slowdowns they experienced when working for American companies, but the coded language also communicated that these factories remained open during strikes.[125] And not every manufacturer was so subtle: in the midst of the ILGWU strike of 1916, for instance, the Badran Bros. Company placed an ad to replace its striking operatives with the promise that "this work will be protected from any labor strike—*any STRIKE*—so the aggressors' hands can never reach our female workers."[126] By including the implication that Syrian women garment workers required company protection from the union, the Badran advertisement leans into a paternalistic thread common to the genre, which characterized the relationship between male owners and their female workers as cooperative, caring, and fatherly. In this view, the ILGWU represented interloping outsiders, "aggressors" who disrupted the proper set of relations between Syrian manufacturers and their female workforce. The union's leadership was overwhelmingly male and composed of Ashkenazi Jewish immigrants, likely compounding the sense that organizers' inroads into the Syrian shops represented an unwelcome gender threat. During the height of the 1916 strike, the Badran firm relocated from Broadway Avenue, moving into the centrally located Syrian Quarter on Washington Street.

As the classified ads here illustrate, garment factory labor was uniformly women's work. The jobs were ubiquitous and employers numerous, and for most young women, these positions offered the most remunerative work available to them. Though Syrian men worked in weaving, woolens, or even large format textiles, garment work was so thoroughly coded as feminized that it was shameful for a man to perform. Writing of her own marriage to Abraham Haddad in 1908, needleworker Nabeha Merhige recalls how her wealthy cousins cornered her, taunting, "Whatever possessed you to marry a factory worker? Had you come to see us, as you should, probably you might have met someone in business who would support you better than a *fellah*." That Merhige had left textile work to assume a role as a school headmistress also distressed them: "Are you satisfied with such wages? Why don't you come and work in a factory where you will be paid much more?" Merhige confessed, "I felt hurt and I started to cry" after this harsh questioning.[127] The implication that marrying a factory worker was shameful but that she should also remain one herself—working in her own family's factory, no less—stung her pride.

Though garment work was seen as shameful for Syrian men, it was viewed as advantageous for Syrian women, particularly the young and unmarried. Following the 1913–1919 strikes, two countervailing discourses about women's factory work prevailed. One of them—readily promoted by merchant-manufacturers—valorized young Syrian women who worked in the garment factories as economic contributors to their households. By working within the ethnic community, furthermore, these young women were advancing the Syrian name in America. Conversely, negative stereotypes about women factory workers circulated, targeting Syrian women for shirking their responsibilities to husbands, households, and children in favor of the financial independence factory work represented. Debate over women's work in the garment industry and its implications for Syrian families spilled across the pages of the Arab American press. On one side of this debate were the reformers who critiqued women's industrial work as undermining Syrian traditions; on the other side were the "new woman" (*al-mar'a al-jadida*) feminists like Victoria Tannous, who took a special interest in the challenges that Syrian women workers faced as they navigated daily life between home, factory, and the ways people talk (*kalam al-nas*).[128]

Originally from Jaffa, Palestine, Tannous came to New York in 1913 at twenty-three years old.[129] In New York she studied bookkeeping before becoming a columnist, publishing in several serials across the mahjar, including *al-Majalla al-'Arabiyya*, *al-Akhlaq*, and *al-Samir* in New York and *Fatat al-Sharq* and *al-Mar'a al-Jadida* in Beirut. A contemporary of 'Afifa Karam, Tannous was primarily known for championing working women and opposing negative portrayals of them in Arab American outlets that otherwise tended toward cultural conservatism.[130] Usually, these discussions over factory work were framed in relation to Syrian women's roles as wives and mothers, reflecting the patriarchal tenor in the mahjari press as well as U.S. social work conversations about immigrant women more broadly.[131] In many Syrian American newspapers, women's factory labor was represented as part of a diasporic amalgam of social ills (*al-amrad al-ijtima'iyya*) which together with divorce and prolonged bachelorhood, produced discontent in the hearts of men and crime on the streets.[132] The factory girl stereotype appeared in newspaper editorials to explain problems suffered in working-class neighborhoods.[133] When New York City's Little Syria neighborhood experienced dramatic increases in male unemployment, vagrancy, and violence in the mid-1920s, for instance, *al-Akhlaq* newspaper's editor Ya'cub Rufa'il described the tendency of Syrian working women to delay marriage as a precipitating factor.[134] Writing in 1923, Rufa'il opined that "marriage has a civilizing effect on the Syrian man," expressing anxieties over the impact of a Syrian woman's industrial employment on her marriageability. Working women were also comparatively freer to obtain a divorce, according to Rufa'il, creating a "larger assault on the family" that threatened the respectability the Syrian community otherwise enjoyed in America.[135] Among his peers, Rufa'il was perceived as a progressive, having elsewhere critiqued the stigma attached to marrying a working woman. He argued that this stigma fed a bride trade that he and his contemporaries found disreputable.[136]

Victoria Tannous combatted these caricatures by relaying the complexities of women's working lives and diagnosing patriarchy as the source of the mahjar's social ills. She inverted negatives tropes about factory girls to make her point. In 1916, for instance, Tannous published a series of interviews with young Syrian women on the topic of marriage and work. Titled "Why I Won't Marry in America," the essays laid out how Syrian men shamed women's labor even as they relied on it to make ends meet. Despite the pervasive image of Syrian factory girls as unmarried and young, Tannous argued most women ended up working after their wedding day, often for their husbands. In marrying a merchant, for instance, one of Victoria's informants believed her days working outside the home were over, only to find herself working in a kimono factory because her husband's business struggled. Spurning factory work was an option for him, though he complained he "was daily on the verge of breaking down in shame" because of his wife's kimono work. One of Tannous's friends married a tailor only to end up taking shifts stitching kimonos to help him keep his business: "The poor woman returned to the factory so that she could earn her living while he stayed at home, and now it's been eight years and they have four children together."[137]

In relaying stories about Syrian women whose husbands turned them into garment workers, Tannous blended Syrian immigrant ideas about proper gender comportment with American progressive discourses about sweated home work as sexually threatening. New York City anti-sweatshop campaigns in this era targeted immigrant "home workshops" as the worst sort of sweated labor, directly contrasting the harsh conditions of this work "with idealized images of 'American' factories."[138] Reformers argued that commingling of male and female workers within "the cramped spaces" of home workshops represented a moral threat to the garment industry. Similarly, in 1911 the American social worker Louise Seymour Houghton concluded of Syrian home workers that "the dependence of men upon their wives and children for support is becoming too common a circumstance ... [when] the men are idle, they prefer to take care of the children while the women peddle."[139] American discourses about this phenomenon emasculated Syrian fathers, likely compounding the sense of gender shame that accompanied dependence on wives' garment work. At the same time, feminists like Tannous used this inversion to criticize what they saw as prideful-but-idle immigrant masculinity.

Victoria Tannous's editorials caricatured Syrian men who valued their personal independence by shunning industrial work as shameful, while privately depending on industrial wages earned by mothers, wives, and daughters to make rent. Tannous was not merely inverting a literary trope; Syrian women who worked in the textile industries widely reported how such gender politics shaped their lives. For instance, Damascene silk weaver Najla Nouhan Simon arrived in Paterson, New Jersey in 1913, and entered the silk mills at fourteen years old. "I learned to weave. I had to work because I was the oldest one [of the children] in the family." She worked alongside her uncles to weave silk georgette. Because it was so physically demanding, silk weaving was generally considered a man's job, but Najla reported, "I seen Syrian women and I seen Syrian men" in the factory, though none as young as herself. In the days "before the union ... they used to cheat us *yaʿani,* the first year I wasn't making much money but the last three years I was making $16 like a man, man wages."[140] Najla's family depended on her earnings. She reports with frustration that her father refused silk work because he was unable to find blacksmithing work in Paterson (his trade in Syria); "I was the only income; he sat home," and this persisted until Najla married and left Paterson in 1918.[141] In Boston, SLAS co-founder Hannah

Sabbagh described how she worked in gingham and dressmaking factories during her adolescence with her mother, paying the rent while her brothers struggled to get their merchant business off the ground.[142] Similarly, garment worker Bahieh Kappaz asserted, "Boston, that is where women came to work," before explaining how she, her sister, and her grandmother were her household's primary earners.[143] Both Najla Simon and Zahdi Barsa believed that marriage would end their days in the factories, only to have their hopes dashed: Simon clerked in her husband's grocery store, and Barsa continued in the garment factory.[144] Simon expressed this frustration in stark terms: "I thought when I got married I'd take it easy, but it was worse than ever!" followed by "they didn't even *ask* me."[145]

Syrian women's industrial labor and marriage almost always appeared together in the press, twin issues that defined mahjari feminist critique through the 1930s. As young immigrants who were simultaneously breadwinners, Syrian women criticized the systems which undervalued them materially via wage theft and culturally via pervasive negative stereotypes about working women. In material terms, Tannous reported on Syrian kimono shops that paid married women less than their unmarried peers, undervaluing their labor on the assumption that their husbands provided for them. She dramatized this wage theft in a 1917 exchange she had with two kimono workers on the train. Sitting down with the young women, she overheard one complain to the other that she was being paid "less than Adele." Her friend replied, "Adele's just a girl; (her wage) is going to her father and brothers. He's a merchant and all of them work all day; what, should they leave their young daughter in the house by herself?" Adele's wages raised up her natal household and were seen as a social good. By contrast, a married woman in the factory was also her husband's dependent, and her labor was discounted on that basis. It is not clear how common this practice was; it certainly was not industry wide, and the prevailing standard collectively undervalued pieceworkers as a class. However, Tannous was angered by the logic that the value of a Syrian woman's labor be measured against her relationships with men. She argued that factory work was virtuous, if grueling labor for all: "To you, my sister, the Syrian girl: there is no shame at all in work. The hardworking girl who does not depend on fathers or brothers for her livelihood is a girl that every family has the right to be proud of."[146]

Similarly, Tannous wrote about how the same paternalistic expectations about who owned women's labor capacity alienated young women from their communities. In part two of "Why I Won't Marry in America," she profiled a young kimono worker who found herself alone in New York after her father died suddenly. The worker explained, "I had been in school, and school made me free!" but when her father passed, she lamented, "I found no open door except for the one on the factory. I spent my days and nights there, wailing and crying, until my strength was lost, my resolve broken."[147] Without a visible tie to a Syrian man, whether father or fiancé, the young woman told Tannous, she became an outcast. Factory work provided freedom, but that "freedom was also the reason for [her] downfall from the Syrian community." Looking out at the street from her sewing machine, she reflected, "I see my sisters walking through life's temptations, one of them holding her brother's hand, another clasping her fiancé's arm. As for me, who am I? A lonely girl, a sitting beast." She was afraid to walk through the Syrian Quarter because of the rumors (*kalam al-nas*) she heard whispered behind her. "The girls look at me with contemptuous eyes. The men treat me scornfully. I don't know why."[148] With this profile, Victoria Tannous laid out the moral jeopardy that young working women experienced each day: their material well-being depended on their industrial labor, but that work also engendered shame, contempt, and alienation. For Tannous, marriage was simultaneously an escape from this wretched existence and a mirage; young women could be spurned by potential suitors or get married, only to face the prospect of working motherhood.

The marriageability of Syrian garment workers was also the topic of a larger conversation in Syrian American print culture. Victoria Tannous confronted stereotypes that factory women were less valuable brides with ferocity, sometimes positioning factory women as contributors and other times emasculating men who derided them. Among Arab American feminist writers, the degraded aging bachelor emerged as a symbol during this period, a caricatured response to the joyless Syrian spinster who also appeared in the popular press. In 1923's "Do You Despise the Working Woman?" for instance, Tannous told the story of a fictional forty-one-year-old bachelor named Wadi' who approached a matchmaker for help finding a bride. The pair walked up and down Washington Street, and Wadi' was introduced to dozens of eligible women, each more well-educated and morally incorruptible than the last. Wadi' begged the matchmaker to find him the "most virtuous" wife, a subtext lost on the matchmaker until: "He told me that he did not want to marry a woman who had worked for her means,

FIGURE 15. Portrait of Victoria Tannous in 1925. A critic of women's exclusion from Arab American political spaces, Tannous wrote about the cultural shaming women garment workers experienced. Her "new woman" feminism put her in conversation with writers like 'Afifa Karam and Julia Dimasqiya. Source: *Al-Akhlaq*, January 1925, 3.

whether she labored in the very best market, or toiled in the lowest of trades. He would not seriously consider a working woman as an option for himself, even if her morals and manners were undisputed."[149] Wadi'ʿ's "scorn for women who work" reduced him to elderly bachelorhood, Tannous argued. His chauvinism rendered him incapable of fulfilling his honorable role as head of household.

Tannous also challenged popular perceptions that working women made poor mothers. A 1923 debate in *al-Akhlaq* illustrates the curves of this debate. In "A Child Cries," Arab American social worker Amira al-Hilu dramatized an interaction with a Syrian street urchin on Washington Street. Approaching the young boy, around three years old, al-Hilu wiped a tear from his face and asked him why he was crying. "I'm hungry," he says, "the door (to my home) is locked, and my mother is at the textile factory working."[150] From this story, al-Hilu warned Syrian American mothers who might be tempted to work not to let their priorities deviate from their primary responsibilities to their children. A lonely child in the street was a sign of failed womanhood. Responding to al-Hilu, Tannous accused her of neglecting the other side of the boy's story. For she, too, met this toddler, but their conversation went more like this:

> "Where is your mother?"
> "At the factory."
> "Well then, where is your father?"
> (between sobs, the child exclaims) "Why, he's at the café!"[151]

Far from shirking her responsibilities, Syrian mothers worked "seated over hot machines with none but God for company" before rushing home to prepare supper. Meanwhile, Tannous depicted their husbands as spending their day at the café playing backgammon, smoking narghile, and reciting *zajal*, coming home only to "complain that things in the homeland are not as they ought to be."[152] By locating the wayward husband in the café, Tannous mocked the homeland nationalist political fraternities which inhabited these spaces, challenging their patrons' masculinity and misplaced priorities.

Victoria Tannous's editorials provoked consumers of her regular columns in *al-Majalla al-'Arabiyya* (1916–1918) and *al-Akhlaq* (1920–1925). Readers wrote in with both further indictments of patriarchal expectations and, conversely, with their rebuttals. Writing in opposition to Tannous's "Why I Won't Marry in America" series, for instance, Nabiha Habib argued that if Syrian women felt that marriage had become oppressive, "that is not the fault of the man, but of the woman." "Man is a powerful force, but woman . . . is the engine, the motivation for man's power" and the one responsible for guiding men's energies appropriately. Habib described Syrian factory women as blinded by their own earning power: "As long as we—as Syrian women—are unable to see anything that lies beyond the factory walls or the wares of the silk purse, it is not appropriate for us to take the freedoms of strangers who want to lead us where ever they are going."[153] By claiming that Tannous's critiques of Syrian immigrant gender politics originated in the reformist discourses of American social work, Habib tapped into mahjari anxieties about assimilation, cultural loss, and the moral threat that these represented among Syrian American elites.[154]

As garment workers, Syrian women and girls in New York earned wages that were crucial to their families' survival. Trade union records, the industry press, Arab American feminist writings, and the oral histories of working women all describe how Syrian women—young and old, married and unmarried, across multiple communities—worked as their households' primary breadwinners, usually in factories owned by Syrian American proprietors. In the so-called Syrian shops, proprietors maintained a shop culture that prioritized ethnic loyalty, patriotic obligation, and a patriarchal claim to the labor power of Syrian women. These ideas served as a bolster against the efforts of American labor organizers, allowing Syrian kimono shops to weather the ILGWU strikes that otherwise unionized the entire New York City garment industry. Ironically, the ILGWU's hesitancy (or perhaps inability) to retain female Syrian organizers and instead rely on Syrian and Jewish men to reach them may have played into claims by shop foremen that the union was a foreign, interloping organization, from whom Syrian women and girls needed protection. Syrian women joined garment worker strikes and walked in pickets in droves, but outside of a strike scenario, these women remained beyond the grasp of organized labor and were, in many ways, discounted by it.

In popular discourse, Syrian American industrialists analogized the textile industries to national development. Women's labor became a patriotic obligation and consequently, trade unionism was cast as a detriment to national development. Syrian factory heads were celebrated by mahjari periodicals which simultaneously tended to gloss over or ignore the demands of striking workers. These labor politics disadvantaged Syrian women workers as they sought to improve working conditions, but it also placed women at the fulcrum of debates over gender, class, and assimilation in Syrian America broadly. In the press, Arab American feminist authors battled stereotypes about female factory workers which characterized them as poor wives, unfit mothers, or hopeless spinsters. These editorialists emphasized the centrality of women's work in upholding the mahjar's economy, and the commitment of Syrian American women to projects of racial uplift and upward social mobility. But by the early 1920s, another thread emerged which directly challenged the assumption that racial respectability was the Syrian community's goal in America. Feminists inverted gender tropes to shame Syrian men for the conditions under which Syrian women labored, resorting to rhetorical emasculation when necessary.

Meanwhile, as the New York City ladies' garment industries weathered strike after strike and the Syrian shops experienced work stoppages, lockouts, reversals, and layoffs, Syrian merchant-manufacturers began to look abroad for sources of textile goods for their brands. It was during the 1916 ILGWU strike that one manufacturer, Elias Mallouk, began acquiring factories abroad, focusing particularly on the North Atlantic island of Madeira. A merchant trading port with a rich heritage industry in handmade embroidered linens, Madeira seemed like the ideal site to supply the packs of Syrian peddlers in the Americas. In 1916, Mallouk boarded a steamship from New York to Funchal, joining dozens of other Syrian American merchant-manufacturers who had also made this trip. Within a year, the Syrian American firms of Washington Street jointly controlled 90 percent of Madeira's namesake linen goods industry. They had all heard the rumor that Madeiran women did not strike; at least, they had not done so yet.

FOUR

LABORING FOR EMPIRE
Madeira Island's Fase Síria

NOVEMBER 1919—AWAKING IN FUNCHAL, William Karsa, the foreman of the Alexander J. Hamrah and Co. embroideries factory on Rua do Comércio on the Portuguese island of Madeira, donned his blackest tuxedo jacket with his whitest shoes before entering the factory. Karsa met the photographer and led him, room by room, through the production process. The Hamrah factory comprised eight rooms organized by their core functions—receiving, perforating, stamping, ironing, finishing—and William posed in each amid dozens of Madeiran women, men, and girls working to refine raw linen into decorated luxury household items destined for export to New York. Karsa commissioned these photographs for the company catalog: each image was carefully staged to showcase the factory's efficiency, its advanced machinery, and the Taylorist industrial arrangement that was the venerated ideal of Syrian manufacturers across the diaspora. The economic magazine *al-Majalla al-Tijariyya al-Suriyya al-Amrikiyya* published the photos in New York, celebrating the Syrian firms of Madeira. Its editor, Sallum Mukarzil, applauded "the Syrian immigrant [who] crowded out those sons of Europe [in the market] . . . showing cunning and resourcefulness enough to even win him over."[1]

Hamrah Bros. was one of over a dozen Syrian commercial houses that arrived in Funchal to take over the island's embroideries industry during World War I, an economic miracle Mukarzil credited to Syrian economic cooperation across the mahjar. But even as Karsa led the photographer through his factory, most of the company's work went unseen: thousands of Madeiran women embroidered Hamrah linens in the island's mountainous hinterlands, in villages accessible only by pack mules, driven by men with loaded *kashehs*. These factories were supply-side extensions of the same commercial networks Syrian peddlers depended on in the Americas. Syrian merchants had followed the source of the wares their peddlers were procuring, a vertical integration strategy Mukarzil described as "storming the lion in its den."[2] The Syrian factories on Madeira provided a proof of concept, an economic model that émigré manufacturers replicated in Florence, Manila, Yokohama, and Shanghai and sought to bring home to Zahle, Tripoli, Damascus, and Aleppo.

This chapter is about the Syrian merchants of Madeira, a network of producers who, after opening successful textile factories in New York, broke into the global embroideries business during World War I. Initially an adjunct to the kimono industry, Syrian lace and embroideries dealers shifted from providing yardage for the garment industry toward the manufacture of household embroidered linens. Driven by the war's economic dislocations and the uncertain period which followed it, Syrian American merchants pursued new sources of handmade needlework like Cluny and Filet laces, and Florentine or Madeira linens, establishing a cottage industry on Madeira Island. As a Syrian diasporic merchant class and as naturalized U.S. citizens, these new commercial elites represented themselves as promoters of American commercial interests abroad. Hunting for markets, lobbying for favorable tariff conditions, and plugging into the politics of U.S. expansionism, Madeira's Syrian merchants carved a niche for themselves. On Madeira, the Syrians represented American capital.

ARRIVING IN FUNCHAL: WAR AND LACE

Syrian merchants linked commercial cooperation with partners across the mahjar to strategic investments upstream in the commodity chain, expanding their share in the global whites markets. The timing was auspicious for several reasons. World War I completely upended the art linen industry, which depended on both free trade and open sea lanes. As European competitors ended up on opposing sides of battle lines, Syrian American merchant-manufacturers were uniquely positioned to conduct wartime trade by virtue of their status as naturalized U.S. citizens and their extensive commercial ties. At the same time, New York City's concurrent labor uprisings prompted Syrian textile elites to reinvest abroad, in alternative sites of production beyond the reach of American labor unions. By acquiring factories in global supply zones to sustain the peddling trades of the mahjar, these merchant-manufacturers exercised supply chain power. During the war, Syrian merchants from New York acquired 75 percent of Madeira's entire export economy and 90 percent of its namesake linens, then valued at $1,780,799 a year.[3]

Madeira's embroidered linens were cultural heritage items with a deep history: Portuguese colonists brought the craft to the island in the sixteenth century, drawing on the traditions of the Minho, Beira Alta, and Algarve regions.[4] Hand embroidery was widely practiced within Madeiran households as traditional methods and designs were passed from women to girls. The craft attracted foreign capital to the island in the nineteenth century when British firms, arriving to supply Irish linens, began exporting hand embroideries to Europe. By the early twentieth century, German merchants had come to the island and replaced the British.[5] Commercializing hand embroideries required scaling up production, and each foreign merchant class imposed more control over the industry's materials, design choices, and labor conditions, transforming Madeiran embroiderers into piece-rate workers over time.[6] As more women took on needlework as their primary income, their independent ownership of the craft dwindled.

The first Syrian American merchant to arrive in Funchal was F. M. Jabara, who established his table linens business there in 1908.[7] During World War I, large Syrian American firms came to dominate the island industry, starting with Elias (Ilyas) and Salim Mallouk. Damascenes who had established a substantial importing business in New York City at the turn of the century, the Mallouk brothers had started as household linens suppliers, importing wholesale German embroideries to hand off to Syrian pack peddlers. Initially a client of several of the island's German embroidery houses, Salim Mallouk came to Madeira in 1914, opened his own shop, and begin hiring Madeiran embroiderers away from the German firms. During peace time, this bold move earned Mallouk some enemies. Recapping this story in the Syrian American press, Sallum Mukarzil wrote, "The German merchants saw the encroachment of this Syrian trader on their circle as damaging, and so they resisted him through every means—legal and illegal—to

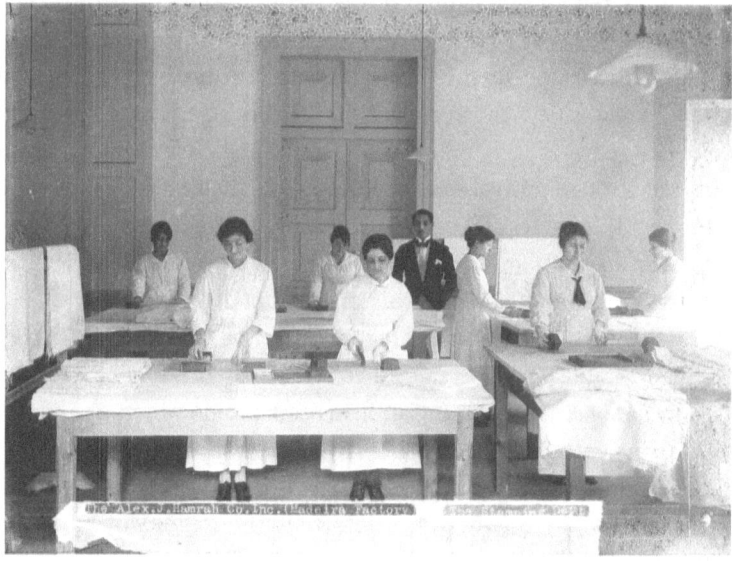

FIGURE 16. Above: William Karsa stands at left next to runners who take linens to the countryside for embroidering, 1919. Below: Hamrah and Co. stamping room, where linens are stamped with ink before distribution to needleworkers. Karsa stands in the background. Source: "Grupo de caixeiros, na rua 5 de Outubro, que levavam para o campo as peças do estabelecimento de bordados Alexandre Hamrah Co. Inc.," 1919-11-18, Museu de Fotografia da Madeira, Atelier Vicente's, on deposit at the Arquivo e Biblioteca da Madeira (hereafter AMB), VIC/D-B/001-002/000003. "Sala de estampagem do estabelecimento de bordados Alexandre Hamrah Co. Inc.," 1919-11-18, Museu de Fotografia da Madeira, Atelier Vicente's, on deposit at AMB, VIC/D-B/001-002/000006.

the extent that they deliberately boycotted every company that did business with Mallouk. They even boycotted any female worker ['*amila*] who had worked for him."[8] But the war intervened to his advantage: the Triple Entente imposed sanctions on German export firms, allowing Syrians to acquire their factories at a deep discount.[9] This hostile takeover came to a head in December 1916: Portugal ordered all German merchants to liquidate their assets and leave the island, and German submarines entered the Bay of Funchal and bombarded the city in retaliation.[10] But as German merchants quit the island, dozens of Syrian Americans arrived to take their place, filling the vacuum created by the new tensions between the European allies and their adversaries.

The drama of this moment fills the pages of the Syrian American press, but another crucial context is absent: New York's strike of 1916 and a wave of labor militancy among Syrian kimono workers as they picketed for better pay, the right to organize, and the adherence to ILGWU protocols. Syrian American manufacturers began outsourcing to hedge against labor unrest in America. They went not only to Madeira; Syrian firms also moved into the Italian lace trades, driven by another wartime trade vacuum. In that case, Italy's decision to enter the conflict seriously strained the country's supply chain for filet, Florentine, and Venetian laces. As the war dragged on, Syrian American manufacturers followed the supply chains to Asia, sending in "some samples of [Italian] filet lace to certain parts of China ... as an experiment" in 1917. The trade journal *Women's Wear* reported that "much to the surprise of the Syrian embroidery houses, the Chinese 'came right back'... and produced what the Syrians today say is better filet lace than the Italians now."[11] By the 1918 armistice, the Italian lace market was "shattered by the war," but the world could still buy Italian-style lace manufactured in Shanghai, made by the same Syrian firms dominating Funchal's linens industry.[12]

Many of Madeira's Syrian merchants who arrived during the war were adjacent, both spatially and socially, to Salim and Elias Mallouk. Amin and Jurj Bardwil opened their first Funchal factory in 1914; Alexander J. Hamrah arrived in 1915, opening a factory with his brother-in-law, William Karsa, who remained on the island as shop manager.[13] Together these were the three largest Syrian firms in Funchal, but there were dozens of smaller companies: Khalil W. Saydah came with his brother, Mikha'il, after the 1916 German bombardment. Like Hamrah, the Saydahs had previously opened a factory in Zahle (in 1910) which failed when the war began; Funchal offered the family a second chance. The Saydah Company was more modest than Hamrah's but gives a sense of what a typical Syrian American embroidery house looked like: at its height, K. W. Saydah employed 150 "runners," launderers, and staff at the Funchal factory and another 5,000 rural women in piecework.[14] By contrast, Hamrah Bros. contracted four times as many pieceworkers, singlehandedly employing 20,000 people in the 1920s.

In addition to their commercial interests, the island's Syrian American merchants were connected through dense networks and held kith, kinship, and personal ties. Many of the importers were Melkites from Zahle who shared businesses.[15] "All of them were from Zahle—Bardwil, Mallouk, Saydah—mostly Zahalni," recalled Chicago-area linen merchant Louis F. Lutfy in an oral history interview, adding that "the most desirable goods" for peddlers to carry came from Funchal.[16] In addition to the Zahle Melkites, there were numerous manufacturers from Damascus and Aleppo on the island. There was also a small Protestant network among them, connected to the First Syrian Protestant Church in Brooklyn.[17] Generationally, these men all represented the "old," "first order" émigré families in Syrian New York, having come in the 1890s and with recent involvement in wholesale peddling businesses. And their families were interlinked through kinship, marriage, or long-term partnership. In other words, the arrival of Syrian American merchants on Madeira did not merely respond to a new economic opportunity, it was also the result of commercial cooperation. Syrian diasporic businesses worked together to close out competitors and protect supply chains, but their success on Madeira was also the result of good geopolitical timing, an export market leaning toward the United States, and most crucially, their access to U.S. citizenship through naturalization.

There is a sizable scholarship on Syrian émigré citizenship practices in the mahjar, illustrating the countervailing forces of racialized immigration restriction versus the maneuverability of nationality laws as they related to Syrian, Lebanese, and Palestinian Ottoman subjects in the Americas.[18] Syrian immigrants in the United States applied for and received citizenship freely until 1908, when a series of legal challenges to their access on racial grounds ultimately culminated in *Dow v. United States* in 1915.[19] Dow set the precedent that Syrians were legally entitled to U.S. citizenship via naturalization, but both during the period of legal challenge (1908–1915) and later, U.S. laws governing the rights of Ottoman nationals in wartime (1917–1919) created an ambiguous legal status for Syrians living in the United States and its colonies.[20] Syrian merchants strategically asserted competing nationality claims and carried multiple foreign passports during the war, a documentary workaround that offered them clear commercial advantages. For the transatlantic Syrian merchants, acquiring U.S. citizenship was a prerequisite to doing business on Madeira. Elias Mallouk, for instance, naturalized in 1906 and carried a U.S. passport on numerous trips to Madeira.[21] Alexander Hamrah naturalized in New Haven in 1904; Jurj Bardwil in New York in 1902.[22] U.S. citizenship enabled Syrian importers to continue their businesses, exempting them from the blockades imposed on German and Ottoman commerce. This surge in Syrian commercial activity was not lost on industry experts: in 1917, for instance, the trade serial *Women's Wear* described how America's war effort halted German businesses while favoring "the rise of the Syrian lace and embroideries markets in Washington Street."[23]

At the same time, the citizenship status of Syrians who commuted between New York and Funchal did not always stick, particularly if they were suspected of having ties to the island's German firms. A visa investigation concerning Suheil Hermos is instructive: born in Syria and having worked briefly in New York, Hermos moved to Funchal in 1916 to work as shop manager for one of Mallouk's subsidiaries, Louis Tweel and Co.[24] When Hermos sought to return to New York in 1919, the Bureau of Investigation flagged him for uncertain citizenship status. The BOI interviewed Elias and Salim Mallouk, another factory manager, Aboussleman, and even Hermos's mother and sister before processing his return visa.[25] Staying abroad for too long was also an occupational risk: the U.S. Consulate routinely reminded merchants to circulate on time, or else face the presumption of expatriation. This is what happened to Naim Abualy and Elias Hamowy; both came to Funchal to manage factories in 1920 and overstayed the return dates stamped on their passports.[26] It required personal intervention by Consul General Stillman Eells, in the form of a letter to the U.S. secretary of state, to restore their citizenship to them.[27]

In addition to U.S. documents, Syrians arriving in Funchal also often carried French or British papers declaring them protected foreign subjects. Chiary Nicola Haddad, a merchant from Brazil, carried a French visa issued in Rio De Janeiro in 1920.[28] Anton Malhoul, a merchant headed to New York City, offered proof that he was "a French subject" in December 1921; he likely carried the French *sauf conduit*, a document used by merchants, repatriates, and refugees.[29] Others relied on British diplomatic protection. F. M. Jabara and Co. manager Emil Mogabgab, for instance, grew up in Cyprus with a Lebanese father and British mother; he was a British citizen who carried an American passport, a double vouchsafe that was also common.[30] Whether through naturalization, colonial possession, or diplomatic protection, achieving a legal tie to the Entente powers was an occupational necessity for Syrian merchants on Madeira. The British began blacklisting firms that were potentially hostile to allied war interests in 1916, and the United States did the same in 1917. Syrians who maintained Ottoman or other neutral nationalities appeared on these blacklists. This is what happened to "Wm Marum" in 1916, the only Syrian listed that month among a cluster of German nationals.[31]

Arriving during the war, then, Syrian merchant-manufacturers monopolized Madeira's hand embroideries industry, initiating a *fase síria* (Syrian phase) which lasted from 1916 until 1925.[32] At its apex, Syrian firms controlled 90 percent of the industry, and nearly all U.S. firms operating on the island were owned by Syrian merchants headquartered in New York City.[33] This was also a period of exponential expansion: Márcia Gomes identifies 100 factories active in Funchal that were active between 1919 and 1923.[34] The *fase síria* ended as abruptly as it began, with the assumption of Madeiran industrial control and the precipitous flight of Syrian American capital in 1925, under accusations of corruption.

Under Syrian control, the United States became the dominant market for Madeiran hand embroideries for the first time, receiving 80 to 90 percent of the island's export linens.[35] The Syrian firms similarly favored American machinery. The Portuguese government had resisted the industry's mechanization before the war, but as Syrian Americans arrived, they brought new stamping and punching machines with them from New York.[36] As wartime bans on iron, steel, and machinery exports expired in 1919, these firms sought to mechanize their Funchal factories completely. They acquired specialized Singer machines which necessitated the arrival of skilled Syrian workers to staff them.[37] The appearance of American machines on the island coincides with the Singer Corporation's aggressive pursuit of global markets; after saturating the home sewing machine market, the company shifted its focus toward specialty machines in U.S. colonies and developing regions. Singer worked closely with U.S. citizens opening factories abroad.[38] New embroidery-finishing machines also reshaped Madeira's production processes around standardized design and grading of needlework according to the export market. This mechanization remained incomplete; most of the needlework continued to be done by hand in Madeiran households to preserve the product's artisanal brand. But something crucial had changed: with machine-made patterns and perforations, creative control shifted firmly from the hands of Madeira embroiderers to the factories in Funchal.

Syrian American firms also replicated the modes of production and labor practices that presided in Syrian factories in the mahjar, particularly the New York kimono factories. In the early 1920s, the culture of Taylorist efficiency, scientific management, and vertical integration dominated among the émigré industrial elite. Syrian American firms in Funchal reimagined their commercial houses as factories, separating distinct facets of production into separate rooms: for cutting, stamping, and perforating raw linen in preparation for distribution; counting, grading, laundering, and finishing piecework; packaging and accounting for exports; and art and design. Though intentionally incomplete, this system of subdivided labor tasks mirrored a larger shift toward a factory system that "undermined the originality and craftsmanship of the maker" in favor of mechanized design and industrial consistency.[39] At the same time, the system's decentralized nature created chains of dependency which empowered the merchant-manufacturers at the expense of the workers. By controlling supply chains, Syrian firms controlled the industry at large.

Workplaces were sex-segregated and situated in sectors defined by hierarchical wage rates. The overwhelming majority of embroidery workers were Madeiran women and girls performing needlework in their homes. Embroiderers almost never traveled to the factory; instead, they depended on factory agents to bring linens and threads to them, agreeing to a piece rate, and then agents collected the pieces once completed. In a 1925 deposition, Alexander J. Hamrah and Co. foreman, João Maria P. Henriques described the process: "During 1919–1921, we employed 100 agents. Each agent had 50 to 100 embroiderers." Hamrah linens came from Ireland, and cotton cloth and threads from the United States; these were collected from the port, "cut, stamped, verified, and distributed to the agents" who carried them into the mountainous countryside.[40] The embroiderer workforce was vast: the Syrian American firms collectively employed 50,000 to 70,000 women across the island, a sum which represented a majority of the island's female population at the time.[41] The Funchal factories were quite small by comparison, each of them employing anywhere from a few dozen to 150–300 waged employees who processed the linens before export to New York.[42] At the height of the *fase síria* in 1922, the entire workforce of Funchal's embroidery factories was 2,500, split between seventy shops.[43] Each room in the Syrian American shops was dedicated to a specific task in the process, the work performed mostly by Madeiran women, who prepared linen bolts for cutting, punching, and stamping of bulk linen, and also laundered, ironed, and prepared finished pieces before export.

Home needleworkers in Madeira were a diverse lot: women and girls from multiple generations and family configurations, embroidering on at-will, part-time, or full-time piece contracts.[44] "These women are working throughout the day," American Consul General William Jenkins described in a 1919 report, adding that if kerosene sales are any indication, "without a doubt they are working [by lamplight] through the night too."[45] Though home workers tended to be of all ages, their counterparts in the Funchal factories tended to be young women, unmarried or recently married to men who had emigrated abroad. Factory work was broadly seen as a job for "women who wait," an association shared by several cultures along the Mediterranean migration circuit. Linda Reeder and Jennifer Guglielmo illustrate this clearly in Italy, and Sarah Gualtieri and Akram Khater in Lebanon and Syria.[46] Madeiran and Azorean men who departed the islands often ended up in factories in New England or New York, working alongside Italian and Syrian migrants as well.[47]

Madeiran women entered piecework contracts to supplement their households in the absence of male relatives or to make up shortfalls in remittances from abroad.[48] As home workers, embroiderers could set down linen work to prioritize other labor as needed, including more lucrative orders by competitor firms. Their pay was determined by handshake contracts usually staked on linen futures, defined as the price of raw linen in relation to projected retail prices on Fifth Avenue. This made earnings sensitive to even small price shifts. Though embroiderers usually finished the lots brought to them in two or three weeks, competition could be fierce during moments of high demand. Despite the reputation that Syrian American firms did not compete with one another, runners frequently poached embroiderers from their rivals. And because linen was an index commodity with a notoriously unstable price, women needleworkers turned rising prices and intense competition to their favor, delaying less remunerative orders in favor of quicker money. The runners who couriered linen pieces between Funchal and women's homes also depended on this unstable index; they drew no salary, earning only 5 to 7 percent on the value of goods delivered to the factories.[49]

Madeiran men also worked for the Syrian embroidery factories, though in specific roles: as runners bringing piecework or payments into the mountains or working with the heavier machinery on site. Madeiran and Syrian men staffed the punching machines and other specialized equipment and commanded higher wages than did their female peers. In the late 1930s, for example, machinists earned an average of five escudos a day, compared to the meager one escudo per day of the average pieceworker.[50] Furthermore, most of the professional and creative work was reserved for Syrian American men hired in New York. Several firms brought their own brand designers to Funchal, Syrian men who developed brand patterns in response to the latest American trends.[51] Retaining designers was expensive, and Syrian firms competed fiercely over artists. This fixation on transatlantic design was borrowed directly from New York kimono factories, where the ability to pivot to the newest trend kept large producers like Macksoud, Bardwil, and Arida on top of Fifth Avenue.[52] In addition to asserting central control over design, the Syrian firms also developed new lines of embroidered pillow shams and bed linens, items not previously produced in Madeira but which had been central to Syrian New York since the 1890s.[53]

Syrian American factory foremen stood at the top of this industrial order. Often, these men were younger relatives of their company's patriarch. William Karsa, for instance, was Alexander Hamrah's brother-in-law and apprentice. In addition to managing daily operations, the foreman also became the industry's public face on the island, mediating between the U.S. Consulate, the Portuguese government, and local labor. Factory managers concerned themselves with the latest trends in industrial management, adopting modern accounting to prevent material loss, stave off labor disputes, and maximize company profits. His job was to see that the "detailing, sewing, ironing, and folding are all accounted for on a regular basis, according to the latest rules of the economy of movement."[54] Just like their cognates in Manila, Shanghai, or Yokohama, Funchal's Syrian factories were dependencies of the mahjari firms of New York, where a specific culture of merchant capitalism emerged in the 1920s. "Our merchants have realized

FIGURE 17. Ironing and stamping rooms of Saydah Importing Co., Funchal, 1922. Both photos were altered to efface three Syrian factory foremen from the scene, preserving the factory's sex segregation in postproduction. Source: "Sala de engomagem do estabelecimento de bordados Saydah Importing Co.," 1922-11-26, Museu de Fotografia da Madeira, Atelier Vicente's, on deposit at AMB, VIC/D-B/001-013/000003. "Sala de estampagem do estabelecimento de bordados Saydah Importing Co.," 1922-11-26, Museu de Fotografia da Madeira, Atelier Vicente's, on deposit at AMB, VIC/D-B/001-0113/000004.

and mastered the details of managing industry," Sallum Mukarzil opined of the new factories, "no one else even comes close." The merchant class's preoccupation with the principles of scientific management led managers like Karsa to reimagine Madeira embroidery factories in ways reminiscent of the Syrian garment shops across the Atlantic: with orderly, distinct zones of production, segmented workforces, and carefully calibrated wage scales.

Standardization and partial mechanization were two legacies of Madeira's *fase síria*; these two shifts allowed Syrian firms to scale up production, doubling the industry's size between 1916 and 1921. At the same time, Syrian firms rearranged the island's labor economy in such a manner that "only the middlemen made reasonable profits."[55] Embroiderers labored as pieceworkers following patterns stamped on linen pieces by the Funchal shops. Rui Carita argues that mass production "lowered the quality of the final product," requiring exporters to focus on the American market rather than on

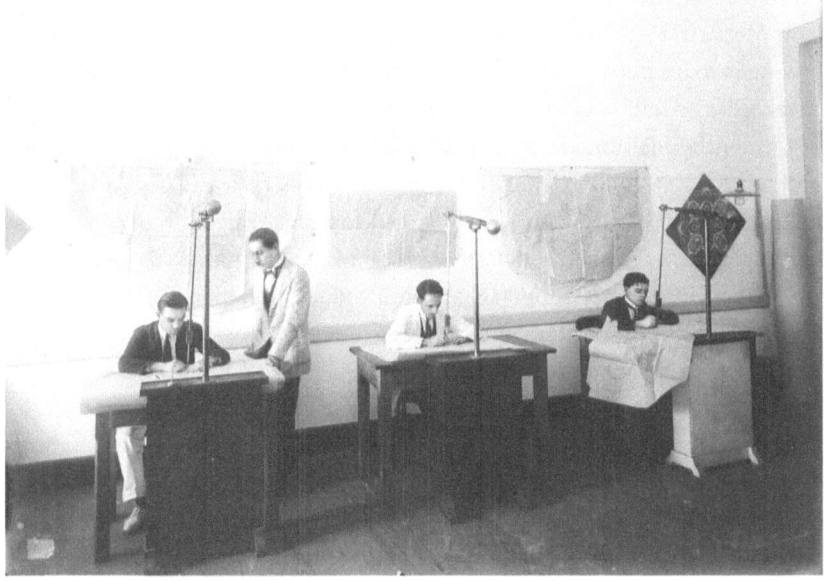

FIGURE 18. The punching room at the Alex Hamrah and Co, 1919. William Karsa stands over Madeiran men punching patterns into the stenciled linen. The patterns are displayed on the wall behind them. Source: "Sala de picotagem do estabelecimento de bordados Alexandre Hamrah Co. Inc.," 1919-11-18, Museu de Fotografia da Madeira, Atelier Vicente's, on deposit at AMB, VIC/D-B/001-002/000009.

more discerning European consumers.[56] New product lines arrived as well. Mallouk, Samara, and Hamrah each negotiated contracts with U.S. department stores for branded bedding and table linens which they marketed as handmade (and thus luxury) items, but with the mass consumer appeal and speed of factory production.[57] These changes came at the expense of Madeiran workers who faced worsening labor conditions, shrinking pay, and infringements on their traditional autonomy. Merchant capitalism was not new on Madeira. But the monopolist approach of the early 1920s deepened rifts between Madeiran workers, linen firms, and the Portuguese state until a collision in 1924–25 led most Syrian firms to abruptly leave the island.

THE MADEIRA EMBROIDERY CLUB

As Syrian American firms created an uncontestable monopoly on Madeiran hand embroideries, the island's U.S. Consulate sought commercial cooperation with them, believing they could offer entry into further American economic expansion. After an early effort to establish a U.S. Chamber of Commerce in Funchal failed in 1919, the consulate resorted to working with private instruments to influence the lucrative export industry. The Madeira Embroidery Club was one of these instruments. Established in 1921 and prominently positioned adjacent to the U.S. Consulate, the Madeira Embroidery Club was conceived first as a men's social club and hotel for Syrian American merchants, agents, sellers, and foremen. The club offered lavish lodging and amenities, a tavern serving Madeira's namesake wines and cigars, and conference rooms where embroidery men met to discuss industry and matters of mutual concern. Theoretically, "anyone who is engaged in the embroidery business is eligible [for membership], whatever his nationality," Jenkins reported to the secretary of state, though, in practice, its members were "exclusively American and Syrian."[58] The Madeira Embroidery Club served as a manufacturers association, representing thirty-two export firms on the island, thirty of them led by Syrian émigrés.[59] Only four American firms on the island were not members. Heavily outnumbered and beholden to decisions made over scotch within the club's walls, the proprietors of these four firms complained to the U.S. Consulate about monopolism, corruption, and possible fraud tied to its membership.[60] To the island's Portuguese majority, meanwhile, the Madeira Embroidery Club was synonymous with the Syrian capitalist presence. Madeiran workers—

and especially Madeiran women workers—were not allowed on the club's grounds, even as their labor formed its raison d'être.

Representing foreign capital, the Madeira Embroidery Club's members acted jointly to reshape the industry in favor of manufacturers. The club's member firms used their majority share of the industry to impose wage cuts, reduce labor costs, and govern industry practices without representation from labor. Lobbying the U.S. Consulate in Funchal and the Portuguese government in Lisbon, the club pushed for lenient customs and valuation standards, and lower taxes on their materials. Madeiran factory workers and embroiderers protested the Madeira Embroidery Club's monopolism, with the trade unionist serial *O Operário* calling it a "house of complot" and a "Syrian Supreme Court" where manufacturers "conspire freely and ... kill all of the competition which is the life of the industry, counting eyelets and dots."[61]

American consular officials had a complex, oftentimes anxious relationship with the Madeira Embroidery Club, cycling between celebration of these manufacturers as vigorous proponents of American economic expansionism and concern over unscrupulous behavior, compounded further by racial anxieties about the club's Syrian identity. A 1922 battle over piece rates throws this dynamic into relief. In April, falling retail demand in New York City threw the Madeira embroideries industry into crisis. The New York City market then accounted for 80 percent of the island's exports; the Madeira Embroidery Club announced it would hold a series of meetings to discuss strategies to protect prices including wage reductions and slowing production. "Composed of the principal embroidery merchants of Funchal," U.S. Consul General Stillman Eells wrote of this meeting, the club "proposed a radical reduction in wages for hand embroidery workers ... caused by the sudden decline in demand and the accumulation of large stocks."[62] Elias Mallouk hastened to Funchal from New York to lead the club's meetings. Though he was Madeira's largest merchant-manufacturer and the Madeira Embroidery Club's president, Mallouk had not visited since 1920.[63] Workers perceived him as the man most responsible for the industry's monopolism, and when his ship arrived at port, Mallouk faced an "insurrection for increased wages" and a general mood that a strike was coming. After several meetings open only to manufacturers, the Madeira Embroidery Club issued its unanimous agreement to cut industry-wide piece rates by 30 percent, to a rate of six reis per eyelet.[64]

Madeira's embroiderers were not formally organized, but those who resented exploitive piece rates found voice among Funchal's syndicalist movement, particularly the União dos Sindicato Operários do Funchal and its serial, *O Operário*. Days after the Madeira Embroidery Club distributed leaflets to the countryside announcing the wage cut, hostile editorials began to appear in *O Operário* attacking Syrian manufacturers as "a rabble of falsified Americans, pariahs without creed and without country [who] only prosper in peaceful places with indigenous people" they exploit. In one essay, John de Vasconselos, himself a bootblack, narrated Elias Mallouk as an interloper, "a Turk, a Bedouin of the desert, a lace man of Bagdad, one that contributed to the embroidery industry's unfortunate situation."[65] Redubbing him "Elias Maluco"—Elias the crazy—Vasconcelos accused the Madeira Embroidery Club of exploiting the island's "slave embroidery women [who] are finishing, in a hurry, a piece of embroidery to mitigate the hunger and illness of her rickety and sorrowful children." Mallouk called himself a "civilizer" coming for the "salvation of Madeira embroidery," but Vasconcelos claimed he was, rather, a threat to the island and its industry.

As Syrian American manufacturers discussed new piece rates, arbitration policies, and industry stances on taxation in closed sessions, Vasconcelos targeted them as "falsified Americans" who weaponized their clout with the U.S. Consulate against native labor. In a public letter to the industry, he pointed to a dual betrayal: first, as a foreign merchant class exploiting Madeiran needleworkers, and second as Syrians, colonized people who aligned with capital instead of fighting the worthier battle against European imperialism in their Middle Eastern homeland. Again addressing Elias Mallouk:

> Oh, Elias, oh prophet of whiskey and of the Abdullas, why are you not going to Syria—which is known only nominally—to flaunt yourself as the savior of your people who are now enslaved and vexed by the ignominious stigma of Great Britain? Why don't you invent, oh wise Maluco, the colors of a banner which, when flown in the Orient, may represent your nationality which has been violated throughout the remotest eras, so you may become a working people in your own dominions, which are not yours? Instead of being verminous parasites who swarm in a foolish flittering to this sacred land, sacred by race and dignity?

At the same time, Vasconcelos evoked the Syrian peddlers of the Atlantic world, begging Mallouk to return there and "take upon yourself the pack and go through the avenues of America, proclaiming your fake embroideries and leaving us to live peacefully forgotten."⁶⁶

Unfavorable editorials multiplied in 1922, and the mood in the Syrian factories turned sour. As they congregated behind the walls of the Madeira Embroidery Club, manufacturers complained about absenteeism at their shops, but simultaneously expressed relief that slow demand for embroidered linens stifled public protest among the thousands of Madeiran women stitching eyelets in their homes.⁶⁷ Meanwhile, Mallouk presented several additional cuts, each previously voted on by linens importers in New York: salary reductions for all factory workers; elimination of salaries for runners (in place of commissions capped at 5 to 7 percent of each item's retail price); elimination of bonuses paid to embroiderers whose work was graded "well made"; and 30 percent discounting on any pieces graded as "badly made." These cuts radically reshaped the labor economy in Madeiran embroideries. The rationale for the change was that existing structures incentivized factory runners to commission and accept badly made linens. The new cuts externalized the risk of contracting linens onto the runners and less directly, onto hand embroiderers themselves, while preserving stable margins for merchant-manufacturers. It was a business model that replicated changing business structures in the Syrian American peddling market; new patterns of credit and debt shifted greater risk onto peddlers in favor of their suppliers. The Madeira Embroidery Club passed the new terms in a unanimous vote and resolved to distribute the news to workers via leaflet. Linen runners carried those flyers across the island by donkey, along with linen pieces stamped to reflect the reduced rate of six reis per eyelet.⁶⁸ The wage cuts were scheduled for May 15, 1922.

Knowing the leaflets were heading into the countryside, the Madeira Embroidery Club approached the U.S. Consulate for help stanching the negative press. On April 18, Ferris Saydah and Elias Mallouk met with Consul General Stillman Eells and presented him with copies of *O Operário* containing inflammatory rhetoric. Though his predecessor, William Jenkins, had been enthusiastic about the club's position as a lever for American economic power, Eells was wary of the organization. Memorandizing the meeting, he recorded that the consulate would investigate the matter of the press maligning Mallouk ("who is an American citizen"), but he was also troubled by the fact that the merchants had simultaneously complained to Funchal's French Consular office "as the Syrians in Funchal are under

French protection."⁶⁹ Mallouk accused *O Operário* of defamation and hired an attorney, prompting Eells to consult with Madeira's civil governor, Coronel Nobre de Veiga. The governor demanded that both *O Operário* and *Correio da Madeira* publish retractions, coercing the most vehement of the editors, Vasconcelos, to write one himself on pain of arrest: "The Syrian colony prevented the closure of our embroidery houses during the war; they feed the industry. To them I solemnly send my apologies and in the same way, deny everything I wrote with respect to the altruistic and respectful industrial heads."⁷⁰ Stating that he had written four editorials based on information he received secondhand, Vasconcelos said his goal was to "agitate among workers"; he also blamed his own "disturbed youth." Meanwhile, a brief series of letters between Eells and Veiga produced their agreement that the insults against Mallouk constituted a "private crime."⁷¹ Neither the Americans nor the Portuguese prosecuted the matter criminally.

The retraction appeared in *Correio da Madeira* on April 30 and was met with the immediate recognition that it had been coerced. *O Operário* refused to publish the retraction, and its editors instead published a new series maligning Civil Governor Veiga for his collusion with foreign capital. In "Portuguese or Syrian?" the serial addressed the governor directly: "We did not think that you were [anything] other than the same genius of all Portuguese . . . if you read the contents of the articles, you will conclude that they are not blasphemies, not defamatory or injurious to the Turkish, Jewish, or Syrian colony that parasitizes on the comfort of our poor, enslaved embroidery women!"⁷² The editors doubled down, calling the embroidery heads "falsified Americans, our violators, our rentiers" before calling on all Portuguese to "beat them back with a broom." To Veiga, the editorial concluded with a threat: "Defend! Dear Governor, our honor that these damned Turks are scandalously compromising, else in another five years our hungry and ignorant embroiderers—mothers and daughters—will be reduced to the rotten path of venereal debauchery. *Either I tear you down or you tear me down.*" To "that turco Maluco" and the Madeiran Embroidery Club, they closed ominously, "And now, Syrian misters, do not forget us, nor forget our colleagues at Trabalho e União. We will continue."⁷³

Summer 1922 commenced with tension at the companies represented by the Madeiran Embroidery Club. Turnover among factory operatives peaked, as did the departure of linens runners who had previously connected Funchal to the home embroiderers in the Madeiran countryside. Reports circulated that Syrian firms had dismissed operatives caught trying to organize a union, particularly at the Mallouk and Saydah houses.[74] But the general strike *O Operário* threatened in May did not materialize. Instead of organizing the needleworkers (a task which seemed insurmountable amid a market contraction), the island's trade unions courted the Madeiran autonomy movement. Autonomists took aim at greater economic separation from the government in Lisbon. Driven by protests against excessive taxes on public utilities and on goods entering Madeiran ports, the movement pointed to the presence of foreign merchant capital and favoritism of foreign businesses to protest "the injustice with which the Government shakes the whole island."[75] Rebellion against rents and fiscal extraction took center stage in Funchal's liberal circles and among the working left. Import duties on wheat and flour similarly induced rage; Funchal weathered weeks of a general strike before a bomb exploded at the Secretary of Funchal's General Council in November 1921. "It is thought," wrote U.S. Consul Eells to the U.S. secretary of state, "that the crime was committed as a protest against the law," before sending a second letter to the Funchal secretary congratulating him on his survival.[76]

Violent acts were uncommon but always a concern; intellectuals and syndicalists sought to translate Madeiran tax revolts into a drive for political autonomy and empowerment of Funchal's municipal legislative structures. But the rage was also palpable. Though the embroideries industry was a tertiary autonomist priority, the discrepancies between high import taxes and low taxes on export linens escaped no one. During a 1924 general strike protesting a new maritime navigation tax, for instance, railway workers, store owners, and day laborers ground "all industrial activities to a standstill" and issued a petition stating "the taxes levied already on shipping are now so burdensome that vessels can no longer afford to call here."[77] Meanwhile, even as the Madeira Embroidery Club lobbied for free trade principles and pushed to keep art linen export duties low, the industry attracted the attention of American and Portuguese regulators.

TARIFF PRESSURE AND LABOR DISPUTES

Though Syrian American embroideries firms represented their businesses as models of mechanized industrial efficiency, the reality remained that most of the production process occurred outside of a factory setting, in the homes of women needleworkers. In the early 1920s, whether art linens were produced under factory or cottage conditions mattered enormously. U.S. legislators mounted protectionist tariff campaigns to halt the entry of foreign goods that posed unfair competition to American products. This context throws the efforts of Syrian American manufacturers into a new light: touting their Funchal factories filled with sleek new American-made machinery for stamping, punching, and packaging fine hand embroideries, they sought to represent this business as modern and industrial, like their American counterparts. Conversely, in New York City and Washington D.C., Syrian industry representatives highlighted Madeira embroideries as a heritage craft, one which could only be created on the island and in the homes of Madeiran women and girls. Both strategies sought to evade stiff tariffs on the industry, which was valued at $2.32 million in 1920 and was almost entirely dependent on an import trade through the Port of New York.[78] To protect this supply chain, Syrian American firms simultaneously argued their Funchal businesses were—and were not—"factories" and that their hand embroiderers both were—and were not—"workers." These tensions came to a head with the U.S. passage of the 1922 Forney-McCumber Tariff.

America's surge of enthusiasm for imported linen goods following the 1918 Armistice dampened as the domestic textile industries struggled with supply chain issues and weathered a new wave of textile labor uprisings between 1919 and 1924. As U.S. manufacturers faced dislocations, wild price swings, and factory stoppages at home, many pointed to imported goods, arguing that these firms had blurred the lines between merchant and manufacturer to exploit cheaper labor abroad for competitive advantage. In 1921, Congress moved on a slate of tariffs, reordering multiple sectors of American industry. Initially titled HR 7456, the bill included new tariffs on import textile components, white goods, garments, and embroideries; it passed first as the Emergency Tariff of May 1921, and a revised version became law in 1922.[79] The bill's sponsors, Joseph Fordney and Porter McCumber, asserted that importers posed unfair competition to domestic industries because they relied on lower labor costs and poor labor standards abroad. Their tariff bill would impose a 37.5 percent ad valorem tariff on all American companies importing embroideries from Madeira and the Azores, a steep rate that led fifteen of the island's American manufacturers to submit a joint protest letter to Congress, led by Madeira Embroidery Club President Elias Mallouk and his lawyer, Thomas Lane.[80] "The undersigned are manufacturers and importers of Madeira embroideries," the letter began, going on to argue that "a duty of 37.5 percent on the American selling price is the equivalent of a duty ... of 100 to 135 percent on the foreign valuation" and would be "destructive of a large and important industry developed abroad by American capital."[81]

The Madeiran importers protested the adoption of the American valuation system, which would set the value of imported embroideries by their New York City retail value rather than their value in Funchal.[82] Testifying before Congress in 1921, Thomas Lane argued that Madeiran embroidery was not a fungible commodity but a cultural heritage item. Madeira's merchants did not oppose the tariff in principle, but "Madeira embroideries are the product of the island of Madeira and adjacent Portuguese possessions." Lane argued, "The commodity is not made in the United States, nor is there manufactured in the United States any comparable product."[83] Additionally, the manufacturers' letter asserted that U.S. valuation was an impossible standard to meet, because "an importer does not know in advance of offering the goods for sale what he can get for them"; by contrast, "he may have a very definite idea as to what they will cost." The island's merchant-manufacturers, three-quarters of them U.S. citizens who "supplanted and superseded German capital" on Madeira during the war, assumed the risks of this trade and could only continue under a favorable tariff regime. American valuation, they concluded, "would result in an embargo upon the importation of Madeira embroideries ... An important industry developed by American capital is [now] threatened with destruction, with no compensating benefit to American industry."[84]

The tariff act's passage required the U.S. Consulate in Funchal to take a direct role in declaring values for embroideries destined for America through a system of dual invoicing. Embroidery firms were required to declare their costs on invoices on color-coded forms. Blue forms were reserved for merchant contractors or consigners, who were required to declare their labor costs. White forms were for manufacturers, who were required to declare their materials costs in addition to labor. Dual invoicing allowed the U.S. Customs House to distinguish among import goods originating from American merchants versus manufacturers abroad and assess tariffs accordingly.[85] The Madeira Embroidery Club protested this system, arguing that it favored consigners over manufacturers, offering them reduced costs when, from the club's perspective, the distinction between firms that manufactured embroideries versus contractors who purchased them on consignment was fuzzy at best. Factory operators were burdened with a duty levied on the cost of materials in addition to labor. "We kindly solicit ... to be placed on equal basis," the Madeira Embroidery Club concluded in a petition letter to U.S. Customs, "otherwise [we] cannot possibly exist against competitors."[86] In a second letter to U.S. Customs, the signatories clarified the matter further, alleging that Portuguese manufacturers were selling their goods to American merchants via the blue forms, which allowed them to evade a 40 percent levy on their materials costs and resulting in Portuguese firms—not American ones—gaining competitive advantage.[87] Blue invoices paid on average 20 percent less on goods moving into the United States, E. Francis of Suigany and Skaf calculated. "Manufacturers of my class with a heavy outlay of capital, paying high wages and big salaries to a large staff" assumed more risk for less profit; Francis concluded, "This is preposterous."[88] In his own letter to Customs, U.S. Consul General Stillman Eells made allegations of his own: "I suspect that the use of the blue [contractor's] form is simply an attempt to evade the adding of the forty percent expenses, and profit on the cost of the material."[89]

Meanwhile, invoices were rife with irregularities on lots of embroideries leaving Funchal, on both blue and white forms. The U.S. Consulate identified a steady 10 to 15 percent undervaluation of labor costs on the white forms submitted by the Madeira Embroidery Club in 1923, leading Consul General Eells to request an investigation by the U.S. Treasury Department (his request was denied).[90] In addition to invoicing fraud, the consulate alleged the Madeiran Embroidery Club engaged in reexport of textiles produced elsewhere, especially in China.[91] After crates of Mallouk laces from Shanghai were discovered to have been illegally reexported from Funchal in 1923, consular staff reported that invoice fraud was an industry-wide problem.[92] Vice Consul Hernan Vogenitz put it this way: "The women of Madeira ... are undoubtedly expert and work quickly, but they cannot perform miracles."[93] With a meager staff of four, the consulate could not accurately certify that goods coming from Funchal were invoiced properly or that they originated in Funchal at all. Ultimately, officials believed the dual invoicing system so incentivized fraud that they scrapped it in 1924 in favor of a system that counted eyelets, dots, flourishes, and embellishments on each linen piece and set duties that way. Embroidery houses exporting to the United States submitted their patterns for inspection at the consulate and then invoiced pieces at "point prices," which the consulate staked to average labor costs submitted weekly by manufacturers.

Though the new system seemed to mitigate the Madeira Embroidery Club's monopoly over the reported value of labor, it also exerted downward pressure on actual labor values. Hand embroiderers who were paid seventeen reis per eyelet in June 1924, for instance, were paid seven to eight reis per eyelet that December.[94] Multiple factors pushed real wages down, including a market contraction in New York, currency fluctuations in the Portuguese escudo, and reduced competitive demand for embroidery labor. However, the consulate noted that Syrian American firms lowered their labor prices in coordination with one another. Allegations mounted as competing firms accused one another of artificially deflating wages, stockpiling finished linens awaiting a market boost, or misleading officials about true eyelet counts on their goods.[95]

Destabilized wages also produced labor disputes, as gains in real needlework wages won between 1918 and 1921 were not only reversed but also "outweighed by [a currency] exchange situation" that favored merchant-manufacturers to the detriment of Madeiran workers.[96] Because the overwhelming majority of embroiderers worked at home, it was difficult to mount formal strikes, but embroiderers nevertheless protested shrinking pay and losses of autonomy through slowdowns, stoppages, and complaints to municipal authorities.[97] One consistent and effective way that embroiderers protested poor pay was by slowing production or withholding finished goods. In testimony taken by the U.S. Consulate in 1925, a foreman at Alexander J. Hamrah and Co. describes how rural embroiderers sometimes changed projects midstream, shifting to pieces consigned by competitors: "We had difficulty [in] having goods which were given out by us at good prices, being put aside by the embroiderer by goods given out later, without our knowledge, at better prices."[98] Runners returning to repossess unfinished pieces from home embroiderers were met with obfuscation or resistance. Hamrah, for instance, paid nothing on linens returned unfinished ("because if she has more profitable work we do not pay," explained the Hamrah foreman), leading home workers to refuse to return the linens at all.[99]

Though organized stoppages in the countryside were uncommon, strikes did halt work in the Funchal factories where the linen was finished, driven by wages that hovered between $0.43–$0.52 (for unskilled workers) and $1.00 (for foremen) per eight-hour work day.[100] Usually, all embroidery factories closed when a general strike was called; a March 1920 strike closed the entire industry for several weeks in protest of import taxes, for instance.[101] However, Syrian American firms occasionally attempted to resist closures, and that refusal fed Madeiran resentment. During a declared general strike in August 1921, for instance, the K. Katen and Co. factory on Rua Dr. Vieira kicked to life at 9:00 a.m. and within a few minutes "was attacked by a tremendous mob comprising mostly of the working class of this city." The shop foreman, a Mr. Fares, was present. Reporting later to the U.S. Consulate, he described how Madeiran syndicalists "unhesitatingly forced their way through the stairway of our factory demanding immediate closure of our premises." Fares spoke to the group's leaders, Armando Franca and Jaoquim de Gouveia, but they refused to disperse the assembly. "Fearing of looting," Fares called the chief of police, who came to the factory only to tell him "that he was powerless to drive the mob away."[102]

It was at that moment that Fares decided to hoist the American flag to the rafters, antagonizing the angry Madeiran strikers occupying the shop floor below. "I ordered flying the American flag," and the demonstrators "ordered pulling down the flag" in response. Fares shouted at them that he would take the flag down once they left his factory. Two of Fares's workers, Jayme Pompilo Gomes and Alfredo Olovo Ferreira, yanked the flag down from the rafters, handing it off to strike leaders. They folded the flag and took it and marched—with the "mob" flanked by the Katen factory's own workforce—out the front door, leaving Fares and a couple of managers alone. K. Katen and Co. had to shut down that day and stayed shuttered until the end of the strike. Relaying the incident to his superiors in Washington, U.S. Consul William Jenkins is clearly critical of the Katen firm: every other U.S. firm, he reported, had obeyed the consulate's order to close shop during the strike. Once the strike ended, Jayme Gomes brought Fares's flag to the consulate, telling Jenkins that "he meant no disrespect" but that his men had taken it to "not have it torn down by the mob."[103] It was probably a savvy move; two flour millers who opened shop were badly beaten by strikers that morning. Fares demanded Jenkins investigate the attack on K. Katen and Co., providing a list of strikers he had identified. Jenkins did not comply.

Amid this climate of monopolism, price speculation, labor disputes, and

FIGURE 19. The finishing room at Hamrah and Co., Funchal, 1919. Madeiran women clean up piece work and add finishing touches in preparation for export. Source: "Sala de acabamentos do estabelecimento de bordados Alexandre Hamrah Co. Inc.," 1919-11-18, Museu de Fotografia da Madeira, Atelier Vicente's, on deposit at AMB, VIC/D-B/001-002/000004.

Madeiran autonomism, fluctuations in the Portuguese escudo most shaped the Madeiran hand embroideries industry during the *fase síria*. Reporting in 1921, William Jenkins argued that the escudo's "constantly decreasing exchange value" was "the main factor hindering the extension of American trade with Madeira," especially for Syrian American embroidery firms which depended on imported linen materials. That year alone, the escudo fell from 3.50 escudos to over 10 escudos to the dollar.[104] By January 1923, the U.S. Consulate reported that the exchange rate between the dollar and the escudo had "dropped to the lowest in the history of the island."[105] The export business ultimately relied upon this exchange rate for profitability; the sliding escudo had incentivized Syrian American firms to buy in and made Madeiran embroideries into a fashionable art linen in the United States. But the worsening exchange rate also drove Madeira's tax revolts and animated the push for autonomy that targeted foreign capitalists on the island. In 1924, the Portuguese Republic announced its plan to institute financial reforms to protect the escudo's value and reverse the losses of the early 1920s. Within two years, most foreign capital in Madeira's embroidery industry took flight; 80 percent of the island's Syrian American merchants left Funchal entirely, leaving only a couple of firms which rebranded to downplay their Syrian origins.[106]

THE END OF THE *FASE SÍRIA*

In late 1923, Portugal's First Republic under Alvaro de Castro announced new currency stabilization policies through sales of gold and silver abroad and the creation of an Exchange Stabilization Fund to intervene in foreign exchanges. Enacted in January 1924, the Castro plan restored the escudo's exchange rate to its 1913 level and, though Portugal experienced additional volatility in 1925–26, the currency stabilized by 1927.[107] On Madeira, meanwhile, the allegations grew against Syrian American embroidery firms. Concluding a yearlong investigation into undervaluation of labor costs on consular invoices, Vice Consul Hernan Vogenitz referred the firms of Abualy, Bardwil, Beyda, Hamrah, Lian and Mubarak, Mallouk, A. G. Samara, and Salamy to the Treasury Department for prosecution.[108] In 1924, the Madeiran governorate similarly detected "financial improprieties" at four large Syrian American firms and ordered them all to liquidate and leave the island. These reversals prompted a flight from Funchal, impacting not only the firms facing allegations but all Syrian American companies. In 1925, for instance, Ameen Samara arrived from New York on an emergency passport for the "purpose of closing my embroidery factory."[109] He sold his firm to his Madeiran shop managers, who continued to produce table linens and bedding "in the Syrian American style" and invoiced them through the U.S. Consulate.[110]

Not every exit from Madeira Island was so dramatic, but between 1924 and 1925, the departure of Syrian American merchants was pronounced. The U.S. Consulate noted these factory sales in quarterly reports to the Department of State. By April 1925, only twelve Syrian American firms remained, and most of those departed the island within the next eighteen months. Meanwhile, new firms managed by Madeiran Portuguese merchants appeared on the scene, each assuming the invoices of Syrian predecessors: J. Alvarez; Freitas Castro and Co.; M. Coito; V. Gouves; M. Jardim

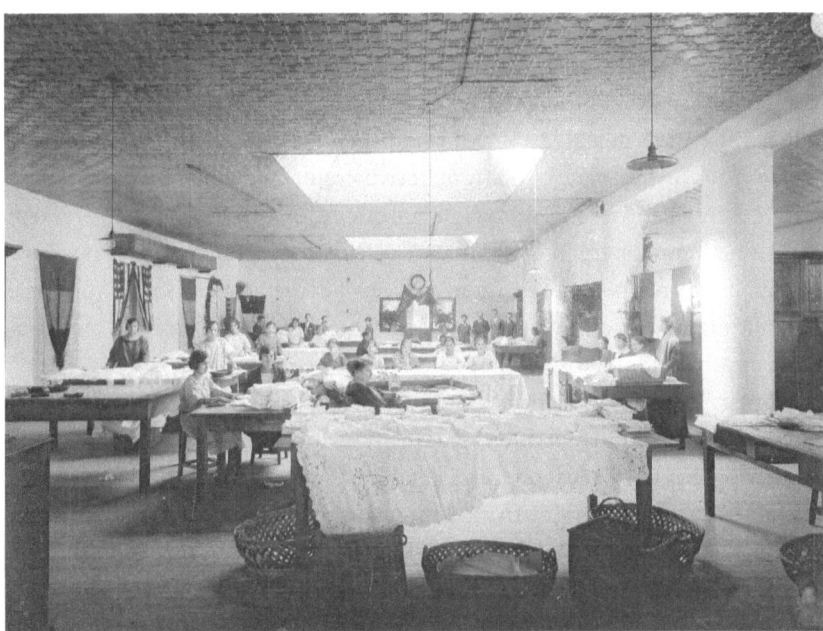

FIGURE 20. The finishing room at A. G. Samara and Company. Ameen Samara stands in the background with shop foremen. In 1925, Ameen sold the company to his Madeiran workers and returned to New York City. Source: "Sala de acabamentos do estabelecimento de bordados A. G. Samara & Cª," s.d., Museu de Fotografia da Madeira, Atelier Vicente's, on deposit at AMB, VIC/D-B/001-001/000001.

of Casa Alema; L. Serruys; and Jose de Costa.[111] The Madeiran governorate instituted protectionist policies to promote the rise of this Madeiran merchant class, including a new guild organization and a residency requirement that exporters must live in Funchal at least six months of the year.[112] The departure of American firms from Madeira also accompanied a shift toward global markets: exporters focused less on preserving a single commercial tie between Funchal and New York City and began exporting embroideries to Portugal, Brazil, and Latin America.[113] The United States' share in imports from Madeira dropped precipitously from $2.8 million in 1924 to $700,000 in 1925, a decline the New York Times attributed to flagging demand and a strengthening escudo.[114] Though workers applauded the industry's shift toward Madeiran ownership, the industry also weathered "one of the most severe depressions in [the island's] history,"[115] rebounding after the institution of protectionist policies in 1926–27 and a compulsory guild system in 1935.[116] As for needleworkers, many of them also left the island: Madeiran women embroiderers followed relatives abroad to California or New England, and others headed to Brazil where an emergent embroidery industry rose to global prominence.[117] This pattern prevailed beyond the places where Syrian émigrés did business; mass labor migration of skilled needleworkers was also a hemispheric story. Aimee Loiselle, for instance, illustrates how similar pressures persuaded Puerto Rican needleworkers to move to the U.S. mainland during this period, becoming a visible part of the New England apparel industry until the region's deindustrialization in the 1980s.[118]

Though over 80 percent of the Syrian American firms left Madeira by 1925, a few Syrian businessmen remained, including Emile Marghab. Born Emil Mogabgab in 1895 on the island of Cyprus, Emile's father, Amin Mogabgab, was an émigré from Ain Zhalta in Lebanon's Chouf district, and his mother was an Anglican missionary.[119] Emile attended the English school in Nicosia and upon graduating, worked as a British intelligence officer during World War I. After the war's end, he came to New York City for a job with the U.S. National Guard. Connecting with Syrian American linens importers instead, he left military life to become a linens agent in Funchal.[120] In Funchal, he worked for F. M. Jabara and Co. and the L. Tweel Company, work that involved intensive steamship travel along linen circuits between Funchal and Liverpool, Nigeria, Mexico, Lisbon, and New York City through the 1920s.[121] Emile's brother, Anis Mogabgab, left Funchal to open an embroidery factory in China.[122] By the late 1920s, Emile partnered with Gabriel Farra to establish Farra and Mogabgab Ltd. (notably, Farra had once served as a Cunard Line steamship ticket agent in Beirut before his own departure to the mahjar almost two decades earlier).[123] In 1931, Emile married an American woman, Vera Way, and together the couple bought Farra out using money Anis sent them from China.[124] Emile also changed his own name from Mogabgab to Marghab, a decision motivated as much by commercial concerns about being identified as "Syrian" in Madeira as by anxieties about being discriminated against in America.[125] In 1933, Casa Marghab reincorporated under Emile and Vera Way Marghab jointly. Producing embroidered table linens with Swiss linen and Egyptian cotton (a combination Casa Marghab trademarked as "Margandie"), the firm was in business for nearly fifty years.[126] Emile passed away in 1947, leaving Vera to manage the business until its closure in 1980. In the interim, Casa Marghab so dominated the linens market that Emile's invented surname remains a genericized, globally recognizable trademark today.

"Shanghai, Venice, and Funchal," *Women's Wear* began in 1918, "Hamrah Bros. are one of the concerns down in the little known Syrian Quarter who are doing an interesting business that has the whole world as its background."[127] Leaving Funchal, several Syrian émigré companies expanded their embroidery businesses in Manila, Yokohama, and Shanghai, cities that industry leaders speculated were "the field of the future." The Mallouk, Bardwil, and Hamrah companies each opened factories in Manila and Shanghai by the 1920s.[128] And just as they had done in Funchal, the firms assertively lobbied their interests in Washington. Elias Mallouk and George Bardwil, for instance, lobbied senators for a carve-out to protect their businesses against a trade embargo on Chinese lace, pushed against tariffs, and (in Bardwil's case) protested restrictions on Asian trade during World War II.[129]

Under U.S. colonial occupation since 1898, the Philippines became an attractive site for Syrian American textile capital, thanks to relaxed export taxes. The islands' only centralized textile mill collapsed in 1923, creating a labor market for the Syrian American model for putting out linen embroideries on piece rate. William Gervase Clarence-Smith describes a production process like that in Funchal: "The cloth was cut and stamped in Manila factories, according to the specifications of American firms. Travelling agents or contractors provided advances of prepared cloth, other inputs and cash to local women," and the work was "part-time, mainly lingerie, handkerchiefs, tablecloths, and children's clothing."[130] Philippine exports like embroideries, coconut oil, and cigars "receive[d] preferential treatment in the United States market," reported a U.S. congressional memo. Though some of these incentives softened in the 1930s, export embroideries continued to enjoy relaxed tariffs until the islands gained independence in 1946.[131] Similarly, the arrival of Syrian American firms reshaped the Chinese embroideries industry: by 1925, China was the single largest source of import white goods into the United States.[132] Two years later, in 1927, 80 percent of Chinese embroideries were exported to the United States. In 1934, the *Syrian World* printed an interview with Halim Azar, a Mallouk Bros. manager from Swatow, exclaiming "millions of Chinese depend on Syrians for their living," before estimating that 95 percent of China's lace and embroideries industry was in the hands of fewer than one dozen Syrian American firms.[133] As they had done in Funchal, the firms brought pattern machines to Shanghai; rather than drawing on traditional designs, they punched fashionable transatlantic designs into linen pieces that needleworkers traced in.[134] As in Funchal, China's Syrian producers maintained "a swanky club of their own" called the Rose and Leaf Club, which doubled as a manufacturers' association.[135]

Syrian American producers also opened factories in Yokohama, Japan, where a similar pattern emerged of standardization, fixation on the U.S. retail market, and American subsidies, until Japan's 1940 declaration of war.[136] That year, U.S. wartime restrictions on trade prompted protest by Syrian American companies who relied on open channels between China and Japan. In one letter to the secretary of state, a Bardwil Industries spokesman emphasized how "the direct result of these restrictions is that American businesses ... are suffering greatly and business is practically paralyzed. The lace and embroidery trade in China [which relied directly on Japan for materials] had been developed by American firms, and these firms have substantial investments greatly jeopardized by these restrictions."[137] Bardwil Industries remained in Shanghai until it was forced to close shop during the 1949 Cultural Revolution. "As soon as I heard the guns," George Bardwil was quoted later, "I knew it was time to get out."[138] These companies pursued global commodity chains and relied on diasporic commercial networks to move goods around the world, but they were so closely tied to American capitalist hegemony abroad that their fortunes waxed and waned in coordination with U.S. expansionism.[139]

There were taboos in this business. On Madeira, Syrian American firms represented their embroidery shops as mechanized factory spaces abroad, showcasing their modern machinery while most of the labor was conducted out of sight, in the homes of women and girls in a cottage-style production uncaptured by company photographers. These workers were unmentionable: they were not congregated in a factory space where they would be meaningfully able to strike. Embroiderers understood their exploitation intimately, identifying the industry as engaged in conflict with a foreign merchant class whose own homeland was colonized by foreign capitalist interests. Outside of general strikes, these workers protested poor wages by deploying strategies unique to the subcontracted nature of their jobs: they worked to rule, pitted factory agents against each other, or picked up and put down piecework autonomously.

Lasting only ten years, Madeira's *fase síria* illustrates the emergence and development of a transatlantic Syrian textile elite. These merchant-manufacturers reinvested profits from the spinning, weaving, and garment industries in the United States abroad and perfected the exercise of supply chain power. As they followed commodity chains across oceans, they acquired Madeira embroidery factories as a check against labor unrest in America. Accidents of nationality facilitated this move: as former Ottoman subjects, as naturalized Americans, and as Syrians with deep diasporic ties to port cities on Mediterranean, Atlantic, and Pacific shores, these elites positioned themselves as agents of an expanding U.S. capitalism, promoting "free trade," opening supply zones, and creating new markets for American machines and finished goods. Embroidered art linens produced on Madeira—like those made in Zahle, Florence, Manila, or Shanghai—were readily absorbed into the same retail markets served by the Syrian shops of New York. Because these firms also commanded the Syrian peddling routes extending across continents, they also relied on a steady supply of new Syrian, Lebanese, and Palestinian migrants who could move these goods to markets.

FIVE

LOGISTICS
Selling Textiles in the US-Mexico Borderlands

"**NO, NO . . . THAT WAS MADEIRA!** Madeira Linen. That's different," exclaimed Zahdi Barsa in her oral history interview with historian Alixa Naff. She had been asked whether she thought peddling was "low work" after insisting "Lebanese people were peddlers, not the Syrians, not a one. I don't see any Damascene people do that, never!" Zahdi still saw her work stitching aprons in a Boston garment factory as less taxing than the physically demanding suitcase trades. "Lebanese peddlers were making money! They [were] trying to make me go with them, but I could never do it. I could never carry that suitcase and walk like that!" She watched them as they came into the Syrian Quarter to procure goods for their packs. Peddlers who sold sewing notions, trinkets, or religious paraphernalia were at the bottom of this trade, Zahdi recalled; those who carried kimonos, laces, or underwear were middling. Only the richest traders carried Madeira linens: "They make money! They put the big suitcase on their shoulder, and they go!"[1] Their *kashehs* full to bursting, they proceeded to the railways; they had a ticket out of town. The more expensive their merchandise, the farther they went. This is how Syrian kimonos, silks, and embroideries went to markets across the continent: to the American South, the Midwest, the U.S.-Mexico borderlands, or across the hemisphere.

Observers across America's industrial centers corroborated Barsa's observations about the peddlers who carried goods across the mahjar. In a

1917 report on New York's kimono shops, the trade journal *Women's Wear* reported "the Syrians have taken another progressive step in the export business to Mexico, West Indies, and in South America," often joining kimonos with white goods manufactured in Syrian-owned factories from Madeira, East Asia, or the Middle East.[2] Riding the rails, peddlers hoisted large suitcases, trunks, or *kashehs* containing the usual items: "ladies' wrappers or house dresses; some lace curtains in ecru shades; some fancy table scarves, such as Syrians sell . . . also ladies wearing apparel consisting largely of negligees . . . cash of $126 mostly in gold pieces; one dark brown suit; a little whiskey for personal use."[3] The most seasoned peddlers knew to head south; the U.S. borderlands with Mexico was the most lucrative site for the textile trades, but breaking into this business could be difficult. One had to know the right suppliers, carry the right papers, and navigate a shifting American border regime.

Though he is rarely thought about as such, the Syrian peddler was also a textile worker: a specialist in logistics who carried garments and goods made in the mahjar's factories to retailers or consumers. The peddler has long been the primary point of mahjari historical narration, a celebrated icon whose entrepreneurialism, grit, and commercial independence are common motifs in novellas and plays, poetry, and hip hop. He also appears in bronze sculpture in both Lebanon and its diaspora.[4] Despite such representations of Syrian peddlers as self-made men, unfettered by the drudgery of waged work, they were closely tied to the mahjar's textile production and dependent on the industrial work of Syrian garment workers, most of them women. "Peddling did not only consist of a travelling salesperson or only a network of peddlers and those who supplied them with goods," Charlotte Karem Albrecht argues in her pathbreaking work on the queer ecology of peddling. "[It] also included stationary work that many Syrian women undertook to make peddling profitable work."[5] Maintaining the mythology of the peddler's independence requires training one's eye away from the garments he sold as well as the hands that produced them. Missing too are the sophisticated patterns of capitalist accumulation, credit, debt, and coercion that undergirded his enterprise. This chapter examines the transnational business of textile peddling, focusing on Syrian border trade from New York City to Mexico. In the borderlands, textile merchants and their peddler employees navigated complex systems of labor migration, wholesale distribution, and the performance of legal legibility in pursuit of a living.

They worked within (and very often for) networks monopolized by the merchant-manufacturers whose goods they distributed. Peddlers did not work in any factory, but they were textile workers, nevertheless.

Arab migrants arrived in Mexico in the late 1880s, and immigration accelerated through the first years of the twentieth century.[6] In the hemispheric mahjar, Mexico was the fourth largest Syrian overseas colony (*jaliyya*), smaller than those of Brazil, Argentina, and the United States but growing swiftly. A survey of population data illustrates this growth: in 1910, 3,000 to 5,000 Syrians lived in Mexico, constituting 2.5 percent of the country's foreign population.[7] Rebeca Rubio estimates around 20,000 Syrians and Lebanese lived in Mexico by 1914.[8] Using French consular records, Kohei Hashimoto identifies 16,489 Lebanese in Mexico in 1926 (though notably, this sum excludes immigrants from Syria and Palestine).[9] About half (49.2 percent) of Arab immigrant men worked as peddlers, *comerciantes ambulantes* in small textiles, textile components, haberdashery, and other sorts of ambulatory commerce.[10] Peddling was the community's largest single occupation before 1949, and Syrians found their niche along existing peddling networks of Sephardi, Spanish, Chinese, and Greek immigrant peddlers, competing for a share of Mexico's textile commerce.[11]

Most Syrian migrants arrived through the Port of Veracruz, transiting along an established Beirut-Marseille-Veracruz line managed by Syrian travel agencies.[12] After making contact with a Syrian runner in France, Syrian men who landed in Veracruz might connect with one of several Syrian Mexican immigration inspectors, who would vouch for them and help them find work in the carrying trade. One such notable Veracruz merchant was Domingo Kuri, who operated a clothing store in Veracruz and worked at the port as an interpreter.[13] Kuri had come to Mexico in 1903 as a teenager, getting his start in peddling and eventually opening the La Fama store next to the port, selling import textiles and ready-wear clothing from around the mahjar. Like many Syrian American merchants, Kuri became an immigration inspector to assist his countrymen, but this work also gave him access to an inbound labor force. He helped Syrian families purchase railway tickets to the U.S. border, and he also hired Syrian men into peddling, outfitting them with wholesale goods acquired from the port.[14] Kuri's peddlers carried embroidered table linens, white goods, and Syrian kimonos imported from New York. These items were packed into suitcases, and peddlers carried them from Veracruz to Mexico City or Monterrey for sale.

There, Syrian peddlers from Veracruz met with their counterparts conducting the next leg of this trip: a north-south carrying trade to the U.S.-Mexico border.

On both sides of the U.S.-Mexico border, the textile trades overlapped with an overland Syrian migration corridor. Peddlers and transmigrants met on the railways, transcontinental routes stretching from the major immigration ports to the U.S.-Mexico borderlands.[15] In the United States, the Immigration Commission reported the movement of both people and textiles from New York's Little Syria neighborhood to the border as early as 1900. In 1909, the U.S. Department of Commerce sought to regulate the Syrian trades by deploying Customs inspectors to the border. Meanwhile, in American border towns like El Paso, Laredo, and Sonora, local Syrian communities emerged, opened shops, and sold textiles to peddlers coming from Mexico to carry them south.[16] 1,051 Syrians had settled in south Texas by 1910, most of them engaged in textile businesses.[17] By 1920, this number had appreciated to 3,200.[18] American policymakers saw the textile trades as a net positive, particularly when they brought new business into borderlands towns. What concerned them, though, was the convergence of Syrian peddling networks with clandestine migration corridors as southbound Syrian textiles established cover for northbound Syrian transmigrants.

OVERLAP: SYRIAN TEXTILES AND BORDERLANDS MIGRANT SMUGGLING

As the borderlands textile trades expanded after 1900, the number of Syrian transmigrants seeking to enter the United States via the southern border also accelerated. Syrian migration through Mexico was substantial: at its peak between 1905 and 1910, 4,000 Syrian migrants entering Mexican ports declared themselves as transit migrants per year.[19] At the land border, Middle Eastern migrants composed a quarter of all recorded crossings: in 1907, for instance, the Immigration Commission recorded 1,360 Syrians, Lebanese, and Palestinians among a total of 5,214 persons.[20] These figures only include immigrants, people who declared their intent to come to the United States permanently. Immigrant crossings were categorized separately by the U.S. Immigration Commission from the thousands of border crossings by Syrian textile peddlers. Border commerce was supposedly categorically distinct from inbound immigration, but immigration officials, suspecting peddlers of moonlighting as migrant smugglers, recognized that moving textiles and moving people operated on fundamentally similar logics. Wholesalers relied on the arrival of crates of fabric as well as migrant workers at the seaports, their businesses functioned on patron-client relationships similar to smuggling rings, peddlers and transmigrants both followed the railways to the borderlands, and both businesses were conducted in cash. While textile merchants did what they could to distinguish themselves from smuggling rings, smugglers operated among them; passing as a peddler provided good cover. Additionally, as both the U.S. and Mexican governments sought to restrict inbound Middle Eastern migrants, the lines between Syrian commerce and clandestine transmigration became even less legible.

As Syrian peddling networks established distinct (if overlapping) routes leading to the borderlands, the U.S. Immigration Commission sought to interdict unwanted Syrian immigration via this border through surveillance of the textile trades. The U.S. Immigration Commission and Bureau of Investigation conducted at least three investigations into this migration corridor, suspecting Syrian merchants of violations of the 1885 Foran Act: at the New York City Barge Office in 1901,[21] the Port of Marseille in 1903,[22] and in Mexico in 1906–07.[23] Rana Razek argues that these reports illustrate Syrian migrant "networks' connections to the growing regime of restrictions at U.S. ports and borders," a system by which Syrian transmigrants were channeled into "labor contracts, poverty, illness, and ultimately, exclusion."[24] These investigators inadvertently captured the mahjar's textile trade in its full transnational contours. Though they were looking for migrant smugglers, they usually found merchants instead.

The route to borderlands trading had two parts: the transatlantic steamship journey to the immigration ports at New York City or Veracruz and from there, the overland trip to the border. Syrians who arrived in New York were processed at immigration stations and released to the Barge Office, where they would meet Syrian American immigration inspector Najib Arbeely. Remembered as the son of one of Little Syria's "first families," Arbeely was an interpreter who introduced new arrivals to the Syrian textile wholesalers congregated on Washington Street.[25] Najib's ties to the city's Syrian white goods firms made him a sought-after migration agent. These same qualities, however, made him vulnerable to accusations of padronism, and, in 1901, his boss at the Barge Office accused him of illegal labor contracting.

The allegations centered on Arbeely's procurement of rail tickets on behalf of Syrian immigrants. Once Syrians were medically cleared at Ellis Island, Arbeely's job was to determine their economic eligibility for entry: he interviewed them about family connections, financial status, and employment prospects. Any Syrians who arrived without funds were in a desperate situation; they could be refused entry under public charge laws, but the 1885 Foran Act simultaneously prohibited them from negotiating labor contracts prior to arrival in America. This contradiction made immigrant inspectors like Arbeely crucial. Relying on his contacts, Arbeely vouched for Syrian workers, found them temporary lodging, and pointed them toward quick employment: either industrial work in weaving, woolens, or textile mills or textile peddling. One week in 1900, Arbeely secured exit passes for forty Syrians, accompanying them to a boardinghouse on Carlisle Street. Once there, the immigrants negotiated peddling contracts with Syrian white goods wholesalers who came to Carlisle Street specifically to receive them. Returning to the Barge Office, Arbeely bought them rail passes departing for points west: Texas and California. Watching from his own desk at the Barge Office, Arbeely's supervisor, Edward McSweeney, reported him on suspicion of illegal labor contracting. After a substantial corruption probe, Najib Arbeely was cleared of all suspicion; instead, McSweeney was found guilty of "abuses and ill treatment" of Syrian immigrants.[26]

Transatlantic travel agencies were similarly subject to Foran Act investigations, including a five-year investigation by Immigration Commission inspector Marcus Braun into migrant smuggling.[27] Between 1903 and 1908, Braun studied Syrian transit migration in Marseille, focusing his energies on Anton Fares, who allegedly worked in cooperation with migrant smugglers in the United States and Mexico.[28] According to Braun's report, the "evil" of migrant smuggling was "contributed to by residents of the United States engaged in the steamship ticket or foreign exchange business." He added, they were frequently "either connected with or publishing some newspaper in a foreign language" (a not-so-subtle nod to Najib Arbeely and his contemporaries). The Immigration Commission was primarily concerned with Syrian transmigrants routed through Veracruz and from there to the U.S.-Mexico land border. Syrians deemed ineligible for entry at New York ended up in Mexico routinely, as did many who had been rejected after arriving there. Braun concluded that Marseille smugglers convinced these Syrians that by heading to Mexico they would "not be subjected to the rigid examinations they would have to undergo at Ellis Island."²⁹ Such assurances were apparently profitable: when Braun interviewed Mexican inspectors at Veracruz in 1903, they told him that 40 percent of their 1,500 arrivals each month were "divided among Syrians and Armenians, [both] classified as 'Turks' by the Mexican people." In his 1907 report delivered to the Immigration Commission, Braun enumerated 4,000 Syrians arriving at Veracruz that year, adding, "almost invariably they do reach our territory."³⁰

Braun also spent several weeks in Mexico, studying the peddling networks between Veracruz, Orizaba, and Mexico City.³¹ He noted how Syrian transmigrants commonly carried textile goods from the ports to the interior, hired by Syrian merchants who profited as much by free shipping as they did by offering them credit. He focused on Mexico City's largest textile firm, Kuri Primos, established by Nasib Kuri in 1880; "I am told [Kuri] is the leading Syrian merchant in the Republic," Braun recounted in his report.³² Braun watched as the firm sent merchant Antonio Sarbo to Veracruz to pick up Syrian workers at the port; he loaded them up with goods to carry to Mexico City, and from there, Kuri Primos peddlers proceeded north on the railway, again outfitted with cases of goods to unload along the way. As the peddlers approached the borderlands, they carried cash and appeared before U.S. immigration officials at the Laredo, Eagle Pass, or El Paso border stations.³³ Once admitted, they purchased more goods and made the reverse trip south.

Noting the informality with which Syrian peddlers were recruited in Veracruz or Mexico City, Marcus Braun's concern was that large Syrian textile firms on the Mexican side of the border might also conduct migrant smuggling operations. However, Braun noted that Syrian clandestine migration was so densely interconnected with the mahjar's peddling trades that untangling legal commerce from unauthorized immigration would be a difficult task.³⁴ The U.S. government was uninterested in restricting border commerce, particularly the flow of American-made textiles and garments into Mexico. So, this became the Immigration Commission's core challenge: how could officials distinguish licit Syrian peddling from illicit Syrian immigration? That work fell to the immigration inspectors and customs officers who staffed the U.S. border stations.

As Marcus Braun reported his findings to the Immigration Commission, another U.S. immigration inspector went undercover. Alcibiades Seraphic came to Mexico with the goal of infiltrating Syrian migrant smuggling networks. An ethnic Greek and naturalized American citizen, Seraphic spent nearly a year posing as a Syrian peddler in Mexico, following the industry's circuit from the Atlantic ports at Veracruz and Tampico to the U.S.-Mexico border before getting himself smuggled into Texas. The intelligence he gathered informed the 1911 Dillingham Commission Report, reshaping the U.S. border regime and leading to an increase in Syrian deportations from the borderlands.[35] He began his work in Tampico, a port city on the southward route of passenger steamships from the U.S. ports of New York City and Tampa. Tampico was one of three Mexican ports where Syrians from Marseille initially landed, second to the port of Veracruz (which took in 58 percent of Syrian arrivals before 1910 and up to 85 percent by 1929).[36] When Seraphic arrived in 1906, Tampico hosted a small community of Syrians, nearly all of whom were in the textile business. He met Skender Ayar, the owner of a local dry goods store who ran a derelict boardinghouse in the back. Ayar employed arriving Syrians as peddlers and, Seraphic alleged, also engaged in migrant smuggling. Posing as a new arrival from Marseille, Seraphic dropped Anton Fares's name and Ayar offered him work. Meeting twenty-one Syrian peddlers at Ayar's boardinghouse that night, Seraphic described them as "liv[ing] in filth under the most unsanitary conditions" and laboring under conditions akin to indenture.[37] Indebtedness was a significant feature of the peddling and migrant smuggling businesses. Transit migrants sometimes took up ad hoc peddling work in exchange for credit toward passage, believing they would "find protection in the hands of their townsman Ayar, but instead he, as they stated, charged them exorbitant prices for their peddling goods." Focused on the traffic of Syrian migrants bound for Texas, Seraphic noted that some of the men had visible, untreated trachoma, the eye infection that commonly resulted in Syrians being debarred at Ellis Island.[38]

After a couple of nights with Ayar, Seraphic and his peers were given cases of goods for delivery to Veracruz. There Seraphic met Nicholas Homsey, a smuggler working with Syrian merchants in town to sell merchandise to peddlers while promising them a pathway to America. Like Ayar, Homsey maintained a small store, and peddlers were his primary customers; he boarded eighty Syrians in his store the night Seraphic arrived. Most of the boarders this time were headed to Yucatán, another hub for Syrian commerce.[39] "While in appearances he seems to be helping [Syrian migrants] to the United States," Seraphic testified that Homsey instead threw "every possible obstacle in their way to induce them to stay in Mexico."[40] Profit was Homsey's motivation: he charged boarders $1–1.50 a night for lodging, $2 for paperwork and interpretation, and lent them wares at usurious rates, creating a cycle of dependency and impoverishment that benefited none but the smugglers. Seraphic asked Homsey for help getting to the United States; Homsey agreed and overcharged him $20 for a rail ticket to Mexico City ($16 was the going rate). Syrians who took this route were usually handed off to smugglers who routed them through Torreon, Chihuahua, or Nuevo Laredo where they would engage in peddling work but would inevitably be charged more. The smugglers' rates of success in getting migrants into the United States were mixed. "The reason is obvious," Seraphic concluded in his report, "when we consider that [the smugglers'] business is dependent, if not entirely, for the greater part on peddlers . . . the more peddlers they can send out on the road the greater the outlet will be for the lines of goods they carry, and the profits in proportion."[41] In Mexico City, Seraphic again posed as a peddler and met Selim Amshiti, Issa Marcos, and Aziz Baroudi, all collecting fares from Syrians traveling to Eagle Pass or Laredo, Texas. Seraphic asked Amshiti if he could help him evade a medical exam; Amshiti replied that he knew a doctor in Eagle Pass who made the way easier for Syrians, regardless of trachoma or other illnesses.[42]

It was at this point in Seraphic's operation that the question of "passing" became relevant. In his report to the U.S. Justice Department, Seraphic described how Syrian migrants' ability to racially pass as Mexican undermined efforts to interdict unwanted immigration. In posing as a Syrian peddler, Seraphic instrumentalized passing himself: he was ethnically Greek, having come to the United States from Meğri (present-day Fethiye, Turkey) in 1893 as a teenager.[43] He took a job at Ellis Island as an immigration interpreter in 1900, gained U.S. citizenship, and subsequently joined the U.S. Navy.[44] His ability to speak English, Spanish, Greek, and Arabic along with his ambiguous complexion was a powerful advantage to his investigative work.[45] Seraphic moved through the worlds of smugglers: to the Syrians he became Syrian; to the Greeks (also numerous in Mexico, especially in Juarez) he was Greek. And as Seraphic approached the border station, he spoke Spanish to officials and was admitted as Mexican.[46] In his testimony, Seraphic described how Syrians routinely evaded immigration interdiction this way. Though U.S. authorities restricted the immigration of Chinese, Turkish, Syrian, and Greek migrants, cross-border travel by

FIGURE 21. Alcibiades A. Seraphic, a naturalized American citizen who worked for the U.S. Immigration Commission. Source: "Conditions on the U.S.-Mexico Border," 8; National Archives and Records Administration.

Mexican nationals was permitted. The smugglers Seraphic hired told him to speak either Spanish or broken English when he arrived at Eagle Pass, to appear more Mexican.

American anxieties mounted over possibilities that Syrians might take "advantage of their swarthy complexion" to evade increased restrictions on Middle Eastern immigration.[47] However, smugglers and migrants were not the only ones who strategically deployed racial passing. Seraphic alleged he witnessed interpreters and employees at the border crossings facilitate this performance by misrepresenting crossers to their superiors, usually while taking fares from them. Because U.S. officials lacked competency in Spanish or other languages, they were unable to discern excludable immigrants. In the worst cases, the Immigration Commission unwittingly hired smugglers, as was alleged of S. M. Mattar, a Syrian interpreter fired from El Paso's border station.[48] Meanwhile, because checkpoint officials did not document each day's crossings systematically, Syrians who were turned away on Thursday tried again on Friday, altering the vowels in the Anglicized rendering of their name to evade detection. In short, Seraphic told the Justice Department that any attempt to police the border via observed ethnic or national categories would fail without better standards of documentation, photography, or other screening technology. His recommendations to the government were specific: to close the border to non-nationals; to replace its inspectors and medical staff with experts from New York City's Ellis Island; and to integrate photography as a means of registering migrants.[49]

Ultimately, both Marcus Braun's and Alcibiades Seraphic's reports on migrant smuggling shaped U.S. border control policies. The Immigration Commission created the Mexican Border District in 1907, centralizing what had been separate enforcement offices in Arizona, New Mexico, and most of Texas into a single administrative unit. Section 24 of the 1907 Immigration Act additionally earmarked more funds for immigration inspectors and bureaucratized the crossing process. Taken together, both measures refocused the goal of border control toward interdiction of unauthorized immigration and contract labor law violations.[50] Border stations hired Arabic speaking investigators, making passing more complicated, though failing to resolve matters of nationality totally. The 1917 detention of Girard Tombray is a swift example: seeking to leave Laredo for Mexico and carrying a Mexican passport, Tombray "claimed to be a Mexican but could talk very little Mexican and had a Jewish or Syrian brogue." After he was initially refused passage, he told Bureau of Investigation (BOI) interrogators he was a French subject and was concluded to be "a Syrian or Turk."[51] Because the BOI could not clarify Tombray's origins further, he was not granted passage. While Tombray's case shows how more staff and standard processes complicated immigration, these changes also fundamentally altered how peddlers conducted their business at the border.

In their reports, both Braun and Seraphic described Syrian mahjari newspapers as engaging in illegal labor contracting. When compared against available serials from the period, this claim clearly represents a dark reading of practices that were exceedingly common; classified ads blurred the lines between sales of wholesale goods, credit and lending, and offers of employment to would-be Syrian peddlers. The 'Assy Shaheen and Sons company of New York, for instance, advertised both goods and territories to their peddlers. Next to images of Shaheen brand embroidered shirts, for instance, a 1918 ad includes, "Wherever you are, tell us right away, and a district of 35,000 people will be allocated to you; we will not sell to anyone but yourself in that district and we will even print advertisements on your behalf at our expense."[52]

This practice was not limited to mail-order garments. Peddlers working across the United States reported such territorial arrangements, negotiated between either manufacturers or wholesale outlets and their peddlers over handshakes. In an oral history interview with Alixa Naff, for instance, Louis

FIGURE 22. Sample kimonos with embroidered appliques advertised by Shaheen and Sons Co. Targeting merchant peddlers and retailers alike, the company marketed their garments with assurances that they would be distributed equitably among Shaheen partners. Source: Shaheen and Sons advertisement, *al-Majalla al-Tijariyya al-Suriyya al-Amrikiyya*, December 1918, 2; New York Public Library.

(Ilyas) F. Lutfy described how he purchased linen goods in New York City for resale in Chicago, adding that the roundtrip ticket was worth it because "the best goods were those coming from the Syrian factories in New York."[53] In midwestern towns, Syrian suppliers competed for territory while assuming the role of patron to their peddlers.[54] In Indiana, Mahomed Wazney described how he quit textile peddling in 1922 because he "couldn't earn a nickel." His Muslim supplier could not compete with the well-organized network of Christians from Zahle who controlled the trade there.[55] In Ohio, rival suppliers battled over market share: Faris Naff described how his supplier, Salem Beshara, controlled much of the state's linens business and staffed it with peddlers from Reshaya, but that an upstart network in Toledo outfitted by the Aytha family offered stiff competition.[56] Syrian manufacturers in New York also sent their middle managers to the Syrian clubs across the United States, reported Nazha Haney; her parents "graduated from *kasheh* to Madeira" that way, when F. M. Jabara and Co. (of New York and Funchal) hired them in Detroit as exclusive agents for their embroideries.[57] It was Jabara linens that led Khalil Goushe to quit his Detroit factory job and move into borderlands peddling. Together with four partners, he shuttled crates of Madeira linen to Texas, walking them across the border for sale in northern Mexico. Goushe did this route for ten years before returning to Palestine to marry in 1929.[58] An intensified regime of passes, passports, and performance of documentation developed at the border in the years between Seraphic's 1907 departure and Goushe's arrival in 1919. A savvy pack peddler knew how to navigate it.

CROSSING: THE POLITICAL ECONOMY OF THE *KASHEH*

As legislators drafted the Immigration Act of 1907, Syrian, Lebanese, and Palestinian crossings mounted, soon constituting a quarter of inbound migration.[59] However, most daily crossings between Mexico and the United States were not by immigrants, but by textile merchants and the peddlers who worked for them. Indeed, Alcibiades Seraphic cautioned against overstating the scale of unauthorized Syrian immigration, adding that his interviews with U.S. consular staff across Mexico convinced him "they all have an exaggerated idea of the number of diseased Syrians who go to the United States."[60] The specter of the diseased smuggled Syrian was fodder for xenophobic immigration discourse, but that stereotype conflated the phenomenon of inbound migration with the daily commercial activities of Syrian peddlers. The borderlands represented a specific node in the mahjar's carrying trades: men moving laces, white goods, and linens into Mexico to be sold at retail or fed into factories. Approaching the border stations from the Mexican side, peddlers carried cash to buy their goods, vouchsafe letters by their employers, and usually, at least one passport document. Border officials admitted peddlers on roundtrip business while simultaneously keeping an eye on them, looking for evidence of smuggling disguised as textile work. The officials' reports, which tracked peddlers' comings and goings, were preserved in Bureau of Investigation records.

These routine crossings generated a specific archival footprint, revealing the regular flow of peddlers and goods in a Syrian textile trade that was simultaneously local and transnational. Peddlers navigated territories between port cities and the land border. This pattern prevailed in both the United States and Mexico after 1900, intensified after 1907, and continued through the 1920s. The Mexican Border District's reorganization in 1907 led to the increased investigatory activity; after 1909, Syrians who crossed here were registered through a system of BOI crossing cards. These men were not legally required to carry passports or other bona fides when traveling—they were peddlers, not immigrants—but Syrian traders nevertheless collected such documents as insurance against arbitrary BOI detention. An examination of crossing cards from between 1909 and 1929 illustrates how border officials' anxieties about potential smuggling led textile peddlers into a performance of vouchsafe, gathering the "right" papers to represent themselves as allies and extensions of American capital abroad.

First, a typical crossing during this period. At crossing stations in Laredo, Eagle Pass, and El Paso, border officials did routine passport checks on Syrian peddlers as a pretext to examine the goods they carried. Familiar with this game, peddlers swiftly offered up documents to signify their pedigree and hasten their release. In 1918, A. B. Abdelnour arrived at the Laredo station and gave officials both his Mexican and French passports. Both passports had been drawn up in New York City, connecting Abdelnour to the Syrian American merchant-manufacturers of that city and staging him as "known" to U.S. allies. In addition to these papers, Abdelnour handed over a second French passport procured from the consulate in Mexico City. As the Laredo officials read over these documents, Abdelnour dramatically offered to hand over his Ottoman passport (*mürûr tezkeresi*) as well (they declined to review this one; America was at war and the Ottoman Empire was allied with Germany). Convinced that the Syrian was a merchant—not an immigrant—border officials admitted him and sent him into Laredo to buy his lace and ribbons.[61]

It was normal for Syrian merchants operating in the borderlands to carry multiple documents, procured from diverse consulates and multiple nation-states. Abdelnour's Ottoman nationality was both meaningless and significant in Laredo: he needed to secure foreign documents to conduct business among allied nations, but the eagerness with which the French, Mexican, and U.S. governments also claimed him suggests a will to facilitate Syrian textile trades even during times of geopolitical conflict. Hundreds of crossings like Abdelnour's honed this process. A clear hierarchy emerged as to which foreign passports were the good ones for peddlers to carry. Ottoman documents carried next to no social capital, either during or after World War I. Syrians arriving from Mexico with only the *mürûr tezkeresi* were coded as immigrants and subjected to a harsher border regime than were their peddler counterparts; those seeking departure opened sticky questions about their draft worthiness. As seen on Madeira, foreign passports enhanced a Syrian's legibility as a trader. However, Mexican and American passports were less favorable than European passports in the borderlands.

Among borderlands peddlers, the French passport was the ideal document to have in one's possession. Eager to claim Syrian and Lebanese merchants across the hemispheric mahjar, France offered them passports to place them under diplomatic protection as potential French colonials.[62] Holding a French passport whitelisted Syrian peddlers and their employers operating in both Mexico and the United States. Textile businesses secured these papers from the French consulates in Mexico City, San Antonio, and New York City, starting in 1915 (notably, five years before the French Mandate emerged in Syria and Lebanon). However, not every French consulate offered these Syrian passports: the El Paso consulate, for example, refused to grant passports to Syrian merchants unless they could prove they also had full French citizenship, a policy written in response to U.S. anxieties about Syrian migrant smuggling in that city.[63] Local, on-the-ground idiosyncrasies shaped and reshaped the system of passes Syrian merchants confronted, channeling mahjari textiles through specific border stations: away from El Paso, for instance, and toward Laredo and onward to San Antonio.

Lacking guidance on how to handle Syrians crossing with foreign passports, U.S. border officials expressed anxiety about Middle Eastern migrants potentially using their leverage with U.S. allies to conduct smuggling operations. The United States government could do very little to halt Syrian crossers who carried French documents, for instance. Textile peddlers leveraged this status widely, using their status as French "protected" people before 1920 and as French colonial subjects after that.[64] The proliferation of French passports among Syrian and Lebanese émigrés after 1920 bolstered the border trades and enabled a second wave of migration into and across the mahjar as merchants pursued expanding opportunities. All of this means that between the war and the quota restrictions of 1924, the French passport was simultaneously the best passport for a Syrian peddler to carry and the most likely to raise U.S. suspicions that its bearer might be a politically connected smuggler.

In addition to carrying foreign passports, some Syrian merchants also achieved U.S. citizenship, another advantageous status in the borderlands trades. A lace dealer named John Jirash, for example, started working as a peddler in New York City after arriving from Tripoli as a boy in 1880.[65] Working as an agent for a Syrian American silk firm, he became a U.S. citizen in 1896[66] and then came to Mexico in 1898 to "to study the business conditions here, because I expect to go into the commission business in the United States."[67] Jirash opened a merchant business in northern Mexico, married in 1911, and settled there permanently. He sent peddlers north to collect garments sent to Texas by his U.S. partners. Though he was a permanent resident of Mexico, Jirash also maintained his U.S. passport by returning intermittently to visit family until his death in 1926.

At the other end of the spectrum were Syrian peddlers who held no documents at all. Undocumented Syrians appeared at the border stations in Laredo, El Paso, and Eagle Pass regularly. Arriving without a passport did not necessarily result in being refused entry; many immigrant Syrians held no records at all. However, for peddlers and traders who made frequent crossings as their business, those who lacked passports also lacked status, and they could be detained for hours or even days as BOI agents investigated their identities. This business of passports created tiers in terms of who had access to the border trades over time: established textile businesses cornered the market, bringing on peddlers and supplying them with documents and contacts designed to facilitate their trade, utterly changing how the business worked in the meantime. Free agents, by contrast, resorted to creative routes and multiple attempts at entry. When Assad Sallom appeared in Laredo in 1917, for instance, he was interrogated for not having a passport and ultimately denied entry on the basis that he was "likely to become a public charge." He returned to Mexico, hit the road, and a couple of weeks later reappeared at a second processing station in Brownsville, seeking entry to purchase goods with $550 in cash. This time he was detained by BOI investigators who interviewed him about his application. "I am a peddler in Mexico," he told his interviewer in Spanish; "yes, sir, this is the first time [I've] applied for admission to the United States"; and "no, sir, I have no passport and no letters." Asked why he opted for Brownsville instead of going to more established Syrian trading channels at Laredo, Sallom told them he knew a Syrian called "Antonio" (no last name) he hoped the visit. Sallom's interrogators knew he had been turned away at Laredo. Ultimately, he was denied entry and sent away. Sallom's paperwork again says he was "likely to become a public charge" if admitted: that he showed up with no baggage and arrived with another debarred Syrian contributed to this assessment.[68] Crucially, only immigrants were debarred on public charge grounds. By declaring Sallom a public charge risk, BOI investigators cast doubts about whether Sallom was even a peddler: what sort of peddler lacks a passport, vouchsafe letters, or the ability to name merchant patrons all while carrying less than $1,000 cash?

The day Sallom was turned around at Brownsville, he told his interrogators he was coming from Chihuahua, a significant waypoint for the Syrian carrying trades in Mexico. BOI investigators watched the flow of Syrian textiles through Chihuahua closely. In 1918, fourteen Syrian stores sent their *comerciantes* to the border from there, and a half dozen more operated in the larger district of Chihuahua. "There are probably more than 100 Syrian peddlers [that] have not been taken into account in compiling the above lists," Consul J. Stewart added. "As a class they are unreliable [and] would not hesitate to trade with the enemy, if possible, to do so without being detected."[69]

While men like Sallom responded to refusal by simply trying their luck elsewhere, others appealed their rejections through diplomatic channels. Mexico City textile merchant Amin Frances was denied entry at Laredo. Amid a spate of reports that Syrians were posing as peddlers to conduct espionage for the enemy, Frances had tried to cross in December 1917. He was summarily denied entry because of his Ottoman nationality, a rare occurrence in a border regime that usually fixated on pretexts other than nationality status. A wealthy merchant of some stature, Frances returned to Mexico City and filed a complaint with the French Consulate; he was issued a French passport, and French officials sent a letter protesting Frances's denial to the U.S. Consulate of that city. In his appeal, Frances argued that as a French-protected merchant, he was exempt from U.S. proscriptions on Ottoman border crossings.[70] Frances returned to the Laredo border station, fully expecting to gain entry into Texas, but despite his efforts and all his letters, he was again rebuffed. Amin's cousin, Eid Frances, was a Texas resident and had come to Laredo to pick him up; Eid was not allowed to cross to the Mexican side either. Instead, Amin and Eid sat on opposite sides of the Laredo station, staring at one another across the border, rent by the ambiguities of America's security regime.[71] After that day, Frances appears in the BOI register only once more: in early 1918, when he was seen purchasing goods in Laredo after somehow smuggling himself in. The BOI deployed thirty Texas Rangers to apprehend Frances in town and deport him back to Mexico.[72]

Finally, some Syrian merchants used the border stations themselves as sites of appeal. Merchant John Jirash (the naturalized U.S. citizen mentioned above) tried this in 1917. Approaching agents at the Laredo crossing, Jirash was denied entry because his U.S. passport had expired. He returned to Laredo the next day with a lawyer at his side. Jirash's lawyer proffered documents showing his ties to the United States to border inspectors: a photograph of his brother, a Florida farmer, and a list of names of U.S. citizens who would vouch for Jirash, including Syrian American business associates. After some argument, Jirash was allowed to pass, revealing that sometimes character references, sheer pluck, and a lawyer's presence trumped formal appeals made through diplomatic channels.[73]

Both the Mexican Revolution and World War I shaped this border performance in significant ways. High-profile cases involving Mexican revolutionaries engaged in ammunition smuggling or political subversion drove official anxieties that Mexico's Syrian merchants might be engaged in similar work, even taking advantage of French protégé status to do it. In 1918, for instance, the U.S. secretary of state instructed border officials to halt the departure of Syrians from U.S. territory into Mexico. "You will report to the Department ... the names and addresses of Syrians seeking to cross the border without the permission of the Department of State, and you will inform them that they must make application to that Department for such permission."[74] In a memo forwarding this order to the BOI field office in El Paso, agent Gus Jones opined that it would assist them "greatly . . . in our efforts to keep 'tab' on these suspects."[75] Syrians "holding French or other passports" were placed under surveillance; the same documents that allowed these merchants to travel freely also made them into targets of suspicion. Having a more formal relationship with the United States did not eliminate suspicion, either. When Madeira linens merchant Elias Sirgany crossed into Mexico in 1919, he was detained on his return trip. He offered the BOI a French passport document and told the officer he was a U.S. resident who had taken his "first papers" in preparation for citizenship. Nevertheless, the BOI communicated with its New York office to confirm Sirgany was indeed "a member of Sirgany & Skaf of 15 Washington Street," and that he "is not in any way connected to any anarchistic or I.W.W. organizations in this country."[76] While such political tests do not appear to have been a standardized directive, Syrians suspected of ties to labor unions risked being refused reentry.

The commercial ties that existed between Mexican revolutionaries, German and German-aligned firms in Mexico, and Syrian borderlands peddlers also alarmed BOI investigators during the war. Syrian textile businesses previously aligned with German American firms had to cut ties with those firms, observe U.S. trading blacklists, and performatively affirm their loyalty to the United States. The transnational implications of this shift are significant: Syrian American manufacturers in New York went from working with German American firms to direct ownership of the Madeiran and Azorean linen factories, producing goods which now filled the suitcases arriving in the borderlands. Many Syrian peddlers detained at the border were stopped on suspicion that their goods—or the profit thereof—might fall into German or Mexican revolutionary hands. Syrians were not the only Middle Eastern group targeted: Turkish Ottoman nationals were prohibited from travel; only those approved by the State Department were granted exceptions. Even then, BOI Special Agent in Charge Robert Barnes ordered that "all Turks entering the United States from Mexico should be watched," because "[he was] informed reliably that they are employed and sent by German organizations."[77] Ottoman Jewish merchants also experienced this BOI sorting of perceived friends from foes, and "American consular officials . . . sought to stem the granting of visas to and limit the trade of those suspected of harboring anti-Entente views."[78]

Syrian American customs inspectors played an important role in regulating borderlands trade, sometimes raising their employers' suspicions. One Laredo customs officer, George Coury, became the subject of a BOI investigation after the agency's surveillance of Arab peddlers revealed bank receipts bearing his name. Banking records showed Coury received $1,160 from the Schikri Hermuda Hnos firm of Guadalajara with the memo to hold onto the sum and "deduct the amount I owe." Coury then withdrew $760 from his account in Laredo, for disbursement to a Schikri Hermuda peddler, after he crossed into Texas. Coury was accused of accepting bribes for smoother border processing. The ensuing investigation revealed he was engaged in lending, investing capital into the stores of Syrian peddlers for a hefty cut. The BOI also learned that Coury had been fired for doing similar work among Syrian businesses at Italian ports before coming to America (Coury is named in Marcus Braun's 1907 Naples investigation, for instance).[79] Though the agency concluded he was not a migrant smuggler, it recommended that he "should not be connected with the immigration services." It is not clear from BOI records, however, whether Coury was fired or charged with any crime.[80] Allegations like this followed Syrian American immigration inspectors everywhere, because many of them did engage in facets of the migration business: lending, translation, boarding, or direct employment. The line between advocacy and corruption shifted only as the Immigration Commission began to see its work as more fundamentally a project of migration interdiction. Though dismissals happened, they were infrequent, particularly on the southern border where maintaining staff was difficult.

Once admitted, inbound peddlers proceeded to the Syrian colonies in south Texas and Arizona to purchase goods carried there from the Syrian factories of New York. Filling suitcases with lace, linen embroideries, garments, and kimonos, peddlers paid wholesale rates according to the contracts negotiated by their employers in Mexico. BOI investigators tailed them and reported on their transactions. Maron Beshara was flagged at the El Paso border station because he was making frequent trips to Chihuahua, and a BOI agent who followed him on his rounds described how "he went first to a Syrian store on S. El Paso Street . . . conducted by Ayoub Bros., Syrians; he was there a half hour, then he went to H. Krupp Wholesale and . . .

Krakauer Zork and Moyo," accumulating merchandise.[81] Routine reports consume a significant portion of the BOI records, demonstrating that U.S. officials blurred the lines between migration control and regulation of foot commerce, both seen as national security concerns at this moment.

As outbound peddlers returned to the border stations, U.S. officials vetted them closely, examining their inventories and looking for contraband or suspicious items. Many peddlers carried laces, ribbons, appliques, or spools of thread destined for Mexican factories, stashed between finished garments, silks, and linen goods for retailers. However, sometimes routine checks of peddlers' cases yielded bizarre objects, leading officials to deny their departure. Syrian peddlers moving, for instance, 300 pounds of chocolate; contraband liquors and distilled spirits; ammunition, pistols, and long guns; or curiously large sums of gold or silver bullion were all flagged as threats. Alejandro Kefuri was detained in Eagle Pass in 1918 because agents discovered $100,000 worth of precious metals buried beneath a false bottom in his suitcase, leading them to conclude he was a migrant smuggler. Kefuri was imprisoned at Leavenworth Penitentiary later that year when the BOI discovered he was actually smuggling arms to Mexican revolutionaries.[82]

Arabic printed materials were also contraband. Shortly after the United States entered the war, the Immigration Commission deployed interpreter H. A. Bishara to Eagle Pass to censor inbound mails. His reports on Syrian newspapers printed in Mexico led to a ban on their importation in 1917 ("nasty sheets" Bishara reported of these papers, "with quite a circulation among the Syrians in this country").[83] Similarly, the BOI investigated "un-American" utterances by peddlers who allegedly met in Mexico to "discuss subversion" against the United States and who smuggled Arabic newspapers. A Syrian BOI informant ("Samora") accused his El Paso neighbor, Dab Kahlele, who was then arrested on suspicion of sedition. During four days of interrogation, Kahlele told the BOI he was selling kimonos to borderlands peddlers and that he was a proud U.S. ally. When police learned that Kahlele had pursued a woman who Samora was dating, they released Kahlele and concluded that "the information" Samora provided was "given out of [personal] prejudice."[84] Kahlele was released, but his business suffered as Syrian peddlers nervously avoided his kimono shop after that. In addition to bad press or rumors (*kalam al-nas*), Syrian peddlers also had to avoid landing on trading blacklists, which could damage their ability to move across the border, get credit, or make transactions. Manuel Nassar from Torreon learned this the hard way when his name turned up on a U.S. trading blacklist in 1919, leading his bank in El Paso to freeze his assets while the BOI investigated him. Nassar was ultimately cleared of any wrongdoing and his rights to cross the border were restored, but like Kahlele, his business subsequently suffered, as his lenders, patrons, and clients all avoided him.[85]

Whether physically crossing a border or not, Syrian merchants traded in a secondary economy of perception, reputation, and trust. These assets were as significant as the lace, linens, and silk goods the peddlers carried, and successful merchants accumulated and managed perception jealously. The American border regime changed over time, and meeting those moving goalposts was also peddlers' work. The primary goal of crossing was to differentiate peddlers from immigrants, but by the 1920s, peddlers also contended with changing politics of nationality, concerns about contraband, trade blacklisting, and immigration quotas. As legal regimes at the border mounted, they required progressively more sophisticated responses, shifting the political economy of Syrian borderlands commerce away from free agency and toward a vertically integrated supply chain that favored large firms. Competing networks of traders increasingly dominated the borderlands trades. Joining a network—while less lucrative than free agency—was a safer way to work. The most well-known networks focused on specific Mexican territories, shaping and reshaping foot crossings through the 1920s. Working in corporation, Syrian men orchestrated signature routes, carried specific documentation, and offered station officials specific narratives about the work they were undertaking. One well-known branch manager, Salim Ayub Noemi crossed on foot into Laredo, Texas, in May 1920, carrying $10,000 in cash with a transit visa declaring that he was headed to Syria via New York City.[86] Eight months later, Noemi reappeared at the port of Veracruz and, proceeding to Mexico City, he picked up his business, hired a dozen *comerciantes ambulantes*, and maintained a successful textile firm there through the 1920s.[87] We will turn to his story next.

PEDDLING AT SCALE: INTERWAR MERCHANT NETWORKS

As the war ended and Mediterranean sea lanes reopened, emigration to Mexico accelerated, quadrupling the rate of Syrian, Lebanese, and Palestinian arrivals into Mexico in the early 1920s. Consulting consular records,

Theresa Alfaro-Velcamp argues that Syrian routes to the U.S. by way of Mexico took on new significance after the passage of immigration quota acts in 1921, 1924, and 1929.[88] Immigration officials continued to express alarm over Syrian immigrants passing through the Mexican land route. As arrivals to Mexico mounted, the Mexican government also banned new immigration from Syria, Lebanon, Palestine, and Turkey in 1927.[89] In 1929, Mexico passed additional laws banning most new labor immigration and requiring foreign nationals working there to register with the Departamento de Migración.[90] Completed between 1930 and 1938, this campaign represents the first systematic attempt to classify Syrian, Lebanese, and Palestinian *comerciantes ambulantes* in Mexico and to limit their trade through a daunting paperwork regime.[91]

Examining the first year of the Departamento de Migración's effort, a few patterns emerge. Registrants were classified according to occupation, nationality and village of origin, date and port of arrival, and race and religious identity. Individuals also identified a sponsor (usually next-of-kin), employer, or institution with which they were associated, allowing the department to locate individual *comerciantes ambulantes* when they were on the road. Men and women are represented: the men overwhelmingly in merchant business or peddling commerce, and most of the women as homemakers or working widows. Most Syrian peddlers registered with the department were men of Catholic faith (Maronite, Roman, and Greek Catholic), who arrived in Mexico during one of two immigration waves: the first between 1900 and 1908, or between 1922 and 1928. This two-wave immigration pattern was typical of the Latin American mahjar. It was driven by the wartime halt in transatlantic migration, intensified with U.S. immigration restrictions after 1921, and ended with the Great Depression of the 1930s.[92] Though Catholics predominated numerically, as a class, Middle Eastern peddlers were a diverse group: Greek Orthodox, Druze, Muslim, and Protestant peddlers are all represented in the registry (in that order), and there was also a minority of self-identified "free thinkers" (*libre pensadores*), a colloquialism that referred to freemasons or secularists but which was also informally associated with anarchism.

The Departamento de Migracion's records reveal that by the late 1920s, the Syrian textile trades had become more vertically integrated and were dominated by large firms with transnational reach, rather than by small independent merchants. Two large Syrian commercial networks are particularly well documented in the department's records: those of textile merchants Salim Ayub Noemi and Constantino Matuk. Originally from Ghazir, Mount Lebanon (born 1885), Salim Ayub Noemi was a prominent merchant living in Capuchinas. On his 1930 registration card, Salim claimed he first arrived in Mexico in 1921 via the port of Veracruz; U.S. records of border crossings, however, document his presence in Mexico much earlier, dating his arrival before World War I.[93] In 1921, Noemi moved to Yucatán with his wife, Filamina Kuri, where he ran a successful textile peddling business connecting Yucatán to Mexico City. He staffed this enterprise with Syrian men recently arriving through Veracruz.[94] Noemi's partner in Mexico City was Jorge Kuri, a Mexico City trader originally from Salima, Lebanon, whose peddlers dominated much of the border trade.[95] Noemi also collaborated with Constantino Matuk (born 1885), the proprietor of Mexico City's Matuk y Hnos, a wholesaler involved in "Syrian embroideries, laces, art goods, and lace curtains" produced by Syrian women workers abroad.[96] Constantino Matuk's registration card is missing from the 1930–33 set. Instead, he frequently appears there as the immigration sponsor, employer, or "next of kin" for Syrian foot peddlers working for him.[97]

From Mexico City, Noemi, Kuri, and Matuk jointly administered three Syrian peddling routes: Veracruz to Yucatán, Veracruz to Mexico City, and between Mexico City and the borderlands. Peddlers working for Noemi and Matuk were overwhelmingly recent immigrants.[98] They spanned out across territories defined by Matuk and Noemi, taking on subcontractors along the way. As elsewhere in the mahjar, ties of kinship blended into commercial networks. Syrian companies operating in Mexico tended to be centrally structured within and across extended families, also relying on fellow travelers from the home village.[99] Constantino Matuk employed younger relatives coming to Mexico from his native Tripoli: brothers Jose and Gorge Matuk both arrived via Veracruz in the 1920s to work as *comerciantes*, though by 1930 Gorge had contracted with Salim Ayub Noemi (according to his registry).[100] Several similar points of connection can be traced between Noemi and Matuk; though the Departamento de Migración cards do not capture direct cooperation between the two men, the easy movement of peddlers between them illustrates a shared network governed by patterns of passage, patronage, and commerce. Such ties bolstered what could otherwise be a chaotic, risky, and diffuse set of commercial relationships. Felipe de Jesus Bello Gomez notes that merchant-peddler relations were easily formed and easily dissolved. Peddlers participated in "the development of linked business networks," but these linkages were less institutional than they were personal, reaffirming that the accumulation and management of trust, perception, and social capital was the merchant's secondary business.[101] At the same time, the Noemi-Matuk network was not exceptional nor singular in its structure. The routes these men worked were common ones, traversed by dozens of Syrian firms by the early 1930s. Large networks like Noemi-Matuk were representative of a continuing trade that Alcibiades Seraphic had observed thirty years earlier.

In Mexico, Syrian merchants also nurtured institutional bodies to protect their trade and, when called upon, to represent the Syrian community to the Mexican state. One such body was the Cámara de Comercio Libanesa, established in Mexico City in 1926 "to protect mahjari economic interests ... in the early years of the [French] Mandate."[102] Camila Pastor assembled charter information for five peer institutions among Syrians and Lebanese in Puebla, Veracruz, and Mexico City, each of them organizing between 1924 and 1932 as representative bodies for the immigrant community.[103] In addition to desires for hemispheric cooperation, local efforts to reorganize Syrian and Lebanese trade drove bodies like the Cámara de Comercio Libanesa. The Cámara represented the old guard, established merchants who sat at the center of their own peddling networks. Pablo Lama, for instance, had been in Mexico since 1901, arriving from Ghazir, Lebanon. He worked with Salim Ayub Noemi before establishing his own firm in Veracruz (Lama was also a witness to Noemi's 1901 marriage to Filomina Kuri).[104] Felipe Abraham of Corregidora similarly listed himself as a Cámara officer, a merchant from Beirut living in Mexico since 1903.[105] Another merchant in Corregidora, Bechara Yazbek, linked himself to the body; Yazbek arrived in Mexico in 1907 at the port of Veracruz.[106]

Across Mexico in the 1920s and 1930s, Syrian communities depended on merchant commerce in textiles.[107] But they were not the first to enter this trade; Syrian peddlers "competed with the Chinese for control of petty trades until the Chinese were either massacred or expelled by the local Mexicans," as a 1944 U.S. intelligence report records bluntly.[108] In the 1930s, nationalist groups targeted foreign merchants in northern Mexico with legal discrimination and extrajudicial violence to force them to flee the region. Chinese Mexicans bore the brunt of these campaigns. A series of anti-Chinese associations in Sonora and Sinaloa produced massive extrajudicial violence targeting Asian neighborhoods, leading to the expulsion of Chinese merchants from those states.[109] In addition to terrorizing Chinese immigrants, the Bloque Nacionalista de Defensa Pro Patria campaigned for "the expedition of a law that will restrain the immigration of Turkish, Syrian-Lebanese, Poles, and Jews, or any other nationalities of the many that are invading the markets with serious injury to the National commerce." The campaign accused Syrian merchants of operating unscrupulously and harming Mexican workers, connecting these claims to racialist arguments against the "degeneration of the race by introduction of Asiatics."[110] Xenophobic flavor, the depiction of Syrians as a perfidious foreign capitalist class, and a concomitant antisemitic rhetoric shaped the Bloque's politics in the 1930s, mirroring depictions of Arab merchants working in West Africa, Argentina, and the Caribbean at the time.[111]

Though the Mexican government "formally restricted the entry of new immigrants from Syria, Lebanon, and Palestine" through immigration quota legislation, these laws did not sanction discrimination against merchants already in the country.[112] In the early 1930s, local campaigns mounted pressure on the government into acting against Syrian traders, especially in Sonora, Sinaloa, and Monterrey. In 1932, Syrians in Guaymas reported that the municipality "is increasing the taxes on businesses operated and owned by nationals or descendants of nationals of countries of the Near East ... seemingly for the purpose of forcing them to close their business establishments or leave."[113] Reporting from the U.S. Consulate in Guaymas, Vice Consul A. F. Yepis connected this move against Syrian businesses to "last year's anti-Chinese campaign" as well as pervasive anti-Syrian propaganda appearing in the press. The tax increase "is sufficient to force these aliens out of business," Yepis concluded, adding that he did not believe the departure of the Syrians from Guaymas would be as devasting as the Chinese massacres of the previous year. Meanwhile, in Mazatlán, the government issued a January 1932 directive that all Chinese, Russian, Syrian, and Turkish immigrants "must present themselves, bringing for inspection all documents which they may possess regarding their legal entry into this country," as well as proof of "activities in which they have engaged."[114] Immigrants were given fifteen days to submit to a government inspection, and noncompliance was criminalized.

Because many Syrian and Lebanese merchants doing business in Mexico were also naturalized American citizens or maintained other legal ties with the United States, they appealed to U.S. consulates for protection when facing such discrimination. While American officials often sympathized with them, the Department of State's policy was to avoid entanglement with the Mexican government over naturalized immigrants doing business there. In 1933, for instance, a prominent Syrian American merchant from Mazatlán appealed to the U.S. Embassy for help after his business was attacked by Pro Nacionalistas. The merchant was named in a series of "articles attacking the local Jewish and Syrian merchants" in *La Voz del Pueblo*, which led to a riot that destroyed his store. A rival store owner, Feliciano Ruiz, subsidized this serial and was behind the incitement. The U.S. Embassy helped place a rebuttal in the Mazatlán *El Demócrata Sinaloense* on the merchant's behalf (specifically refuting the claim that Syrian merchants paid less taxes than their Mexican counterparts), but embassy officials were also briefed on the need to "discreetly cooperate with Mexican authorities" and avoid going beyond the limits of Mexican state interests in protecting foreign merchants.[115]

Mounting Mexican restrictions on Syrian businesses also shaped travel and immigration regimes at the border, and these changes impacted naturalized Syrian Americans in particular. Where in the 1920s, achieving U.S. citizenship eased Syrian commerce in both directions, this changed as Mexico restricted immigration of all individuals of Syrian, Lebanese, Palestinian, and Turkish origin in the early 1930s. A capacious category which included naturalized Syrian American merchants, tourists, and travelers, the new border policy mirrored U.S. laws adopted alongside the immigration quotas after 1924. State Department memoranda record new difficulties faced by Syrian American merchants seeking entry into Mexico. In 1934, for instance, a Syrian American businessman arrived in Laredo, Texas, planning to cross into Mexico for a trip with several colleagues when, as the only Arab American, he was singled out and denied passage. His lawyer, Philip Kazen of Laredo, appealed to Secretary of State Cordell Hull "on behalf of myself and 225,000 Syrian Americans of the United States" to protest "the discriminatory Mexican immigration laws dealing with American tourists of Syrian and Arabian extraction." Kazen's client was "very much embarrassed" to be denied entry on the basis that Mexico's law "was based on origin and extraction and not on citizenship." Kazen also noted that even though he was also Arab American, the law was "never once applied" to him.[116]

Receiving Kazen's letter, Cordell Hull requested that the Embassy in Mexico City investigate the allegation of discrimination. Promoting the economic interests of U.S. nationals in Mexico was a hallmark of Hull's term as secretary of state; he was concurrently challenging Mexico's nationalist expropriation of farmland owned by American citizens in 1934, a context which informed his concern for Syrian Americans.[117] Upon Hull's request, U.S. Ambassador Josephus Daniels met with the Migration Department and reported back that Mexico was indeed restricting businessmen of Syrian, Lebanese, and Palestinian origin, regardless of their naturalization status.[118] However, the Mexican government claimed this treatment mirrored U.S. border practices: "When aliens ... have presented themselves at ports of entry in the United States as non-immigrants, [they] likewise have been denied admission on the assumption that they might seek to evade the United States quota restrictions on the pleas that they were Mexicans." Turnabout was fair play. This logic convinced Ambassador Daniels, who told Hull he believed it would be unfair to protest, as it was U.S. "treatment [that] presumably prompted the Mexican Government to retaliate by restricting the entry into Mexico of American citizens of like racial strains."[119]

It was during this period in the early 1930s that several Syrian merchants pivoted from borderlands trading to direct manufacturing, opening factories in Mexico producing women's garments, shoes, hats, and other goods locally.[120] The rising cost of doing business in the borderlands was only one incentive. Racial quota restrictions adopted by both the United States and Mexico made peddling labor less lucrative for peddlers and merchants alike. Responding to the Great Depression's broader economic downturn, fewer new immigrants arrived in Mexico. Those who did come did so under family sponsorships and had few incentives to enter the ambulatory trades. Return migration to the Middle East attenuated these numbers further.[121] And in the United States, the Great Depression led textile manufacturers there—including Syrian Americans—to downsize or to relocate production abroad, especially to Latin America and Asia. Syrian borderlands trading depended on both robust transatlantic transit migration and the mass production of garments in Syrian New York. As those manufacturing centers moved, more than a dozen new Syrian garment, haberdashery, and footwear factories opened in Mexico in the early 1930s, owned by merchant-manufacturers previously tied to peddling.[122]

Miguel Abed, a merchant from Puebla, exemplifies this trend. Abed was born in Syria in 1897 and arrived in Mexico just before World War I. Working as a peddler, Abed was once detained by U.S. border officials at El Paso in 1917; he handed them a packet of reference letters by Syrian American merchants and was allowed a one-day pass to buy merchandise. Abed became a prosperous textile dealer, and in the early 1930s he established a textile factory in Patriotismo and subsequently founded a Mexico City bank in 1935.[123] Like other merchant-manufacturers of his class, Abed circumnavigated the world in the 1930s, traveling to textile centers in New York, Europe, and the Mediterranean. His itineraries mirror those of major New York City manufacturers like Elias Mallouk, George Bardwil, or Alexander Hamrah, confirming his arrival into the mahjar's textile industrial elite and integration into textile supply chains across the Arab Atlantic. At the same time, an older, recognizable pattern of "passing via passport" is evident in Abed's personal records. Abed's 1934 passport lists his nationality as French and his race as Syrian; the following year, in 1935, he traveled again as a French national carrying a Mexican diplomatic passport (suggesting this trip involved official state business).[124] And in 1936, Abed hit the Atlantic again with his son, Miguel Abed Varga, this time as a naturalized Mexican citizen.[125]

A similar pattern is observable across Mexico and the Latin American mahjar. In Puebla, Lebanese immigrants took over that city's textile industry, buying out the Spanish firms which previously dominated manufacturing.[126] Upstart companies appeared across the hemisphere: the Hasbun factory in Costa Rica, the Safie factory in Guatemala, or the Samar and Shihab plants in Nicaragua are some examples.[127] In Honduras, Palestinian immigrants owned 20 percent of that country's fifty-eight garment factories in the 1930s.[128] In Chile, the Palestinian Yarur family opened what became that country's first modern cotton mill in 1937, but as Cecilia Baeza notes, the Yarur plant was just one of nearly one hundred textile factories established by Arab immigrants in Chile.[129] The legacy of Middle Eastern dominance in Latin American textiles persisted through the postwar period, in the massive factories of Jafet (in Brazil), Yarur (Chile), or Abusaid (Colombia), or in the smaller garment workshops proliferating across Mexico, Central America, and the Caribbean.[130] As Middle Eastern immigrant workers in the United States transitioned out of textile and garment industries, this sector expanded across the rest of the hemisphere, seemingly without limit.

In Syrian Mexico, the transition from borderlands peddler to mahjari merchant, and from merchant to manufacturer, reveals a pattern of supply chain pursuit shared with diasporic capitalists operating across the Arab Atlantic. Just as Syrian American kimono bosses in New York looked abroad when their workers struck, Syrian merchants in Mexico made their living through deft navigation of supply chains and strategic negotiation of the land border. Working from U.S. and Mexican immigration and consular records, this chapter has argued that Syrian borderlands peddlers represented the final leg of the mahjar's textile industry. Though embodied as a plucky entrepreneur and a racially respectable symbol of commercial success in nostalgic Arab Americana (and by contrast, as unscrupulous, venal, or racially degraded in xenophobic nationalist discourses), the Syrian peddler was engaged in the work of labor reproduction, textile logistics, and retail. Subcontracting with kimono shops, embroidered linens manufacturers, or lace and underwear importers around the Syrian diaspora, peddlers managed the border trades through the strategic use of racial passing, a politics of documentary vouchsafe, and the accumulation of trust and logistical know-how.

This work was progressively professionalized, arranged around transnational flows of capital investment, credit, debt, and risk. If the trade began in the 1890s with petty merchants carrying laces made by their wives, sisters, and nieces in the home, by the 1920s, this corridor was monopolized by a hierarchical network of large merchants and their employees. This pattern of hemispheric—and then global—consolidation relied on women's work, spreading across a variety of industrial labor arrangements. Though this chapter has focused on the borderlands as one site of transnational supply chain power, Syrian firms in Mexico similarly coaxed a niche monopoly on white goods manufacturing in the 1930s. The textile trade allowed Arab immigrants to enter the Mexican elite, but it simultaneously made them the target of populist Mexican nationalism.

In all this work to preserve supply chains, facets of the business remained unmentionable, accessible only through the whispered reportage of later generations, who heard stories about their parents as children. "The story we liked about Uncle Jimmy Simon and his brother Charlie," Joseph Kneiser told historian Alixa Naff, was about "the trouble they had in crossing the border, *legally, of course.*" Jimmy was admitted to the United States, but Charlie was rebuffed "because he was good friends with the Mexican bandit Pancho Villa... he stayed in Mexico and married a Mexican woman" instead. Working in borderlands textiles, Charlie reportedly told his family "Pancho was not a bad guy" and suggested that Mexican revolutionaries were his best customers. Charlie and Jimmy spent time in Mexico and "worked [their] way across the country and had some very interesting experiences."[131] In another of her interviews, Naff asked Mayme Farris about her relatives in Mexico; they worked there because they were unable to get into America. Yes, they peddled, but when asked why they did so, Farris said the Lebanese "are merchants by heritage, from the Phoenicians."[132] Apocryphal family lore aside, most aspects of the early twentieth-century borderlands textile trades were preserved only in the occasional Bureau of Investigation intelligence report. This unintelligibility protected Syrian peddlers as they did their work; the same unintelligibility facilitated celebratory myths about their racial proclivities toward commerce. In other words, the "Phoenician" origins of the modern Syrian merchant became part of the mahjar's historical mythology; the context of Mexico, despite its importance to itinerant textile workers and their trade, did not.

CONCLUSION

SYRIAN SHOPS FOR THE SYRIANS

Benefit the sons of your homeland and profit!
AL-MAJALLA AL-TIJARIYYA AL-SURIYYA AL-AMRIKIYYA, 1919[1]

THE REOPENING OF SEA LANES in 1919 was an auspicious moment for the mahjar. For emigrant workers, this was their first opportunity to return to Syria, Lebanon, or Palestine, and many jumped at the chance. "Immigrants from America are starting to return to their homelands," reported Sallum Mukarzil in April of 1919, adding that the Port of New York recorded 3,000 departures for the Mediterranean each month. Factory operatives and needleworkers were represented in these early numbers, suggesting to Mukarzil that Middle Eastern labor was coming home.[2] Their return from the mahjar offered an unprecedented opportunity to revitalize the region's textile industries, which had collapsed during the war. Mukarzil applauded returning migrants for bringing their labor power home, adding: "The success of Syria's industrial projects depends on them. Who doubts the willingness of Syrians to meet this challenge of the homeland? Even if not driven to help Syria's industries by patriotic considerations, there are personal motivations that tempt them to return and help the homeland's revival. Because we—like all other immigrants—came to the mahjar but our souls are ready to go home."[3] Mukarzil believed the mass repatriation of textile operatives, weavers, and garment workers would "help Syria realize its place in the world economy, its spot in the sun."⁴ This was an expression of postwar developmentalist optimism, but it was simultaneously an elite claim on the diaspora's labor power, mostly women workers who were not consulted or quoted in these editorials. A genre was emerging, embraced by the diaspora's industrial elites, which redeployed mahjari labor control tropes in service to homeland economic projects.

Meanwhile, the early interwar period was a moment of colonial capitalist restructuring. The League of Nations Mandate administrations emerged in Syria, Lebanon, and Palestine and focused on regulating the flows of migrants, money, and machines between Mashriq and mahjar.⁵ The Mandates similarly fixated on commercial ties which bound the region to its diasporas abroad, particularly in textiles. The appearance of émigré investors was not totally unwelcome, but the ties those elites maintained with American capitalist expansion created significant anxiety. This moment also reshaped the mahjar's textile industries, which rose to global prominence in the 1920s and 1930s. This book has captured the key events of that story: the arrival of Arab workers in American textile factories; the emergence of the "Syrian shops"; the ability of diasporan elites to acquire garment shops on the embroidery islands of the North Atlantic; and the opening of Syrian firms in Asia and Latin America. As I have argued, the mahjar's commercial activities enabled an émigré industrialist class to exercise supply chain power. When one sector of this industry weathered strikes, merchant-manufacturers shifted production elsewhere; when unfavorable tariff conditions discouraged maritime trade, they relied on foot peddlers, railways, and land borders; when Ottoman passports no longer worked, they used French ones, and when these, in turn, ceased to be favorable, they used American ones. The ability to claim and command labor power across multiple nodes in the Arab Atlantic world was the centerpiece of these firms' business model. They looked at the Syrian and Lebanese textile industries, factories that had employed 12,000 women and girls before 1914, as the sites to begin postwar reconstruction.⁶

This dual set of contexts—the need for reconstruction and a desire to return from abroad—influenced a series of efforts by the mahjar's elites. In New York City, merchant-manufacturers hoped to join capital from the diaspora with U.S. desires to open the Middle East to foreign trade. One early campaign by 'Assy Shaheen is illustrative. Three weeks after the armistice was declared in November 1918, Shaheen wrote an anonymous editorial enjoining "our Syrian merchants, those who are financially able, [to] take advantage of their presence in America to expand the scope of their trade, opening new doors that [will] bring them great profit and great benefit." Reduced trade barriers between Syria and America would enable these manufacturers to revitalize their homes: "Fate has put us here to be the mediator of new contracts between the trade of the United States and that of our ancient homeland, recently extracted from the yoke of political oppression but awaiting removal from the yoke of commercial injustice."[7] Shaheen opposed tariffs and bans on machine imports specifically; extracting favorable terms on both had been the basis for Syrian manufacturing in Madeira, the Philippines, China, and Japan. He was hoping to produce a similar economic miracle in Syria.

By the time the Mandate system had emerged after 1920, Shaheen and Sons' plants in New York City, Brooklyn, and New Jersey had expanded beyond kimonos and into silk weaving, including silk-cotton blend fabrics, which the company exported across the Americas.[8] The brand was valued at $2 million. The two Shaheen sons, George and Tawfik, were of different minds about whether to return to Lebanon. George had come to New York City reluctantly and in 1919 announced his intention to reinvest his share of the company in Lebanon. "When the allies collectively decided Syria would not be returned to the Turkish yoke," Sallum Mukarzil described, "the idea came to George that establishing a factory would be a significant contribution to Syria's national economic revival."[9] In June 1920, George Shaheen traveled to Baʿabda and met with Habib Pasha Saʿad, securing the Administrative Council's support for construction of a new silk factory in Mount Lebanon.[10] Announcing the meeting in the Beiruti and mahjari press, the Shaheen company described it as a "key first step for the cause of promotion of national industry in Syria and Lebanon" and established the Shaheen and Sons joint stock company, pledging $1 million in direct investment and seeking a match from Syrian investors across the Americas.[11]

The Shaheen "Proposal for a National Syrian Knitting Factory" consumed the attention of Syrian elites across the diaspora for two years. In New York, the Syrian American Chamber of Commerce held special sessions on the Shaheen Plan. The factory George sought to build would be a mirror of the firm's plant in Cranford, New Jersey: it would make kimonos, negligees, and a variety of ready-wear white garments.[12] It was noted at the time, though "Assy Shaheen enjoys a national reputation for commercial savvy and has the financial capacity and determination to undertake" the plan, "he refuses to complete the factory project unilaterally, and is suggesting the creation of a national company" in the "name of the national good."[13] The firm spent two years lobbying "to revive the national industry in Syria."[14] The company advertised in the press in the mahjar and Middle East, looking for investors as well as mill owners who might subcontract with the brand. "We are now the largest Syrian manufacturer in America," one 1919 advertisement read. "If you are a mill owner or would like to open a workshop with us, we will help you with capital, information, or the sale of goods: contact us. We already serve several sons of the homeland [*ibna' al-watan*] who have gained expertise in the needs of our dignified citizens."[15] The invitation was intentionally transnational: small Syrian manufacturers could contract with Shaheen and Sons and gain access to a global supply chain and diasporic retail market managed by the company. The language of the ads merged the patriotic with the commercial: partnering with Shaheen made good business sense while benefiting the homeland.

Ultimately, the dream for a Shaheen silk plant in Lebanon did not come to fruition. The plan's early history is recorded enthusiastically in the press, but its demise is not. A confluence of geopolitical factors helps explain it. First, barely three weeks after Shaheen met with Lebanon's Administrative Council, French military authorities dissolved that body, arrested seven of its leaders, and exiled them. In September 1920, the state of Greater Lebanon was established and its French high commissioner wavered between wariness of émigré commercial appeals and hostility to American attempts to impose free trade on Syria and Lebanon. Meanwhile, east Asian silks continued to expand and dominated the Middle Eastern silk market by the mid-1920s, undercutting one of the revenue sources the Shaheen plan depended upon (in an interesting wrinkle, Bardwil Bros. was among the firms engaged in Chinese silk importing).[16] So, instead of building in Lebanon, George Shaheen moved his family—and his silk factory—to California. The California Shaheen plant imported silks from Yokohama, necessitating frequent trips to Guam and Hawaii, where George Shaheen and his wife, Mary, relocated in 1938. In 1946, their son, Alfred Shaheen, followed them to Honolulu, and it was there that the Shaheen family business innovated a postwar American classic: the printed Hawaiian shirt. Notably, Alfred Shaheen's aloha shirts were manufactured in "one factory that handled all the manufacturing processes. He bought his plain fabrics, created his dyes . . . created textile design and fashion departments, sewed, and distributed."[17]

In other words, the company's "cocoon to finished garment" manufacturing shifted from Mediterranean to Pacific climes as the Shaheen company pursued global supply chains.[18]

Though Lebanon's silk processing industries struggled, the Arida Brothers Corporation established a series of successful cotton mills, including a 300-employee factory at Tripoli described by the *Syrian World* as "the largest cotton weaving factory in Syria and Lebanon."[19] The Tripoli mill started as a yarn factory in 1927, founded with a half-million-dollar initial investment by Solomon, Joseph, and George Arida, wealthy merchants from Australia with ties to Mexican textile manufacturing.[20] Richard (Rashid) Arida also capitalized the Arida Corporation from abroad, and the company enjoyed a connection to Antoun Arida, Tripoli's archbishop and, after his 1932 elevation, the Maronite Patriarch.[21] As Patriarch, Antoun Arida encouraged several development projects that bolstered the Tripoli mill's success, including hydroelectric power to enable adoption of power loom technology.[22] The Tripoli plant spun yarns on 20,000 spindles imported from Boston via émigré channels.[23] It was also the first in Lebanon to adopt mechanized looms, machines acquired from U.S. firms as they downsized.[24] By the early 1930s, their company was producing the equivalent of 12 percent of Syrian and Lebanese imports. The timing of the Aridas' industrial investment "suggests the impact of the Depression," Carolyn Gates concludes, "which reduced import competition and allowed industrialists to exploit local advantages."[25] Hicham Safieddine observes that "wealthy Lebanese emigrants seeking to repatriate their foreign-earned capital" offered a significant source of capitalization that, after independence, underpinned the national central bank.[26]

The Arida Corporation mills were strong enough to pull the state toward policies that—for a time—protected the industry from foreign competition. Shortly after the Tripoli mill opened, the Great Depression began, challenging textile companies worldwide. In the mahjar, many smaller textile firms closed, leaving their workers unemployed. The production of cotton piece goods fell in Syria and Lebanon as well, from 225,000 in 1929, to 179,500 in 1931, to 109,550 pieces in 1933.[27] From Tripoli, Michel Arida argued that imports challenged the industry further, and he lobbied the French Mandate for increased tariff protections for cotton and silk materials, particularly those coming from Asia.[28] Japan was then the largest importer of textile components to Syria and Lebanon, its silk thread out-competing local manufacture. However, because Japan was also a League of Nations member state, it enjoyed favored nation status in European Mandate territories, and the French balked at demands to regulate foreign goods entering regional markets. A dispute emerged: failing to get the French to impose tariffs, the Arida Brothers Corporation shut down its mills in 1933, citing "competition of Japanese goods . . . making it impossible to keep up work without great loss."[29] Writing as an observer from New York, Sallum Mukarzil opined that Japan's "low standard of living and wages has enabled it to compete easily with French, British, and Italian products, and, as it now appears, has threatened the economic future of the newly-founded and flourishing national firms."[30] The Mandate relented the following year, imposing new tariffs under Decree No. 271/LR to protect local production. Satisfied with the new duties, Arida Brothers Corporation pursued a fresh round of émigré investment and reopened factories in Tripoli and Aleppo.[31] They also aggressively produced local textiles at prices far lower than those which foreign importers could meet. In a letter from 1935, the American vice consul reported that the new yarn duties were so disadvantageous that no American yarns could be sold in Syria for less than 220 piasters per ten-pound package, compared to 180 piasters for the local Arida yarns. Complaining about the "aggressiveness" of the Arida Brothers Corporation, he warned "this firm is beginning to control the market." Unless the French could be persuaded to relax tariffs, "it will be practically impossible for foreign manufacturers to compete." The vice consul suggested that U.S. cotton producers should invest in one of Arida's rivals to secure their commitment to buying American yarns abroad, an idea that ultimately came to naught.[32] All told, this combination of émigré investment, lobbying for tariffs, and accelerated production produced a late 1930s boom in Lebanese textiles that was, in Carolyn Gates's words, "instrumental in establishing import-substitution industries" in post-independence Lebanon.[33]

The goals of the mahjar's textile elite often conflicted with the French Mandate's interest in feeding the European export market. France received 90 percent of Lebanon's silk crop each year and invested in cotton primarily to compete with Great Britain and the United States.[34] French desires for export fiber dampened most projects for expanding Syrian or Lebanese infrastructure in reeling, weaving, or finishing cloth, and this stance changed little before the 1930s, when the U.S. textile industries disintegrated, and machinery liquidated from the mahjar was more easily imported. When

George Shaheen sought to import silk power looms to Beirut in 1920, for instance, he was stymied by early Mandate regulations prohibiting machining imports.

This shifted in 1924, as the Mandate abolished tariffs on machine imports to facilitate state-led projects to modernize select industries.[35] When the Arida Corporation imported Saco-Lowell Shops weaving machines from Boston in 1931, the company found the port authority more receptive. Nicholas G. Mobayed served as Arida's purchasing agent in 1931. Born to Lebanese émigré parents in Alexandria, Egypt, Mobayed learned the jobbing business as a teenager working for Malaxos Freres.[36] He relocated to New York some time before 1914, first employed as a merchant and later as a foreman for a factory in Brooklyn.[37] According to ship records, Mobayed spent considerable time in the 1920s and 1930s between Tripoli and New York, facilitating transactions like the Saco-Lowell machining deal. The new Arida machines were previously installed at shops where Syrian workers ordered stoppages with IWW and AWCA. Now, under the ownership of émigré merchant-manufacturers, they were bargained through customs to be operated in Tripoli and Aleppo.[38]

Transactions like these illustrate how mahjari capital returned home during the French Mandate period through multiple avenues, but what about mahjari labor? Despite the optimism of newspapermen like Sallum Mukarzil that émigré workers and manufacturers alike would return to Syrian and Lebanese factories "on a mission of regeneration," most permanent repatriates were not interested in industrial labor.[39] In a 1923 report on return migration to Syria, the U.S. Consulate in Beirut described repatriates as driven by "the ease of life in Syria" made possible by "his means, moderate or otherwise, accumulated in the United States. His wants are few and simple. He eats bread and *labni*, grapes and figs, he sleeps during the day and drinks *arack* with his friends in the village café in the evening. *He does not work.*" The report coded Syrian repatriates as both physically and politically idle. Arguing for revocation of naturalization, it warned of a "very marked tendency ... to return to Syria immediately after securing [U.S. citizenship]" while "evading all taxation and all duties of citizenship."[40] This pessimism was shared by Lebanese economists of the time. Writing in 1927, Alsharif Munir argued that the region's economic woes were exacerbated as much by "the importation of millionaires from abroad" as by slow growth in local manufacturing.[41]

Low wages also presented a problem, frustrating the desires of émigré investors to mechanize textile production. A 1924 project to introduce power looms in Damascus failed because manufacturers were unable to pay sufficient wages to retain weavers with technical expertise.[42] Noting this problem, *al-Majalla al-Tijariyya al-Suriyya al-Amrikiyya* argued that imposing a minimum wage was crucial for Syria's economic revival. The journal argued, "If a man works, he does so not only to improve his own condition but also the material conditions of his country, raising his nation's standard of life." [43] Skilled weavers were likelier to leave for the mahjar, where wages were higher, than they were to remain in Syria or Lebanon where "laws regulating the number of hours or a minimum wage do not exist."[44] As the industry flagged in the United States and immigration quotas mounted, more workers went to Mexico, Central America, Brazil, or Argentina.

Meanwhile, the early 1930s were another moment of labor unrest in the mahjar, as Syrian workers again shuttered New York City garment factories and New Jersey silk plants. In 1933, a round of ILGWU strikes closed twenty-five Syrian negligee factories. "The strike started brewing at the firm of Barsa and Company [just] as it did in 1919," the *Syrian World* reported, "as the union's Syrian organizer, Fred Habib, campaigned among the garment workers."[45] Then working for the Barsa plant, Habib pushed for Syrian shops across the city to observe the new minimum wage laws established under the National Recovery Act (NRA).[46] The usual methods were employed: thousands of workers left their machines, gathered in the streets, and proceeded from factory to factory, compelling others to stop work and join the strike. "Jebaily-Lonschein was the first firm to be invaded by the strike leaders and then quickly the workers from every other firm were lined up, the majority of them forced to join the union by threats. The workers, most of whom are Syrian women, are snatched at the doorway of a building and bundled into waiting taxi cabs. The employers themselves are bewildered, not knowing how the strike will end, not even having heard officially of the terms to be demanded." Invoking the coercion of Syrian women from their sewing machines, the *Syrian World* likened the industrial action to kidnapping, repeating well-worn tropes about compliant workers being "forced to join" a strike by violent threats. These narratives echo the public statements of bosses. George Kateb, for instance, claimed ILGWU Local 62 was "hiring gangsters" to expel workers from his factory. Michael Hadad told the *Syrian World* that "he was going to fight to the last." C. N. Macksoud said his workers had been "forced to join" the union. Macksoud, then president of the Negligee Manufacturing Association in New York, was the man ILGWU was calling to the bargaining table.[47]

The *Syrian World*'s pro-management stance shifted over the four weeks of this strike, especially as its reporters discovered that "according to our investigation, Syrian negligee manufacturers pay the lowest wages in the industry." Skilled cutters, for instance, were paid $12–$17 in Syrian shops, compared to the $40–$50 their counterparts earned in closed union shops. Unskilled operatives were paid as little as $6 per week, less than half of the new $13 minimum wage mandated by the NRA. Syrian workers pushed ILGWU demands for a thirty-five-hour week and wages ranging from $25 for operatives to $47 for skilled cutters.[48] When the *Syrian World*'s labor reporter went to ILGWU Local 62's union hall he found it staffed by Syrian women, and "one striker after another denied they had been brought there by coercion, saying they were glad the strike was on." They told him about a Syrian negligee industry that netted $20 million that year, but which paid them only $12–$13 a week. Organizers Fred Habib and Sadie Shalhoub "vehemently denied" rumors that the strike was "a Communist plot."[49] These revelations challenged the *Syrian World*'s pro-management politics. The periodical's editor, Sallum Mukarzil, eventually published his own support for the strikers' demands, noting the strike "involved a majority of Syrian employers and employees [and] there were no radical manifestations, nor stubborn reactionism." He nevertheless added that the 1933 strike "is quite a contrast with another strike in the same industry in 1919, when strife and violence blinded the judgment of many and substituted unreasonableness."[50]

The *Syrian World*'s support for women strikers in 1933 was unprecedented. At the same time, both in this publication and in the Syrian American press generally, the politics of labor paternalism still prevailed. When one reporter's interview revealed that "Syrian manufacturers fear that once the Syrian workers are unionized, they will find that preference will not be given them when union workers are in demand," the *Syrian World* suggested that "if unionization of the Syrian negligee industry is inevitable, they advise that Syrian strikers should make some provision to be given preference with Syrian employers."[51] Editorialist Habib Ibrahim Katibah endorsed this idea, writing, "We are in hearty approval of a suggestion made by a sensible Syrian employer that should the unionization of Syrian workers become inevitable, a provision should be made that Syrian workers have preference of employment with Syrian firms." This preference to keep the Syrian shops Syrian was an explicit claim to command the labor power of the community's women workers. Katibah argued that Syrian Americans had a duty to denounce "evidence of gross abuse from employers" and urged his countrymen to take "a more friendly attitude" toward their striking workers and the NRA, but he also claimed Syrian employers had an ethnic interest to protect their operatives from interloping labor unions. "Almost all nationalities, excepting the Syrians, in this country have recognized the labor unions and benefitted by them," he asserted in 1933. "We commend employers who give preference to their own countrymen, as long as blue-blooded Americans make distinctions against 'foreigners' in employment."[52]

The negligee strike ended with union victory, and a contract ensuring a wage scale of $15 to $42 per 35.5 hour work week.[53] Mukarzil congratulated "both employers and employees [who] behaved in the best traditions of eastern wisdom" in negotiations, adding "any strike is an abnormal condition which should be avoided as much as possible."[54] Six weeks later, 2,000 Syrian workers led another successful strike in Paterson, New Jersey, in protest of minimum wage violations by silk manufacturers there. The American Federation of Labor local leading the strike told the press that "the Syrians of Paterson are like one big family." They worked together and went on strike together.[55] Such instances of labor solidarity belie the racial stereotypes employed by union historians during this period, who continued to assert that Syrian immigrants were "industrially stagnant ... completely lacked a background in labor ideology," and "had to be taught that as wage earners they had certain economic interests which they had to defend as a solidly organized group."[56] Syrian labor was both powerful and unmentionable.

> ... the third man is a dead man, and yet he speaks to
> live men all the time. *Answer: writing in a book.*[57]

John Ramey is buried in Lawrence, Massachusetts; his grave marker bears the words, "a victim of the 1912 textile strike."[58] For a century, Ramey's life history has served as the emblem of working-class life in the Arab American mahjar, a counternarrative that offers relief from the hegemonic histories of peddlers, proprietors, and public men whose papers dominate the diaspora's archives. As a young man whose death was an act of defiance against a racial regime upheld by American employers, Ramey's history is individualized. He is a masculinist hero, a striker whose union affiliation has since been obscured, one of three martyrs at the strike for Bread and Roses. Because his bosses were American and not Syrian, his story was intelligible. Because Ramey is rendered alone, he is made exceptional; because he is exceptional, he is contained. The mahjar's larger labor history remains unmentionable, because it is a history of collective action, strategic invisibility, effacement of origins, and a struggle between labor and capital that occurred within an ethnic community. As this book has argued, elite cultural politics governed when and whether Syrian labor histories were put to print. Retrieving working class formation in the mahjar has required pulling it from the hegemonies of this diaspora's archives. It is not enough to call these hidden histories; the historian must also account for the class politics of hiding.

Unmentionability was both a coercive force for labor control and a crucial survival strategy for textile workers in the mahjar. In the woolens mills, weaving factories, and garment shops of America, Syrian workers understood the consequences of being observed organizing among the radical wings of the labor movement. American manufacturers and their political allies customarily threatened Syrian labor organizers with removal. Syrian activists had to navigate around the stock racial trope of the bomb-throwing anarchist, even when their white bosses were the ones planting dynamite. In Massachusetts mill towns, Syrian workers found safety in numbers, organizing within trusted ethnic spaces, nurturing mutual aid networks, and liaising with labor unions through representatives who were invulnerable to employer retaliation. In New York City's Garment District, Syrian women workers joined pickets in numbers large enough to take a strike general, interfere with the industry's profitability, and impose terms on unorganized kimono shops. During times of industrial peace, mutual aid societies pooled resources, provided social insurance, and served the working class as a powerful redistributive institution. Interracial solidarity was central to Syrian labor organizing when it came to coordinating work stoppages, but otherwise workers performed most of their organizational work within the ethnic community, raising bail money, paying strike wages, feeding picketers, and hosting strike meetings while opting out of formal union politics. If Syrian workers appear in the mahjar's counterarchives as isolated individuals, they appear only as staggering aggregates in union records. This leaderless, intradiasporic quality to Syrian American labor organizing was a self-protective strategy, a play on unmentionability that makes sense given the specific risks that Syrian immigrants faced and the reality that many of them held strong diasporic ties to their Syrian employers.

At the other end of the supply chain, Syrian textile peddlers also managed public perceptions of their work, especially in the borderlands where racial passing was a core facet of the business. Carrying multiple passports and patronage letters, and staying off trading blacklists, required both local expertise and transnational savvy. Borderlands peddlers navigated in zones of migration interdiction as U.S. and Mexican authorities expanded their surveillance of cross-border travel. Success in this setting required that peddlers be instantly recognizable as agents of American commerce, and unworthy of mention otherwise. This book has asserted that peddlers were also textile workers, representing the logistics side of a supply chain where manufacturers increasingly controlled the flow of raw material, piece goods, and capital investment between the mahjar and supply zones in the North Atlantic, Asia, and the Middle East.

Even the ascendant merchant-manufacturer class operated in a world which demanded a strategic politics of mention and omission. In part, this book is an economic history that addresses the emergence, domination, and hegemony of transnational textile elites, Syrian merchant firms that began as small workshops or importing businesses in the Americas. By the 1920s, these businesses had expanded into global firms by virtue of international connections, diasporic labor control, and a timely geopolitical alignment with American capitalist expansion abroad. In this period, Syrian American firms commanded not only a hemispheric industry in kimonos, negligees, and white goods, but also monopolized Madeiran hand-embroidered linens and held controlling shares of Philippine undergarments, Chinese laces and white goods, and Japanese export silks. But effacement of origins was a key part of the business, both the origins of the goods and of their Syrian producers. On Madeira Island, embroidery workers protesting poor wages pointed to the Syrian ethnicity of their owners. Firms like Alexander J. Hamrah and Co., K. W. Saydah, and the Mallouk Corporation asserted their American nationality, lobbied the U.S. Consulate, and situated themselves as agents of America's economic mission in the world. But Madeiran resentment of foreign merchant control precipitated the Syrians' abrupt departure. Only a few Syrian firms remained after 1925, rebranding themselves and becoming less recognizably Syrian.

Capturing the diasporic interplay among Syrian industrial workers, peddlers, and merchant-manufacturers in the Atlantic textile industries, this book has sought to make mention of uncomfortable intersections of patriarchy, racialization, and respectability politics as facets of Arab American class formation. Plotting these actors across an expanding hemispheric supply chain around their shared business—the weaving, cutting, stitching, and selling of garments and textile goods—clarifies the role of the mahjar as a zone of economic production where transnational networks conditioned industrial shop culture as well as labor activism. I have also plotted a Syrian class politics that set itself against the hegemony of upwardly mobile commercial elites disproportionately represented by the mahjar's print culture, while considering the ways that Arab Americans identified one another not only as migrants, but as workers. This is a powerful caution against overdetermining the act of migration as *the* moment around which overseas Syrians arranged the rest of their lives. Syrians everywhere engaged in the manufacture and movement of textiles. This work was so common, it was unremarkable, but it was also recognizable. Whether they met on the factory floor, on steamships, on the railways, on opposing sides of picket lines, or on the U.S.-Mexico border, Syrians working on all sides of the Arab Atlantic recognized one another by their position within the mahjar's textile industry. Sometimes this act of recognition passed by subtly, silently among friends. Other times it occurred more forcefully, in acts of defiance between workers and bosses. And in a mahjar where the Syrians' right to remain was still challenged, such rebellions, though seen and heard, went unmentioned.

NOTES

Introduction

1. Howard Barrett Wilson, "Notes of Syrian Folk-Lore Collected in Boston," *Journal of American Folklore* 16, no. 62 (1903): 135.

2. Ramy's death certificate declares he was twenty years old. His grave marker (installed by the American Lebanese Awareness Association later) estimates he was sixteen or seventeen. 1913 Congressional testimony records him variously as sixteen, eighteen, or twenty; notably, John's parents were not among those who testified. The Massachusetts State Guard's 1912 incident report was neither released to city police nor made public. Additional speculation about Ramey's age is fueled by two trends: the regularity with which immigrant workers overreported their ages to secure adult wages and the will of legislators seeking to expand or limit the use of child operatives in mills. John Ramey Certificate of Death, January 30, 1912, Commonwealth of Massachusetts, County of Essex, book 12, page 12, no. 129, Lawrence History Center, Arab American Collection (hereafter LHC/AAC); communication with Kathy Flynn, October 23, 2021, Lawrence History Center, Lawrence, Massachusetts.

3. There was a version where John Ramey became a cautionary tale. The daughter of Sicilian mill workers, Laura Peters recalls her parents warning her not to be out late because of "that Syrian boy from Elm Street" felled by bayonet. Ramey's ghost haunted her childhood. Laura Peters Oral History, Lawrence, MA; Faris and Yamna Naff Arab-American Collection Archives Center, National Museum of American History (hereafter NMAH/NC), box 80, folder 19.

4. Ramey's biography appears in generations of historiography, one of a sparse number of Syrian workers' life histories linked by a clear citational chain. In chronological order, see Evelyn Menconi, "The Bread and Roses Strike: Syrian

Connections," *William G. Abdalah Library Newsletter* (Fall 1987): 1–3, LHC/AAC, box 2, folder 6; Michael W. Suleiman, "The Arab American Left," in *The Immigrant Left in the United States*, ed. Dan Georgakas and Paul Buhle (Albany: State University of New York Press, 1996), 242–43; Evelyn Shakir, *Bint Arab: Arab and Arab American Women in the United States* (Westport, CT: Praeger, 1997), 48; Bruce Watson, *Bread and Roses: Mills, Migrants, and the Struggle for the American Dream* (New York: Penguin, 2006), 150; Elizabeth Boosahda, *Arab-American Faces and Voices: The Origins of an Immigrant Community* (Austin: University of Texas Press, 2010), 3–26; Ethan Snow, "Voices of Labor Militancy in Lawrence, 1912–1931," in *The Great Lawrence Textile Strike of 1912: New Scholarship on the Bread and Roses Strike*, ed. Robert Forrant and Jurj Siegenthaler (New York: Taylor and Francis, 2014), 135–53; Donald Cole, *Immigrant City: Lawrence, Massachusetts, 1845–1921* (Chapel Hill: University of North Carolina Press, 2017), 180; Khayrallah Center for Lebanese Diaspora Studies, "Legacies of Labor: Lebanese Workers in America, Lawrence Massachusetts," 2018; and Dominique Cadinot, "Integrated Laborers but Marginal Figures: The Untold Story of Early Syrian-American Factory Workers," *Labor History* (2022): 234–47. Evelyn Menconi originally credits Lawrence Immigrant City Archivist Eartha Dengler for this biography, which was also the focus of a 1989 ethnic history exhibit put together by the Lawrence Lebanese American Awareness Society.

5. Though Arab migrants were usually referred to as "Syrian" during this period, the term denoted an ethnic, racial identity across the Americas, both before and during the establishment of League of Nations Mandates in Syria, Lebanon, and Palestine. This book uses the term capaciously, as is typical in historical writing on the mahjar. However, the "Syrian" community was a blended one, comprising Lebanese, Palestinian, and Syrian immigrants; where possible, I identify the origins of individuals named in this book.

6. Philip K. Hitti, *The Syrians in America* (New York: Doran Company, 1924), 56.

7. Habib Ibrahim Katibeh and Farhat Jacob Ziadeh, *Arabic-Speaking Americans* (New York: Institute of Arab American Affairs, 1946), 5.

8. Hitti, *The Syrians in America*, 57.

9. Mae Ngai, "The Architecture of Race in American Immigration Law: A Reexamination of the Reed Johnson Act of 1924," *Journal of American History* 86, no. 1 (1999): 67–70.

10. James R. Barrett, *History from the Bottom Up and Inside Out: Ethnicity, Race, and Identity in Working Class History* (Durham, NC: Duke University Press, 2017), 127.

11. "Silks: Mixed Situation Develops When Paterson Mills Open for Work, Radicals Refuse to go in until Eight O'clock," *Women's Wear* 19, no. 29 (August 4, 1919), 6–7, 21.

12. Katibeh and Ziadeh, *Arabic-Speaking Americans*, 7.

13. Sallum Mukarzil, *Tarikh al-Tijara al-Suriyya al-Amrikiyya* (New York: Matbaʿat al-Suriyya al-Amrikiyya al-Tijariyya, 1921), 20.

14. Alixa Naff, *Becoming American: The Early Arab Immigrant Experience* (Carbondale: Southern Illinois University Press, 1985), 128–61. Evelyn Shakir challenges this tendency in *Bint Arab*, 46–47, as does Sarah M.A. Gualtieri, "Gendering the Chain Migration Thesis: Women and Syrian Transatlantic Migration, 1878–1924," *Comparative Studies of South Asia, Africa and the Middle East* 24, no. 1 (2004): 71–74.

15. Gualtieri, "Gendering the Chain Migration Thesis," 67–78.

16. Charlotte Karem Albrecht, *Possible Histories: Arab Americans and the Queer Ecology of Peddling* (Oakland: University of California Press, 2023); Stacy D. Fahrenthold, "Ladies Aid as Labor History: Working-Class Formation in the Mahjar," *Journal of Middle East Women's Studies* 17, no. 3 (2021): 327; Sarah M. A. Gualtieri, *Arab Routes: Pathways to Syrian California* (Stanford, CA: Stanford University Press, 2019); Charlotte Karem Albrecht, "An Archive of Difference: Syrian Women, the Peddling Economy, and US Social Welfare, 1880–1935," *Gender & History* 28, no. 1 (2016): 127–49; Sally Howell, *Old Islam in Detroit: Rediscovering the Muslim American Past* (New York: Oxford University Press, 2014); Jacob Rama Berman, *American Arabesque: Arabs, Islam, and the Nineteenth Century Imaginary* (New York: New York University Press, 2012), 180; Akram Fouad Khater, *Inventing Home: Emigration, Gender, and the Middle Class in Lebanon, 1870–1920* (Berkeley: University of California Press, 2001), 82–83; Shakir, *Bint Arab*, 38–41; Naff, *Becoming American*, 128–61. The term Mayflowerism originates in Rudolph Vecoli, "Problems in Comparative Studies of International Emigrant Communities," in *Lebanese in the World*, ed. Albert Hourani and Nadhim Shehadi (London: Centre for Lebanese Studies and I. B. Tauris, 1992), 721.

17. Sarah M. A. Gualtieri, *Between Arab and White: Race and Ethnicity in the Early Syrian American Diaspora* (Oakland: University of California Press, 2009), 66–73; Matthew Frye Jacobsen, *Whiteness of a Different Color: European Immigration and the Alchemy of Race* (Cambridge, MA: Harvard University Press, 1998), 239.

18. David Camfield, "Re-Orienting Class Analysis: Working Classes as Historical Formations," *Science & Society* 68, no. 4 (2005): 422–25.

19. One notable exception is Peter Winn, *Weavers of Revolution: The Yarur Workers and Chile's Road to Socialism* (New York: Oxford University Press, 1986).

20. Nadim Bawalsa, *Transnational Palestine: Migration and the Right of Return Before 1948* (Stanford, CA: Stanford University Press, 2022); Reem Bailony, "Transnationalism and the Syrian Migrant Community: The Case of the 1925 Syrian Revolt," *Mashriq and Mahjar: Journal of Middle East and North African Mi-

gration Studies 1, no. 1 (2013), 9–31; Stacy D. Fahrenthold, "Transnational Modes and Media: the Syrian Press in the Mahjar and Emigrant Activism during World War I," *Mashriq and Mahjar: Journal of Middle East Migration Studies* 1, no. 1 (2013), 32–57; Ilham Khuri-Makdisi, *The Eastern Mediterranean and the Making of Global Radicalism* (Berkeley: University of California Press, 2010).

21. Stacy D. Fahrenthold, *Between the Ottomans and the Entente: The First World War in the Syrian and Lebanese Diaspora, 1908–1925* (New York: Oxford University Press, 2019); Camila Pastor, *The Mexican Mahjar: Transnational Maronites, Jews, and Arabs under the French Mandate* (Austin: University of Texas Press, 2017); Hani Bawardi, *The Making of Arab Americans: From Syrian Nationalism to U.S. Citizenship* (Austin: University of Texas Press, 2014); Simon Jackson, "Diasporic Politics and Developmental Empire: The Syro-Lebanese at the League of Nations," *Arab Studies Journal* 21, no. 1 (2013): 166–90; Andrew Arsan, "'This Age Is the Age of Associations': Committees, Petitions, and the Roots of Interwar Middle Eastern Internationalism," *Journal of Global History* 7, no. 2 (2012): 166–88.

22. A similar pattern shapes narratives about working women in Lebanon, particularly when they went on strike; Malek Hassan Abisaab, "'Unruly' Factory Women in Lebanon: Contesting French Colonialism in the National State, 1940–1946," *Journal of Women's History* 16, no. 3 (2004): 58–60.

23. Naff, *Becoming American*, 109.

24. David Gutman, "Travel Documents, Mobility Control, and the Ottoman State in an Age of Global Migration, 1880–1915," *Journal of the Ottoman and Turkish Studies Association* 3, no. 2 (2016): 347–68; Kemal H. Karpat, "The Ottoman Migration to America, 1860–1914," *International Journal of Middle East Studies* 17, no. 2 (1985): 175–209; Hatice Ayse Polat, "Contending Sovereigns, Contentious Spaces: Illicit Migration and Urban Governance in the Late Ottoman Empire," *Global Histories: A Student Journal* 3, no. 1 (2017): 108–26.

25. Randa Tawil, "A 'Flying Carpet to Doom': Retracing Gender and Orientalism through the Transnational Journeys of a Syrian Migrant Woman, 1912–1949," *Frontiers: A Journal of Women Studies* 43, no. 1 (2022): 120–44.

26. See advice manuals like Jamil Butrus Hulwah, *al-Muhajir al-Suri: wa-ma Yajibu an-Ya'arifahu wa-Ya'amalu bihi* (New York: Matba'at al-Huda, 1909); Ibrahim Hitti, *Khulasat Shar'i al-Muhajara*, and Jamil Butrus Hulwah, *Nizam al-Wilayat al-Mutahida*, and *Huquq wa-Wajibata al-Jinsiyya al-Amrikiyya* (New York: Matba'at al-Huda, n.d.).

27. Engin Akarli, "Ottoman Attitudes towards Emigration," in *Lebanese in the World: A Century of Emigration*, 130–31. See also Khater, *Inventing Home*, 53–56.

28. Céline Regnard, "The Transit Stage as a Migratory Experience: The Syrians in Marseille," in *Migrants and the Making of the Urban-Maritime World: Agency and Mobility in Port Cities, c. 1570–1940*, ed. Christina Reimann and Martin Öhman (New York: Routledge, 2020), 154–155.

29. Regnard, "The Transit Stage as a Migratory Experience," 154.
30. Charles Shagoury family history, private manuscript (s.d.), 3–4.
31. Laurice Maloley, *Destiny by Default: A Memoir* (Boston: First Books, 2002), 10–11.
32. Charles Shagoury family history, private manuscript, 4.
33. Mukarzil, *Tarijkh al-Tijara*, 21.
34. The child, Rose Homsy, later eloped with this couple's son, Albert Homsy, in 1921. Albert had an apron factory where sisters Rose Homsy and Mary Shagoury worked. Maloley, *Destiny by Default*, 35.
35. Maloley, *Destiny by Default*, 11.
36. Laurice Maloley, family history, private manuscript, 3.
37. Charles Shagoury, family history, private manuscript, 2.
38. Regnard, "The Transit Stage as a Migratory Experience," 161.
39. Maloley, *Destiny by Default*, 131. Joseph Shagoury achieved American citizenship in the early 1920s, as did Wadia Shagoury in the 1940s.
40. Batal Family History Narrative, 1–3; LHC/AAC, box 1. Batal's rescuer was Bashara Forzley, a peddler from Karhoun. In his memoirs, Forzley describes a 1908 trip to Jerusalem to visit his mother; it is likely he encountered Batal in Marseille on his way home and connected him with a Worcester cousin, Shaker Syiek. Bashara Kalil Forzley, *An Autobiography of Bashara Kalil Forzley*, ed. Philip Forzley (Worcester: Self-published 1958), 10–11. See also Najib E Saliba, *Emigration from Syria and the Syrian-Lebanese Community of Worcester, Massachusetts* (Antakya Press, 1992).
41. Batal Family History Narrative, 2–3.
42. A representative sample of the historiography on this hemispheric trade includes (in reverse chronological order) John Ermer, "Our Representative on This Island: Local Belonging and Transnational Citizenship among Syrian and Lebanese Cubans, 1880–1980," (Ph.D. dissertation, Florida International University, 2021); Lily Pearl Balloffet, *Argentina in the Global Middle East* (Stanford, CA: Stanford University Press, 2020); Steven Hyland Jr., *More Argentine Than You: Arabic-Speaking Immigrants in Argentina* (Albuquerque: University of New Mexico Press, 2017); Pastor, *The Mexican Mahjar*; Evelyn Alsultany and Ella Shohat, eds., *Between the Middle East and the Americas: the Cultural Politics of Diaspora* (Ann Arbor: University of Michigan Press, 2013); Gildas Brégain, *Syriens et Libanais d'Amérique du Sud, 1918–1945* (Paris: l'Harmattan, 2008); Theresa Alfaro-Velcamp, *So Far from Allah, So Close to Mexico: Middle Eastern Immigrants in Modern Mexico* (Austin: University of Texas Press, 2007); John Tofik Karam, *Another Arabesque: Syrian-Lebanese Ethnicity in Neoliberal Brazil* (Philadelphia: Temple University Press, 2007); Sofia D. Martos, "The Balancing Act: Ethnicity, Commerce, and Politics among Syrian and Lebanese Immigrants in Argentina, 1890–1955" (Ph.D. Dissertation, University of California, Los Angeles, 2007); Maria Narbona, "The Development of Nationalist Identities in French Syria and Lebanon: A Transnational

Dialogue with Arab Immigrants to Argentina and Brazil, 1915–1929" (Ph.D. Dissertation, University of California, Santa Barbara, 2007); Cristina Civantos, *Between Argentines and Arabs: Argentine Orientalism, Arab Immigrants, and the Writing of Identity* (Albany: State University of New York Press, 2006); ʿAbd al-Wahad Akmir, *al-ʿArab fi-l-Arjintin: al-Nashuʾ wa-l-Tatawwur* (Beirut: Markaz Dirasat al-Wahda al-ʿArabiyya, 2000); Liliana Cazorla, *Presencia de inmigrantes Sirios y Libaneses en el desarrollo industrial Argentino* (Buenos Aires: Fundacion los Cedros, 2000); Oswaldo Truzzi, *Patricios: Sirios e libaneses em São Paulo* (São Paulo: Editorial Hucitac, 1997); María Cruz Burdiel de las Heras, *La emigración libanesa en Costa Rica* (Madrid: Cantarabia D.L., 1991); Mintaha Alcuri Campos, *Turco Pobre, Sírio Remediado, Libanês Rico: Trajetória do Imigrante Libanês no Espirito Santo* (Vitória: Instituto Jones dos Santos Neves, 1987); Clark Knowlton, *Sirios e libaneses em São Paulo* (São Paulo: Editoria Anhembi, 1961).

43. Kohei Hashimoto, "Lebanese Population Movement 1920–1939," 107; Charles Issawi, "The Historical Background of Lebanese Emigration, 1800–1914," 29–31; Karpat, "The Ottoman Emigration to America," 183–84; Élie Safa, *L'émigration libanaise* (Ph.D. Dissertation, Université Saint Joseph, Beirut, 1960), 188–91.

44. Anthony Ramey oral history interview with Juliet Bistany, Methuen, MA, June 5, 1985; LHC/OH121–121A. Anthony and Maria Ramey were married in Lebanon in April 1925.

45. Andrew Arsan, *Interlopers of Empire: The Lebanese Diapora in Colonial French West Africa* (Oxford: Oxford University Press, 2014); William Gervase Clarence-Smith, "Middle Eastern Migrants in the Philippines: Entrepreneurs and Cultural Brokers," *Asian Journal of Social Science* 32, no. 3 (2004): 425–57.

46. Balloffet, *Argentina in the Global Middle East*; Tawil, "ʿA Flying Carpet to Doom',"120–44: Campos, *Turco Pobre*; Cazorla, *Presencia de imigrantes sirios y libaneses*; Edward Curtis, *Muslims of the Heartland: How Syrian Immigrants Made a Home in the American Midwest* (New York: New York University Press, 2022).

47. Marcel Van der Linden, "The Promise and Challenges of Global Labor History," *International Labor and Working-Class History* 82 (2012): 66–67. See also Aviva Chomsky, *Linked Labor Histories: New England, Colombia, and the Making of a Global Working Class* (Durham, NC: Duke University Press, 2008).

48. Emmanuel Wallerstein, "The Rise and Future Demise of the World-Capitalism System: Concepts for Comparative Analysis," *Comparative Studies in Society and History* 16, no. 4 (1974): 387–415; as cited in Nelson Lichtenstein, "The Return of Merchant Capitalism," *International Labor and Working-Class History* 81 (2012): 13–20.

49. Abdallah Hanna, *al-Haraka al-ʿUmmaliyya fi-Suriya wa-Lubnan, 1900–1945* (Damascus: Dar Dimashq, 1973), 12; Munira D. Atyah, "Cotton Textile Industry in Lebanon" (MBA, American University of Beirut, 1964), 12.

50. Khater, "ʿHouse' to 'Goddess of the House,'" 325–48; Malek Abisaab, *Mili-

tant Women in a Fragile Nation (Syracuse, NY: Syracuse University Press, 2010), 9–12; Joel Beinin, *Workers and Peasants in the Modern Middle East* (Cambridge: Cambridge University Press, 2010), 71–73; Donald Quataert, "Labor History and the Ottoman Empire, 1700–1922," *International Labor and Working-Class History* 60 (2001): 93–109; Roger Owen, *The Middle East in the World Economy, 1800–1914* (New York: I. B. Tauris, 1981), 158–61.

51. "Occupation before Coming to the United States of Foreign-Born Females Who Were Sixteen Years of Age or Over at the Time of Coming, by Race of Individual," in *Immigrants in Industries* (Washington D.C.: Government Printing Office, 1911), 33.

52. Abisaab, "'Unruly' Factory Women," 61–62.

53. *Reports of the Industrial Commission on Immigration* (Washington D.C.: Government Printing Office, 1901), 443–44.

54. Joel Beinin describes a similar transition in Egypt in "Egyptian Textile Workers: From Craft Artisans Facing European Competition to Proletarians Contending with the State," in *The Ashgate Companion to the History of Textile Workers, 1650–2000*, ed. Els Hiemstra-Kuperus and Lex Heerma van Voss (Ann Arbor, MI: Taylor and Francis, 2010), 182. See also John T. Chalcraft, *The Striking Cabbies of Cairo and Other Stories: Crafts and Guilds in Egypt, 1863–1914* (Albany: State University of New York Press, 2004), 111–13.

55. Karem Albrecht, *Possible Histories*, 4.

56. Devi Mays, *Forging Ties, Forging Passports: Migration and the Modern Sephardi Diaspora* (Stanford, CA: Stanford University Press, 2020), 10.

57. W. Jett Lauck and Edgar Sydenstricker, "Conditions of Labor in Principal Industries: A Summarization of the Results of Recent Investigations" (New York: Funk & Wagnalls, 1917), 10.

58. Evelyn Shakir, "Syrian-Lebanese Tell Their Story," *Frontiers: A Journal of Women Studies* 7, no. 1 (1983): 11.

59. Sabbagh Family Reunion Book, Arab American National Museum, Dearborn, MI, Evelyn Shakir Collection (herafter AANM/ES), box 1, folder 4.

60. Maloley, *Destiny by Default*, 35.

61. On Jewish American garment workshops, for instance, see Daniel Bender, *Sweated Work, Weak Bodies: Anti-Sweatshop Campaigns and Languages of Labor* (New Brunswick, NJ: Rutgers University Press, 2004), 8.

62. Mukarzil, *Tarihh al-Tijara*, 22–25.

63. Khater, "'House' to 'Goddess of the House,'" 329–31.

64. A similar pattern of supply chain control and accumulation appeared among Ottoman Armenians; see Yasar Tolga Cora, "Female Labor, Merchant Capital, and Resilient Manufacturing: Rethinking Ottoman Armenian Communities through Labor and Business," *Journal of the Economic and Social History of the Orient* 61, no. 3 (2018): 361–95.

65. Sherene Seikaly, *Men of Capital: Scarcity and Economy in Mandate Palestine* (Stanford, CA: Stanford University Press, 2015), 13–15.

66. Seikaly, *Men of Capital*, 20.

67. Charlotte Karem Albrecht, "Narrating Arab American History: The Peddling Thesis," *Arab Studies Journal* 37, no. 1 (2015): 100–17; Berman, *American Arabesque*, 180–82; Naff, *Becoming American*, 199.

68. James L. Gelvin and Nile Green, eds., *Global Muslims in the Age of Steam and Print* (Oakland: University of California Press, 2014); Adam McKeown, "Global Migration, 1846–1940," *Journal of World History* 15, no. 2 (2004): 155–89.

69. Fredy González, *Paisanos Chinos: Transpacific Politics among Chinese Immigrants in Mexico* (Oakland: University of California Press, 2017); Julian Lim, *Porous Borders: Multiracial Migrations and the Law in the U.S.-Mexico Borderlands* (Chapel Hill: University of North Carolina Press, 2017); Adam McKeown, *Melancholy Order: Asian Migration and the Globalization of Borders* (New York: Columbia University Press, 2008).

70. Craig Robertson, *The Passport in America: The History of a Document* (New York: Oxford University Press, 2010).

71. David R. Roediger and Elizabeth D. Esch, *The Production of Difference: Race and the Management of Labor in U.S. History* (New York: Oxford University Press, 2012).

72. David M. Struthers, Kenyon Zimmer, and Peter Cole, eds., *Wobblies of the World: A Global History of the IWW* (London: Pluto Press, 2017); Kenyon Zimmer, *Immigrants against the State: Yiddish and Italian Anarchism in America* (Urbana: University of Illinois Press, 2015).

73. *Reports of the Industrial Commission on Immigration*, 446.

74. *Reports of the Industrial Commission on Immigration*, 445–46.

75. "Escape Bullets and Dynamite: Syrians Near Death in an Attack at Camden," *Boston Globe* March 209, 1910, 9.

76. "Will Waterville Have a Race War? Syrians and Greeks Appear to Have Tribal Hatred for One Another," *Bangor Daily News*, August 15, 1907, 2. See also Eric J. Hooglund, "From the Near East to the Down East," in *Crossing the Waters: Arabic-Speaking Immigrants to the United States Before 1940*, ed. Eric Hooglund (Washington D.C.: Smithsonian Institution Press, 1987), 85–103.

77. "Review of Special Reports: Syrians," in *Reports of the Industrial Commission on Immigration*, xli.

Chapter 1

1. *Reports of the Industrial Commission on Immigration*, 442.

2. "One Man Is Responsible," *Lawrence Evening Tribune*, January 24, 1912, 1; Bruce Watson, *Bread and Roses: Mills, Migrants, and the Struggle for the American Dream* (New York: Penguin, 2010), 104.

3. "Put Match to Dynamite," *Los Angeles Times*, May 29, 1913, 18. Assef's testimony is recorded here, indicating the friend was probably Dr. Iskandar Hajjar.

4. The Syrians arrested: Faris Marad, Joseph Assef, Marc Boched, David Bishara, Mary Bochell, Mary Suizy. One Trinedad Bushon (from Puerto Rico) was also arrested.

5. "Cache of Dynamite in Lawrence Strike," *New York Times*, January 21, 1912, 9. Marad was originally from Jdita in the Bekaa Valley. He was born in 1889, making him twenty-two years old at the time of the dynamite incident. By the 1940s, Marad owned the Farris Café at 41 White St., Lawrence. "Farris Marad," Lawrence, MA, 1942; World War II Draft Cards (Fourth Registration), M2090, entry no. 5434; RG 147, National Archives and Record Administration (hereafter NARA), St. Louis. Farris was married in 1913 to factory operative Lamia S. Lahoud; Marriage Record for Farris Marad Razouk and Lamia Lahoud, Lawrence, January 31, 1913. New England Historic Genealogical Society; Boston; Massachusetts Vital Records, 1911–1915; volume 618, entry 97, p. 6.

6. "Cache of Dynamite," 9.

7. Watson, *Bread and Roses*, 100–101.

8. Melvyn Dubofsky, *We Shall Be All: A History of the Industrial Workers of the World*, abridged edition, ed. Joseph A. McCartin (Urbana: University of Illinois Press, 2000), 136–38.

9. "Cache of Dynamite," 9.

10. Walter Merriam Pratt, *New England Magazine*. Pratt was dispatched to Lawrence for twenty-eight days and later published his criticisms of the militias' handling of the Lawrence strike in a memoir titled *Tin Soldiers?* (1912), capitalization in original.

11. Lawrence police seized illegal *araq* in the tenements and jailed its Syrian distillers. State Department of Health in Massachusetts, "Fortieth Annual Report of the State Board of Health of Massachusetts, 1910" (Boston, 1911), 374.

12. "Doubt Dynamite Case," *Boston Globe*, January 23, 1912, 4.

13. "High Rents Behind Lawrence Strike," *New York Times*, February 1, 1912, 3.

14. Michael Mark Cohen, *The Conspiracy of Capital: Law, Violence, and American Popular Radicalism in the Age of Monopoly* (Amherst: University of Massachusetts Press, 2019), 142–88; Erik Loomis, *A History of America in Ten Strikes* (New York: The New Press, 2018), 120–45; Peter Cole, David Struthers, and Kenyon Zimmer, eds., *Wobblies of the World: A Global History of the IWW* (London: Pluto Press, 2017); Robert Forrant and Jurj Siegenthaler, eds., *The Great Lawrence Textile Strike of 1912: New Scholarship on the Bread and Roses Strike* (Amityville, NY: Baywood Publishing, 2014); Watson, *Bread and Roses*; Ardis Cameron, *Radicals of the Worst Sort: Laboring Women in Lawrence, Massachusetts, 1860–1912* (Urbana: University of Illinois Press, 1993); Peter B. Cole, *Immigrant City: Lawrence, Massachusetts, 1845–1921* (Chapel Hill: University of North Carolina Press, 1963).

15. Stefano Luconi, "Crossing Borders on the Picket Line: Italian-American Workers and the 1912 Strike in Lawrence, Massachusetts," *Italian Americana* 28, no. 2 (2010): 149–61; James R. Green, *The World of the Worker: Labor in Twentieth Century America* (Urbana: University of Illinois Press, 1998), 67–99.

16. In addition, French consular estimates from 1920 recorded an estimated 3,150 Syrians and Lebanese in Boston and 1,448 in Worcester, but their data did not include a count for Lawrence and their Fall River estimate (971) was certainly too low; see Kohei Hashimoto, "Lebanese Population Movement 1920–1939," table A.4, 95. Najib Saliba estimates Worcester's Syrian community was 2,000 people by 1930 in *Emigration from Syria and the Syrian-Lebanese Community of Worcester, Massachusetts* (Antakya Press, 1992), 26–27. The Fall River *Evening Standard* counted 2,400 Syrians lived in Fall River in 1916, 35 percent of them working in the town's cotton mills and dress factory; "Assyrians Urged to Be Citizens: 2400 Here," *Evening Standard* (Fall River, MA), February 28, 1916, 2.

17. Massachusetts Bureau of Statistics, "Forty-Third Annual Report on the Statistics of Labor for the Year 1912," (Boston 1913), 54. Twenty-five percent of those counted in 1895 were children younger than sixteen.

18. Massachusetts Bureau of Statistics, "Forty-Third Annual Report," 63.

19. Nagib T. Abdou, *Dr. Abdou's Travels in America* (Self-published, 1910), 65.

20. Daniel Goldberg, *A Tale of Three Cities: Labor Organization, and Protest in Paterson, Passaic, and Lawrence, 1916–1921* (New Brunswick, NJ: Rutgers University Press, 1989), 89–91.

21. Sarah M.A. Gualtieri, "Gendering the Chain Migration Thesis: Women and Syrian Transatlantic Migration, 1878–1924," *Comparative Studies of South Asia, Africa and the Middle East* 24, no. 1 (2004): 67–78.

22. Rosaline Beshara Habeeb oral history interview with Juliet Bistany, Methuen, MA, June 12, 1985. Lawrence History Center, Oral History Collection, tape 124 (hereafter LHC/OH124).

23. Roger Aziz oral history interview with Paul Hudon, Lawrence, MA, June 30, 1979, LHC/OH46.

24. Anthony Ramey oral history interview with Juliet Bistany, Methuen, MA, June 5, 1985, LHC/OH121–121A.

25. Anthony Ramey, LHC/OH121. Anthony trails off after "everybody who came from" in the original. Ramey was born in Lawrence in 1906; he was a butcher and member of the Syrian Young Men's Association in town.

26. Abdou, *Dr. Abdou's Travels*, 68.

27. Abdou, *Dr. Abdou's Travels*, 77.

28. Massachusetts Bureau of Statistics, "Forty-First Annual Report on the Statistics of Labor for the Year 1910," (Boston: Wright and Potter Printing Co., 1911), 295. Philip Hitti's 1924 estimates for each of these rites across the entire United

States were as follows: Maronites: 90,000; Greek Orthodox: 85,000; and Melkites: 10,000; Philip K. Hitti, *The Syrians in America* (New York: Doran and Co., 1924), 62.

29. In a 1912 interview, Rev. Clark Carter of the Lawrence City Mission attributed the arrival of Syrians in Lawrence to the presence of W. E. Wolcott, a Presbyterian minister. Wolcott was the son of Rev. Samuel Wolcott, who was a missionary in Beirut and the head of the Congregational College there; "The Lawrence Mill Workers: Carter Tells How the Foreign Element in the City Has Grown Up," *Boston Evening Transcript,* February 1, 1912, 5.

30. "Forty-First Annual Report on the Statistics of Labor," 295–97. On Turkish workers, see Işil Acehan, "'Ottoman Street' in America: Turkish Leatherworkers in Peabody, Massachusetts," *International Review of Social History* 54 (2009): 19–44.

31. "Forty-First Annual Report on the Statistics of Labor," 297.

32. Adele Younis, *The Coming of the Arabic-Speaking People to the United States* (New York City: Center for Migration Studies, 1995), 205. Linda Jacobs cites an additional early periodical Ghusn Ghusn started in 1905, *al-Bustan*, in *Strangers No More: Syrians in the United States, 1880–1900* (New York: Kalimah Press, 2019), 205. Ghusn Ghusn's son, Yusuf Ghusn, also founded *al-Fajr* as a young man before moving to New York to become editor of *Mirat al-Gharb* in 1937.

33. Anthony Ramey, LHC/OH121A.

34. "High Rents Behind Lawrence Strike," 3.

35. State Department of Health in Massachusetts, *Fortieth Annual Report of the State Board of Health of Massachusetts, 1908* (Boston, 1909), 705.

36. W. Jett Lauck and Edgar Sydenstricker, "Conditions of Labor in Principal Industries: A Summarization of the Results of Recent Investigations" (New York: Funk & Wagnalls, 1917), 161.

37. Juliet Bistany, LHC/OH120.

38. Anthony Ramey, LHC/OH121.

39. Thomas Kattar and Victoria Kattar oral history interview with Juliet Bistany, Lawrence, MA, June 22, 1985, LHC/OH131.

40. Thomas Kattar, LHC/OH131.

41. Juliet Bistany oral history interview with Mary Blewett, Lowell, MA, May 21, 1985, LHC/OH120.

42. Commonwealth of Massachusetts, "1907 Senate Bill 0250. Continuation of the Investigation of Conditions Affecting the Health or Safety of Employees in Factories and Other Establishments," Boston, 1907, 39–41.

43. Massachusetts District Police, "Report of the Chief of the Massachusetts District Police, for the Year Ending December 31, 1903, Including the Inspection and Detective Departments," Boston 1904, 57.

44. "High Rents Behind Lawrence Strike," 3.
45. Roger Aziz, LHC/OH46.
46. "High Rents Behind Lawrence Strike," 3. See also William Moran, *The Belles of New England: The Women of the Textile Mills and the Families Whose Wealth They Wove* (New York: St. Martin's Press, 2002), 183.
47. Massachusetts Bureau of Statistics, "Forty-Third Annual Report," 61.
48. Mary Ead oral history interview with Jonas Stundza, Lawrence, MA, June 29, 1979, LHC/OH33.
49. Massachusetts Bureau of Statistics, "Forty-Third Annual Report," 61–62.
50. Inéz Valdez, "Socialism and Empire: Labor Mobility, Racial Capitalism, and the Political Theory of Migration," *Political Theory* 49, no. 6 (2021): 12–13.
51. "The Padrone System and Common Labor: The Syrians," in *Reports of the U.S. Industrial Commission on Immigration*, volume 15 (Washington D.C.: Government Printing Office, 1901), 445–46. On nativist complaints about contract labor during this period, see Hidetaka Hirota, *Expelling the Poor: Atlantic Seaboard States and the Nineteenth Century Origins of American Immigration Policy* (New York: Oxford University Press, 2017); Andrew Urban, *Brokering Servitude: Migration and the Politics of Domestic Labor in the Long Nineteenth Century* (New York: New York University Press, 2017).
52. John Golden testimony to Mr. Stanley, March 1912, United States Congress, House, Committee on Rules. *The Strike at Lawrence, Mass. Hearings Before the Commission on Rules of the House of Representatives on House Resolutions 409 and 433, March 2–7, 1912* (Washington, D.C.: Government Printing Office, 1912), 82–83. Golden's UTW had also been trying for years to organize AWC's skilled workers, only to be "instantly stamped on by mill superintendents and their subordinates"; see Dubofsky, *We Shall Be All*, 135.
53. Robert Asher and Charles Stephenson, "American Capitalism, Labor Organization, and the Racial-Ethnic Factor: An Exploration," in *Labor Divided: Race and Ethnicity in United States Labor Struggles, 1835–1960*, ed. Robert Asher and Charles Stephenson (Albany: State University of New York Press, 1990), 11–25.
54. James Barrett and David R. Roediger, "Inbetween Peoples: Race, Nationality, and the 'New Immigrant' Working Class," in *History from the Bottom Up and Inside Out: Ethnicity, Race, and Identity in Working Class History*, ed. James R. Barrett (Durham, NC: Duke University Press, 2017), 169.
55. E. G. Dunnell, "Industry a Civilizing Force" 36, no. 16, 302; reprinted from *Gunton's Magazine* March 1904 issue.
56. Rudolph J. Vecoli, "Anthony Capraro and the Lawrence Strike of 1919," in *Labor Divided: Race and Ethnicity in United States Labor Struggles, 1835–1960*, ed. Robert Asher and Charles Stephenson (Albany: State University of New York Press, 1990), 267–70.

57. Dubofsky, *We Shall Be All*, 132–33.

58. Watson, *Bread and Roses*, 21–22.

59. "Textile Workers on Anxious Seat," *Lawrence Telegram*, January 5, 1912, 4; as cited by Watson, *Bread and Roses*, 23; Phillips Russell," "The Dynamite Job at Lawrence," *International Socialist Review* 1912, 310–11; Dubofsky, *We Shall Be All*, 135–36.

60. Samuel Lipson testimony to Mr. Berger, Committee on Rules. *The Strike at Lawrence*, 34.

61. Ray Stannard Baker, "The Revolutionary Strike," *American Magazine* June 1912, 2; as cited by Watson, *Bread and Roses*, 20.

62. "Mob Runs Riots in Mills at Lawrence: Foreign Employes [sic] Drive Men and Women Out of Four Plants," *Boston Globe*, January 13, 1912, 1.

63. "Big Strike in New England," *Industrial Worker* 3, no. 44 (January 25, 1912): 1.

64. Clarise A. Poirier, "The Committee of Ten: The Local Heroes Who Faced Lawrence's Mill Men and Won in 1912," in *The Great Lawrence Textile Strike of 1912: New Scholarship on the Bread and Roses Strike*, ed. Robert Forrant and Jurg Siegenthaler (Amityville, NY: Baywood Publishing, 2014), 48–49.

65. Iskendar Hajjar, wife Susan E. Hajjar, adopted son William F. Hajjar, Lawrence, enumeration district 214, Fourteenth Census of the United States 1920; T625, roll 689, page 23b; RG 29, NARA. Susan Hajjar was a Canadian American, naturalized in Lawrence in 1915.

66. "The Congregational Circle," *The Congregationalist and Christian World* vol. 100, May 6, 1915, 576. Also LHC/PC, "Syrian Protestant Church."

67. Massachusetts Grand Lodge of Masons Membership Card, Iskandar Abdalla Hajjar, February 7, 1910; New England Historic Genealogical Society, Boston, MA.

68. "al-Hafle al-Suriyya li-ʿUmal Sharikat al-Suf al-Amrikiyya," *Al-Fajr* March 19, 1921, 2. In 1921, these men were cited as representing the Syrian workers of AWC: Wadiʿ Baʿqlini, Asʿad Hajjar, Najib Husrani, Amin Abinader, Yusuf Hatem, Salim Qadri, Yusuf Haddad, Jurj Skaff, Yusuf al-Hajjar, Halim Shibli, Ilya Nafiʿ, Yusu Saʿad Nassif, Faris Yusuf, and Khalil Niqula ʿAssi.

69. Cole, *Immigrant City*, 188; Ken Skulski, *Images of America: Lawrence, Massachusetts*, vol. 2 (Arcadia Publishing), 52.

70. Passport application for James Brox, Boston, May 31, 1900; U.S. Passport Applications, 1795–1925 (hereafter M1490), roll 553, no. 25945; NARA. James's passport application was made the week of his naturalization, in preparation for a one-year trip to return to Zahle. Achieving U.S. citizenship appears to have ensured that James would be allowed to return to the United States. See also naturalization petition for James Brox, Boston, May 29, 1900; Index to New England Naturalization Petitions, roll 52, no. B620; M1299, NARA.

71. Ardis Cameron, "Comments on 'Cleansing History,'" *Radical History Review* 65 (1996), 91–97.

72. James Brox was president of the Syrian National Club of Lawrence in 1919; see *Lawrence City Directory, 1919* (R. L. Polk and Company, 1919), 91. Before the Bread and Roses Strike, James also served as president of the Lawrence Young Men of Zahle, *Lawrence Directory, 1911*, 65.

73. Both men were from Zahle, according to Edwin Fenton's interview with James Brox. Edwin Fenton, *Immigrants and Unions, a Case Study: Italians and American Labor, 1870–1920* (New York: Arno Publishing, 1975), 355–56. Shaheen was also the IWW local's treasurer.

74. Akram Khater, "'Like a Wolf Who Fell upon Sheep': Arab Diaspora and Religion in America," *Diaspora: A Journal of Transnational Studies* 21, no. 1 (2021): 9; Dominique Cadinot, "Integrated Laborers but Marginal Figures: The Untold Story of Early Syrian-American Factory Workers," *Labor History* (2022), 1–12.

75. Justus Ebert, *The Trial of a New Society* (Cleveland: Ohio I.W.W., s.d.), 70. Capitalization and emphasis in the original.

76. The Presbyterian Reverend Clark Carter and Irish Catholic priest Father O'Reilly publicly opposed the strike, discouraging their parishioners from civil disobedience; Dubofsky, *We Shall Be All*, 142. St. Anthony's Father Jibrail al-Bustany was a vocal supporter of strikers, particularly following John Ramey's death; see Khater, "'Like a Wolf Who Fell upon Sheep,'" 9. The reverend at the Lithuanian church, St. Francis, also supported the strikers; James J. Kenneally, "Catholic Clerical Quandary: The Lawrence Strike of 1912," *American Catholic Studies* 117, no. 4 (2006), 45.

77. Fenton, *Immigrants and Unions*, 345n192.

78. Cameron, *Radicals of the Worst Sort*, 126.

79. Evelyn Shakir, *Bint Arab: Arab and Arab American Women in the United States* (Westport, CT: Praeger, 1997), 48.

80. Dubovsky, *We Shall Be All*, 141.

81. Anne F. Mattina and Dominique Ciavettone, "Striking Women: Massachusetts Mill Workers in the Wake of Bread and Roses," in *The Great Lawrence Textile Strike of 1912: New Scholarship on the Bread and Roses Strike*, ed. Robert Forrant and Jurg Siegenthaler (Amityville, NY: Baywood Publishing, 2014), 156.

82. "M. Sonian," Lawrence, January 29, 1912; Essex County Jail Records, box 1, case no. 14270; Lawrence History Center (hereafter LHC/ECJ). *Given names removed to protect the privacy of the accused.

83. "A. Yazza," Lawrence, March 7, 1912; LHC/ECJ, box 1, case no. 14342.

84. "P. Ackeryonia," Lawrence, January 31, 1912; LHC/ECJ, box 1, case no. 14272.

85. "V. Lomastro," Lawrence, January 15, 1912; LHC/ECJ, box 1, case no. 14220.

86. "Globe Woman in Lawrence Finds No Suffering among Strikers," *Boston Globe* January 23, 1912, 4.
87. "Globe Woman in Lawrence Finds No Suffering," 4.
88. Cameron, *Radicals of the Worst Sort*, 161–62.
89. "Globe Woman in Lawrence Finds No Suffering," 4.
90. Loretta Hall, *Arab American Voices* (University Park: Pennsylvania State University Press, 2000), 21–23.
91. "Globe Woman in Lawrence Finds No Suffering," 4.
92. "High Rents Behind Lawrence Strike," 3.
93. Shakir, *Bint Arab*, 48.
94. Mattina and Ciavattone, "Striking Women," 154.
95. "Indorse Plan to Meet Mill Owners," *Boston Globe*, January 23, 1912, 4.
96. "Strike Still on at Lawrence," *Industrial Worker* 3, no. 52 (March 21, 1912), 1.
97. Rev. Clark Carter testimony to Representative Thomas Hardwick, March 1912, United States Congress, House, Committee on Rules. *The Strike at Lawrence, Mass. Hearings before the Commission on Rules of the House of Representatives on House Resolutions 409 and 433, March 2–7, 1912* (Washington, D.C.: Government Printing Office, 1912), 376–77.
98. Dubofsky, *We Shall Be All*, 140.
99. Dubofsky, *We Shall Be All*, 141.
100. Massachusetts Bureau of Statistics, "Forty-Third Annual Report," 25.
101. "Cache of Dynamite," 9. Evelyn Menconi adds that John Breen was the man who tipped the police off to the presence of dynamite at Marad's tenement; Menconi, "Bread and Roses, Syrian Connections" unpublished draft dated 1987, 1–2; LHC/AAC, box 2, folder 6.
102. "Sent Another Try at 'Placing,'" *Boston Globe*, January 22, 1912, 2. The third lot, found in a cemetery, was originally destined for Samya's Oak Street home. Bruce Watson claims that Mrs. Samya knew David Rashad, one of Assef's roommates; Watson, *Bread and Roses*, 122.
103. "Doubt Dynamite Case," 4.
104. "Lawrence Slayer Might Be a Soldier," *Boston Globe*, February 4, 1912, 1.
105. "Lawrence Slayer Might Be a Soldier," 1.
106. "Wood Glad to Meet His Men, Replies to Strikers' Statement," *Boston Globe*, January 23, 1912, 4.
107. "W. M. Wood Is Held in Dynamite Plot," *New York Times*, August 31, 1912, 3.
108. Poirier, "The Committee of Ten," 55. Portions of the dynamite conspiracy story are also narrated in exhibitions, including at the Lawrence History Center and Digital Public Library of America, "Bread and Roses Strike of 1912: Two Months in Lawrence, Massachusetts, that Changed Labor History" (April 2013), https://dp.la/exhibitions/breadandroses; and Khayrallah Center for Lebanese Di-

aspora Studies, "Legacies of Labor: Lebanese Workers in Lawrence, Massachusetts" (2018), https://lebanesestudies.ncsu.edu/projects/lawrence.php

109. The name of the press is not included in court filings, but the location suggest he targeted *al-Wafa'*.

110. "Admits He Helped to Plant Dynamite," *New York Times*, May 21, 1913, 4.

111. "Haywood to Lead Lawrence Strikers: Both Sides Remain Firm," *New York Times*, January 23, 1912, 20.

112. "Haywood to Lead Lawrence Strikers," 20.

113. "Joseph Ettor," Lawrence, January 31, 1912, LHC/ECJ, box 1, case no. 14275; "Antonio Giovannitti," Lawrence, January 31, 1912, LHC/ECJ, box 1, case no. 14274.

114. "Troops Surrounded, Checked a Riot," *Boston Globe*, January 30, 1912, 2

115. "One Striker Killed, Two Leaders Held: Ettor and Giovannitti Accused of Being Accessories to Murder in Lawrence," *New York Times*, January 31, 1912, 1.

116. "Second Death in Strike," *Boston Globe*, January 31, 1912, 5. See also Shakir, *Bint Arab*, 48.

117. John Ramey Certificate of Death, January 30, 1912, Commonwealth of Massachusetts, County of Essex, Book 12, Page 12, No. 129, LHC/AAC; Charles Neil, *Report on Strike of Textile Workers in Lawrence, Massachusetts* (Washington, D.C.: Government Printing Office, 1912), 45.

118. "One Striker Killed, Two Leaders Held," 1.

119. Mattina and Ciavettone, "Striking Women," 156.

120. "Ill Feeling by Strikers," *Boston Globe*, January 30, 1912, 2.

121. "One Striker Killed, Two Leaders Held," 1. Capitalization in the original. See Emily Pope-Obeda, "Expelling the Foreign-Born Menace: Immigrant Dissent, the Early Deportation State, and the First American Red Scare," *Journal of the Gilded Age and Progressive Era* 18 (2019): 32–55.

122. "Class War Rages in Lawrence," *Industrial Worker* 3, no. 47 (February 15, 1912), 1. See also Cadinot, "Integrated Laborers But Marginal Figures," 7–8.

123. Dubofsky, *We Shall Be All*, 145–46.

124. Joseph Bedard, Secretary, Textile Workers Strike Committee, "Strike Assistance Needed," *Industrial Worker* 3, no. 46 (February 8, 1912), 4.

125. Lawrence Cappello, "In Harm's Way: The Lawrence Textile Strike's Children's Affair," in *The Great Lawrence Textile Strike of 1912: New Scholarship on the Bread and Roses Strike*, ed. Robert Forrant and Jurg Siegenthaler (Amityville, NY: Baywood Publishing, 2014), 59–78; Watson, *Bread and Roses*, 141–62.

126. Cappello, "In Harm's Way," 61.

127. "Lawrence Strikers Move to Free Ettor," *New York Times*, February 3, 1912, 5.

128. "New Police Head for Lawrence," *Boston Globe*, February 20, 1912, 1.

129. "Textile Workers Active," *Boston Globe*, February 20, 1912, 1.

130. Elizabeth Boosahda, *Arab-American Faces and Voices: The Origins of an Immigrant Community* (Austin: University of Texas Press, 2010), 76–77.

131. "Textile Strike a Revolution," *Industrial Worker* 3, no. 49 (February 29, 1912), 1.

132. Mr. John Dalzell to John J Sullivan, March 1912. United States Congress, House Committee on Rules, *The Strike at Lawrence, Mass. Hearings Before the Commission on Rules of the House of Representatives on House Resolutions 409 and 433, March 2–7, 1912* (Washington, D.C.: Government Printing Office, 1912), 296.

133. John J. Sullivan testimony to Mr. John Dalzell, *The Strike at Lawrence*, 296. Sullivan represented both the Lawrence City Police Department (as acting chief) and the state militia (deputized as assistant marshal by Sweetser) to Congress. Kenneally, "Catholic Clerical Quandary," 45.

134. Cappello, "In Harm's Way," 60–61.

135. "W. M. Wood Held in Dynamite Plot," *New York Times*, August 31, 1912, 3.

136. Excerpts of Samuel Goldberg's testimony, for instance, appeared in "Congressmen Heard Strikers' Children," *New York Times*, March 5, 1912, 5.

137. Samuel Goldberg testimony to Chairman Robert L. Henry, *The Strike at Lawrence*, 139–40.

138. John J. Sullivan testimony to Representative Thomas Hardwick, Committee on Rules. *The Strike at Lawrence*, 344.

139. John J. Sullivan testimony to Representative Thomas Hardwick, *The Strike at Lawrence*, 301.

140. "Strike Still on at Lawrence," *Industrial Worker* 3, no. 52 (March 21, 1912), 1.

141. "Striker Ranks Remain Unbroken," *Industrial Worker* 3, no. 51 (March 14, 1912), 1. Emphasis mine.

142. "Congressmen Heard Strikers' Children," 5.

143. Samuel Lipson testimony to Representative Thomas Hardwick, *The Strike at Lawrence*, 98–99.

144. John Sullivan testimony to Mr. Stanley, *The Strike at Lawrence*, 326.

145. John Sullivan testimony to Mr. Stanley, *The Strike at Lawrence*, 327. The state militia's incident report has not been made public and was never released to the City of Lawrence. Communication with Kathy Flynn, October 23, 2021, Lawrence History Center, Lawrence, Massachusetts.

146. John Sullivan testimony, *The Strike at Lawrence*, 314, spellings in original. Sullivan clarified that he did not hear the utterances, but that "everybody talked about it here, it was a matter of public knowledge in Lawrence."

147. The lawyer had confused Dr. Ibrahim Hajjar with James Brox, two Syrian members of the Committee of Ten. Neither Brox nor Hajjar appeared. Rev. Clark Carter testimony to Mr. Wilson, *The Strike at Lawrence*, 396.

148. Samuel Lipson testimony to Mr. Berger, *The Strike at Lawrence*, 42.

149. Katherine Benton-Cohen, *Inventing the Immigration Problem: The Dillingham Commission and Its Legacy* (Cambridge, MA: Harvard University Press, 2018), 133.

150. Frank Sibley, "Vote to Work in Six Mills," *Boston Globe*, March 15, 1912, 1.

151. Russell, "The Dynamite Job at Lawrence," 311.

152. "al-Sinaʿa wa-l-ʿAmal," *Majalla al-Tijariyya al-Suriyya al-Amrikiyya*, July 1924, 24.

153. "Boston Strike of Clothiers is Successful," *Daily Worker*, August 20, 1924, 2.

154. Young Men of Deir el Kamar society ledger, 462–63, LHC/AAC.

155. "Boston Strike of Clothiers Is Successful," *Daily Worker*, August 20, 1924, 2.

156. Fall River was then home to the second largest Portuguese community in the United States, overwhelmingly comprised of Azorean cotton mill workers; Leo Pap, *The Portuguese-Americans* (Boston: Twayne Publishers, 1981), 62.

157. Robert Minor, "Cotton Mills Strikers Will Continue Fight," *Daily Worker*, February 10, 1925, 2.

158. The following men also served as officers for the Syrian National Club between 1912 and 1927: Fred J. Ghusn, Karim Salem, William Brux, Aziz Hasbany, Joseph Batal; *The Lawrence Directory, 1913* (Boston: RL and Polk, 1913), 68; *The Lawrence Directory, 1919* (Boston: A. L. Cole and Company, 1919), 69. See also Goldberg, *A Tale of Three Cities*, 96; Cole, *Immigrant City*, 188.

159. *The Lawrence Directory, 1919*, 68.

160. Farid Ghusn, "Nahda al-Muntada al-Suri," *al-Fajr*, December 17, 1921, 8. See also "al-Muntada al-Suri al-ʾUmumi," *al-Saʾih*, May 15, 1916, 1–2.

161. Munayyir also wrote political novellas, including one about a French peasant who defies the feudalist social order and his low birth to marry his beloved, printed by Lawrence's *al-Rawda* and dedicated to his father, Faris Tannous al-Munayyir of Qab Ilyas. Khalil Munayyir, *Riwayat al-Thar wa-la-ʿar* (Lawrence: Matbaʿat al-Rawda, 1921), LHC/AAC, box 2.

162. Commonwealth of Massachusetts, *Annual Report of the Department of Public Welfare for the Year Ending November 30, 1929* (Boston: Wright & Potter Printing Co., 1929), 98; Commonwealth of Massachusetts, *Annual Report of the Department of Public Welfare for the Year Ending November 30, 1930* (Boston: Wright & Potter Printing Co., 1930), 102.

163. Arab American National Museum (Dearborn, MI), Michael Suleiman Collection, box 147, Syrian National Club Advertisement in *Fatat Boston*, September 6, 1918, 3. See also Massachusetts House of Representatives No. 1215 (1926), 57.

Chapter 2

1. Reem Bailony, "Donating in the Name of the Nation: Charity, Sectarianism, and the Mahjar," in *Practicing Sectarianism: Archival and Ethnographic Interventions on Lebanon*, ed. Lara Deeb, Tsolin Nalbantian, and Nadya Sbaiti (Stanford, CA: Stanford University Press, 2023), 81–97; Lily Balloffet, "From the Pampa to the Mashriq: Arab-Argentine Philanthropy Networks," *Mashriq and Mahjar: Jour-

nal of Middle East Migration Studies 4, no. 1 (2017): 4–28; Andrew Arsan, " 'This Age Is the Age of Associations': Committees, Petitions, and the Roots of Interwar Middle Eastern Internationalism," *Journal of Global History* 7, no. 2 (2012): 166–88.

2. Stacy D. Fahrenthold, *Between the Ottomans and the Entente: The First World War in the Syrian and Lebanese Diaspora, 1908–1925* (New York: Oxford University Press, 2019), 86. See also Camila Pastor de Maria Campos, "The Great Arab Revolt, Palestine and a Phoenicianist Civilizing Mission: Transregional Debates in the Mexican Mahjar Press," *Revue des mondes musulmanes et de la Méditerranée* 152 (2022): 85–114; Nadim Bawalsa, *Transnational Palestine: Migration and the Right of Return Before 1948* (Stanford, CA: Stanford University Press, 2022).

3. Ann Laura Stoler, "Colonial Archives and the Arts of Governance: on the Content in the Form," in *Refiguring the Archive*, ed. Carolyn Hamilton, Verne Harris, Michéle Pickover, Graeme Reed, Razia Shah, and Jane Taylor (Dordrecht: Springer Netherlands, 2002), 85–86, as cited by Adalaine Holton, "Decolonizing History: Arthur Schomberg's Afrodiasporic Archive," *Journal of African American History* 92, no. 2 (2007): 224.

4. Sonja Luehrmann, *Religion in Secular Archives: Soviet Atheism and Historical Knowledge* (New York: Oxford University Press, 2015), 137–38.

5. Holton, "Decolonizing History," 220.

6. Luehrmann, *Religion in Secular Archives*, 138–39.

7. Rajbir Singh Judge and Jasdeep Singh Brar, "Critique of Archived Life: Toward a Hesitation of Sikh Immigrant Accumulation," *Positions: Asia Critique* 29, no. 2 (2021): 319–46.

8. Sarah M. A. Gualtieri, *Arab Routes: Pathways to Syrian California* (Stanford, CA: Stanford University Press, 2019), 91–109; Suad Joseph, "Arab American Women: Intersectional Genealogies and Trajectories," in *Arab American Women: Representation and Refusal*, ed. Michael W. Suleiman, Suad Joseph, and Louise Cainkar (Syracuse, NY: Syracuse University Press, 2021), 1–17; Jess Bier, "Mapping the Archive for Arab American Women's Labor in the New York Metropolitan Area, 1880–1930," in *Arab American Women: Representation and Refusal*, ed. Michael W. Suleiman, Suad Joseph, and Louise Cainkar, 55–83 (Syracuse, NY: Syracuse University Press, 2021).

9. Gualtieri, *Arab Routes*, 97–98.

10. Evelyn Shakir, "Good Works, Good Times: The Syrian Ladies' Aid Society of Boston, 1917–1932," in *Crossing the Waters: Arabic-Speaking Immigrants to the United States before 1940*, ed. Eric J. Hooglund, 133–43. Washington D.C.: Smithsonian Institution Press, 1987. ; Evelyn Shakir, *Bint Arab: Arab and Arab American Women in the United States* (Westport, CT: Praeger, 1997), 59–65; Alixa Naff, *Becoming American: The Early Arab Immigrant Experience* (Carbondale: Southern Il-

linois University Press, 1985); Elizabeth Boosahda, *Arab-American Faces and Voices: The Origins of an Immigrant Community* (Austin: University of Texas Press, 2003), 131–70.

11. Reem Bailony, "From Mandate Borders to the Diaspora: Rashaya's Transnational Suffering and the Making of Lebanon in 1925," *Arab Studies Journal* 26, no. 2 (2018): 44–73; Balloffet, "From the Pampa to the Mashriq: Arab-Argentine Philanthropy Networks," 5–7; Stacy Fahrenthold, "Sound Minds in Sound Bodies: Transnational Philanthropy and Patriotic Masculinity in *al-Nadi al-Homsi* and Syrian Brazil," *International Journal of Middle East Studies* 46, no. 2 (2014): 259–83.

12. Daniel Soyer, "Mutual Aid Societies and Fraternal Orders," in *A Companion to American Immigration*, ed. Reed Ueda (Malden: Blackwell, 2006), 529.

13. David T. Beito, "Mutual Aid for Social Welfare: The Case of American Fraternal Societies," *Critical Review* 4, no. 4 (1990): 710.

14. Soyer, "Mutual Aid Societies," 529–30; Beito, "Mutual Aid for Social Welfare," 713.

15. "Industrial Condition of Foreign-Born Male Employees in Each Specified Occupation before Coming to the United States, by Race," in *Immigrants in Industries, Parts 3–4, 61st Congress 2d Session 1909–1910, Senate Documents*, vol. 72, 73.

16. However, it is notable that U.S. statistics do not consider the home textile work of Syrian women before arrival; see "Industrial Condition before Coming to the United States of Foreign-Born Males Who Were 16 Years of Age at Time of Coming, by Race of Individual," *Immigrants in Industries, Parts 5–7, 61st Congress 2d Session 1909–1910, Senate Documents*, vol. 73, 31.

17. "Industrial Conditions before Coming to the United States of Foreign-Born Males Who Were 16 Years of Age or Over at Time of Coming, by Race of Individual," *Immigrants in Industries, Parts 8–10, 61st Congress 2d Session 1909–1910, Senate Documents*, vol. 74, 35.

18. Paul D. Garrett and Kathleen A. Purpura. *Frank Maria: A Search for Justice and Peace in the Middle East* (Bloomington, IN: Authorhouse, 2007), 14; Jennifer Guglielmo, *Living the Revolution: Italian Women's Resistance and Radicalism in New York City, 1880–1945* (Chapel Hill: University of North Carolina Press, 2010), 76.

19. "Yearly Earnings of Males 18 Years of Age or Aver, by General Nativity and Race of Individual," *Immigrants in Industries, Senate Documents*, vol. 74, 50.

20. "Affiliation with Trade Unions of Males 21 Years of Age or Over Who are Working for Wages, by General Nativity and Race of Individual," *Immigrants in Industries, Parts 8–10, 61st Congress 2d Session 1909–1910, Senate Documents*, vol. 74, 62.

21. Sarah M. A. Gualtieri, *Between Arab and White: Race and Ethnicity in the Early Syrian American Diaspora* (Oakland: University of California Press, 2009), 52–80.

22. Bahieh Kappaz (Khabbaz) oral history interview with Alixa Naff, Detroit, May 10, 1980. Faris and Yamna Naff Arab-American Collection Archives Center, National Museum of American History (hereafter NMAH/NC), box 277. Kappaz had been previously detained and deported on medical grounds in 1910. Though he is better known for his legal activism in the interwar period, Faris Saleem Malouf's first jobs in Boston were at a glass factory followed by the Thomas G. Plant Shoe factory in Jamaica Plain; Charles Malouf Samaha, *Faris Saleem Malouf (1892–1958): A Voice in the Dark, One Man's Arab American Activism* (Self-published, 2019), 28.

23. Bahieh Kappaz, NMAH/NC, box 277.

24. Zahdi Barsa oral history interview with Alixa Naff, May 21, 1980; NMAH/NC, box 274. Though she never names her employer, it is likely she worked for the Albert Homsy Apron Factory.

25. Nancy L. Green, *Ready-to-Wear, Ready-to-Work: A Century of Industry and Immigrants in Paris and New York* (Durham, NC: Duke University Press), 140–41.

26. On Turks, see "Months Worked during the Past Year by Persons 16 Years of Age or Over Employed Away from Home, by Sex and by General Nativity and Race of Individual," *Immigrants in Industries, Senate Documents*, vol. 74, 147; on Syrians, see "Months Worked during the Past Year by Males 16 Years of Age or Over Employed Away from Home, by General Nativity and Race of Individual," *Immigrants in Industries, Senate Documents*, vol. 74, 271.

27. Jeremiah Whipple Jenks and William Jett Lauck, *The Immigration Problem: A Study of American Immigration Conditions and Needs* (New York: Funk and Wagnalls, 1913), 50–51.

28. Akram Fouad Khater, *Inventing Home: Emigration, Gender, and the Middle Class in Lebanon, 1870–1920* (Berkeley: University of California Press, 2001), 19–48.

29. W. Jett Lauck and Edgar Sydenstricker, "Conditions of Labor in Principal Industries: A Summarization of the Results of Recent Investigations" (New York: Funk & Wagnalls, 1917), 90.

30. "Number and Percent of Households Keeping Boarders or Lodgers, by General Nativity and Race of Head of Household," *Immigrants in Industries, Senate Documents*, vol. 74, 264. See also Shakir, *Bint Arab*, 48–49.

31. Khater, *Inventing Home*, 5–6.

32. Laurice Shagoury Maloley family history, private manuscript, 6–7.

33. Nancy W. Jabbra, "Household and Family Among Lebanese Immigrants in Nova Scotia: Continuity, Change, and Adaptation," *Journal of Comparative Family Studies* 22, no. 1 (1991): 40–41.

34. Charlotte Karem Albrecht, "An Archive of Difference: Syrian Women, the Peddling Economy and U.S. Social Welfare," *Gender and History* 28, no. 1 (2016): 136; William Moran, *The Belles of New England: The Women of the Textile Mills and*

the Families Whose Wealth They Wove (New York: St. Martin's Press, 2002), 179–80.

35. "Number and Percent of Households Keeping Boarders or Lodgers, by General Nativity and Race of Head of Household," *Immigrants in Industries, Senate Documents*, vol. 74, 279.

36. Rates of female labor varied, but as a general trend, roughly half of Arab women (44.3 percent) whose husbands worked in industry also worked themselves. This represents a higher rate of female wage work than other immigrant groups: 30.9 percent (all immigrants) to 44.3 percent (Syrian women); "Wives at Work, by General Nativity and Race of Head of Family," *Immigrants in Industries, Parts 3–4, 61st Congress 2d Session 1909–1910, Senate Documents*, vol. 72, 683. See also Nabeel Abraham and Andrew Shryock, *Arab Detroit: From Margin to Mainstream* (Detroit, MI: Wayne State University Press, 2000), 156–58.

37. "G. Hassoud," Lawrence, October 11, 1912; Lawrence History Center, Essex Country Jail Records (hereafter LHC/ECJ), box 1, case no. 14650. *Given names are removed to protect the privacy of the accused.

38. "E. Saab," Lawrence, April 29, 1913; LHC/ECJ, box 1, case no. 14877.

39. "E. Saab," Lawrence, July 29, 1913; LHC/ECJ, box 1, case no. 148777.

40. Roger Aziz oral history interview with Paul Hudon, Lawrence, MA, June 30, 1979, LHC/OH46.

41. Roger Aziz oral history, LHC/OH46.

42. Roger Aziz oral history, LHC/OH46.

43. Its founders were Aziz A. Aziz, Abdo A. Aziz, Abdo Saliby, Abdalla A. Aziz, Solomon E. Aziz, George A. Peters, Joseph Riashieie, Joseph Farage, and Ferris Jaheely. In 1907, the organizers met in members' homes in the Syrian tenements on Elm and Oak Streets. Lawrence Public Library (hereafter LPL), *United Syrian Charitable Society Fortieth Anniversary Jubilee Program*, 20–21.

44. Early club officers include Kalil Moraway (who served as president several times between 1911 and 1922), Kalil Matta, Nicolas Hassey; *The Lawrence Directory, 1919* (Boston: RL and Polk, 1919), 69.

45. "Al-Maqbura al-Suriyya al-Umumiyya," *al-Wafa'*, March 16, 1909, 3; "al-Akhbar al-Mahliyya," *al-Wafa'*, March 19, 1909, 2–3.

46. Hajjar and Finnegan Undertakers advertisement, *al-Fajr*, March 4, 1922, 6; LCH/AAC.

47. Roger Aziz, LHC/OH46.

48. At time of writing, 372 (about 67 percent) of the grave sites have been photographed and are viewable online: https://www.findagrave.com/cemetery/91762/syrian-cemetery.

49. The Syrian Burial Society was registered at 15 Edinboro Street, under officers Elias H. Maloof, Rasheed A. Maloof, and Charles H. Maloof. Commonwealth

of Massachusetts, *Thirty-Fourth Annual Report: State Board of Charity, Year Ending November 30, 1912* (Boston: Wright & Potter, Co., 1913), 162–63. See also Amy E. Rowe, "A Trace of Arabic in Granite: Lebanese Migration to the Green Mountains, 1890–1940," *Vermont History* 76, no. 2 (2008): 91–129; Rosina Hassoun, "Religion, Family, and Relocation: Arab American Burial Practices," in *Till Death Do Us Part: American Ethnic Cemeteries as Borders Uncrossed*, ed. Allan Amanik and Kami Fletcher (Jackson: University of Mississippi Press, 2020) 247–70.

50. *United Syrian Charitable Society, 40th Anniversary Program*, March 23, 1947, LPL.

51. Roger Aziz, LHC/OH46.

52. Roger Aziz, LHC/OH46. The charter is recorded in Commonwealth of Massachusetts, *Thirty-Fourth Annual Report: State Board of Charity*, 200.

53. Roger Aziz, LHC/OH46.

54. Roger Aziz, LHC/OH46.

55. *al-Fajr*, March 11, 1922, 3, LHC/AAC.

56. *Lawrence Directory, 1904* (Boston: RL and Polk, 1904), 485. Kalil arrived with a Joseph Moraway. The boarding house on 485 Valley recurs in the oral histories taken by the Lawrence History Center as the first place new immigrants settled into before finding housing of their own.

57. Anthony Ramey, LHC/OH121–121A.

58. Anthony Ramey, LHC/OH121A. Anthony never joined the society, but he did join the Young Syrian Men's Association, which was tied to the society and engaged in mutual charity and fundraising.

59. Roger Aziz, LHC/OH46.

60. Graham Auman Pitts, "The Ecology of Migration: Remittances in World War I Mount Lebanon," *Arab Studies Journal* 26, no. 2 (2018): 102–29; Sevan N. Yousefian, "Picnics for Patriots: The Transnational Activism of an Armenian Hometown Association," *Journal of American Ethnic History* 34, no. 1 (2014): 32; Stacy Fahrenthold, "Sound Minds in Sound Bodies," 259–83.

61. Young Men of Deir el Kamar (hereafter YMDK) society ledger, James Shebaby, "History of Young Men of Deir el Kamar and Suburbs," LHC/AAC.

62. YMDK society ledger, 456–61, LHC/AAC.

63. YMDK society ledger, 461–64, LHC/AAC. YMDK member Yusuf al-Tahan founded the Mexico chapter after he moved there from Lawrence in 1920.

64. YMDK society ledger, 432–53, LHC/AAC. This rate is from 1931; it is higher than dues payments would have been in the club's first years.

65. YMDK society ledger,12–13, 28, 452, LHC/AAC.

66. YMDK society ledger, 124, LHC/AAC.

67. Rudolph J. Vecoli, "Anthony Capraro and the Lawrence Strike of 1919," in *Labor Divided: Race and Ethnicity in United States Labor Struggles, 1835–1960*, ed.

Robert Asher and Charles Stephenson (Albany: State University of New York Press, 1990), 269.

68. Daniel Goldberg, *A Tale of Three Cities: Labor Organization, and Protest in Paterson, Passaic, and Lawrence, 1916–1921* (New Brunswick, NJ: Rutgers University Press, 1989), 95–97.

69. Adam Walaszek, "Was the Polish Worker Asleep? Immigrants, Unions, and Workers' Control of America, 1900–1922," *Polish American Studies* 46, no. 1 (1989), 82–83; Ethan J. Snow, "Strike City: An Oral History of the Legacy of Labor Militancy in Lawrence, Massachusetts," (M.A. thesis, University of Massachusetts Lowell, 2012), 46–74.

70. Vecoli, "Anthony Capraro and the Lawrence Strike of 1919," 269–70.

71. Sgt. John H. O'Neil, "Proposed Plan for an Eight Hour Day, Bolshevik Agitation," Boston, MA, January 1–7, 1919, 2; Reports on Radical Activities in New England, 1918–1919, U.S. Military Intelligence Reports: Surveillance of Radicals in the United States, roll 11, series 10110–913, document 558; RG 165, NARA.

72. Green, *Ready-to-Wear, Ready-to-Work*, 52.

73. Goldberg, *A Tale of Three Cities*, 121.

74. "Lawrence Strike Leader Released," *Boston Globe*, February 11, 1919, 1–2; "Conference Today on Lawrence Strike," *Boston Globe*, April 10, 1919, 10; Walaszek, "Was the Polish Worker Asleep?" 89.

75. YMDK society ledger, 465, LHC/AAC.

76. "Trouble with Syrians," *Boston Globe*, April 10, 1919, 10.

77. Goldberg, *A Tale of Three Cities*, 121; Vecoli, "Anthony Capraro and the Lawrence Strike of 1919," 275–76; "Carlo Tresca Smuggled into the City and Out Again Last Night," *Lawrence Telegram*, May 3, 1919. Sponsored by the IWW, the event prompted discord among Syrians who felt the union was responsible for the retaliatory repression they faced in the aftermath of the speech. Many Syrians defected from IWW in favor of ATWA after Tresca's visit.

78. "Early Morning Disturbance," *Boston Globe*, April 10, 1919, 10.

79. "State to Delve into the Lawrence Strike," *Boston Globe*, April 3, 1922, 8.

80. "Labor Strikes and Boycotts," *The New Learned History*, vol. 6 (Springfield: C. A. Nichols and Company, 1923), 5116–17.

81. YMDK society ledger, 462–63, LHC/AAC.

82. YMDK society ledger, 452, LHC/AAC.

83. "No Charter for this Club," *Boston Globe*, September 22, 1913, 9. See also Emily Pope-Obeda, "Expelling the Foreign Born Menace: Immigrant Dissent, the Early Deportation State, and the First American Red Scare," *Journal of the Gilded Age and Progressive Era* 18 (2019): 32–55.

84. YMDK society ledger, 462–63, LHC/AAC.

85. Portions of this section draw upon Stacy D. Fahrenthold, "Ladies Aid as

Labor History: Working Class Formation in the Mahjar," *Journal of Middle East Women's Studies* 17, no. 3 (2021): 326–47.

86. Shakir, *Bint Arab*, 38.

87. Moran, *The Belles of New England*, 176; Alixa Naff, "New York: The Mother Colony," in *A Community of Many Worlds: Arab Americans in New York City*, ed. Kathleen Benson and Philip M. Kayal, 7–10 (Syracuse, NY: Syracuse University Press, 1994).

88. *Report on the Effect of the Child Labor Law of 1913*, 84.

89. *Report on the Effect of the Child Labor Law of 1913*, 180.

90. Laurice Maloley, *Destiny by Default: A Memoir* (Boston: First Books, 2002), 15–16.

91. Charles Teebagy (Khalil Tubbaji), oral history interview with Alixa Naff, Dorchester, MA, August 1962; NMAH/NC, box 280.

92. Maloley, *Destiny by Default*, 15–18.

93. Rose Homsy was born in 1904, making her five at the time; her sister Mary was four. "Rose Homsy," Boston City Ward 22, enumeration district 250, Fifteenth Census of the United States, 1930, T626, page 18b, line 63; RG 29, NARA.

94. Maloley, *Destiny by Default*, 19.

95. Shakir, "Good Works, Good Times," 139.

96. Maloley, *Destiny by Default*, 22–23.

97. Shakir, "Good Works, Good Times," 133–43; Shakir, *Bint Arab*, 38–47.

98. Polly Welts Kaufman, Jean Gibran, Sylvia McDowell, and Mary Howland Smoyer, "Chinatown/South Cove Walk," in *Boston Women's Heritage Trail* (Corona, CA: Applewood Books, 2006), 46; Loretta Hall, *Arab American Voices* (University Park: Pennsylvania State University Press, 2000), 20.

99. Sabbagh family reunion book, 2–3; Arab American National Museum (Dearborn, MI), Evelyn Shakir Collection (hereafter AANM/ES), box 1, folder 4. See also Kaufmann et al., "Chinatown/South Cove Walk," 47.

100. Dominique Cadinot and Jeffrey Burkholder, "The Reconfiguration of Gender Relations in Syrian American Feminist Discourse in the Diasporic Conditions of the Late Nineteenth Century," *Clio* 37 (2013): 177; Shakir, *Bint Arab*, 38.

101. Hannah Sabbagh Shakir oral history, 7; AANM/ES box 1 folder 4.

102. Hannah Sabbagh Shakir oral history, 5; AANM/ES box 1, folder 4.

103. Two skirts sewn at the Parkway Manufacturing, AANM/ES box 3.

104. Hannah Sabbagh Shakir oral history, 5–6; AANM/ES box 1, folder 4.

105. Fahrenthold, *Between the Ottomans and the Entente*, 51–56; Bawardi, *The Making of Arab Americans: From Syrian Nationalism to U.S. Citizenship* (Austin: University of Texas Press, 2014), 106, 134.

106. Goldberg, *A Tale of Three Cities*, 13.

107. Syrian Ladies' Aid Society (hereafter SLAS) meeting minutes, March 5,

1918, Lebanese Syrian Ladies' Aid Society Records, 1917–2005, Schlesinger Library, Radcliffe Institute, Harvard University (hereafter LSLAS/SL/RI); MC 574, folder 1.

108. SLAS meeting minutes, May 20, 1919; LSLAS/SL/RI.

109. SLAS meeting minutes, October 28, 1919; LSLAS/SL/RI.

110. SLAS meeting minutes, April 7, 1920; LSLAS/SL/RI.

111. Commonwealth of Massachusetts, *Annual Report of the Department of Public Welfare for the Year Ending November 30, 1921* (Boston: Wright & Potter, 1921), 144; SLAS Meeting Minutes, May 25, 1920; LSLAS/SL/RI. The officers on the 1920 state incorporation paperwork are Adele Shayeb, Sadie Beshara, and Latifee Khoury.

112. SLAS meeting minutes, June 2, 1920; LSLAS/SL/RI.

113. Ibrahim Kousa began offering Arabic languages classes for children there in 1920; SLAS meeting minutes, October 14, 1920; LSLAS/SL/RI.

114. SLAS meeting minutes, January 5, 1922; LSLAS/SL/RI.

115. Charles Shagoury family history, private manuscript, 6; Laurice Shagoury Maloley family history, private manuscript, 6–7.

116. Matthew Stiffler, "A Brief History of Arab Immigrant Textile Production in the U.S.," Arab American National Museum, October 2010. https://issuu.com/alaa.boston/docs/textile_history_aanm_arab_american_.

117. Laurice Shagoury Maloley family history, private manuscript, 13. Rose and Albert Homsy were married in 1919, having eloped because her immigration paperwork erroneously listed Rose as Albert's sister; New England Historical Genealogical Society, Boston, Massachusetts, Department of Public Health, Registry of Vital Records, Index to Marriages in Massachusetts, 1916–1920, 205. Sister Mary passed away suddenly in 1929 of congenital heart failure. Wadia Shagoury continued her stitching job until she was seventy-two years old; Maloley, *Destiny by Default*, 106.

118. SLAS meeting minutes, September 9, 1920; LSLAS/SL/RI.

119. SLAS meeting minutes, September 22, 1920; LSLAS/SL/RI. The first Work Committee in 1920 included Yasmine Firan, Sara Sa'ada, Adma Maluf, Rose As'ad, and Hannah Sabbagh.

120. SLAS meeting minutes, February 18, 1921; LSLAS/SL/RI. This pattern of society employment of Syrian women also appeared in Worcester, where Nabeha Merhije Haddad describes working on hand embroideries at the Friendly House from 1920 to 1926, see Nabeha Merhije Haddad, *Nabeha: Remembrances, an Autobiography* (Worcester: Self-published, 1993), 175–77.

121. Sabbagh Bros. accounting ledger (c. 1930s), AANM/ES, box 1, folder 6.

122. Sabbagh Bros. accounting ledger (c. 1930s), AANM/ES, box 1, folder 6.

123. SLAS meeting minutes, October 28, 1920; LSLAS/SL/RI. See also "Syrian

Ladies' Aid Society's Bazar: Laces and Embroideries Being Sold," *Boston Globe*, December 13, 1923, 14.

124. Per its charter, the SLAS declared its assets to the state each year. Massachusetts records record redistributive assets of $2,788 (1921); $2,136 (1923); $2,076 (1926); $3,312 (1927); $2,012 (1929); $3,193 (1930); and $3,181 (1931). See Commonwealth of Massachusetts, *Annual Report of the Department of Public Welfare for the Year* (Boston: Wright & Potter Printing Co.), years 1921–1931.

125. Author's note: names of SLAS relief recipients have been changed to respect privacy. This is in accordance with the organization's wishes and archival policy. All such pseudonyms are indicated with an asterisk* in the first instance.

126. SLAS meeting minutes, February 24, 1921; LSLAS/SL/RI.

127. SLAS meeting minutes, September 1, 1925; LSLAS/SL/RI. See also Evelyn Shakir's index to SLAS meeting minutes 1925; AANM/ES, box 1, folder 15.

128. SLAS meeting minutes, November 4, 1926; LSLAS/SL/RI. See also Evelyn Shakir's index to SLAS meeting minutes 1926; AANM/ES, box 1, folder 15.

129. Garrett and Purpura, *Frank Maria*, 85.

130. SLAS meeting minutes January 7, 1926; LSLAS/SL/RI. See also AANM/ES, box 1, folder 15.

131. YMDK society ledger, 458–59; LHC/AAC.

132. SLAS meeting minutes, May 26, 1926; LSLAS/SL/RI. See also AANM/ES, box 1, folder 15.

133. SLAS meeting minutes, June 8, 1920; LSLAS/SL/RI.

134. Sarah Deutsch, "Learning to Talk More Like a Man: Boston Women's Class-Bridging Organizations, 1870–1940," *American Historical Review* 97, no. 2 (1992): 398–400.

135. "Syrian Ladies' Aid to Hold South End Supper," *Boston Globe*, November 4, 1925, 4; "Syrian Ladies' Aid Society Serves Luncheon, Dinner," *Boston Globe*, December 7, 1934, 15. See also "Evening Classes for Women," Denison House Pamphlet, 1907. Denison House Records, Daily Activity Reports, B-27, series 3, folder 72. https://iiif.lib.harvard.edu/manifests/view/drs:428082582$250i.

136. SLAS meeting minutes, May 19, 1921; LSLAS/SL/RI. See also Shakir, *Bint Arab*, 59–60.

137. Laurice Shagoury Maloley family history, private manuscript, 10. The SLAS also partnered with the Denison House to provide childcare services at Tyler Street. The societies organized jointly under the auspices of the Society for the Care of Syrian Children (*Jam'iyyat al-I'tina' al-Atfal al-Suri*). SLAS meeting minutes, October 4, 1934; LSLAS/SL/RI.

138. "Ladies Aid Society Looks Back Over 27 Years," *Syrian World*, November 16, 1934, 2. The New York SLAS was established in 1908. Its Ells Island women's interpreter, named "Mrs. Arbeely," was presumably related to Najib Arbeely, who

then served as an U.S. Immigration Inspector. See also Mary Basila, "Jam'iyyat al-Sayyidat al-Suriyya fi-Amrika," *al-Jami'a*, June 20, 1908, 6.

Chapter 3

1. R. Tahan and Bros. classified ad, al-*Sa'ih*, August 23, 1917, 3.
2. Kiamie Bros. classified ad, *al-Nasr*, July 19, 1918, 3.
3. Eddy Cury and Bros. classified ad, *al-Nasr*, April 12, 1916, 2.
4. Alixa Naff, *Becoming American: The Early Arab Immigrant Experience* (Carbondale: Southern Illinois University Press, 1985), 129.
5. Naff, *Becoming American*; Sarah Gualtieri, "Gendering the Chain Migration Thesis: Women and Syrian Transatlantic Migration," *Comparative Studies of South Asia, Africa and the Middle East* 24, no.1 (2004): 68–71; Jacob Norris, "Exporting the Holy Land: Artisans and Merchant Migrants in Ottoman-era Bethlehem," *Mashriq and Mahjar: Journal of Middle Eastern and North African Migration Studies* 1, no. 2 (2013): 17–45.
6. Sallum Mukarzil, *Tarikh al-Tijara al-Suriyya al-Amrikiyya* (New York: Matba'at al-Suriyya al-Amrikiyya al-Tijariyya, 1921), 31.
7. American Catholic History Research Center and University Archives, Terence Vincent Powderly Papers (Knights of Labor), box 166, folder 4, testimony given by Edward F. McSweeney, March 21, 1900, page 428-R.
8. Mukarzil, *Tarikh al-Tijara*, 33–34.
9. "American Exhibits in Syria and Turkey," *Ice and Refrigeration* 41, no. 4 (October 1911), 115; "The American-Syrian Chamber of Commerce," *Dun's Review* 18, no. 6 (February 1912), 68.
10. Linda Jacobs, *Strangers in the West: The Syrian Colony of New York City, 1880–1900* (New York: Kalimah Press, 2015), 182–96, 203–5.
11. Mukarzil, *Tarikh al-Tijara*, 63.
12. Mukarzil, *Tarikh al-Tijara*, 61–62.
13. Fred Halliday, "The Millet of Manchester: Arab Merchants and Cotton Trade," *British Journal of Middle Eastern Studies* 12, no. 2 (1992): 159–76; William Gervase Clarence-Smith, "Middle Eastern Migrants in the Philippines: Entrepreneurs and Cultural Brokers," *Asian Journal of Social Science* 32, no. 3 (2004): 425–57.
14. *Levant Trade Review* vol. 4 (1920), 97.
15. *Levant Trade Review* vol. 4 (1920), 97.
16. Arriving Passenger and Crew List for the S.S. *Kaiserin Aug Victoria*, New York, June 19, 1913; Records of the Customs Service, Passenger Lists of Vessels Arriving at New York (hereafter T715), 1913, page 10, line 49, Alexander Hamrah; RG36, NARA.
17. Mukarzil, *Tarikh al-Tijara*, 76. Passport records describe Alexander Hamrah

as traveling between England, France, Italy, Spain, Madeira, and Belgium in search of supply materials between 1910 and 1921; see Passport Application for Alexander Joseph Hamrah, Washington D.C., January 26, 1921; U.S. Passport Applications, 1795–1925 (hereafter M1490), roll 1475, no. 134610; NARA.

18. Nabeha Merhige Haddad, *Nabeha: Remembrances, an Autobiography* (Worcester: Self-published, 1993), 79–80.

19. Mukarzil, *Tarikh al-Tijara*, 59–60.

20. Elizabeth McLean Petras, "The Shirt on Your Back: Immigrant Workers and the Reorganization of the Garment Industry," *Social Justice* 15, no. 1 (1992): 77–78.

21. Lucius H. Miller, *Our Syrian Population: A Study of the Syrian Communities of Greater New York*, (New York: n.p., 1904), 9–10; Jacobs, *Strangers in the West*, 299–304; Gregory J. Shibley, "New York's Little Syria, 1880–1935," (M.A. thesis, Florida Atlantic University, 2014), 55.

22. Alixa Naff, "New York: the Mother Colony," in *A Community of Many Worlds: Arab Americans in New York City*, ed. Kathleen Benson and Philip M. Kayal (Syracuse, NY: Syracuse University Press, 1994), 7.

23. Adele Younis, *The Coming of the Arabic-Speaking People to the United States* (New York: Center for Migration Studies, 1995), 197–98.

24. House, *Reports of the Industrial Commission*, 445; as cited by Shibley, "New York's Little Syria," 65.

25. Jeremiah Whipple Jenks and William Jett Lauck, *The Immigration Problem: A Study of American Immigration Conditions and Needs* (New York: Funk and Wagnalls, 1913), 51.

26. Evelyn Shakir, *Bint Arab: Arab and Arab American Women in the United States* (Westport, CT: Praeger, 1997), 38.

27. Akram Fouad Khater, "'House' to 'Goddess of the House': Gender, Class, and Silk in 19th-Century Mount Lebanon," *International Journal of Middle East Studies* 28, no. 3 (1994): 325–48.

28. Petition for Naturalization for Michael Nassif Arida, New York, April 17, 1903; Records of District Courts of the United States (hereafter M1972), roll 110, case no. 12351; RG21, NARA.

29. The Jafet family undertook a similar venture in 1903, sending Nami Jafet to scout sites for a weaving and stamping factory in Syrian São Paulo, see Molly Ball, "Wife, Mother, and Worker: The Decision to Work in Early Twentieth Century São Paulo," *Journal of Women's History* 29, no. 4 (2017): 109–32; Fahrenthold, *Between the Ottomans and the Entente*, 20–23.

30. Mukarzil, *Tarikh al-Tijara*, 45.

31. McSweeney testimony to Investigating Committee of the New York Immigration Commission, New York City, March 21, 1900. In "Terence Powderly Mis-

cellaneous Legal Report and Testimony: Luigi Graziano Case Regarding Corruption in the Bureau of Immigration" 1900), p. 428-R. See also Cohen, "Smuggling, Globalization, and America's Outward State, 1870–1909," *Journal of American History* 97, no. 2 (2010): 371–98; Sarah M. A. Gualtieri, *Arab Routes: Pathways to Syrian California* (Stanford, CA: Stanford University Press, 2019).

32. New York State Department of Labor, "Register of Factories, 1913," in *Annual Industrial Directory of New York State*, vol. 2 (New York: 1915), 524.

33. Mukarzil, *Tarikh al-Tijara*, 45–46.

34. *New York Times*, July 14, 1913, 1. The elder brother, Kamel Arida was born in 1876. Kamel split his time between New York and Buenos Aires, where the family also maintained silk businesses. He was of French nationality until naturalizing in 1926. Petition for Naturalization for Kamal Arida, New York, March 30, 1926; M1972, petition no. 2346166; RG26, NARA.

35. Mukarzil, *Tarikh al-Tijara*, 48. Nasib Arida was simultaneously editor of *al-Funun*, a literary journal established in 1913; he later became editor of *al-Sa'ih* newspaper.

36. *Syrian Business Directory* (New York: S. A. Mokarzel and H. F. Otash, 1908), 3–29; Shibley, "New York's Little Syria," 65.

37. *Syrian American Directory Almanac* (New York: Arida and Andria, 1930), as cited by Adele Younis, "The Challenge of Commerce: The Syrian-American Almanac," *International Migration Review* 302 (1995), 302.

38. Declaration of Intention for Abdalla Barsa, New York, April 27, 1911; Declarations of Intention, Eastern District of New York, roll 137, petition no. 130060; RG 21, NARA.

39. The date of Simon Barsa's arrival to New York via El Paso is unclear. According to naturalization paperwork, he arrived in 1906. However, he also appeared at El Paso's border crossing in October 1905, stating his intent to move to New York to work in manufacturing; in the 1905 manifest, Barsa's sponsor was Elias Mouakad, another New York kimono merchant-manufacturer. See Arrival Manifest for Simon Barsa, El Paso, October 1905, 93; Manifests of Alien Passengers for the U.S. Immigration Officer at Port of Arrival, roll 1, list 3, page 93, line 18; RG 85, NARA. See also Declaration of Intention for Simon Barsa, New York, April 25, 1916; Declarations of Intention, Eastern District of New York, roll 98, petition no. 48528; RG21, NARA.

40. *Trow's General Directory of the Borough of Manhattan and Bronx, New York City, for the Year Ending August 1, 1913* (New York: Trow Directory Printing, 1913), 91.

41. "Register of Factories, 1913," 524.

42. Mukarzil, *Tarikh al-Tijara*, 52.

43. Mukarzil, *Tarikh al-Tijara*, 52.

44. "Silks: From the Cocoon to the Finished Garment Is Comprehensive Plan of A. Shaheen & Sons Co.," *Women's Wear* 20, no. 73 (March 29, 1920), 6.
45. "Shaheen A. Shaheen," 1910 United States Federal Census (hereafter T624), roll 955, Kings County, Brooklyn Ward 3, District 23, Sheet 8b, entries 81–90; NARA.
46. "Akbar Maʿmal fi-l-ʿAlam," *al-Nasr,* November 18, 1919, 7.
47. Mukarzil, *Tarikh al-Tijara,* 55.
48. Mukarzil, *Tarikh al-Tijara,* 56–57.
49. Philip Kiamie arrived in New York in 1912. He declared his intention to naturalize in 1921 and became a U.S. citizen in 1927. Petition for Naturalization for Philip Kiamie, New York City, October 5, 1921; Records of District Courts of the United States, roll 405, no. 83359; RG 21, NARA.
50. Mukarzil, *Tarikh al-Tijara,* 58.
51. "Kiamie Bros, Philip and Najib," *New York City Directory* (1917), 1141.
52. Mukarzil, *Tarikh al-Tijara,* 58.
53. "Lingerie: Kiamie Bros. Leases Space on Madison Avenue." *Women's Wear Daily* 43, no. 37 (August 20, 1931), SII11; "Negligees and Pajamas: Kiamie Bros., Inc., Opens Chicago Office," *Women's Wear Daily* 43, no. 81, October 22, 1931, SII3.
54. Mukarzil, *Tarikh al-Tijara,* 43.
55. These prices average to around $2,000 a piece in 2021 U.S. dollars, illustrating that before mass production the kimono was primarily an art object accessible only to the wealthy.
56. Mukarzil, *Tarikh al-Tijara,* 44.
57. Mukarzil, *Tarikh al-Tijara,* 61.
58. Petras, "The Shirt on Your Back," 79–80.
59. Mukarzil, *Tarikh al-Tijara,* 44.
60. Habib Ibrahim Katibeh and Ferhat Jacob Ziadeh, *Arabic-Speaking Americans* (New York: Institute of Arab American Affairs, 1946), 8. The Mouakad factory employed 267 operatives in the 1920s: 140 men and 127 women.
61. Katibeh and Ziadeh, *Arabic-Speaking Americans,* 8; "Register of Factories, 1913," 524–26. In addition to these names, Katibeh and Ziadeh enumerated New York City producers Sayour, Kateb, Hadad, Jebaily, Kiamie, and Malouf (the Malouf brothers relocated their factory to Los Angeles).
62. Habib Katibeh, "Arab American Activities and Politics," New York City, 1941, 5. U.S. Office of Strategic Services, Records of the Foreign Nationalities Branch, Near East, no. INT-2AB; RG 226, NARA.
63. Edgar Sydenstricker Draft Report, "Conditions of Labor in the Principal Industries," *Draft Report to the Commission on Industrial Relations No. 3015* (1915), 180; Records of the U.S. Commission on Industrial Relations, T4; RG174.6.1, NARA.

64. Annelise Orleck, "The Needle Trades and the Uprising of Women Workers," in *City of Workers, City of Struggle: How Labor Movements Changed New York*, ed. Joshua B. Freeman (New York: Columbia University Press, 2019), 91.

65. Daniel Katz, *All Together Different: Yiddish Socialists, Garment Workers, and the Labor Roots of Multiculturalism* (New York: New York University Press, 2011), 46–72.

66. Orleck, "The Needle Trades," 85–86.

67. Lewis L. Lorwin, *The Women's Garment Workers: A History of the International Ladies' Garment Workers' Union* (New York: B. W. Huebsch, 1924), 219–20.

68. Orleck, "The Needle Trades," 92–94.

69. "The Children's Crusade: The New York Strikers are Winning Fights," *Ladies' Garment Worker*, February 1913, 1–3.

70. Lorwin, *The Women's Garment Workers*, 220–21. The campaign simultaneously targeted Spanish and Sephardi kimono shops, another ethnically segmented garment workforce.

71. "Garment Strike Grows: Kimono and Wrapper Workers Walk Out," *Baltimore Sun*, January 9, 1913, 1.

72. Lorwin, *The Women's Garment Workers*, 227.

73. Boris Emmet, "Trade Agreements in the Women's Clothing Industries in New York City," *Monthly Review of the U.S. Bureau of Labor Statistics* 5, no. 6 (December 1917), 20–21.

74. "Report of the General Executive Board to the Thirteenth Conventions of the International Ladies' Garment Workers Union," *Thirteenth Convention of the I.L.G.W.U.* (Philadelphia: September 15, 1916), 25.

75. "Resolution No. 107," *Officers' Reports to the Twelfth Convention of the I.L.G.W.U.* (Self-published: Screiber Press, 1913), 195.

76. "Officers' Reports to the Fourteenth Convention of the International Ladies' Garment Workers Union," *Fourteen Convention of the I.L.G.W.U.* (Boston: May 20, 1918), 97–98.

77. "Our Women Workers: Wrapper and Kimono Workers Union Local No. 41," *Ladies' Garment Worker* 4, no. 2 (November 1913), 21.

78. Allen M. Wakstein, "The Origins of the Open-Shop Movement, 1919–1920," *Journal of American History* 51, no. 3 (1964), 460–62.

79. "Resolution No. 107," 195–96, emphasis mine.

80. "Our Women Workers: Among the Wrapper and Kimono Workers," *Ladies' Garment Worker* (July 1913), 22.

81. Pauline M. Newman, "Our Women Workers," *Ladies' Garment Workers* (August 1913), 26. Capitalization in original. A Lithuanian Jewish immigrant who worked in the New York needle trades, Newman rose to prominence during the 1909–10 uprising. She was appointed ILGWU's first women's organizer in 1913;

Annelise Orleck, *Common Sense and a Little Fire: Women and Working-Class Politics in the United States, 1900–1965* (Chapel Hill: University of North Carolina Press, 1994), 121–65.

82. Newman, "Our Women Workers," 27. Emphasis in original.

83. "Wrapper and Kimono Makers Union, Local 41," *Ladies' Garment Worker* (February 1914), 25.

84. "Wrapper and Kimono Makers Local No. 41," *Ladies' Garment Worker* (June 1914), 25–26.

85. "Communications and Requests," *Ladies' Garment Worker* (March 1915), 19; Resolution No. 92 in "Report of the General Executive Board to the Thirteenth Convention of the International Ladies' Garment Workers Union," *Thirteen Convention of the I.L.G.W.U.*, (Philadelphia, Self-published September 15, 1916), 146.

86. "Agitation among the Children-Dress and Wrapper Makers," *Ladies' Garment Worker*, (December 1915), 26.

87. A. Baroff, ILGWU General Secretary, "Reports," *Ladies' Garment Worker*, (February 1916), 9.

88. This draft of the appeal letter includes a crossed-out portion indicated here. "Union" is rendered both in the Arabic *al-ittihad* as well as transliterated English *al-union*. Strike is similarly rendered, as both *idrab* and *strike*. Benjamin Schlesinger, President. Records, 1914–1923. File re: Local 41, 5780/009 box 4, folder 1, Kheel Center for Labor-Management Documentation and Archives, Martin P. Catherwood Library, Cornell University. My thanks are due to Devin Naar, who shared this letter with me while consulting the collection.

89. "Report of the General Executive Board to the Thirteenth Convention of the International Ladies' Garment Workers Union," 26.

90. Emmet, "Trade Agreements in the Women's Clothing Industry in New York City," 35–36.

91. "More Strikes Mapped out by Garment Union: 200 Resolutions at Convention Promises Many Changes in Women's Wear Trades," *Women's Wear* 13, no. 97 (October 25, 1916), 1, 8.

92. A. Baroff, "Workers Claiming Rightful Share," *Ladies' Garment Worker*, March 1916, 14.

93. "10,000 Women on Strike Here Fear Violence," *Brooklyn Daily Times*, February 9, 1916, 1–2.

94. A. Baroff, "A Strenuous Period in the Life of Our International: Police Partiality to Employers," *Ladies' Garment Worker* (March 1916), 14.

95. "House Dress, Wrapper and Kimono Strike Ends," *Women's Wear*, 12, no. 40 (February 18, 1916), 35. See also Lorwin, *The Women's Garment Workers*, 296–98.

96. "Report of the General Executive Board to the Thirteenth Conventions of the International Ladies' Garment Workers Union," 26.

97. "Matters of Interest to the Entire Industry," *Ladies' Garment Worker*, December 1916, 14.

98. "Officers' Reports to the Fourteenth Convention of the International Ladies' Garment Workers Union," *Fourteenth Convention of the I.L.G.W.U.*, (Boston: Self-published, May 20, 1918), 22.

99. "Housedress and Kimono Workers Local 41," *Ladies' Garment Worker*, December 1918, 27.

100. "House Dress and Kimono Workers of New York," *Report of the General Executive Board to the Fifteenth Biennial Convention of the International Ladies' Garment Workers' Union*, Chicago, May 3, 1920, 36–37.

101. "Kimono Union Ready to Present Demands: Forty-Four Hour Week and Increased Pay Chief among Concerns," *Women's Wear* 18, no. 12 (January 15, 1919), 1, 4. See also "Kimono Workers Numbers 3,000 on Strike Now: Associate Factory Heads for Not Oppose," *Women's Wear* 18, no. 39 (February 17, 1919), 1.

102. The trade journal uses "Assyrian" and "Syrian" indiscriminately, reflecting American confusion between Middle Eastern workers. The usage of "Spanish" also likely refers to Sephardi Jewish manufacturers, another Ottoman group that prevailed in the kimono sector. "House Dress Workers May Agree with Mfrs: Strike, However, Considered Likely among Assyrian and Spanish Element," *Women's Wear* 18, no. 31 (February 6, 1919), 2.

103. See also "Syrian and Spanish Workers Reported Out," *Women's Wear* 18, no. 40 (February 18, 1919), 1. This represents perhaps a third of the Syrian shops affected by prior ILGWU actions, most notably 1916, which shuttered 35 Syrian factories.

104. "Kimono Workers to Strike," *New York Times*, February 17, 1919, 9.

105. "Union Refuses to Meet Kimono Men to Settle," *Women's Wear* 18, no. 42 (February 20, 1919), 4.

106. "Waist Strikers Say Disorder Charges are 'Fairy Tales,'" *New York Tribune*, February 21, 1919, 8. The *Tribune* also reports lectures held in Armenian, Greek, Italian, Ladino, and Yiddish.

107. Lorwin, *The Women's Garment Workers*, 330; "Conferences Called to Settle Kimono Strike: Manufacturers to Concede to Shorter Working Week but Not Wage Increase," *Women's Wear* 18, no. 44 (February 24, 1919), 1–2.

108. Orleck, "The Needle Trades and the Uprising of Women Workers," 85–86; Petras, "The Shirt on Your Back," 80.

109. Harry Best, "Extent of Organization in the Women's Garment Making Industries of New York," *American Economic Review* 9, no. 4 (December 1919), 782–83; Theresa Wolfson, "Role of the ILGWU in Stabilizing the Women's Garment Industry," *ILR Review* 4, no. 1 (1950), 37.

110. Mukarzil, *Tarikh al-Tijara*, 56.

111. Richard M. Breaux, "Mahjari Musicians: The Recorded Sounds of Arab Americans in the Early Twentieth Century, 1912–1936," in *Arab Worlds Beyond the Middle East and North Africa*, ed. Mariam F. Alkazen and Claudia E. Youakim, 151–70 (New York: Lexington Books, 2021).

112. Mukarzil, *Tarikh al-Tijara*, 56.

113. In *Al-Majalla al-Tijariyya al-Suriyya al-Amrikiyya*, Mukarzil collated monthly reports in a section, "Aham Hawadith al-Shahr al-Tijariyya wa-l-Sinaʿiyya," January 1919, 37. See also features like "Hal al-Qatan al-Mawjud yikfi hajja al-ʿalam?" January 1919, 16–20; "al-Tijari al-Suriyya fi-Niyu Yurk," January 1919, 41; or Mikhaʾil Abi Sulaiman, "Tijara Thugri Bayrut wa-Tarablus Qabl al-Harb," January 1919, 32–36.

114. Sallum Mukarzil, "Bab al-Tahrir: al-Muhajira wa-l-Tijara," *al-Majalla al-Tijariyya al-Suriyya al-Amrikiyya* May 1920, 24.

115. Khalil Bey al-Aswad, "Tijaratna fi-l-Mahjar," *al-Majalla al-ʿArabiyya* November 1916, 62–63.

116. Sallum Mukarzil, "al-Taʿwin al-Tijari bayna al-Suriyyin," *al-Majalla al-Tijariyya al-Suriyya al-Amrikiyya* January 1919, 24–29.

117. Sallum Mukzarzil, "al-Bunyan li-l-Mustaqbal," *al-Majalla al-Tijariyya al-Suriyya al-Amrikiyya* March 1919, 25.

118. Sallum Mukarzil, "Al-Usul wa-l-Adab wa-l-Turaʾiq al-Tijariyya," *al-Majalla al-Tijariyya al-Suriyya al-Amrikiyya* January 1920, 29.

119. Wakstein, "The Origins of the Open-Shop Movement," 467.

120. Abdalla Barsa and Bros. classified advertisement, "bi-Haja ila-ʿAmilat," *al-Saʾih*, January 11, 1917, 3.

121. Classified advertisement, *Al-Saʾih*, August 30, 1917, 6.

122. Kiamie Bros. classified advertisement, *al-Nasr*, July 19, 1918, 3.

123. Eddy Cury and Bros. classified advertisement, *al-Nasr*, April 12, 1916, 2.

124. Mikhaʾil Arida and Co. classified advertisement, *al-Saʾih*, August 2, 1915, 2.

125. Petras, "The Shirt on Your Back," 78.

126. Badran Bros. classified advertisement, "Amilat!," *al-Nasr*, February 18, 1916, 3. The repetition of "any strike" is in the original, rendered first in Arabic and then in transliterated English for emphasis: "*Mahfouz min-kull idrab ʿan al-Amal—Ayy-l-Strike!*"

127. Haddad, *Nabeha: Remembrances*, 129–32.

128. Victoria Tannous, "Limatha la atazawwaj fi-Amrika, Part 2" *al-Majalla al-ʿArabiyya*, November 1916, 74–76.

129. Tannous became a U.S. citizen in 1925, after a four-year process. Petition for Naturalization for Victoria Tannous, Jersey City, May 13, 1925; Records of District Courts of the United States, roll 283, no. 42288; RG 21, NARA.

130. Michael W. Suleiman, "A Brief History of Arab American Women, 1890s to World War II," in *Arab American Women: Representation and Refusal*, ed. Louise

Cainkar, Michael W. Suleiman, and Suad Joseph, 39–42 (Syracuse, NY: Syracuse University Press, 2021); Sarah M. A. Gualtieri, "From Lebanon to Louisiana: Afifa Karam and Arab Women's Writing in Diaspora," in *Arab American Women: Representation and Refusal*, ed. Michael W. Suleiman, Suad Joseph, and Louise Cainkar, 169–88 (Syracuse, NY: Syracuse University Press, 2021); Elizabeth Claire Saylor, "Gender, Hybridity, and Transnationalism in 'Afifa Karam's Fatima al-Badawiyya," *Journal of Middle East Women's Studies* 15, no. 1 (2019): 3–23.

131. Louise Seymour Houghton, "The Syrians in the United States II: Business Activities," *The Survey*, August 5, 1911, 660.

132. Ya'cub Rufa'il, "Nazarat: al-Talaq," *al-Akhlaq*, January 1923, 3.

133. Akram Fouad Khater, *Inventing Home: Emigration, Gender, and the Middle Class in Lebanon, 1870–1920* (Berkeley: University of California Press, 2001), 34–38.

134. "Crime Boards Tell How Boy Gangs Rise in New York Slums," *New York Times*, March 20, 1927, 1; "Shot by Police in Chase: Prisoner Accused of Wounding Man in Fight in Brooklyn," *New York Times*, December 27, 1927, 2.

135. Rufa'il, "Nazarat: al-Talaq," 3–4. His periodical also ran a serialized translation of Leonard McGee's "Nine Causes for Misery in Marriage" in *al-Akhlaq* through 1923.

136. Shakir, *Bint Arab*, 68–71.

137. Victoria Tannous, "Limatha la atazawwaj fi-Amrika," *al-Majalla al-'Arabiyya*, October 1916, 29–30.

138. Daniel Bender, *Sweated Work, Weak Bodies: Anti-Sweatshop Campaigns and Languages of Labor* (New Brunswick, NJ: Rutgers University Press, 2004), 4–5, 9.

139. Houghton, "The Syrians in the United States II," 661.

140. Notably, Najla arrived in Paterson just before the silk strike of 1913; though she does not mention the strikers or whether she or her family participated, she attributes the rise in wages to her own advancement in skill as well as "when the union came." Najla Simon oral history interview with Alixa Naff, Ann Arbor, MI, May 23, 1980; Faris and Yamna Naff Arab-American Collection, Archives Center, National Museum of American History (hereafter NMAH/NC), box 279.

141. Najla Simon, NMAH/NC, box 279.

142. Hannah Sabbagh Shakir oral history with Evelyn Shakir, 7; Arab American National Museum (Dearborn, MI), Evelyn Shakir Collection (hereafter AANM/ES), box 1, folder 4.

143. Bahieh Kappaz (Khabbaz) oral history interview with Alixa Naff, Detroit, May 21, 1980; NMAH/NC, box 277.

144. Zahdi (Fallaha) Barsa oral history interview with Alixa Naff, Detroit, May 21, 1980; NMAH/NC, box 280, 1a.

145. Najla Simon, NMAH/NC, box 279. Emphasis in original.

146. Victoria Tannous, "al-Marʾa Qabl al-Zawaj wa-Baʿdiha," *al-Majalla al-ʿArabiyya*, May 1917, 375–80.

147. Victoria Tannous, "Limatha la-Atazawwaj fi-Amrika 2," *al-Majalla al-ʿArabiyya*, November 1916, 74–76.

148. Tannous, "Limatha la-Atazawwaj fi-Amrika 2," 76.

149. Victoria Tannous, "Hal Tuhtaqar al-Fatat al-ʿAmila?" *al-Akhlaq*, January 1924, 18–19.

150. Amira Jamal Faylun al-Hilu, "Tifl Yabki," *al-Akhlaq*, May 1923, 15.

151. Victoria Tannous, "Tifl Yabki," *al-Akhlaq*, June 1923, 12.

152. Tannous, "Tifl Yabki," 12.

153. Nabiha Habib, "Limatha la-Natazawwaj fi-Amrika," *al-Majalla al-ʿArabiyya*, February 1917, 218–20.

154. Raouf J. Halaby, "Dr. Michael Shadid and the Debate over Identity in *The Syrian World*," in *Crossing the Waters: Arabic-Speaking Immigrants in the United States Before 1940*, ed. Eric J. Hooglund (Washington D.C.: Smithsonian Institution Press, 1987), 55–68.

Chapter 4

1. Sallum Mukarzil, *Tarikh al-Tijara al-Suriyya al-Amrikiyya* (New York: Matbaʾat al-Suriyya al-Amrikiyya al-Tijariyya, 1921), 62.

2. Mukarzil, *Tarikh al-Tijara*, 65.

3. "Lace and Embroideries: Madeira Embroidery Exports Show Gain," *Women's Wear* 21, no. 11 (July 14, 1920): 17, 48. This figure is up from America's wartime share of the trade: $968,778 in 1916; $831,368 in 1917; $1,494,320 in 1918; and $1,780,799 in 1919; "Tuqaddim Sinaʾa Mutarazat Madira," *al-Majalla al-Tijariyya al-Suriyya al-Amrikiyya* March 1920, 18.

4. Georgina da Conceição Branco Garrido, "Dos Conventos ao Economuseu: Patrício & Gouveia Lda., Fábrica de Bordados," (M.A. thesis, Universidade do Lisboa, 2015), 23; Alberto Vieira, *Bordado Madeira* (Funchal: Tip. Peres, SA, 2007), 15–23.

5. Vieira, *Bordado Madeira*, 38.

6. Viera, *Bordado Madeira*, 38–39.

7. Vieira, *Bordado Madeira*, 60–61; "Tuqaddim Sinaʾa Mutarazat Madira," *al-Majalla al-Tijariyya al-Suriyya al-Amrikiyya*, March 1920, 17.

8. Mukarzil, *Tarikh al-Tijara*, 65; Vice Consul K. Kemp memo to Madeiran embroidery manufacturers, Funchal, April 1, 1925; Consular Posts, Funchal, Madeira Island, box 70 (1925), vol. 2, no. 621; Record Group 84, Record of Foreign Service Posts; National Archives and Records Administration (hereafter RG84, NARA).

9. "Tuqaddim Sinaʾa Mutarazat Madira," 18.

10. Vieira, *Bordado Madeira*, 39–40; Rui Carita, *História da Madeira séc. XX: o caminho para a autonomia*, vol. 6 (Funchal: Impressa Académica, 2020), 70–77.

11. "Syrians Forcing to Front in Lace and Embroideries," *Women's Wear*, November 12, 1917, 4.

12. "Iskandar Abu Hamra," *Majallat al-Tijariyya al-Suriyya al-Amrikiyya*, January 1919, 7. "Iskandar Abu Hamra," *al-Sa'ih*, January 1923, 64.

13. Mukarzil, *Tarikh al-Tijara*, 70–71. William and his mother, Amina, previously lived with Alexander Hamrah and Lillian (Karsa) Hamrah in Brooklyn. "Alexander J Hamrah," T624 (1910), roll 957, Kings County, Brooklyn Ward 6, sheet 2a. See also "Laces and Embroideries," *Dry Goods Economist* no. 3905, May 10, 1919, 78. Ellis Basha was Hamrah's third partner in this period.

14. Mukarzil, *Tarikh al-Tijara*, 132–33.

15. Madeira linen played an important role in New York's Little Syria neighborhood. St. George's Syrian Catholic Church at 103 Washington Street currently stands as the immigrant neighborhood's principal landmark. George Ilyas Bardwil purchased the building for the community in 1920; Michael D. Caratzas report for the Landmarks Preservation Commission, "(Former) St. George's Syrian Catholic Church," New York City, July 14, 2009, 6; https://melkite.org/wp-content/uploads/2012/02/stgeorgechurch.pdf.

16. Louis F. Lutfy oral history interview with Alixa Naff, Detroit, May 2, 1980; Faris and Yamna Naff Arab-American Collection Archives Center, National Museum of American History (hereafter NMAH/NC), box 277.

17. First Syrian Presbyterian Church, meeting minutes, Brooklyn, February 16, 1908; NMAH/NC, box 280. The Saydah and Karsa families also donated to the Syrian Ladies' Aid Society of Brooklyn (Khalil Saydah's wife was the SLAS president in 1938); Syrian Ladies' Aid Society Financial Statement (1938), folder 1; Syrian Ladies' Aid Society (Brooklyn, NY) Records, Near Eastern Collection, Immigration History Research Center Archives, University of Minnesota (IHRC2567).

18. For a survey, see A. Ebru Akcasu, "Nation and Migration in Late Ottoman Spheres of Legal Belonging: A Comparative Look at Laws on Nationality," *Nationalities Papers* 49, no. 6 (2021): 1113–31. For close discussion of Palestinian, Syrian, and Ottoman cases, see Nadim Bawalsa, "To Be Denied a Homeland: British Mandate Policy and the Making of the Palestinian Diaspora in Chile," in *Routledge Handbook of Middle Eastern Diasporas*, ed. Dalia Abdelhady and Ramy Aly, 23–38 (London: Routledge, 2022); Chris Gratien and Emily Pope Obeda, "Ottoman Migrants, US Deportation Law, and Statelessness during the Interwar Era," *Mashriq and Mahjar: Journal of Middle Eastern and North African Migration Studies* 5, no. 2 (2018): 105–39; Jacob Norris, "Return Migration and the Rise of the Palestinian Nouveaux Riche, 1870–1925," *Journal of Palestine Studies* 46, no. 2 (2017): 60–75; Camila Pastor, *The Mexican Mahjar: Transnational Maronites, Jews, and Arabs under the French Mandate* (Austin: University of Texas Press, 2017), 43–49, 96.

19. Sarah M. A. Gualtieri, *Between Arab and White: Race and Ethnicity in the*

Early Syrian American Diaspora (Oakland: University of California Press, 2009), 66–73; John Tehranian, *Whitewashed: America's Invisible Middle Eastern Minority* (New York: New York University Press, 2010), 55–56.

20. Stacy D. Fahrenthold, "'Claimed by Turkey as Subjects': Ottoman Migrants, Foreign Passports, and Syrian Nationality in the Americas, 1915–1925," in *The Subjects of Ottoman International Law*, ed. Lâle Can, Michael Christopher Low, Kent Schull, and Robert Zens, 216–37 (Bloomington: University of Indiana Press, 2020).

21. Elias Mallouk and Katherine Mallouk, October 1920, Passaportes caixa 255, no. processo 108, passaporte 167. Arquivo Regional da Madeira.

22. Passport Application for Alexander Joseph Hamrah, Washington D.C., January 26, 1921; U.S. Passport Applications, 1795–1925 (hereafter M1490), roll 1475, no. 134610; NARA. See also Passport Application for George Elias Bardwil, Washington D.C., November 10, 1922; M1490, roll 2130, no. 230281; NARA.

23. "Syrians Forging to the Front in Lace and Embroideries," *Women's Wear* 15, no. 111 (November 12, 1917), 1, 14.

24. L. Tweel and Co. was the namesake of Ilyas Tawil, Mallouk's partner from Brooklyn. Born in 1880 in Syria and arriving in New York in 1895, Tweel became a U.S. citizen in 1904. By 1920, his firm in Madeira was among the largest in art linens. Passport application for Louis Tweel, New York City, May 29, 1920; M1490, roll 1233, no. 44147; NARA. See also "Ila-man yahumuhum baiʿ Madira," *al-Akhlaq*, January 1922, 64. Tweel retired from Madeira imports in 1919, but Salim and Elias Mallouk operated his namesake brand through the 1920s; "al-Tijara al-Suriyya fi-Niyu Yurk," *al-Majalla al-Tijariyya al-Suriyya al-Amrikiyya*, March 1919, 44.

25. W. Poling, "Suhail Hermos," New York, August 11, 1919, 1–6; General Records of the Federal Bureau of Investigation, Investigative Records, Old German Files (hereafter M1085), roll 803, case no. 364266; RG 65.2.2, NARA.

26. Affidavit to Explain Protracted Foreign Residents and to Overcome Presumption of Expatriation for Naim Abualy, Funchal, March 31, 1922; Consular Correspondence, Funchal, Madeira Island, Box 57 (1922), vol. 2, no. 130; RG 84, NARA. See also Affidavit to Explain Protracted Foreign Residents and to Overcome Presumption of Expatriation for Elias Hamowy, Funchal, February 22, 1922; Consular Correspondence, Funchal, Madeira Island, Box 57 (1922), vol. 2, no. 130; RG 84, NARA.

27. Consul General Stillman Eells to Department of State, "Registration of Naim Abualy," Funchal, August 16, 1922; Consular Correspondence, Funchal, Madeira Island, Box 57 (1922), vol. 2, no. 130; RG 84, NARA.

28. Chiary Nicola Haddad, October 1920, Passaportes Caixa 257, no. processo 108, s.n. passaporte. Arquivo Regional da Madeira.

29. Anton Malhoul, December 1921, Passaportes Caixa 267, no. processo 97, passport 597. Arquivo Regional da Madeira.

30. D. J. Cline, *Perfection, Never Less: The Vera Way Marghab Story* (Brookings: South Dakota Art Museum, 1998), 25.

31. "Marum, Wm," Statutory List of Persons and Firms with Whom Persons and Firms in the United Kingdom are Prohibited from Trading," Trading with the Enemy, Consolidating Statutory List (London, 1917), 62. Records of the Department of State, Pro-German Activities, 1916–1918, vol. 345, entry 348; RG59, NARA. See also "Removals from List: Government Notices Affecting Trade," *Board of Trade Journals* (London, October 1917), 122.

32. Garrido, "Dos Conventos ao Economuseu," 21. See also Márcia Cristina Sousa Gomes, "O Bordado Madeira: Preservação De Uma Técnica Artesanal," (M.A. thesis, Universidade do Lisboa, 2019), 19–20.

33. Consul General William L. Jenks, "Annual Report on Commerce and Industries for 1920," Funchal, April 4, 1921; Consular Correspondence, Funchal, Madeira Island, Box 54 (1921), vol. 2, no. 600; RG 84, NARA. See also "Tuqaddim Sina'a Mutarazat Madira," 18.

34. Garrido, "Dos Conventos ao Economuseu," 36.

35. Maria Benedita Almada Câmara, "Madeira Embroidery: A Failed Collective Brand, 1935–1959," *Business History* 53, no. 4 (2011): 586.

36. Vieira, *Bordado Madeira*, 23.

37. "Isti'dad Amrika al-Tijari ba'd al-Harb," *al-Majalla al-Tijariyya al-Suriyya al-Amrikiyya*, December 1918, 29–30.

38. Paula A. de La Cruz, "Marketing the Hearth: Ornamental Embroidery and the Building of the Multinational Singer Sewing Machine Company," *Enterprise and Society* 15, no. 3 (2014): 447.

39. Cruz, "Marketing the Hearth," 448.

40. Deposition of J. Maria P. Henriques of Alex Hamrah and Co., Inc. taken by Vice Consul J. Lord, Funchal, December 12, 1925, 1–3; Consular Correspondence, Funchal, Madeira Island, Box 70 (1925), vol. 2, no. 804.5; RG 84, NARA.

41. William Jenks to Secretary of State, Funchal, April 1921, Consular Correspondence, Funchal, Madeira Island, Box 54 (1921), vol. 2, no. 310; RG 84, NARA. See also "Commerce and Industries of Madeira Island during 1920," in *Commerce Reports* August 6, 1921, 684–690; Vieira, *Bordado Madeira*, 110; Mukarzil, *Tarikh al-Tijara*, 62. See also Garrido, "Dos Conventos ao Economuseu," 36.

42. Deposition of J. Maria P. Henriques, 4.

43. Vieira, *Bordado Madeira*, 70.

44. Clive Glaser, "Home, Farm, and Shop: The Migration of Madeiran Women to South Africa," *Journal of Southern African Studies* 38, no. 4 (2012), 889; Charles P. do Rego, "Portuguese Labor Migration to Curacao," *Caribbean Studies* 42, no. 2 (2014), 157–58; Alberto Vieira, *Historia e Autonomía da Madeira* (Funchal: CEHA-Biblioteca, 2003), 133.

45. "Tuqaddim Sina'a Mutarazat Madira," 17.

46. Linda Reeder, "When the Men Left Sutera: Sicilian Women and Mass Migration," *Women, Gender, and Transnational Lives: Italian Workers of the World*, ed. Donna Gabaccia and Franca Iacovetta, 57–61 (Toronto: University of Toronto Press, 2002); Jennifer Guglielmo, *Living the Revolution: Italian Women's Resistance and Radicalism in New York* (Chapel Hill: University of North Carolina Press, 2010); Sarah Gualtieri, "Gendering the Chain Migration Thesis: Women and Syrian Transatlantic Migration, 1878–1924," *Comparative Studies of South Asia, Africa and the Middle East* 24, no.1 (2004): 68–71; Akram Fouad Khater, "'House' to 'Goddess of the House:' Gender, Class, and Silk in 19th-Century Mount Lebanon," *International Journal of Middle East Studies* 28, no. 3 (1996): 330–33.

47. Migrant labor from the Portuguese islands accounted for 75 percent of all Portuguese immigration to the United States before World War I; see Leo Pap, *The Portuguese-Americans* (Boston: Twayne Publishers, 1981), 56.

48. Glaser, "Home, Farm, and Shop," 887.

49. Madeira Embroidery Club meeting minutes, Funchal, April 6, 1922, 1; Consular Correspondence, Funchal, Madeira Island, box 59 (1922), vol. 4, no. 850.4; RG 84, NARA.

50. Câmara, "Madeira Embroidery," 585.

51. Vieira, *Bordado Madeira*, 35–39.

52. Mukarzil, *Tarikh al-Tijara*, 44.

53. Garrido, "Dos Conventos ao Economuseu," 35.

54. Mukarzil, *Tarikh al-Tijara*, 44.

55. Glaser, "Home, Farm, and Shop," 887.

56. Carita, *História da Madeira*, 124.

57. "Durur al-Mudarba fi-Matrazat Madira," *al-Majalla al-Tijariyya al-Suriyya al-Amrikiyya*, July 1920, 33–34.

58. William Jenkins to Secretary of State, Funchal, September 30, 1921, 1; Consular Correspondence, Funchal, Madeira Island, box 54 (1921), vol. 2, no. 610; RG 84; NARA.

59. Consul General Stillman Eells to Secretary of State, Funchal, April 12, 1922, 1–2; Consular Correspondence, Funchal, Madeira Island, box 59 (1922), vol. 4, no. 850; RG 84, NARA.

60. These four firms were Madeira Embroidery Company; British Embroidery Company; Madeira House of Reid, Castro, and Co.; and H. C. Payne. Stillman Eells to Secretary of State, Funchal, April 12, 1922, 2.

61. J. De Vasconcelos, "Esvocandao ... em Redor da Industria de Bordados," *O Operario*, April 15, 1922, 1.

62. S. W. Eells, "World Textile News in Brief: Reducing Madeira Embroidery Workers' Wages," in *Commerce Reports*, May 22, 1922, 470.

63. Mallouk's businesses in Funchal included the Elias Mallouk and Bros. firm; the Mallouk Corporation; and H. Mallouk and Co. Murad L. Carter on behalf of Elias Mallouk to Consul General Stillman Eells, Funchal, January 3, 1922; Consular Correspondence, Funchal, Madeira Island, box 60 (1922), vol. 5, no. 865.5. RG 84, NARA.

64. Madeira Embroidery Club meeting minutes, Funchal, April 11, 1922, 1–2; Consular Correspondence, Funchal, Madeira Island, box 59 (1922), vol. 4, no. 850.4; RG 84, NARA. See also Consul General Stillman Eells to Secretary of State, Funchal, April 5, 1922; Consular Correspondence, Funchal, Madeira Island, box 59 (1922), vol. 4, no. 850.4; RG 84, NARA.

65. J. De Vasconcelos, "Esvocandao", 1.

66. Vasconcelos, "Esvocandao," 1. Underlining in original. The author evokes British colonialism as vexing Syria, confusing the British Mandate in Palestine with the French Mandate in Syria and Lebanon.

67. Madeira Embroidery Club meeting minutes, Funchal, December 22, 1922, 1–2; Consular Correspondence, Funchal, Madeira Island, box 60 (1922), vol. 5, no. 851; RG 84, NARA.

68. Madeira Embroidery Club meeting minutes, April 6, 1922, 1; Consular Correspondence, Funchal, Madeira Island, box 59 (1922), vol. 4, no. 850.4; RG 84, NARA.

69. Consul General Stillman W Eells memorandum, Funchal, s.d., 1–2; Consular Correspondence, Funchal, Madeira Island, box 57 (1922), vol. 2, no. 340; RG 84, NARA.

70. Vasconcelos retraction excerpted in Stillman Eells memorandum, Funchal, s.d.

71. Consul General Stillman Eells to Governor Civil Coronel Nobre de Veiga, Funchal, May 9, 1922; Consular Correspondence, Funchal, Madeira Island, box 57 (1922), vol. 2, no. 430; RG 84, NARA; and Governor Civil Coronel Nobre de Veiga reply to Consul General Stillman Eells, Funchal, June 14, 1922; Consular Correspondence, Funchal, Madeira Island, box 57 (1922), vol. 2, no. 430; RG 84, NARA.

72. "A Verdade Nua: Portugeses ou Sirios?" *O Operario*, May 7, 1922, clipping; Consular Correspondence, Funchal, Madeira Island, box 57 (1922), vol. 2, no. 340; RG 84, NARA.

73. "A Verdade Nua," May 7, 1922.

74. "A Verdade Nua," May 7, 1922.

75. Consul General Stillman Eells consular report no. 195, "Discrimination by the Central Government in Lisbon against the District of Funchal," Funchal, February 7, 1923, 1–2; Consular Correspondence, Funchal, Madeira Island, box 66 (1923), vol. 6, no. 810.8; RG 84, NARA.

76. Stillman Eells to Secretary of State, Funchal, November 23, 1921, 1; Con-

sular Correspondence, Funchal, Madeira Island, box 54 (1921), vol. 2, no. 810.8; RG 84, NARA.

77. Draft American Foreign Service Report on Decree No. 10046, Funchal, s.d., pp. 2–3; Consular Correspondence, Funchal, Madeira Island, box 69 (1924), vol. 4, no. 621; RG 84, NARA.

78. William Jenkins, "Commerce and Industries of Madeira Islands during 1920," *Commerce Reports*, August 6, 1921, 685.

79. Department of State Memo, "Emergency Tariff Act of May 27, 1921," Washington D.C., June 15, 1921; Consular Correspondence, Funchal, Madeira Island, box 54 (1921), vol. 2, no. 621; RG 84, NARA.

80. Bryan Garrett discusses this hearing closely and identifies the Syrian merchant signatories: Elias Mallouk and Brothers, the Mallouk Corporation, Habib Mallouk and Company, Saydah Importing Company, Alexander J. Hamrah, Kemal Katen and Company, F. M. Jabara and Company, the Bardwil Brothers, Joseph Balesh and Brothers, Massabni Brothers, M. N. Abualy, Shalom and Company, Dweck and Hafif, Amin Samara Company, A. M. Salamy and Company, and Azoon and Bonany. See Bryan Garrett, "Otherness and Belonging in 'Democratic Empires': The Syrian Diaspora and Transatlantic Discourses of Identity," (Ph.D. dissertation, University of Texas Arlington, 2016), 275–79.

81. United States Senate Committee on Finance, "Tariff Hearing on H.R. 7456" (Washington D.C.: Government Printing Office, 1921), 179.

82. The prevailing tariff structure before 1921 was set by the McKinley Tariff (1890) and Dingley Act (1907), which set a tariff of no more than 60 percent of the goods' foreign value before export, rather than their American retail price.

83. "Tariff Hearing on H.R. 7456," 179–80.

84. "Tariff Hearing on H.R. 7456," 181.

85. Department of State Memo, "Emergency Tariff Act of May 27, 1921," Washington D.C., June 15, 1921.

86. Madeira Embroidery Club petition to Agent in Charge, Customs House of New York City and Consul General Stillman Eells, Funchal, June 18, 1923; Consular Correspondence, Funchal, Madeira Island, box 63 (1923), vol. 3, no. 621; RG 84, NARA. The letters signatories include: S. G. Samara (club secretary); Elias Haddad of K. Katen and Co.; Mallouk Bros.; Gabriel Shami of J. Balesh and Co.; B. Francis of Suigany and Skaf; Lian and Mubarak; H. Mallouk and Co.; F. M. Jabara and Bros.; Bardwil Bros.; Saydah Importing; A. G. Samara Co.; J. R. Beyda and Sons; Antoun Messara (for Elias Mallouk); Alex J. Hamrah; Shalom and Co; E. N. Massabni; Tweel Importing; A. Hougaz; and Salamy Corporation.

87. E. Francis (Suigany and Skaf) and G. Farra (Salamy Corp and B. Kassab) letter to James Barnes, U.S. Customs, Funchal, May 28, 1923, 2–3; Consular Correspondence, Funchal, Madeira Island, box 63 (1923), vol. 3, no. 621; RG 84, NARA.

88. E. Francis (Suigany and Skaf) and G. Farra (Salamy Corp and B. Kassab) letter to James Barnes, U.S. Customs, Funchal, May 28, 1923, 6.

89. Stillman Eells to Special Agent in Charge, United States Customs Service, Funchal, April 4, 1923; Consular Correspondence, Funchal, Madeira Island, box 63 (1923), vol. 3, no. 621; RG 84, NARA.

90. Stillman Eells to Secretary of State, "Report No. 216: Suspected Undervaluation of Embroideries Exported from Madeira," Funchal, February 28, 1923, 4–5; Consular Correspondence, Funchal, Madeira Island, box 63 (1923), vol. 3, no. 621; RG 84, NARA. In this report, Eells alleges coordinated undervaluation by twenty-two of the club's thirty-two members, all Syrian American firms from New York.

91. Vice Consul Hernan Vogenitz to Secretary of State, "Report No. 291: Gross Undervaluation of Labor Costs by Embroidery Exporting Houses," Funchal, November 17, 1923, 1–4; Consular Correspondence, Funchal, Madeira Island, box 63 (1923), vol. 3, no. 621; RG 84, NARA.

92. The Chinese-made embroideries mimicked the Madeiran style, and similar patterns occurred in the Azores and the Philippines. The purported goal of reexporting goods was to adhere to new trade regulations governing origin provenance, and between 1922 and 1924, Chinese goods under the Mallouk, Bardwil, and Hamrah brands were discovered to have been routed through Funchal. See E. N. Massabni to Consul General Stillman Eells, Funchal, February 8, 1922, 1; Consular Correspondence, Funchal, Madeira Island, box 58 (1922), vol. 3, no. 621; RG 84, NARA; and U.S. Treasury Department to Stillman Eells, New York City, September 28, 1923; Consular Correspondence, Funchal, Madeira Island, box 63 (1923), vol. 3, no. 621; RG 84, NARA.

93. Vogenitz, "Report No. 291: Gross Undervaluation of Labor Costs," 4.

94. Vice Consul Kemp reported weekly labor costs among embroiderers to the U.S. Customs Information Exchange for two years after the introduction of per-point pricing. See Kemp to U.S. Custom Information Exchange, Funchal; Consular Correspondence, Funchal, Madeira Island, box 67 (1924), vol. 2, no. 621; RG 84, NARA.

95. Carl Stern, attorney L. Tweel and Co., to Secretary of State, New York City, October 6, 1924, 1–2; Consular Correspondence, Funchal, Madeira Island, box 67 (1924), vol. 2, no. 621; RG 84, NARA.

96. "Madeira Embroideries: Gain in Exports of Them, Though Qualities Are Inferior," *New York Times*, February 15, 1920, e12.

97. Vieria, *Bordado Madeira*, 71.

98. Deposition of J. Maria P. Henriques of Alex Hamrah and Co., Inc. taken by Vice Consul J. Lord, Funchal, December 12, 1925, 7; Consular Correspondence, Funchal, Madeira Island, box 70 (1925), vol. 2, no. 804.5; RG 84, NARA.

99. Deposition of J. Maria P. Henriques, 13.

100. "Madeira, Wages in Various Occupations," *Wages in Foreign Countries: A Compilation of the Latest Available Data Regarding Wages in Industrial and Agricultural Employments* (Washington D.C.: Government Printing Office, 1929), 178–79.

101. "General Strike in Madeira," *The Times* (London), April 3, 1920, 9.

102. Fares of K. Katen and Co. to Consul General William Jenkins, Funchal, August 6, 1921, 1–3; Consular Correspondence, Funchal, Madeira Island, box 54 (1921), vol. 2, no. 621; RG 84, NARA. K. Katen and Co. was headquartered at 80 Washington Street in New York, "Madira," *al-Sa'ih*, April 24, 1922, 3. It is likely (but not certain), this was Fares Saydah, who worked for a few related firms in Funchal before returning to New York to supervise kimono factories in the mid-1920s.

103. Consul General William Jenkins to Secretary of State, Funchal, August 19, 1921, 1; Consular Correspondence, Funchal, Madeira Island, box 54 (1921), vol. 2, no. 621; RG 84, NARA.

104. Jenkins, "Commerce and Industries of Madeira Islands during 1920," 684. See also Câmara, "Madeira Embroidery," 586–87; "Tuqaddim Sina'a Mutarazat Madira," *al-Majalla al-Tijariyya al-Suriyya al-Amrikiyya* March 1920, 18.

105. Stillman Eells to Secretary of State, Funchal, January 8, 1923; Consular Correspondence, Funchal, Madeira Island, box 60 (1923), vol. 5, no. 851.5; RG 84, NARA.

106. Carita, *Historia da Madeira*, 124–25.

107. Jorge Braga de Macedo, "Paper No. 320: Portuguese Currency Experience: A Historical Perspective," paper given at the Yale University Economic Growth Center, September 1979, 7.

108. Vogenitz, "Report No. 291: Gross Undervaluation of Labor Costs, 4.

109. Passport application for Ameen Samara, Funchal, January 17, 1925; Consular Correspondence, Funchal, Madeira Island, box 70 (1925), vol. 2, no. 130.8; RG 84, NARA. Samara was from Mardjoun, Syria, and had emigrated to the United States in 1897, where he became a citizen in 1908. The A. G. Samara firm was modest compared to the Mallouk, Massabni, Katen, Balesh, and Saydah companies (each of them invoicing two to three times the volume of Samara and Co.); see Consul General Stillman Eells to Department of State, "Marking of Embroidery Made in Azores and Shipped from Madeira," Funchal, July 25, 1922, 3.

110. Garrido, "Dos Conventos ao Economuseu," 37. The sale is registered in the Diário de Notícias, 1925-01-01, n.º 15.183, p. 3. PT/ABM/VIC/D-B/001-001/000001.

111. Vice Consul K. Kemp to Scretary of State, Funchal, April 22, 1925, 1–2; Consular Correspondence, Funchal, Madeira Island, box 70 (1925), vol. 2, no 621; RG 84, NARA. I list the top seven firms here, but fifty new Madeiran Portuguese merchants submitted U.S. invoices during the first quarter of 1925.

112. Cline, *Perfection, Never Less*, 64.

113. Edward Pickard, "World Textile New in Brief," *Commerce Reports: A Weekly Survey of Foreign Trade*, February 23, 1931, 498.

114. Vice Consul K. Kemp to Secretary of State, Funchal, March 25, 1925, 1; Consular Correspondence, Funchal, Madeira Island, box 70 (1925), vol. 2, no. 621; RG 84, NARA; "Drop in Madeira Embroideries," *New York Times*, December 12, 1925, E21.

115. "Drop in Madeira Embroideries," E21.

116. Câmara, "Madeira Embroidery," 583, 588–89.

117. Vieira, *Bordado Madeira*, 72–73.

118. Aimee Loiselle, "Puerto Rican Needle Workers and Colonial Migrations, Deindustrialization as Pathways Lost," *Journal of Working Class Studies* 4, no. 2 (2019): 40–54.

119. Cline, *Perfection, Never Less*, 35.

120. "Mogabgab, Emil," May 9, 1921. New York State Archives, Albany, New York. New York, New York National Guard Service Cards, 1917–1954, series B2001, roll 17. See also a 1923 letter from Emil published in "107th Infantry Company Notes," *Seventh Regiment Gazette* 38, no. 1 (October 1923), 38.

121. For a representative sample of ship itineraries, see National Archives, Kew, England, BT27 Board of Trade: Commercial and Statistical Department, Outwards Passenger Lists, Series BT27 entries: "Emile Mogabgab," September 29, 1924, departure Natal (Brazil) to Southampton; "Emile Mogabgab," October 31, 1924, Southampton to Madeira; "Mogabgab, Emile and Farro, Gabriel," June 27, 1928, departure Southampton to New York. See also "Jabara, F. M. and Bros.," *Syrian American Business Directory* (New York: Arida and Andria, 1930), 21.

122. Cline, *Perfection, Never Less*, 51.

123. Cline, *Perfection, Never Less*, 30, 50. The partnership went awry in 1928, resulting in the departure of Jabara and Farra from the island. On Farra, see U.S. House of Representatives, "Certain Reports of Immigration Inspector Marcus Braun," Document No. 884, 59th Congress, 1st Session (1906), 16. In the Michael Suleiman Collection, box 66, Arab American National Museum (Dearborn, MI). See also Georges Gabriel Farra, September 1920, Passaportes caixa 349, no. processo 126, passaporte 55. Arquivo Regional da Madeira.

124. Cline, *Perfection, Never Less*, 69.

125. Some of this anxiety is captured in a 1928 letter Vera sent to Emile, stating her concern that should they marry: "the people from your country...are not popular in our country. You know that as well as I do." Emile's family settled on Marghab, reasoning that it was the name of a Hospitaller fortress from the crusading era. Cline, *Perfection, Never Less*, 53–61.

126. Copyrights KK100444 and KK100445 of 4 September 1954. United States Copyright Office, 1946–1954 Copyright Registration Cards (1946), 1310.

127. "Laces And Embroideries: Chinese Filet Superior in Design and Workmanship to Italian, Says Importer," *Women's Wear* 16, no. 19 (January 23, 1918), 3.

128. Ilyas Mallouk announcement, *al-Sa'ih*, April 26, 1920, 4; Bardwil Bros. announcement, "al-Tijara al-Suriyya fi-Niyu Yurk," *al-Majalla al-Tijariyya al-Suriyya al-Amrikiyya*, April 1919, i. See also William Gervase Clarence-Smith, "Middle Eastern Migrants in the Philippines: Entrepreneurs and Cultural Brokers," *Asian Journal of Social Science* 32, no. 3 (2004): 425–57; Isa Blumi, *Ottoman Refugees 1878–1939: Migration in a Post-Imperial World* (London: Bloomsbury, 2013), 109–10; Timothy Marr, "Diasporic Intelligences in the American Philippine Empire: The Transnational Career of Dr. Najeeb Mitry Saleeby," *Mashriq and Mahjar: Journal of Middle East and North African Migration Studies* 2, no. 1 (2014): 78–106.

129. "May Import Lace from European Ports," *Women's Wear*, April 9, 1918, 1.

130. Clarence-Smith, "Middle Eastern Migrants in the Philippines," 449–50. He enumerates the major Syrian exporters of embroidered linen in 1927 as: E. Awad and Co.; Antonio A Brimo; G. K. Jureidini; Mallouk, Elias and Brother; R .G. Meluk; Shalom and Co. Philippine; and Juan Ysmael and Co. Inc. See also Blumi, *Ottoman Refugees*, 108–14; Jacob Norris, *The Lives and Deaths of Jubrail Dabdoub: or, How the Bethlehemites Discovered Amerka* (Stanford, CA: Stanford University Press, 2023), 113–15.

131. "Memorandum of the Interdepartmental Committee on Philippine Affairs in Regard to Various Problems Concerning the Relations between the United States and the Philippine Islands," 1940, 6–7. Series Diplomatic Correspondence, Philippines (1937–1940), Presidential Papers of Franklin D. Roosevelt, Franklin D. Roosevelt Library, New York. See also Clarence-Smith, "Middle Eastern Migrants in the Philippines," 450.

132. "Tijarat al-Bayad fi-l-Alam wa-Tanawi' Ahamiyyatha," *al-Majalla al-Tijariyya al-Suriyya al-Amrikiyya*, March 1925, 10–11.

133. "Millions of Chinese," *Syrian World*, March 16, 1934, 2.

134. "The Chinese Embroidery Industry," *Journal of the Royal Society of Arts* 75, no. 3870 (January 21, 1927): 259–60. Interestingly, the society reported Madeiran designs had fallen from fashion.

135. "Millions of Chinese," 2. The club's president was Ellis Basha, of El-Baroideries.

136. Ambassador Frank Lockhart to Secretary of State, "Administrative Measures Affecting Export Trade: Linen," Peking, February 2, 1940, 1–3; Consular Correspondence, Tokyo, Japan, (1940), no. 690; RG 84, NARA.

137. Frank Lockhart telegram to Secretary of State, February 2, 1940, 3.

138. Thomas Derdak, *International Directory of Company Histories* (Farmington Hills: St. James Press/Centgage, 2009), 15–16. Bardwil Industries returned to China in the 1960s.

139. Karine Walther, *Sacred Interests: The United States and the Islamic World, 1821–1921* (Chapel Hill: University of North Carolina Press, 2015), 191–237.

Chapter 5

1. Zahdi (Fallaha) Barsa oral history interview with Alixa Naff, Detroit, May 21, 1980; Faris and Yamna Naff Arab-American Collection Archives Center, National Museum of American History (hereafter NMAH/NC), box 280.

2. "Syrians Forcing to the Front in Lace and Embroideries," *Women's Wear*, November 12, 1917, 4.

3. P. E. Marrinan, "Re Theft from Interstate Shipment," Boise, August 16, 1919, 4–6; Investigative Casefiles of the Bureau of Investigation, Miscellaneous Files, 1908–1922 (hereafter M1085), case no. 36757; record group 65, National Archives and Records Administration (hereafter RG 65, NARA).

4. John Tofik Karam, *Another Arabesque: Syrian-Lebanese Ethnicity in Neoliberal Brazil* (Philadelphia: Temple University Press, 2007), 31–35; Camila Pastor, *The Mexican Mahjar: Transnational Maronites, Jews, and Arabs under the French Mandate* (Austin: University of Texas Press, 2017), 35–39; Theresa Alfaro-Velcamp, *So Far from Allah, So Close to Mexico: Middle Eastern Immigrants in Modern Mexico* (Austin: University of Texas Press, 2007), 70–109; Sarah Gualtieri, "Gendering the Chain Migration Thesis: Women and Syrian Transatlantic Migration, 1878–1924," *Comparative Studies of South Asia, Africa and the Middle East* 24, no.1 (2004): 67–78; Akram Fouad Khater, *Inventing Home: Emigration, Gender, and the Middle Class in Lebanon, 1870–1920* (Berkeley: University of California Press, 2001), 82–83; Alixa Naff, *Becoming American: The Early Arab Immigrant Experience* (Carbondale: Southern Illinois University Press, 1985), 128–61. On the peddler statues in Mexico and Lebanon, see "Plaza of the Lebanese Migrant, Veracruz, Mexico," *Atlas Obscura*, September 3, 2019, https://www.atlasobscura.com/places/plaza-of-the-lebanese-migrant.

5. Charlotte Karem Albrecht, *Possible Histories: Arab Americans and the Queer Ecology of Peddling* (Oakland: University of California Press, 2023), 4.

6. Ascertaining arrival rates before 1900 is difficult because the Mexican Foreign Affairs Ministry did not yet register Syrians, Lebanese, or Palestinians by nationality. Employing family histories, Martha Díaz de Kuri and Lourdes Macluf estimate the first Arab migrants arrived in 1879 or 1880; Martha Díaz De Kuri and Lourdes Macluf, *De Líbano a México: un crónica de un pueblo emigrante / Min-Lubnan ila-l-Maksik: Qusus Shaʻb Yuhajir* (Mexico City: n.p, 1999), 46–47.

7. Moisés González Navarro, *Los extranjeros en México y los mexicanos en el extranjero, 1821–1970*, vol. 2 (Mexico City: El Colegio de Mexico, 1993), 274–75; Luis Alfonso Ramírez Carrillo, "De Buhoneros a empresarios: La inmigración libanesa en el sureste de México," *Historia Mexicana* 43, no. 3 (1994): 456.

8. Rebeca Inclán Rubio, "La migración libanesa en México," in *El Medio Oriente en la Ciudad de México* (Mexico City: Instituto de Cultura de la Ciudad de México, 1999); Felipe de Jesús Bello Gómez, "Inmigración y capacidad empresarial en los albores de la industrialización de México," *Secuencia* 68 (2007): 9–54.

9. This figure is almost certainly conservative, as the French sought to limit the inclusion of non-Lebanese emigrants from the territories under its Mandate during the 1920s; Kohei Hashimoto, "Lebanese Population Movement 1920–1939," in *Lebanese in the World: A Century of Emigration*, ed. Albert Hourani and Nadim Shehadi (London: I.B. Tauris and Centre for Lebanese Studies, 1992), 109.

10. Carmen Mercedes Páez Oropeza, *Los libaneses en México: Asimilación de un grupo étnico* (Mexico City: Institutico Nacional de Antropología e Historia, 1984), 173.

11. Oropeza, *Los libaneses en México*, 173. See also Díaz De Kuri and Macluf, *De Líbano a México / Min-Lubnan ila-l-Maksik*, 45–46; Gómez, "Emigración a México y Capacidad Empresarial," 30; Doris Musalem Rahal, "La migración palestina a México, 1893–1949," *Destine México: un estudio de las migraciones asiáticas a México, siglos XIX y XX*, ed. Maria Elena Ota Mashima (Mexico City: El Colegio de Mexico, 1997), 316; Devi Mays, *Forging Ties, Forging Passports: Migration and the Modern Sephardi Diaspora* (Stanford, CA: Stanford University Press, 2020), 44; Evelyn Hu-DeHart, "On Coolies and Shopkeepers," in *Displacements and Diasporas: Asians in the Americas* (New Brunswick, NJ: Rutgers University Press, 2005), 78–111; Erika Lee, "Enforcing the Borders: Chinese Exclusion along the U.S. Borders with Canada and Mexico, 1882–1924," *Journal of American History* 89, no. 1 (2002): 54–86; Gómez, "Emigración a México y Capacidad Empresarial," 10.

12. Marcus Braun, "Report of the Special Immigrant Inspector Marcus Braun," to Hon. Frank P. Sargent, Commissioner-General of Immigration, New York City, September 20, 1903, 3–5; Immigration and Naturalization Service, Subject Correspondence Files, European Investigations, case 52320/47, folder 2; RG 85, NARA.

13. Carlos Martínez Assad and Martha Díaz Kuri, "Los libaneses, un modelo de adaptación," in *Veracruz, puerto de llegada*, ed. Carlos Martínez Assad (Mexico City: H. Ayuntamiento de Veracruz, 2007), 70–71; Gómez, "Inmigración y capacidad empresarial," 21n42; Díaz De Kuri and Macluf, *De Líbano a México / Min-Lubnan ila-l-Maksik*, 55–56; Pastor, *The Mexican Mahjar*, 44–45.

14. U.S. Consul of Veracruz to Secretary of State, "List of Syrians and Turks in Veracruz," Washington D.C., January 24, 1918, 2–3; Records of the Department of State, M 367, roll 222, no. 763.72112/6778; RG 59, NARA.

15. This pattern—ports to railways peddling—was also evident in Argentina, see Lily Pearl Balloffet, *Argentina in the Global Middle East* (Stanford, CA: Stanford University Press, 2020), 35–46.

16. Sarah E. John, "Arabic-Speaking Immigration to the El Paso Area," in *Cross-

ing the Waters: Arabic-Speaking Immigrants to the United States Before 1940, ed. Eric Hooglund (Washington D.C.: Smithsonian Institution Press, 1987), 105–18. See also Sarah E. John, "'Trade Will Lead a Man Far: Syrian Immigration to El Paso, 1900–1935," (M.A. thesis, University of Texas at El Paso, 1982); Alfaro-Velcamp, *So Far from Allah*, 58.

17. Ann R. Gabbert, "El Paso, a Sight for Sore Eyes: Medical and Legal Aspects of Syrian Immigration to El Paso, 1906–1907," *The Historian* 65, no. 1 (2002): 15–42.

18. Ann Louise Bragdon, "Early Arabic-Speaking Immigrant Communities in Texas," *Arab Studies Quarterly* 11, no. 2/3 (1989): 87.

19. Carrillo, "De Buhoneros a empresarios," 456.

20. Patrick Ettinger, *Imaginary Lines: Border Enforcement and the Origins of Undocumented Immigration, 1882–1930* (Austin: University of Texas Press, 2010), 97.

21. Immigration and Naturalization Service, Subject Correspondence Files, Ellis Island, 1900–1933, case no. 52707, "Edward F. McSweeney Hearing, Deportation Cases," 1902, 66pp. M1904; RG 85, NARA.

22. Immigration and Naturalization Service, Subject Correspondence Files, European Investigations, 1898–1936, case no. 52320/47, "Marcus Braun European Investigation Including Hungarian Border Police, Falck & Company, and Booking of Undesirable Aliens to the United States via Mexico," 1903, 129pp. M1904; RG 85, NARA.

23. Immigration and Naturalization Service, Subject Correspondence Files, Mexican Immigration, 1906–1930, case no. 51423/1, "Seraphic Report Regarding Conditions on Mexican Border, 1906–07," 1907, 86pp. M1904; RG 85, NARA.

24. Rana Razek, "Trails and Fences: Syrian Migration Networks and Immigration Restriction, 1885–1907," *Amerasia Journal* 44, no. 1 (2018): 113.

25. Naff, *Becoming American*, 138. Najib Arbeely is also recalled as the editor of *Kawkab Amrika* (est. 1892), a serial he edited with his brother, Ibrahim.

26. Nageeb Arbeely testimony given to Mr. Campbell, New York City, March 22, 1900, 440-R. Terence Vincent Powderly Papers, Series 3 Immigration Miscellaneous, "Legal Report and Testimony: Luigi Graziano Case Regarding Corruption in the Bureau of Immigration," ACHA-DC.

27. Several historians have written about Braun's work, including Margot Canaday, *The Straight State: Sexuality and Citizenship in Twentieth-Century America* (Princeton, NJ: Princeton University Press, 2009); Ettinger, *Imaginary Lines*; Lee, "Enforcing the Borders"; Gunther Peck, "Feminizing White Slavery in the United States: Marcus Braun and the Transnational Traffic in White Bodies," *Workers across the Americas*, ed. Leon Fink, 221–44; and Razek, "Trails and Fences."

28. Marcus Braun, "Report about Alien Seamen and Other Immigration from Europe," Department of Commerce and Labor, Bureau of Immigration and Naturalization, Washington D.C., July 5, 1908, 22–23; Immigration and Naturalization

Service, Subject Correspondence Files, European Investigations, case 52320/47, folder 2; RG 85, NARA. For deeper discussion of Braun's investigation, see Razek, "Trails and Fences," 105–26.

29. Braun, "Report of the Special Immigrant Inspector Marcus Braun," 9–10.

30. "Marcus Braun Investigation of Illegal Immigration from Mexico to United States," 13. After concluding the Fares case, Braun redispatched to Europe in 1909 to pursue the "problem of white slavery"; see Canaday, *The Straight State*, 19–25.

31. Braun, "Report of the Special Immigrant Inspector Marcus Braun," 2–3.

32. "Marcus Braun Investigation of Illegal Immigration from Mexico to United States," 17. See also Díaz de Kuri and Macluf, *De Líbano a México*, 160.

33. U.S. House of Representatives, "Certain Reports of Immigration Inspector Marcus Braun," Document No. 884, 59th Congress, 1st Session (1906), 24–25. In the Michael Suleiman Collection, box 66, Arab American National Museum (Dearborn, MI).

34. Braun, "Report of the Special Immigrant Inspector Marcus Braun," 4.

35. Seraphic's 1911 report was titled "The Greek Padrone Syrian in the United States," in *Abstracts of the Immigration Commission*, vol. 2, ed. William Paul Dillingham (1911), 391–97. See also Katherine Benton-Cohen, *Inventing the Immigration Problem: The Dillingham Commission and Its Legacy* (Cambridge, MA: Harvard University Press, 2018), 217–31; Razek, "Trails and Fences," 120–21.

36. The third port was Progreso, adjacent to Syrian colony in Mérida. See Pastor, *The Mexican Mahjar*, 13.

37. A. A. Seraphic, Immigration Inspector to Commissioner General of Immigration, "Report re Conditions on Mexican Border," Washington D.C., January 8, 1907, 1; Immigration and Naturalization Service, Subject Correspondence Files, Mexican Immigration, case no. 51423/1; M1904; RG 85, NARA.

38. Randa Tawil, "A 'Flying Carpet to Doom': Retracing Gender and Orientalism through the Transnational Journeys of a Syrian Migrant Woman, 1912–1949," *Frontiers: A Journal of Women Studies* 43, no. 1 (2022): 133–34.

39. On Syrians in Yucatán, see Luis A. Ramírez Carillo, *De cómo los libaneses conquistaron la península de Yucatán: Migración, identidad étnica y cultura empresarial* (Mérida: Centro Peninsular en Humanidad y Ciencias Sociales; Universidad Nacional Autonomía de México, 2012).

40. Seraphic, "Report re Conditions on Mexican Border," 2; see also Razek, "Trails and Fences," 118.

41. Seraphic, "Report re Conditions on Mexican Border," 2.

42. Seraphic, "Report re Conditions on Mexican Border," 4–5; see also Razek, "Trails and Fences," 119.

43. Passport application for Alcibiades Seraphic, New York City, November 7, 1918; U.S. Passport Applications, 1795–1925, volume 9, Military, Civilian, Federal

Employees and Dependents, no. 295; M1490, RG 59, NARA. Meğri was among the towns subject to the Lausanne population exchange of 1923–24; it was renamed Fethiye in 1934.

44. Passport application for Alcibiades Seraphic, New York City, October 22, 1922; M1490, roll 2123, no. 227596; NARA. Alcibiades's younger brother, Achilles, lived in New York and worked in a cigarette factory; he also briefly worked as an immigration interpreter. See Petition for Naturalization for Achilles Seraphic, New York City, June 17, 1915; Records of District Courts of the United States, 1685–2009, roll 129, no. 17022; RG 21, NARA.

45. Seraphic's appearance also created trouble for him. Years after this investigation, military police detained Seraphic in Rhode Island because he made small talk with a stranger near the naval base; that stranger reported him to the BOI as a suspicious person who "was apparently a Mexican." "In Re: A. Seraphic," Newport, May 11, 1917, 5; General Records of the Federal Bureau of Investigation, Investigative Records, Miscellaneous Files, M1085, case no. 11359; RG 65.2.2, NARA.

46. Razek, "Trails and Fences," 113; Ettinger, *Imaginary Lines*, 109; George T. Díaz and Holly M. Karibo, *Border Policing: A History of Enforcement and Evasion in North America* (Austin: University of Texas Press, 2020), 124–25.

47. "Report to the Immigration Section Commonwealth Club of California," San Francisco, June 26, 1926, 7–8. Immigration and Naturalization Service, Subject Correspondence Files, Asian Immigration and Exclusion, case 53244/1E; RG 85, NARA. See also Tawil, "A 'Flying Carpet to Doom'," 120–144; Sarah M. A. Gualtieri, *Arab Routes: Pathways to Syrian California* (Stanford, CA: Stanford University Press, 2019), 36; Elliot Young, *Alien Nation: Chinese Migration in the Americas from the Coolie Era through World War II* (Chapel Hill: University of North Carolina Press, 2014), 130.

48. Statement of E. D. Winks concerning the Extortion of Money from Immigrants, El Paso, December 31, 1906, 1–4; Immigration and Naturalization Service, Subject Correspondence Files, Mexican Immigration, case no. 51423/1; M1904; RG 85, NARA.

49. Seraphic, "Report re Conditions on Mexican Border," 24–25. See also Anna Pegler-Gordon, *In Sight of America: Photography and the Development of U.S. Immigration Policy, 1880–1930* (Berkeley: University of California Press, 2009), 174–91; and Amy L. Fairchild, *Science at the Borders: Immigrant Medical Inspection and the Shaping of the Modern Industrial Labor Force* (Baltimore, MD: Johns Hopkins University Press, 2003), 157–62.

50. Diaz and Karibo, *Border Policing*, 116; Erika Lee, *The Making of Asian America* (New York City: Simon and Schuster, 2015), 200–201.

51. Miller, "In re: Passport Matters," Laredo, December 14, 1917, 181; General Records of the Federal Bureau of Investigation, Investigative Records, Old

German Files (hereafter M1085), case no. 58623; RG 65.2.2, NARA. The details of Tombray's case suggest he may have been Sephardi, another Ottoman diaspora community with close ties to borderlands commerce.

52. 'Assy Shaheen and Sons advertisement, *al-Majalla al-Tijariyya al-Suriyya al-Amrikiyya*, December 1918, 48–49.

53. Louis F. Lutfy oral history interview with Alixa Naff, Detroit, May 2, 1980; Faris and Yamna Naff Arab-American Collection Archives Center, National Museum of American History (hereafter NMAH/NC), box 277.

54. Ashley Johnson Bavery, "Lifetimes of Instability: The Consequences of Excluding Syrian Boys on the Progressive Era U.S.-Mexico Border, *Mashriq and Mahjar: Journal of Middle East and North African Migration Studies* 11, no. 2 (2024); Ashley Johnson Bavery, "The Unauthorized Mahjar: Syrian Muslim Migrations between the Midwest and Mexico in the Twentieth Century," talk given at the Newberry Library (Chicago, IL), April 29, 2022.

55. Mahomed Wazney oral history interview with Alixa Naff, Detroit, June 3, 1980; NMAH/NC, box 279.

56. Faris Naff Memoir, "The Story of My Life" (Los Angeles: Self-published, 1952); NMAH/NC, box 279, series 1, folder 9.

57. Nazha Haney oral history interview with Alixa Naff, Detroit, MI, July 1962, NMAH/NC, box 262.

58. Khalil Goushe oral history interview with Alixa Naff, Oxen Hill, MD, January 1981, NMAH/NC, box 280.

59. Ettinger, *Imaginary Lines*, 97.

60. Seraphic, "Report re Conditions on Mexican Border," 4.

61. Bureau of Investigation Chief Bielaski to W. M. Offley, "Re A. B. Abdelnour," New York, February 14, 1918, 46–47; M1085, roll 323, case no. 7198; RG 65.2.2, NARA.

62. Pastor, *The Mexican Mahjar*, 56–59; Stacy D. Fahrenthold, "'Claimed by Turkey as Subjects': Ottoman Migrants, Foreign Passports, and Syrian Nationality in the Americas, 1915–1925," in *The Subjects of Ottoman International Law*, ed. Lâle Can, Michael Christopher Low, Kent Schull, and Robert Zens (Bloomington: University of Indiana Press, 2020), 229.

63. Agent Van. V. Curtis report, "Re Bahid Karaham, Syrian suspect," Nogales, December 3, 1917, 2; M1085, roll 257, case no. 96779; RG 65.2.2, NARA.

64. Pastor, *The Mexican Mahjar*, 52–55.

65. Passport Application for John Jirash, Mexico, March 6, 1901; M1490, roll 17, vol. 28, no. 53, NARA.

66. John J. Jirash Naturalization Record Index entry, September 29, 1896; Index to Naturalization Petitions for the United States District and Circuit Courts, Northern District of Illinois, District 9, M1295, roll 91; RG 85, NARA.

67. Affidavit to Overcome Presumption of Expatriation for John J. Jirash, Teziutlán, February 13, 1912; General Records of the Department of State, U.S. Consular Registration Certificates, 1907–1918, no. 30581; RG 59, NARA.

68. Inspector E. P. Reynolds and F. A. Thomas (interpreter), "Re Assad Sallom," Brownsville, November 2, 1917, 1–5; M1085, roll 257, case no. 90833; RG 65.2.2, NARA.

69. U.S. Consul Stewart to the War Trade Board to Secretary of State, "Syrians Established in this Consular District," Washington D.C., March 18, 1918, 1–4; Records of the Department of Status Relating to World War I and Its Termination, M367, roll 224, document 763.72112/7690; RG 59, NARA. Syrian firms recorded in this report: La Casa Blanca (Gabriel Ayub y Cia); La Violeta (S. Ayub y Cia); El Nuevo Mundo (Salomon Abraham Ayub); La Palestina (Felipe Ayub); Monte Líbano (Kellet Azar); and La Ciudad de Mexico (Miguel Atta).

70. J. J. Lawrence, "Re: Amin Frances, Syrian suspect," Laredo, December 13, 1917, 3–4; M1085, roll 484, case no. 105982; RG 65.2.2, NARA.

71. A. H. Miller, "Re: Amin Frances (Syrian)," Laredo, January 9, 1918, 1; M1085, roll 484, case nos. 113458 and 113458; RG 65.2.2, NARA.

72. Miller, "Re: Amin Frances (Syrian)," 1.

73. J. J. Lawrence report, "Re: J. J. Jarash, Syrian suspect," Laredo, December 20, 1917, 1; M1085, case no. 106596; RG 65.2.2, NARA.

74. Z. L. Cobb, "Copy of Circular Letter from Treasury Department Dated February 18, 1918," El Paso, 1–2; M1085, case no. 8000–111684; RG 65.2.2, NARA. See also Randa Tawil, "Racial Borderlines: Ameen Rihani, Mexico, and World War I," *Amerasia Journal* 44, no. 1 (2018): 98–99.

75. Gus T. Jones, "Re: Syrian Activities: Order Refusing Permission to Depart for Mexico," El Paso, March 15, 1918, 2; M1085, case no. 8000-111684; RG 65.2.2, NARA.

76. H. Jenteer, "In Re: Elias Sirgany," New York City, September 3, 1919, 1; M1085, reel 737, case no. 8000-316294; RG 65.2.2, NARA. Sirgany & Skaf also had a factory on Madeira Island and was a member of the Madeira Embroidery Club; see E. C. Frances and G. Farra, Madeira Embroidery Club to James Barnes, U.S. Consulate, Funchal, May 28, 1923, 1. Consular Correspondence, Funchal, Madeira Island, box 63 (1923), vol. 3, no. 621; RG 84, NARA.

77. Robert L. Barnes, "In Re: Turks Entering the U.S.," Washington D.C., September 17, 1918, 1–2; M1085, case no. 8000-71817; RG 65.2.2, NARA.

78. Mays, *Forging Ties, Forging Passports*, 82.

79. Braun, "Report about Alien Seamen and Other Immigration from Europe," 23.

80. Hubert S. Newton, Lieutenant, USNRF, to Major Barnes, Military Intelligence Officer, "Subject George Coury," San Antonio, June 15, 1918, 6. Case no. 232-3145, M1086 Mexican Files, roll 870.

81. Harris, "Re: Maron Beshara," El Paso, September 15, 1917, 1; M1085, case no. 58606; RG 65.2.2, NARA.
82. A. H. Miller, "Re: Alejandro Kefuri (Syrian), Susp- German matter," Eagle Pass, August 26, 1918, 2–13; M1085, roll 681, case no. 8000-266922; RG 65.2.2, NARA.
83. "Re: Syrian Newspaper, Mexico City," Eagle Pass, September 11, 1917, 1; M1085, Mexican Files, roll 862, case no. 2282; RG 65.2.2, NARA.
84. O. L. Tinklepaugh, "Re Dab Kahlele," El Paso, April 26, 1918, 1–2; M1085, roll 589, case no. 8000-186186; RG 65.2.2, NARA.
85. Bates, "Re Manuel Nassar," El Paso, April 24, 1919, 1–2; M1085, roll 705, case no. 287693; RG 65.2.2, NARA.
86. Shuttle Manifest for Selim A Noemi, Laredo, TX, May 29, 1920; Records of the Immigration and Naturalization Service, Statistical and Nonstatistical Manifests of Alien Arrivals at Laredo, Texas, M1502, roll 70, no. 20845; RG 85, NARA. In 1920, he was headed to Ghazir, Mount Lebanon.
87. Salim Ayub Noemy, registry no. 5422, in Archivo General de La Nación (Mexico City), *Libaneses en México*, comp. Stella Maria Gonzalez Cicero, Jorge Nacif Mina, and Raul Gonzalez Lezama (Dicot S.A. de C.V. Digitalicion, 2001).
88. Alfaro-Velcamp, *So Far from Allah*, 95–96.
89. Pastor, *The Mexican Mahjar*, 90–96.
90. Teresa Cuevas Seba and Miguel Mañana Plasencio, *Los libaneses de Yucatán* (Mexico City: n.p, 1990), 36–38; Fitzgerald, *Culling the Masses*, 230–31.
91. The dataset is digitally published as Archivo General de La Nación (Mexico City), *Libaneses en México*, comp. Stella Maria Gonzalez Cicero, Jorge Nacif Mina, and Raul Gonzalez Lezama (Dicot S.A. de C.V. Digitalicion, 2001). This section builds on entries numbered 589–8111, listed with nationalities Libanesa, Siria Libanesa, or Siria.
92. Hashimoto, "Lebanese Population Movement," 87–107; Rahal, "La migración palestina," 312–13.
93. Compare Selim Ayub Noemy, registry no. 5422, in Cicero, Mina, and Lezama, *Libaneses en México*; and Shuttle Manifest for Selim A Noemi, Laredo, TX, May 29, 1920; Records of the Immigration and Naturalization Service, Statistical and Nonstatistical Manifests of Alien Arrivals at Laredo, Texas, M1502, roll 70, no. 20845; RG 85, NARA.
94. Civil Registration of Marriage for Salim Ayub Noemi and Filamina Kuri, Mexico City, August 4, 1921; Archivo de Registro Civil de Distrito Federal, México, 1921, no. 139, 125–26. Jorge Abraham, Pablo Lama, Elias Sarquiz, and Mansur Juan served as witnesses, each affiliated with Noemi's merchant business.
95. Jorge Kuri, registry no. 5428, in Cicero, Mina, and Lezama, *Libaneses en México*.
96. Fred Reiser, Loeb and Schoenfeld company letter and client list to U.S. War

Board, New York, May 23, 1918, P18. NARA, RG 59, M367, roll 261, document no. 763.72112a/5895, 15–18. This document is an appeal application after Loeb and Schoenfeld were added to the Enemy Trading List; dozens of Syrian clients in Latin America (including Matuk) cosigned. Constantino's approximate date of birth is published in his 1930 civil registration of marriage to Narcisa Mazur; see Archivo de Registro Civil de Distrito Federal, Mexico, 1930 Civil Registration Marriages, 91–92. Constantino Matuk died (likely from a stroke) in Mexico City on August 11, 1936; Archivo de Registro Civil de Distrito Federal, Mexico, 1936 Civil Registration Deaths, 147–48.

97. For instance, a Jose K. Matuk—perhaps one of the Matuk brothers in the company's namesake, or perhaps a nephew—was born in Tripoli, Lebanon in 1895, arrived at Tampico on July 26, 1913, and lived in Mexico City in 1930. Jose lists Constantino as his next of kin. Jose K. Matuk, registry no. 6004, in Cicero, Mina, and Lezama, *Libaneses en México*.

98. Matuk y Hnos. peddlers Simon G. Youssef Cheick (from Akkar) and Juan Kuji (from Beirut) both arrived in 1924, Miguel Boulos Kuri in 1928, and so forth. See Simon George Youssef Cheick, registry no. 6357, in Cicero, Mina, and Lezama, *Libaneses en México*. Juan Kuji, registry no. 2337, in Cicero, Mina, and Lezama, *Libaneses en México*. Miguel Boulos Kuri, registry no. 2742, in Cicero, Mina, and Lezama, *Libaneses en México*.

99. Gómez, "Inmigración y capacidad empresarial," 17.

100. Jorge Matuk, registry no. 7999, in Cicero, Mina, and Lezama, *Libaneses en México*.

101. Gómez, "Emigración a México y Capacidad Empresarial," 31–32.

102. Pastor, *The Mexican Mahjar*, 156–57.

103. Pastor, *The Mexican Mahjar*, 157.

104. Pablo Lama, registry no. 2771, in Cicero, Mina, and Lezama, *Libaneses en México*. Lama's stamp and signature also appears among two dozen Lebanese merchants and peddlers in a 1921 petition to the Patriarch of the Maronite Church, Ilyas Huwayyik, asking that a priest be sent to Mexico City to establish a church; Maronite Patriarchal Archive, Bkerke, Lebanon, Ilyas Huwayyik Correspondence, folder 87, document 001ED. Petition letter from Mexico City to Huwayyik, Mexico City, August 27, 1921.

105. Felipe Abraham, registry no. 2965, in Cicero, Mina, and Lezama, *Libaneses en México*.

106. Bechara Yazbek, registration no. 4568, in Cicero, Mina, and Lezama, *Libaneses en México*.

107. Oropeza, *Los libaneses en México*, 141.

108. Office of Strategic Services Research and Analysis Branch, "No. 1186: The Arabic Speaking Communities in Latin America," Washington D.C., January 1,

1944, 22–23; U.S. Office of Strategic Services, Records of the Foreign Nationalities Branch, Near East, no. INT-2AB; RG 226, NARA. See also Fredy Gonzáles, *Paisanos Chinos: Transpacific Politics among Chinese Immigrants in Mexico* (Oakland: University of California Press, 2017), 15–42.

109. González, *Paisanos Chinos.*

110. Henry T. Unverzagt, Vice Consul to Secretary of State, San Luis Potosi, February 11, 1932. Records of the Department of State Relating to Internal Affairs of Mexico, 1930–1939 (hereafter M1379), roll 203, document 176; RG 59, NARA.

111. Arsan, *Interlopers of Empire*; Michael Humphrey, "Ethnic History, Nationalism and Transnationalism in Argentine Arab and Jewish cultures," *Immigrants & Minorities* 16 (1997):1–2, 167–88; David Nicholls, "No Hawkers and Pedlars: Levantines of the Caribbean," *Ethnic and Racial Studies* 4, no. 4 (1981): 415–31.

112. Office of Strategic Services Research and Analysis Branch, "No. 1186: The Arabic Speaking Communities in Latin America," 23. On Mexican immigration restrictions see Alfaro-Velcamp, "*Arab Amirka*: Exploring Arab Diasporas in Mexico and the United States," *Comparative Studies of South Asia, Africa and the Middle East* 31, no. 2 (2011): 290–91; Oropeza, *Los libaneses en México*, 125–26.

113. U.S. Vice Consul A. F. Yepis to Secretary of State, Guaymas, July 5, 1932, 1–2. M1379, roll 175; RG 59, NARA.

114. Guillermo B. Gomez, "Notice to Aliens of Chinese, Russian, Syrian, Bulgarian, Hungarian, Turkish Nationality Issued by Presidente Municipal," Mazatlán, January 7, 1931, 1. M1379, roll 30, document 335; RG 59, NARA. See also Alfaro-Velcamp, "*Arab Amirka*," 291.

115. Frederick Hinke, Consul General to Josephus Daniels, U.S. Ambassador, Mazatlán, September 5, 1933, 2. M1379, roll 39, document 4016/63; RG 59, NARA.

116. Philip A. Kazen to Secretary of State Cordell Hull, Laredo, September 27, 1934, 1–3. M1379, roll 30, document 454; RG 59, NARA.

117. John J. Dwyer, "Diplomatic Weapons of the Weak: Mexican Policymaking during the U.S.-Mexican Agrarian Dispute, 1934–1941," *Diplomatic History* 26, no. 2 (2002): 383–86.

118. Josephus Daniels, "Discrimination by Mexican Immigration Authorities against Certain Classes of American Citizens," Mexico City, October 19, 1934, 2–3. M1379, roll 30, document 459; RG 59, NARA.

119. Josephus Daniels to Secretary of State, Mexico City, February 1, 1935, 1. M1379, roll 30, document 473; RG 59, NARA.

120. "al-Sada Dumit Akhwan," *al-Ghurbal*, April 24, 1935, 18–19.

121. Khater, *Inventing Home*, 112.

122. Gómez, "Inmigración y capacidad empresarial," 10.

123. Office of Strategic Services Research and Analysis Branch, "No. 1186: The Arabic Speaking Communities in Latin America," 23. In 1937, Abed was a founding

member of the Lebanese Union (El Centro Libanes) in Mexico City, see Pastor, *The Mexican Mahjar,* 169; Alfaro-Velcamp, *So Far from Allah,* 137.

124. Arriving Passenger and Crew List for the S.S. *Bremen,* New York, October 10, 1924; Records of the Customs Service, Passenger Lists of Vessels Arriving at New York (hereafter T715), *Bremen,* 1934, page 10, line 5, Miguel Abed; RG 36, NARA; Arriving Passenger and Crew List for the S.S. *Bremen,* New York, November 30, 1935; T715, *Bremen,* 1935, page 43, line 1, Miguel Abed; RG 36, NARA.

125. Arriving Passenger and Crew List for the S.S. *Bremen,* New York, August 20, 1936; T715, *Bremen,* 1936, page 32, line 26, Miguel Abed; RG 36, NARA.

126. Angelina Alonso Palacios, *Los libaneses y la industria textil en Puebla* (Mexico City: Centro de Investigaciones y Estudios Superiores en Antropología Social, 1983); Gómez, "Emigración a México y Capacidad Empresarial," 10.

127. Roberto Marín Guzmán, *A Century of Palestinian Immigration into Central America: A Study of Their Economic and Cultural Contributions* (San Jose: Ed. de la Univ. Costa Rica, 2000), 27, 51–52, 60–61.

128. Guzmán, *A Century of Palestinian Immigration into Central America,* 82.

129. Cecilia Baeza, "Palestinians in Latin America," *Journal of Palestine Studies* 43, no. 2 (2014): 61; Peter Winn, *Weavers of Revolution: The Yarur Workers and Chile's Road to Socialism* (New York: Oxford University Press, 1986).

130. Oswaldo Truzzi, *Syrian and Lebanese Patrícios in São Paulo: From the Levant to Brazil,* trans. Ramon Stern (Urbana: University of Illinois Press, 2018), 75; Winn, *Weavers of Revolution;* Alfaro-Velcamp, *So Far from Allah,* 157; Nicholls, "No Hawkers and Pedlars," 415–31.

131. Joseph Kneiser typescript memoir, NMAH/NC, box 22, folder 5, 18. Emphasis mine.

132. Mayme Farris oral history interview with Elaine Hughes, Vickburg, MS, March 21, 1979; NMAH/NC, box 267.

Conclusion

1. Syrian American Merchants Association, "Nafiʿ ibn Watanak wa-Intafaʿi," *al-Majalla al-Tijariyya al-Suriyya al-Amrikiyya,* May 1919, 48.

2. "Safar al-Ajanib min-Amrika," *al-Majalla al-Tijariyya al-Suriyya al-Amrikiyya,* April 1919, 34.

3. Sallum Mukarzil, "Markaz Suriya fi-l-Shams," *al-Majalla al-Tijariyya al-Suriyya al-Amrikiyya,* February 1920, 39.

4. Mukarzil, "Markaz Suriya fi-l-Shams," 40.

5. Sherene Seikaly, *Men of Capital: Scarcity and Economy in Mandate Palestine* (Stanford, CA: Stanford University Press, 2015), 5–8; Lauren Banko, *The Invention of Palestinian Citizenship, 1918–1947* (Edinburgh: Edinburgh University Press, 2016), 46–54; Nadim Bawalsa, *Transnational Palestine: Migration and the Right of*

Return Before 1948 (Stanford, CA: Stanford University Press, 2022), 77–90; Stacy D. Fahrenthold, *Between the Ottomans and the Entente: The First World War in the Syrian and Lebanese Diaspora, 1908–1925* (New York: Oxford University Press, 2019), 155–57.

6. Abdallah Hanna, *al-Haraka al-ʿUmmaliyya fi-Suriya wa-Lubnan, 1900–1945* (Damascus: Dar Dimashq, 1973), 13.

7. "Istiʿidad Amrika al-Tijari baʿd-l-Harb," *al-Majalla al-Tijariyya al-Suriyya al-Amrikiyya*, December 1918, 29–30. The editorial was penned by "A Syrian merchant of New York," identified later as the Shaheen plan went public.

8. Johnston Export Publishing Company, *Export Trade Directory* (New York City, 1912), 74, 123; See also Johnston Export Publishing Company, *Export Trade Directory* (New York City, 1917), 176.

9. Sallum Mukarzil, *Tarikh al-Tijara al-Suriyya al-Amrikiyya* (New York: Matbaʾat al-Suriyya al-Amrikiyya al-Tijariyya, 1921),,, 55.

10. A copy of the Administrative Council's letter of support for the factory appears in a Shaheen and Sons pamphlet, *Sharika ʿAssi Shahin wa-Awladihu al-Musahama* (New York: al-Matbaʿa al-Suriyya al-Amrikiyya, s.d. circa 1921), 16. Smithsonian Libraries Trade Literature Collections, National Museum of American History (hereafter NMAHTL); Mukarzil, *Tarikh al-Tijara*, 52.

11. "al-Khutwa al-Ula," *al-Akhlaq*, June 1920, 31. The advertisement ran monthly in *al-Akhlaq* through 1921.

12. *Sharika ʿAssi Shahin wa-Awladihu al-Musahama*, 1–5, NMAHTL.

13. Mukarzil, "Iqtira al-Sharika al-Suriyya li-Muʿamil al-Hiyaka al-Wataniyya," *al-Majalla al-Tijariyya al-Suriyya al-Amrikiyya*, February 1920, 41–42.

14. Mukarzil, *Tarikh al-Tijara*, 52.

15. Shaheen and Sons advertisement, *al-Majalla al-Tijariyya al-Suriyya al-Amrikiyya*, June 1919, 1.

16. E. M. Groth, "The Syrian Silk Industry," Beirut, October 13, 1924, 15; Records of the Department of State Relating to Internal Affairs of Asia, reel 16, doc. 890d.6552/1; RG 59, NARA.

17. Geoff Alexander, *America Goes Hawaiian: The Influence of Pacific Island Culture on the Mainland* (Jefferson, NC: McFarland, 2019), 165–68. See also Joe Challita, "The Godfather of the Hawaiian Shirt: Trace Alfred Shaheen's Journey from Lebanon to Honolulu," *Vogue Arabia*, May 5, 2023, https://en.vogue.me/fashion/godfather-hawaiian-shirt-alfred-shaheen-journey-lebanon-honolulu/.

18. "Silks: From the Cocoon to the Finished Garment is Comprehensive Plan of A. Shaheen & Sons Co.," *Women's Wear* 20, no. 73 (March 29, 1920), 6.

19. "Industrialists in New York," *Syrian World*, April 25, 1935, 1.

20. Carolyn L. Gates, *The Merchant Republic of Lebanon: Rise of an Open Economy* (The Center for Lebanese Studies, 1998), 26; Arida Brothers Corporation 1935

certificate, author's collection. See also Anne Monsour, "Undesirable Alien to Good Citizen: Syrian/Lebanese in a 'White' Australia," *Mashriq and Mahjar: Journal of Middle Eastern and North African Migration Studies* 3, no. 1 (2015): 130–56.

21. "Richard Arida, First Lebanese Citizen of Australia, Benefactor of Old Homeland," *Syrian World,* July 25, 1935, 1; Arida Brothers Shut Down Mills," *Syrian World,* December 1, 1933, 6.

22. "The New Patriarch a Staunch Patriot," *Syrian World,* January 1932, 50; "Beirut Engineering," *Syrian World,* December 1937, 2–3.

23. "Beirut Textile Industry: Cotton Products," 2; Confidential U.S. Diplomatic Post Records, Middle East, 1925–1941: Beirut, reel 13, doc. 868.11; RG 84, NARA. See also Munira D. Atyah, "Cotton Textile Industry in Lebanon" (MBA, American University of Beirut, 1964).

24. U.S. Consulate General, "Review of Commerce and Industries in Syria," Beirut, February 14, 1931, 1–2; Confidential U.S. Diplomatic Post Records, Middle East, 1925–1941: Beirut, reel 13, doc. 868.11; RG 84, NARA.

25. Gates, *The Merchant Republic,* 26.

26. Hicham Safieddine, *Banking on the State: The Financial Foundations of Lebanon* (Stanford, CA: Stanford University Press, 2019), 75.

27. Hiroshi Shimizu, *Anglo-Japanese Trade Rivalry in the Middle East in the Interwar Period* (Oxford: Middle East Centre, 1986), 194.

28. "Review of Commerce and Industries in Syria," 1–2.

29. "Arida Brothers Shut Down Mills," *Syrian World,* December 1, 1933, 6.

30. "Arida Brothers Shut Down Mills," 6.

31. Arida Brothers Corporation 1935 certificate (author's collection).

32. "Beirut Textile Industry: Cotton Products," 4–6.

33. Gates, *The Merchant Republic,* 26.

34. Malek Abisaab, *Militant Women of a Fragile Nation* (Syracuse, NY: Syracuse University Press, 2020), 4–5.

35. Abisaab, *Militant Women,* 19; Hanna, *al-Haraka al-ʿUmmaliyya fi-Suriya wa-Lubnan,* 146.

36. Arriving Passenger and Crew List for the S.S. *Patria,* New York, June 9, 1921; T715, 1921, page 306, line 10, Nicholas Mobayed; RG 36, NARA.

37. "Nicholas Mobayed," Brooklyn, NY, June 8, 1918; World War I Draft Registration Cards, M1509, entry no. 537-156; NARA.

38. Saco-Lowell Shops to P. Knabenshue, Boston, June 12, 1931, 1. Confidential Consular Correspondence, Beirut, Lebanon, volume 471, no. 866.12; RG 84, NARA.

39. Sallum Mukarzil, "Kilma ila-l-Tujar al-Raghibin fi-Fatih ʿAlaʾiq maʿa-Amrika," *Majallat al-Tijariyya al-Suriyya al-Amrikiyya,* July 1919, 24–25.

40. Vice Consul A. C. Martin, "Naturalized Americans of Syrian Origin against Whom the Presumption of Expatriation Has Arisen," Beirut, December 19, 1923, 1; Confidential Consular Correspondence, Beirut, Lebanon, volume 463; RG 84, NARA.

41. Alsharif Munir, *al-Daʾiqa al-Iqtisadiyya al-Suriyya, Asbabiha wa-ʿAlajiha* (Damascus, 1927), as cited by Hanna, *al-Haraka al-ʿUmmaliyya fi-Suriya wa-Lubnan*, 164.

42. "The Syrian Silk Industry," 14. Malek Abisaab notes this mixed experience with mechanization in French Lebanon; see *Militant Women*, 17.

43. Sallum Mukarzil, "Rafaʿ Muqayis al-Maʿasha," *al-Majalla al-Tijariyya al-Suriyya al-Amrikiyya*, September 1924, 27.

44. "The Syrian Silk Industry," 16.

45. "Syrian Negligee Industry Crippled by Violent Strike," *Syrian World*, September 15, 1933, 1.

46. Fred Habib Obituary, *New York Times* March 31, 1954, 27. Both the ILGWU Local 62 and Amalgamated Ladies' Garment Cutters Union placed memorials for Habib in the *New York Times*, April 1, 1954, 31. See also Harry Lang, *"62": Biography of a Union* (New York: ILGWU Local 62, 1940), 216.

47. "Syrian Negligee Industry Crippled by Violent Strike," 1.

48. "25,000 to Strike in 500 Shops Here," *New York Times*, September 10, 1933, 26.

49. "Two Week Strike of Negligee Workers Still Unsettled," *Syrian World*, September 22, 1933, 1.

50. "Negligee Strike Over, Girls Return to Work," *Syrian World*, September 29, 1933, 1; "Underwear Strike Ended with NRA Aid," *New York Times*, September 26, 1933, 4.

51. "Two Week Strike of Negligee Workers Still Unsettled," *Syrian World*, September 22, 1933, 2.

52. Habib I. Katibah, "The Syrian Laborer Had His Day," *Syrian World*, September 22, 1933, 4.

53. "Negligee Strike Over, Girls Return to Work," 1; "Underwear Strike Ended with NRA Aid," 4.

54. "In the Best Traditions of Eastern Wisdom," *Syrian World*, September 29, 1933, 4.

55. "Syrians of Paterson, N.J. Hit by Bitter Silk Strike," *Syrian World*, November 4, 1933, 3. Ninety percent of Syrian silk weavers in Paterson by 1933 were from Aleppo.

56. Lang, *"62"*, 203–4.

57. Howard Barrett Wilson, "Notes of Syrian Folk-Lore Collected in Boston," *Journal of American Folklore* 16, no. 62 (1903): 135.

58. Image of John Ramey's grave marker, in Lawrence History Center, University of Massachusetts Lowell History Department. Bread and Roses Strike of 1912: Two Months in Lawrence, Massachusetts, That Changed Labor History. Digital Public Library of America. April 2013, https://dp.la/exhibitions/breadandroses.

BIBLIOGRAPHY

Archival Collections Consulted
Lebanon

NAMI JAFET MEMORIAL LIBRARY, American University of Beirut
  Nami Jafet Serial Collection

LEBANESE EMIGRATION RESEARCH CENTER, Notre Dame University, Louaize

Madeira

ARQUIVO E BIBLIOTECA DA MADEIRA, Funchal
  Museu de Fotografia da Madeira, Atelier Vicente's
  Registo de Passaportes, 1907–1926

United States

ARAB AMERICAN NATIONAL MUSEUM, Dearborn, Michigan
  Evelyn Shakir Collection
  Michael Suleiman Collection

ARTHUR AND ELIZABETH SCHLESINGER LIBRARY, Harvard University, Cambridge, Massachusetts
  Lebanese Syrian Ladies' Aid Society Records, 1917–2005

HARRY ELKINS WIDENER MEMORIAL LIBRARY, Harvard University, Cambridge, Massachusetts
  Nasib Aridah, Abdel Massih Haddad, and Nadra Haddad Collection

IMMIGRATION HISTORY RESEARCH CENTER ARCHIVES, University of Minnesota, Minneapolis
  James Ansara Papers, IHRC208
  Philip Khuri Hitti Papers, IHRC894
  Frank (Francis) Maria Papers, IHRC1469
  Near Eastern Collection, IHRC2567

LAWRENCE HISTORY CENTER, Lawrence, Massachusetts
  Arab American Collection
  Oral History Collection
  Photography Collection

NATIONAL ARCHIVES AND RECORDS ADMINISTRATION, College Park, Maryland
  Records of the Foreign Service Posts of the Department of State (RG 84)
  Records of the Department of State (RG 59)
  Records of the Federal Bureau of Investigation (RG 65, M1085)

NATIONAL MUSEUM OF AMERICAN HISTORY, Smithsonian Institution
  Faris and Yamna Naff Arab-American Collection
  Smithsonian Libraries Trade Literature Collections

NEW YORK PUBLIC LIBRARY MANUSCRIPTS AND ARCHIVES DIVISION, New York, New York
  International Ladies' Garment Workers' Union Education Department Records
  Fannia M. Cohn Papers, 1914–1962

STATE LIBRARY OF MASSACHUSETTS, Boston, Massachusetts

Serials Consulted

CENTER FOR RESEARCH LIBRARIES, Chicago, Illinois
  al-Nasr (Brooklyn, New York)
  al-Wafa' (Lawrence, Massachusetts)
  Fatat Boston (Boston, Massachusetts)
  Mirat al-Gharb (New York, New York)

NEW YORK PUBLIC LIBRARY, New York, New York
  al-Majalla al-Tijariyya al-Suriyya al-Amrikiyya (New York, New York)
  Women's Wear/Women's Wear Daily (New York, New York)

LAWRENCE HISTORY CENTER, Lawrence, Massachusetts
  al-Fajr (Lawrence, Massachusetts)

OTHER REPOSITORIES
al-Akhlaq (New York, New York)
al-Ghurbal (Mexico City, Mexico)
al-Majalla al-'Arabiyya (New York, New York)
al-Sa'ih (New York, New York)
Syrian World (New York, New York)
Boston Globe (Boston, Massachusetts)

Published Secondary Literature
Abdelhady, Dalia, and Ramy Aly, eds. *Routledge Handbook of Middle Eastern Diasporas.* London: Routledge, 2022.
Abraham, Nabeel, and Andrew Shryock. *Arab Detroit: From Margin to Mainstream.* Detroit, MI: Wayne State University Press, 2000.
Abisaab, Malek. *Militant Women of a Fragile Nation.* Syracuse, NY: Syracuse University Press, 2020.
———. "'Unruly' Factory Women in Lebanon: Contesting French Colonialism in the National State, 1940–1946." *Journal of Women's History* 16, no. 3 (2004): 55–82.
Acehan, Işil. "'Ottoman Street' in America: Turkish Leatherworkers in Peabody, Massachusetts." *International Review of Social History* 54 (2009): 19–44.
Akarli, Engin. "Ottoman Attitudes Towards Emigration." In *Lebanese in the World: A Century of Emigration,* edited by Albert Hourani and Nadim Shehadi, 109–38. London: I. B. Tauris and Centre for Lebanese Studies, 1992.
Akcasu, A. Ebru. "Nation and Migration in Late Ottoman Spheres of Legal Belonging: A Comparative Look at Laws on Nationality." *Nationalities Papers* 49, no. 6 (2021): 1113–31.
Akmir, 'Abd al-Wahad. *al-'Arab fi-l-Arjintin: al-Nashu' wa-l-Tatawwur.* Beirut: Markaz Dirasat al-Wahda al-'Arabiyya, 2000.
Alexander, Geoff. *America Goes Hawaiian: The Influence of Pacific Island Culture on the Mainland.* Jefferson, NC: McFarland, 2019.
Alfaro-Velcamp, Theresa. "Arab *Amirka*: Exploring Arab Diasporas in Mexico and the United States." *Comparative Studies of South Asian, Africa and the Middle East* 31, no. 2 (2011): 282–95.
———. *So Far from Allah, So Close to Mexico: Middle Eastern Immigrants in Modern Mexico.* Austin: University of Texas Press, 2007.
Almada Câmara, Maria Benedita. "Madeira Embroidery: A Failed Collective Brand, 1935–1959." *Business History* 53, no. 4 (2011): 583–99.
Alsultany, Evelyn, and Shohat, Ella, eds. *Between the Middle East and the Americas: The Cultural Politics of Diaspora.* Ann Arbor: University of Michigan Press, 2013.

Arsan, Andrew. *Interlopers of Empire: the Lebanese Diaspora in Colonial French West Africa.* New York: Oxford University Press, 2014.

———. "'This Age Is the Age of Associations': Committees, Petitions, and the Roots of Interwar Middle Eastern Internationalism." *Journal of Global History* 7, no. 2 (2012): 166–88.

Asher, Robert, and Charles Stephenson. "American Capitalism, Labor Organization, and the Racial-Ethnic Factor: An Exploration." In *Labor Divided: Race and Ethnicity in United States Labor Struggles, 1835–1960*, edited by Robert Asher and Charles Stephenson, 1–27. Albany: State University of New York Press, 1990.

Assad, Carlos Martínez, and Martha Díaz Kuri. "Los libaneses, un modelo de adaptación." *Veracruz, puerto de llegada*, edited by Carlos Martínez Assad. Mexico City: H. Ayuntamiento de Veracruz, 2000.

Baeza, Cecilia. "Palestinians in Latin America," *Journal of Palestine Studies* 43, no. 2 (2014): 59–72.

Bailony, Reem. "Donating in the Name of the Nation: Charity, Sectarianism, and the Mahjar." In *Practicing Sectarianism: Archival and Ethnographic Interventions on Lebanon,* edited by Lara Deeb, Tsolin Nalbantian, and Nadya Sbaiti, 81–97. Stanford, CA: Stanford University Press, 2023.

———. "From Mandate Borders to the Diaspora: Rashaya's Transnational Suffering and the Making of Lebanon in 1925." *Arab Studies Journal* 26, no. 2 (2018): 44–73.

———. "Transnationalism and the Syrian Migrant Public: The Case of the 1925 Syrian Revolt." *Mashriq and Mahjar: Journal of Middle East and North African Migration Studies* 1, no. 1 (2013): 8–29.

Ball, Molly C. "Wife, Mother, and Worker: The Decision to Work in Early-Twentieth Century São Paulo." *Journal of Women's History* 29, no. 4 (2017): 109–32.

Balloffet, Lily. *Argentina in the Global Middle East.* Stanford, CA: Stanford University Press, 2020.

———. "From the Pampa to the Mashriq: Arab-Argentine Philanthropy Networks." *Mashriq and Mahjar: Journal of Middle East Migration Studies* 4, no. 1 (2017): 4–28.

Banko, Lauren. *The Invention of Palestinian Citizenship, 1918–1947.* Edinburgh: Edinburgh University Press, 2016.

Barrett, James R. *History from the Bottom Up and Inside Out: Ethnicity, Race, and Identity in Working Class History.* Durham, NC: Duke University Press, 2017.

Bawalsa, Nadim. "To Be Denied a Homeland: British Mandate Policy and the Making of the Palestinian Diaspora in Chile." In *Routledge Handbook of Middle Eastern Diasporas,* edited by Dalia Abdelhady and Ramy Aly, 23–38. London: Routledge, 2022.

———. *Transnational Palestine: Migration and the Right of Return Before 1948.* Stanford, CA: Stanford University Press, 2022.
Bawardi, Hani. *The Making of Arab Americans: From Syrian Nationalism to U.S. Citizenship.* Austin: University of Texas Press, 2014.
Bender, Daniel E. *Sweated Work, Weak Bodies: Anti-Sweatshop Campaigns and Languages of Labor.* New Brunswick, NJ: Rutgers University Press, 2004.
Beinin, Joel. "Egyptian Textile Workers: from Craft Artisans Facing European Competition to Proletarians Contending with the State." In *The Ashgate Companion to the History of Textile Workers, 1650–2000*, edited by Els Hiemstra-Kuperus and Lex Heerma van Voss, 171–97. Ann Arbor, MI: Taylor and Francis, 2010.
———. *Workers and Peasants in the Modern Middle East.* Cambridge: Cambridge University Press, 2010.
Beito, David T. "Mutual Aid for Social Welfare: The Case of American Fraternal Societies." *Critical Review* 4, no. 4 (1990): 709–36.
Benton-Cohen, Katherine. *Inventing the Immigration Problem: The Dillingham Commission and Its Legacy.* Cambridge, MA: Harvard University Press, 2018.
Berman, Jacob Rama. *American Arabesque: Arabs, Islam, and the Nineteenth Century Imaginary.* New York: New York University Press, 2012.
Bier, Jess. "Mapping the Archive for Arab American Women's Labor in the New York Metropolitan Area, 1880–1930." In *Arab American Women: Representation and Refusal*, edited by Michael W. Suleiman, Suad Joseph, and Louise Cainkar, 55–83. Syracuse, NY: Syracuse University Press, 2021.
Blumi, Isa. *Ottoman Refugees 1878–1939: Migration in a Post-Imperial World.* London: Bloomsbury, 2013.
Boosahda, Elizabeth. *Arab-American Faces and Voices: The Origins of an Immigrant Community.* Austin: University of Texas Press, 2003.
Bragdon, Ann Louise. "Early Arabic-Speaking Immigrant Communities in Texas." *Arab Studies Quarterly* 11, no. 2/3 (1989): 83–101.
Breaux, Richard M. "Mahjari Musicians: The Recorded Sounds of Arab Americans in the Early Twentieth Century, 1912–1936." In *Arab Worlds beyond the Middle East and North Africa*, edited by Mariam F Alkazen and Claudia E. Youakim, 151–70. New York: Lexington Books, 2021.
Brégain, Gildas. *Syriens et Libanais d'Amérique du Sud, 1918–1945.* Paris: l'Harmattan, 2008.
Buwayri, Ilyas. *Tarikh al-Haraka al-'Ummaliyya wa-l-Niqabiyya fi-Lubnan, 1908–1946.* Beirut: Dar al-Farabi, 1980.
Cadinot, Dominique. "Integrated Laborers but Marginal Figures: The Untold Story of Early Syrian-American Factory Workers," *Labor History* 63, no. 2 (2022): 234–47.

Cadinot, Dominique, and Jeffrey Burkholder. "The Reconfiguration of Gender Relations in Syrian American Feminist Discourse in the Diasporic Conditions of the Late Nineteenth Century." *Clio* 37 (2013): 170–87.

Cameron, Ardis. "Comments on 'Cleansing History.'" *Radical History Review* 65 (1996): 91–97.

———. *Radicals of the Worst Sort: Laboring Women in Lawrence, Massachusetts, 1860–1912*. Champaign: University of Illinois Press, 1995.

Camfield, David. "Re-Orienting Class Analysis: Working Classes as Historical Formations." *Science & Society* 68, no. 4 (2005): 421–46.

Campos, Mintaha Alcuri. *Turco Pobre, Sírio Remediado, Libanês Rico: Trajetória do Imigrante Libanês no Espirito Santo*. Vitória: Instituto Jones dos Santos Neves, 1987.

Can, Lâle, Michael Christopher Low, Kent Schull, and Robert Zens, eds. *The Subjects of Ottoman International Law*. Bloomington: University of Indiana Press, 2020.

Canaday, Margot. *The Straight State: Sexuality and Citizenship in Twentieth-Century America*. Princeton, NJ: Princeton University Press, 2009.

Cappello, Lawrence. "In Harm's Way: The Lawrence Textile Strike's Children's Affair." In *The Great Lawrence Textile Strike of 1912: New Scholarship on the Bread and Roses Strike*, edited by Robert Forrant and Jurg Siegenthaler, 59–78. Amityville, NY: Baywood Publishing, 2014.

Carita, Rui. *História da Madeira Séc. XX O Caminho para a Autonomia*. Funchal: Imprensa Académica, 2020.

Carrillo, Luis Alfonso Ramírez. "De Buhoneros a empresarios: la inmigración libanesa en el sureste de México." *Historia Mexicana* 43, no. 3 (1994): 451–86.

———. *Secretos de familia: libaneses y élites empresariales en Yucatán*. Mexico City: Consejo Nacional para la Cultura y las Artes, 1994.

Cazorla, Liliana. *Presencia de inmigrantes Sirios y Libaneses en el desarrollo industrial Argentino*. Buenos Aires: Fundación los Cedros, 2000.

Chalcraft, John T. *The Striking Cabbies of Cairo of and Other Stories: Crafts and Guilds in Egypt, 1863–1914*. Albany: State University of New York Press, 2004.

Chomsky, Aviva. *Linked Labor Histories: New England, Colombia, and the Making of a Global Working Class*. Durham, NC: Duke University Press, 2008.

Cicero, Stella Maria Gonzalez, Jorge Nacif Mina, and Raul Gonzalez, comps. *Libaneses en México*. Mexico City: Archivo General de la Nación and Instituto Cultural Mexicano Libanés, 2001.

Civantos, Cristina. *Between Argentines and Arabs: Argentine Orientalism, Arab Immigrants, and the Writing of Identity*. Albany: State University of New York Press, 2006.

Clarence-Smith, William Gervase. "Middle Eastern Migrants in the Philippines:

Entrepreneurs and Cultural Brokers." *Asian Journal of Social Science* 32, no. 3 (2004): 425–57.
Cohen, Michael Mark. *The Conspiracy of Capital: Law, Violence, and American Popular Radicalism in the Age of Monopoly.* Amherst: University of Massachusetts Press, 2019.
Cole, Donald. *Immigrant City: Lawrence, Massachusetts 1845–1921.* Chapel Hill: University of North Carolina Press, 1963.
Cora, Yasar Tolga. "Female Labor, Merchant Capital, and Resilient Manufacturing: Rethinking Ottoman Armenian Communities through Labor and Business." *Journal of the Economic and Social History of the Orient* 61, no. 3 (2018): 361–95.
Cuevas Seba, Teresa, and Miguel Mañana Plasencio. *Los libaneses de Yucatán.* Mexico City: n.p., 1990.
Cruz, Paula A. de La. "Marketing the Hearth: Ornamental Embroidery and the Building of the Multinational Singer Sewing Machine Company." *Enterprise and Society* 15, no. 3 (2014): 442–71.
Curtis, Edward. *Muslims of the Heartland: How Syrian Immigrants Made a Home in the American Midwest.* New York: New York University Press, 2022.
Diaz de Khuri, Martha, and Lourdes Macluf. *De Líbano a México: Crónica de un pueblo emigrante.* Mexico City: n.p., 1997.
Díaz, George T., and Holly M. Karibo. *Border Policing: A History of Enforcement and Evasion in North America.* Austin: University of Texas Press, 2020.
Donovan, Joshua. "The Syro-Lebanese from 'Syriban': Nostalgia, Partition, and Coexistence in Eveline Bustros' Imagined Homeland," *Mashriq and Mahjar: Journal of Middle East and North African Migration Studies* 10, no. 1 (2023): 106–36.
Dubofsky, Melvyn. *We Shall Be All: A History of the Industrial Workers of the World.* Abridged edition, edited by Joseph A. McCartin. Urbana: University of Illinois Press, 2000.
Dwyer, John J. "Diplomatic Weapons of the Weak: Mexican Policymaking during the U.S.-Mexican Agrarian Dispute, 1934–1941." *Diplomatic History* 26, no. 2 (2002): 375–95.
Ettinger, Patrick. "We Sometimes Wonder What They Will Spring on Us Next: Immigrants and Border Enforcement in the American West." *Western Historical Quarterly* 37, no. 2 (2006): 159–81.
———. *Imaginary Lines: Border Enforcement and the Origins of Undocumented Immigration, 1882–1930.* Austin: University of Texas Press, 2010.
Fahrenthold, Stacy D. *Between the Ottomans and the Entente: The First World War in the Syrian and Lebanese Diaspora, 1908–1925.* New York: Oxford University Press, 2019.

———. "'Claimed by Turkey as Subjects': Ottoman Migrants, Foreign Passports, and Syrian Nationality in the Americas, 1915–1925." In *The Subjects of Ottoman International Law*, edited by Lâle Can, Michael Christopher Low, Kent Schull, and Robert Zens, 216–37. Bloomington: University of Indiana Press, 2020.

———. "Ladies Aid as Labor History: Working-Class Formation in the Mahjar." *Journal of Middle East Women's Studies* 17, no. 3 (2021): 326–47.

———. "Sound Minds in Sound Bodies: Transnational Philanthropy and Patriotic Masculinity in *al-Nadi al-Homsi* and Syrian Brazil." *International Journal of Middle East Studies* 46, no. 2 (2014): 259–83.

———. "Transnational Modes and Media: The Syrian Press in the Mahjar and Emigrant Activism during World War I." *Mashriq and Mahjar: Journal of Middle East Migration Studies* 1, no. 1 (2013): 32–57.

Fairchild, Amy L. *Science at the Borders: Immigrant Medical Inspection and the Shaping of the Modern Industrial Labor Force*. Baltimore, MD: Johns Hopkins University Press, 2003.

Fenton, Edwin. *Immigrants and Unions, a Case Study: Italians and American Labor, 1870–1920*. New York: Arno Publishing, 1975.

Forrant, Robert, and Jurj Siegenthaler, eds. *The Great Lawrence Textile Strike of 1912: New Scholarship on the Bread and Roses Strike*. Amityville, NY: Baywood Publishing, 2014.

Gabbert, Ann R. "El Paso, a Sight for Sore Eyes: Medical and Legal Aspects of Syrian Immigration to El Paso, 1906–1907." *The Historian* 65, no. 1 (2002): 15–42.

Gates, Carolyn L. *The Merchant Republic of Lebanon: Rise of an Open Economy*. The Center for Lebanese Studies, 1998.

Gelvin, James L., and Nile Green, eds. *Global Muslims in the Age of Steam and Print*. Oakland: University of California Press, 2014.

Gibson-Graham, J. K., Stephan Resnick, and Richard Wolff. *Class and Its Others*. Minneapolis: University of Minnesota Press, 2000.

Glaser, Clive. "Home, Farm, and Shop: The Migration of Madeiran Women to South Africa." *Journal of Southern African Studies* 38, no. 4 (2012): 885–97.

Goldberg, Daniel. *A Tale of Three Cities: Labor Organization and Protest in Paterson, Passaic, and Lawrence, 1916–1921*. New Brunswick, NJ: Rutgers University Press, 1989.

Gómez, Felipe de Jesús Bello. "Inmigración y capacidad empresarial en los albores de la industrialización de México." *Secuencia* 68 (2007): 9–54.

González, Fredy. *Paisanos Chinos: Transpacific Politics among Chinese Immigrants in Mexico*. Oakland: University of California Press, 2017.

———. "The Rise and Spread of the Hong Men Chee Kung Tong in the Cantonese Pacific and Beyond." *Pacific Historical Review* 92, no. 1 (2023): 1–29.

Gratien, Chris, and Emily Pope Obeda. "Ottoman Migrants, US Deportation Law, and Statelessness during the Interwar Era." *Mashriq and Mahjar: Journal of Middle Eastern and North African Migration Studies* 5, no. 2 (2018): 105–39.
Green, James R. *The World of the Worker: Labor in Twentieth Century America.* Urbana: University of Illinois Press, 1998.
Green, Nancy L. *Ready-to-Wear, Ready-to-Work: A Century of Industry and Immigrants in Paris and New York.* Durham, NC: Duke University Press, 1997.
Gualtieri, Sarah M. A. *Arab Routes: Pathways to Syrian California.* Stanford, CA: Stanford University Press, 2019.
———. *Between Arab and White: Race and Ethnicity in the Early Syrian American Diaspora.* Oakland: University of California Press, 2009.
———. "From Lebanon to Louisiana: Afifa Karam and Arab Women's Writing in Diaspora." In *Arab American Women: Representation and Refusal*, edited by Michael W. Suleiman, Suad Joseph, and Louise Cainkar, 169–88. Syracuse, NY: Syracuse University Press, 2021.
———. "Gendering the Chain Migration Thesis: Women and Syrian Transatlantic Migration, 1878–1924." *Comparative Studies of South Asia, Africa and the Middle East* 24, no. 1 (2004): 67–78.
Guglielmo, Jennifer. *Living the Revolution: Italian Women's Resistance and Radicalism in New York City, 1880–1945.* Chapel Hill: University of North Carolina Press, 2010.
Gutman, David. "Travel Documents, Mobility Control, and the Ottoman State in an Age of Global Migration, 1880–1915." *Journal of the Ottoman and Turkish Studies Association* 3, no. 2 (2016): 347–68.
Guzmán, Roberto Marín. *A Century of Palestinian Immigration into Central America: A Study of Their Economic and Cultural Contributions.* San Jose: Ed. de la Univ. Costa Rica, 2000.
Halaby, Raouf J. "Dr. Michael Shadid and the Debate over Identity in the *Syrian World*." In *Crossing the Waters: Arabic-Speaking Immigrants to the United States before 1940*, edited by Eric J. Hooglund, 55–68. Washington D.C.: Smithsonian Institution Press, 1987.
Hall, Loretta. *Arab American Voices.* University Park: Pennsylvania State University Press, 2000.
Halliday, Fred. "The Millet of Manchester: Arab Merchants and Cotton Trade." *British Journal of Middle Eastern Studies* 12, no. 2 (1992): 159–76.
Hanna, Abdallah. *al-Haraka al-'Ummaliyya fi-Suriya wa-Lubnan, 1900–1945.* Damascus: Dar Dimashq, 1976.
Hashimoto, Kohei. "Lebanese Population Movement 1920–1939." In *Lebanese in the World: A Century of Emigration*, edited by Albert Hourani and Nadim Shehadi, 87–107. London: I. B. Tauris and Centre for Lebanese Studies, 1992.

Hassoun, Rosina. "Religion, Family, and Relocation: Arab American Burial Practices." In *Till Death Do Us Part: American Ethnic Cemeteries as Borders Uncrossed*, edited by Allan Amanik and Kami Fletcher, 247–70. Jackson: University of Mississippi Press, 2020.

Heras, María Cruz Burdiel de las. *La emigración libanesa en Costa Rica*. Madrid: Cantarabia D.L., 1991.

Hirota, Hidetaka. *Expelling the Poor: Atlantic Seaboard States and the Nineteenth-Century Origins of American Immigration Policy*. New York: Oxford University Press, 2017.

Hitti, Philip K. *The Syrians in America*. New York: George H. Doran Company, 1924.

Holton, Adalaine. "Decolonizing History: Arthur Schomberg's Afrodiasporic Archive." *Journal of African American History* 92, no. 2 (2007): 218–38.

Honig, Emily. "Women at Farah Revisited: Political Mobilization and Its Aftermath among Chicana Workers in El Paso, Texas, 1972–1992." *Feminist Studies* 22, no. 2 (1996): 425–52.

Hooglund, Eric, ed. *Crossing the Waters: Arabic-Speaking Immigrants to the United States before 1940*. Washington, D.C.: Smithsonian Institution Press, 1987.

———. "From the New East to the Down East." In *Crossing the Waters: Arabic-Speaking Immigrants to the United States before 1940*, edited by Eric J. Hooglund, 85–103. Washington D.C.: Smithsonian Institution Press.

Houghton, Louise S. "Syrians in the United States." *The Survey* 26 (1911): 480–95, 786–803, 957–68.

Howell, Sally. *Old Islam in Detroit: Rediscovering the Muslim American Past*. New York: Oxford University Press, 2014.

Hourani, Albert, and Nadim Shehadi, eds. *The Lebanese in the World: A Century of Emigration*. London: I. B. Tauris and Centre for Lebanese Studies, 1992.

Hu-DeHart, Evelyn. "On Coolies and Shopkeepers." In *Displacements and Diasporas: Asians in the Americas*, edited by Wanni W. Anderson and Robert G. Lee, 78–111. New Brunswick, NJ: Rutgers University Press, 2005.

Humphrey, Michael. "Ethnic History, Nationalism and Transnationalism in Argentine Arab and Jewish cultures." *Immigrants and Minorities* 16 (1997): 1–2, 167–88.

Hyland, Steven. *More Argentine than You: Arabic-Speaking Immigrants in Argentina*. Albuquerque: University of New Mexico Press, 2017.

Issawi, Charles. *The Economic History of the Middle East, 1800–1914*. Chicago: University of Chicago Press, 1975.

———. "The Historical Background of Lebanese Emigration, 1800–1914." In *Lebanese in the World: A Century of Emigration*, edited by Albert Hourani and Nadim Shehadi, 13–32. London: I. B. Tauris and Centre for Lebanese Studies, 1992.

Jackson, Simon. "Diasporic Politics and Developmental Empire: The Syro-Lebanese at the League of Nations." *Arab Studies Journal* 21, no. 1 (2013): 166–90.
Jabbra, Nancy W. "Household and Family among Lebanese Immigrants in Nova Scotia: Continuity, Change, and Adaptation." *Journal of Comparative Family Studies* 22, no. 1 (1991): 39–56.
Jacobs, Linda K. *Strangers in the West: The Syrian Colony of New York City, 1880–1900.* New York: Kalimah Press, 2015.
———. *Strangers No More: Syrians in the United States, 1880–1900.* New York, Kalimah Press, 2019.
Jacobsen, Matthew Frye. *Whiteness of a Different Color: European Immigration and the Alchemy of Race.* Cambridge, MA: Harvard University Press, 1998.
John, Sarah E. "Arabic-Speaking Immigration to the El Paso Area, 1900–1935." In *Crossing the Waters: Arabic-Speaking Immigrants to the United States Before 1940*, edited by Eric Hooglund, 105–18. Washington D.C.: Smithsonian Institution Press, 1987.
Johnson Bavery, Ashley. "Lifetimes of Instability: The Consequences of Excluding Syrian Boys on the Progressive Era U.S.-Mexico Border." *Mashriq and Mahjar: Journal of Middle East and North African Migration Studies* 11, no. 2 (2024): 1–21.
Joseph, Suad. "Arab American Women: Intersectional Genealogies and Trajectories." In *Arab American Women: Representation and Refusal*, edited by Michael W. Suleiman, Suad Joseph, and Louise Cainkar, 1–17. Syracuse, NY: Syracuse University Press, 2021.
Judge, Rajbir Singh, and Jasdeep Singh Brar. "Critique of Archived Life: Toward a Hesitation of Sikh Immigrant Accumulation." *Positions: Asia Critique* 29, no. 2 (2021): 319–46.
Karam, John Tofik. *Another Arabesque: Syrian-Lebanese Ethnicity in Neoliberal Brazil.* Philadelphia: Temple University Press, 2007.
Karem Albrecht, Charlotte. "An Archive of Difference: Syrian Women, the Peddling Economy, and US Social Welfare, 1880–1935." *Gender & History* 28, no. 1 (2016): 127–49.
———. "Narrating Arab American History: The Peddling Thesis." *Arab Studies Quarterly* 37, no. 1 (2015): 100–117.
———. *Possible Histories: Arab Americans and the Queer Ecology of Peddling.* Oakland: University of California Press, 2023.
Karpat, Kemal H. "The Ottoman Emigration to America, 1860–1914." *International Journal of Middle East Studies* 17, no. 2 (1985): 175–209.
Katibeh, Habib Ibrahim, and Farhat Jacob Ziadeh. *Arabic-Speaking Americans.* New York: Institute of Arab American Affairs, 1946.
Katz, Daniel. *All Together Different: Yiddish Socialists, Garment Workers, and the*

Labor Roots of Multiculturalism. New York: New York University Press, 2011.

Kaufman, Polly Welts, Jean Gibran, Sylvia McDowell, and Mary Howland Smoyer. "Chinatown/South Cove Walk." In *Boston Women's Heritage Trail*, 43–51. Corona, CA: Applewood Books, 2006.

Kayal, Philip. "Syrian Migration, Peddling, and 'Little Syria.'" *International Migration Review* 29, no. 2 (1995): 110–41.

Kenneally, James. "Catholic Clerical Quandary: The Lawrence Strike of 1912." *American Catholic Studies* 117, no. 4 (2006): 33–54.

Kessler-Harris, Alice. *Gendering Labor History*. Chicago: University of Illinois Press, 2007.

Khater, Akram. "'House' to 'Goddess of the House': Gender, Class, and Silk in 19th-Century Mount Lebanon." *International Journal of Middle East Studies* 28, no. 3 (1996): 329–31.

———. *Inventing Home: Emigration, Gender, and the Working Class in Lebanon*. Berkeley: University of California Press, 2001.

———. "'Like a Wolf Who Fell upon Sheep': Arab Diaspora and Religion in America, 1880–1930." *Diaspora: A Journal of Transnational Studies* 21, no. 1 (2021): 1–26.

Khuri-Makdisi, Ilham. *The Eastern Mediterranean and the Making of Global Radicalism*. Oakland: University of California Press, 2010.

Knowlton, Clark. *Sirios e libaneses em São Paulo*. São Paulo: Editoria Anhembi, 1961.

Kupferschmidt, Uri M. "The Social History of the Sewing Machine in the Middle East." *Die Welts des Islams* 44, no. 2 (2004): 195–213.

Lauck, W. Jett, and Edgar Sydenstricker. "Conditions of Labor in Principal Industries: A Summarization of the Results of Recent Investigations." New York: Funk & Wagnalls, 1917.

Lang, Harry. *"62:" Biography of a Union*. New York: ILGWU Local 62, 1940.

Lee, Erika. "Enforcing the Borders: Chinese Exclusion along the U.S. Borders with Canada and Mexico, 1882–1924." *Journal of American History* 89, no. 1 (2002): 54–86.

———. *The Making of Asian America*. New York City: Simon and Schuster, 2015.

Lichtenstein, Nelson. "The Return of Merchant Capitalism." *International Labor and Working-Class History* 81 (2012): 8–27.

Lim, Julian. *Porous Borders: Multiracial Migrations and the Law in the U.S.-Mexico Borderlands*. Chapel Hill: University of North Carolina Press, 2017.

Loiselle, Aimee. "Puerto Rican Needle Workers and Colonial Migrations, Deindustrialization as Pathways Lost." *Journal of Working Class Studies* 4, no. 2 (2019): 40–54.

Loomis, Erik. *A History of America in Ten Strikes*. New York: The New Press, 2018.

Lorwin, Lewis L. *The Women's Garment Workers: A History of the International Ladies' Garment Workers' Union.* New York: B. W. Huebsch, 1924.
Luconi, Stefano. "Crossing Borders on the Picket Line: Italian-American Workers and the 1912 Strike in Lawrence, Massachusetts." *Italian Americana* 28, no. 2 (2010): 149–61.
Luehrmann, Sonja. *Religion in Secular Archives: Soviet Atheism and Historical Knowledge.* New York: Oxford University Press, 2015.
Marr, Timothy. "Diasporic Intelligences in the American Philippine Empire: The Transnational Career of Dr. Najeeb Mitry Saleeby." *Mashriq and Mahjar: Journal of Middle East and North African Migration Studies* 2, no. 1 (2014): 78–106.
Mattina, Anne F., and Dominique Ciavettone. "Striking Women: Massachusetts Mill Workers in the Wake of Bread and Roses." In *The Great Lawrence Textile Strike of 1912: New Scholarship on the Bread and Roses Strike,* edited by Robert Forrant and Jurg Siegenthaler, 153–170. Amityville, NY: Baywood Publishing, 2014.
Mays, Devi. "Becoming Illegal: Sephardi Jews and the Opiates Trade." *Jewish Social Studies* 25, no. 3 (2020): 1–34.
———. *Forging Ties, Forging Passports: Migration and the Modern Sephardi Diaspora.* Stanford, CA: Stanford University Press, 2020.
McKeown, Adam. "Global Migration, 1846–1940." *Journal of World History* 15, no. 2 (2004): 155–89.
———. *Melancholy Order: Asian Migration and the Globalization of Borders.* New York: Columbia University Press, 2008.
Monsour, Anne. "Undesirable Alien to Good Citizen: Syrian/Lebanese in a 'White' Australia." *Mashriq and Mahjar: Journal of Middle Eastern and North African Migration Studies* 3, no. 1 (2015); 130–56.
Moran, William. *The Belles of New England: The Women of the Textile Mills and the Families Whose Wealth They Wove.* New York: St. Martin's Press, 2002.
Mukarzil, Sallum. *Tarikh al-Tijara al-Suriyya al-Amrikiyya.* New York: Matbaʿat al-Suriyya al-Amrikiyya al-Tijariyya, 1921.
Naar, Devin. "Turkinos beyond the Empire: Ottoman Jews in America, 1893 to 1924." *Jewish Quarterly Review* 105, no. 2 (2015): 174–205.
Naff, Alixa. *Becoming American: The Early Arab Immigrant Experience.* Carbondale: University of Illinois Press, 1985.
———. "New York: The Mother Colony." In *A Community of Many Worlds: Arab Americans in New York City,* edited by Kathleen Benson and Philip M. Kayal, 3–10. Syracuse, NY: Syracuse University Press, 1994.
Navarro, Moisés González. *Los Extranjeros en México y los mexicanos en el extranjero, 1821–1970.* Volume 2. Mexico City: El Colegio de Mexico, 1993.
Ngai, Mae. "The Architecture of Race in American Immigration Law: A Reexam-

ination of the Reed Johnson Act of 1924," *Journal of American History* 86, no. 1 (1999): 67–92.

Nicholls, David. "No Hawkers and Pedlars: Levantines of the Caribbean." *Ethnic and Racial Studies* 4, no. 4 (1981): 415–31.

Norris, Jacob. "Exporting the Holy Land: Artisans and Merchant Migrants in Ottoman-Era Bethlehem." *Mashriq and Mahjar: Journal of Middle Eastern and North African Migration Studies* 1, no. 2 (2013): 17–45.

———. *The Lives and Deaths of Jubrail Dabdoub: or, How the Bethlehemites Discovered Amerka*. Stanford, CA: Stanford University Press, 2023.

———. "Return Migration and the Rise of the Palestinian *nouveaux riche*, 1870–1925." *Journal of Palestine Studies* 46, no. 2 (2017): 60–75.

Orleck, Annalise. *Common Sense and a Little Fire: Women and Working-Class Politics in the United States, 1900–1965*. Chapel Hill: University of North Carolina Press, 1994.

———. "The Needle Trades and the Uprising of Women Workers." In *City of Workers, City of Struggle: How Labor Movements Changed New York*, edited by Joshua B. Freeman, 84–95. New York: Columbia University Press, 2019.

Oropeza, Carmen Mercedes Páez. *Los libaneses en México: asimilación de un grupo étnico*. Mexico City: Instituto Nacional de Antropología e Historia, 1984.

Owen, Roger. *The Middle East in the World Economy, 1800–1914*. New York: I. B. Tauris, 1981.

Palacios, Angelina Alonso. *Los libaneses y la industria textil en Puebla*. Mexico City: Centro de Investigaciones y Estudios Superiores en Antropología Social, 1983.

Pap, Leo. *The Portuguese-Americans*. Boston: Twayne Publishers, 1981.

Pastor de Maria y Campos, Camila. "The Great Arab Revolt, Palestine and a Phoenicianist Civilizing Mission: Transregional Debates in the Mexican Mahjar Press." *Revue des mondes musulmanes et de la Méditerranée* 152 (2022): 85–114.

———. *The Mexican Mahjar: Transnational Maronites, Jews, and Arabs under the French Mandate*. Austin: University of Texas Press, 2017.

Peck, Gunther. "Feminizing White Slavery in the United States: Marcus Braun and the Transnational Traffic in White Bodies." *Workers across the Americas*, edited by Leon Fink, 221–44. New York: Oxford University Press, 2011.

Pegler-Gordon, Anna. *In Sight of America: Photography and the Development of U.S. Immigration Policy, 1880–1930*. Berkeley: University of California Press, 2009.

Petras, Elizabeth McLean. "The Shirt on Your Back: Immigrant Workers and the Reorganization of the Garment Industry." *Social Justice* 15, no. 1 (1992): 76–114.

Pitts, Graham Auman. "The Ecology of Migration: Remittances in World War I Mount Lebanon." *Arab Studies Journal* 26, no. 2 (2018): 102–29.

Polat, Hatice Ayse. "Contending Sovereigns, Contentious Spaces: Illicit Migration

and Urban Governance in the Late Ottoman Empire." *Global Histories: A Student Journal* 3, no. 1 (2017): 108–26.
Pope-Obeda, Emily. "Expelling the Foreign-Born Menace: Immigrant Dissent, the Early Deportation State, and the First American Red Scare." *Journal of the Gilded Age and Progressive Era* 18 (2019): 32–55.
Poirier, Clarise A. "The Committee of Ten: The Local Heroes Who Faced Lawrence's Mill Men and Won in 1912." In *The Great Lawrence Textile Strike of 1912: New Scholarship on the Bread and Roses Strike*, edited by Robert Forrant and Jurg Siegenthaler, 37–58. Amityville, NY: Baywood Publishing, 2014.
Quataert, Donald. "Labor History and the Ottoman Empire, 1700–1922." *International Labor and Working-Class History* 60 (2001): 93–109.
Rahal, Doris Musalem. "La migración palestina a México, 1893–1949." In *Destine México: un estudio de las migraciones asiáticas a México, siglos XIX y XX*, edited by Maria Elena Ota Mashima, 305–65. Mexico City: El Colegio de Mexico, 1997.
Ramírez Carillo, Luis A. *De cómo los libaneses conquistaron la península de Yucatán: Migración, identidad étnica y cultura empresarial*. Mérida: Centro Peninsular en Humanidad y Ciencias Sociales; Universidad Nacional Autonomía de México, 2012.
Razek, Rana. "Trails and Fences: Syrian Migration Networks and Immigration Restriction, 1885–1907." *Amerasia Journal* 44, no. 1 (2018): 105–26.
Reeder, Linda. "When the Men Left Sutera: Sicilian Women and Mass Migration." In *Women, Gender, and Transnational Lives: Italian Workers of the World*, edited by Donna Gabaccia and Franca Iacovetta, 45–75. Toronto: University of Toronto Press, 2002.
Regnard, Céline. "The Transit Stage as a Migratory Experience: The Syrians in Marseille." In *Migrants and the Making of the Urban-Maritime World: Agency and Mobility in Port Cities, c. 1570–1940*, edited by Christina Reimann and Martin Öhman, 153–71. New York: Routledge, 2020.
Rego, Charles P. do. "Portuguese Labor Migration to Curacao." *Caribbean Studies* 42, no. 2 (2014): 155–79.
Robertson, Craig. *The Passport in America: The History of a Document*. New York: Oxford University Press, 2010.
Roediger, David R., and Elizabeth D. Esch. *The Production of Difference: Race and the Management of Labor in U.S. History*. New York: Oxford University Press, 2012.
Rowe, Amy E. "A Trace of Arabic in Granite: Lebanese Migration to the Green Mountains, 1890–1940." *Vermont History* 76, no. 2 (2008): 91–129.
Rubio, Rebeca Inclán, "La migración libanesa en México." *El Medio Oriente en la Ciudad de México*. Mexico City: México, Gobierno del Distrito Federal/Instituto de Cultura de la Ciudad de México, 1999.

Safieddine, Hicham. *Banking on the State: The Financial Foundations of Lebanon.* Stanford, CA: Stanford University Press, 2019.

Saliba, Najib E. *Emigration from Syria and the Syrian-Lebanese Community of Worcester, Massachusetts.* Antakya Press, 1992.

Samaha, Charles Malouf. *Faris Saleem Maloof (1892–1958): A Voice in the Dark, One Man's Arab American Activism.* Self-published, 2019.

Saylor, Elizabeth Claire. "Gender, Hybridity, and Transnationalism in 'Afifa Karam's Fatima al-Badawiyya (Fatima the Bedouin, 1909)." *Journal of Middle East Women's Studies* 15, no. 1 (2019): 3–23.

Seikaly, Sherene. *Men of Capital: Scarcity and Economy in Mandate Palestine.* Stanford, CA: Stanford University Press, 2015.

Shakir, Evelyn. *Bint Arab: Arab and Arab American Women in the United States.* Westport, CT: Praeger, 1997.

———. "Good Works, Good Times: The Syrian Ladies' Aid Society of Boston, 1917–1932." In *Crossing the Waters: Arabic-Speaking Immigrants to the United States before 1940*, edited by Eric J. Hooglund, 133–143. Washington D.C.: Smithsonian Institution Press, 1987.

———. "Syrian-Lebanese Women Tell Their Story," *Frontiers: A Journal of Women Studies* 7, no. 1 (1983): 9–13.

Shimizu, Hiroshi. *Anglo-Japanese Trade Rivalry in the Middle East in the Interwar Period.* Oxford: Middle East Centre, 1986.

Snow, Ethan. "Voices of Labor Militancy in Lawrence, 1912–1931." In *The Great Lawrence Textile Strike of 1912: New Scholarship on the Bread and Roses Strike*, edited by Robert Forrant and Jurj Siegenthaler, 135–53. New York: Taylor and Francis, 2014.

Soyer, Daniel. "Mutual Aid Societies and Fraternal Orders." In *A Companion to American Immigration,* edited by Reed Ueda, 528–46. Malden, MA: Blackwell, 2006.

Stiffler, Matthew Jaber. "A Brief History of Arab Immigrant Textile Production in the U.S." Arab American National Museum, October 2010.

———. "Consuming Orientalism: Public Foodways of Arab American Christians." *Mashriq and Mahjar: Journal of Middle East and North African Migration Studies* 2, no. 2 (2015): 111–38.

Struthers, David M., Kenyon Zimmer, and Peter Cole, eds. *Wobblies of the World: A Global History of the IWW.* London: Pluto Press, 2017.

Suleiman, Michael W. "The Arab American Left." In *The Immigrant Left in the United States*, eds. Dan Georgakas and Paul Buhle, 233–55. Albany: State University of New York Press, 1996.

———. "A Brief History of Arab American Women, 1890s to World War II." In *Arab American Women: Representation and Refusal,* edited by Michael W. Suleiman, Suad Joseph, and Louise Cainkar, 21–54. Syracuse, NY: Syracuse University Press, 2021.

Suleiman, Michael W., Suad Joseph, and Louise Cainkar, eds. *Arab American Women: Representation and Refusal*. Syracuse, NY: Syracuse University Press, 2021.

Tawil, Randa. "A 'Flying Carpet to Doom': Retracing Gender and Orientalism through the Transnational Journeys of a Syrian Migrant Woman, 1912–1949." *Frontiers: A Journal of Women Studies* 43, no. 1 (2022): 120–44.

———. "Racial Borderlines: Ameen Rihani, Mexico, and World War I." *Amerasia Journal* 44, no. 1 (2018): 85–104.

Tehranian, John. *Whitewashed: America's Invisible Middle Eastern Minority*. New York: New York University Press, 2010.

Truzzi, Oswaldo. *Syrian and Lebanese Patrícios in São Paulo: from the Levant to Brazil*. Translated by Ramon Stern. Urbana: University of Illinois Press, 2018.

Urban, Andrew. *Brokering Servitude: Migration and the Politics of Domestic Labor in the Long Nineteenth Century*. New York: New York University Press, 2017.

Valdez, Inéz. "Socialism and Empire: Labor Mobility, Racial Capitalism, and the Political Theory of Migration." *Political Theory* 49, no. 6 (2021): 902–33.

Van der Linden, Marcel. "The Promise and Challenges of Global Labor History." *International Labor and Working-Class History* 82 (2012): 57–76.

Vecoli, Rudolph J. "Anthony Capraro and the Lawrence Strike of 1919." In *Labor Divided: Race and Ethnicity in United States Labor Struggles, 1835–1960*, edited by Robert Asher and Charles Stephenson, 267–282. Albany: State University of New York Press, 1990.

———. "Problems in Comparative Studies of International Emigrant Communities." In *Lebanese in the World*, edited by Albert Hourani and Nadhim Shehadi, 717–25. London: Centre for Lebanese Studies and I. B. Tauris, 1992.

Vieira, Alberto. *Bordado Madeira*. Funchal: Tipografia Peres, 2007.

———. *História e Autonomia da Madeira*. Funchal: CEHA-Biblioteca, 2003.

Wakstein, Allen M. "The Origins of the Open-Shop Movement, 1919–1920." *Journal of American History* 51, no. 3 (1964): 460–75.

Walaszek, Adam. "Was the Polish Worker Asleep? Immigrants, Unions, and Workers' Control of America, 1900–1922." *Polish American Studies* 46, no. 1 (1989): 74–96.

Wallerstein, Emmanuel. "The Rise and Future Demise of the World-Capitalism System: Concepts for Comparative Analysis." *Comparative Studies in Society and History* 16, no. 4 (1974): 387–415.

Walther, Karine. *Sacred Interests: The United States and the Islamic World, 1821–1921*. Chapel Hill: University of North Carolina Press, 2015.

Watson, Bruce. *Bread and Roses: Mills, Migrants, and the Struggle for the American Dream*. New York: Penguin, 2006.

Wilson, Howard Barrett. "Notes of Syrian Folk-Lore Collected in Boston." *Journal of American Folklore*, 16, no. 62 (1903): 133–47.

Winn, Peter. *Weavers of Revolution: The Yarur Workers and Chile's Road to Socialism*. New York: Oxford University Press, 1986.
Wolfson, Theresa. "Role of the ILGWU in Stabilizing the Women's Garment Industry." *ILR Review* 4, no. 1 (1950): 33–43.
Young, Elliot. *Alien Nation: Chinese Migration in the Americas from the Coolie Era through World War II*. Chapel Hill: University of North Carolina Press, 2014.
Younis, Adele. "The Challenge of Commerce: The Syrian-American Almanac." *International Migration Review* 29, no. 2 (1995): 302–3.
———. *The Coming of the Arabic-Speaking People to the United States*. New York: Center for Migration Studies, 1995.
Yousefian, Sevan N. "Picnics for Patriots: The Transnational Activism of an Armenian Hometown Association." *Journal of American Ethnic History* 34, no. 1 (2014): 31–52.
Zimmer, Kenyon. *Immigrants against the State: Yiddish and Italian Anarchism in America*. Urbana: University of Illinois Press, 2015.

Published Memoirs and Biographies
Cline, D. J. *Perfection, Never Less: The Vera Way Marghab Story*. Brookings: South Dakota Art Museum, 1998.
Forzley, Bashara Kalil. *An Autobiography of Bashara Kalil Forzley*. Edited by Philip Forzley. Worcester: Self-published, 1958.
Garrett, Paul D., and Kathleen A. Purpura. *Frank Maria: A Search for Justice and Peace in the Middle East*. Bloomington, IN: Authorhouse, 2007.
Haddad, Nabeha Merhige. *Nabeha: Remembrances, an Autobiography*. Edited by Margaret Haddad George. Worcester: Self-published, 1993.
Maloley, Laurice B. *Destiny by Default: A Memoir*. Bloomington, IN: First Book Library, 2002.

Unpublished Theses and Dissertations
Atyah, Munira D. "Cotton Textile Industry in Lebanon." M.B.A. thesis, American University of Beirut, 1964.
Ermer, John. "Our Representative on This Island: Local Belonging and Transnational Citizenship among Syrian and Lebanese Cubans, 1880–1980." Ph.D. dissertation, Florida International University, 2021.
Gomes, Márcia Cristina Sousa. "O Bordado Madeira: Preservação De Uma Técnica Artesanal." M.A. thesis, Universidade do Lisboa, 2019.
Garrett, Bryan. "Otherness and Belonging in 'Democratic Empires:' The Syrian Diaspora and Transatlantic Discourses of Identity." Ph.D. dissertation, University of Texas Arlington, 2016.
Garrido, Georgina da Conceição Branco. "Dos Conventos ao Economuseu:

Patrício & Gouveia Lda, Fábrica de Bordados." M.A. thesis, Universidade do Lisboa, 2015.

John, Sarah E. " 'Trade Will Lead a Man Far: Syrian Immigration to El Paso, 1900–1935." M.A. thesis, University of Texas at El Paso, 1982.

Martos, Sofia D. "The Balancing Act: Ethnicity, Commerce, and Politics among Syrian and Lebanese Immigrants in Argentina, 1890–1955." Ph.D. dissertation, University of California, Los Angeles, 2007.

Narbona, Maria. "The Development of Nationalist Identities in French Syria and Lebanon: A Transnational Dialogue with Arab Immigrants to Argentina and Brazil, 1915–1929." Ph.D. dissertation, University of California, Santa Barbara, 2007.

Safa, Élie. "L'émigration libanaise." Ph.D. dissertation, Université Saint Joseph, Beirut, 1960.

Shibley, Gregory J. "New York's Little Syria, 1880–1935." M.A. thesis, Florida Atlantic University, 2014.

Snow, Ethan J. "Strike City: An Oral History of the Legacy of Labor Militancy in Lawrence, Massachusetts." M.A. thesis, University of Massachusetts, Lowell, 2012.

INDEX

Abdalla Barsa and Brothers, 96, 98–99, 111, 114, 194. *See also* Barsa, Abdalla & Simon
Abdelnour, A. B., 169–70
Abdelnour, Rasheed, 85
Abed, Miguel, 183–84
Abraham, Felipe, 180
Abualy, Naim, 131, 150
Abusaid factory (Colombia), 184
Acadia Mill, 67
A. G. Samara and Company, 138, 150–51, 245n109. *See also* Samara, Ameen
A. J. Macksoud Records, 112
al-Akhlaq, 116–17, 121–22
al-Alam al-Jadid, 115
Aleppo, 126, 130, 192–93
Alexander J. Hamrah and Company, 91–92, 125–26, 128–30, 133, 137–38, 147, 149–50, 153, 198. *See also* Hamrah, Alexander & Peter
al-Fajr, 56
Alfaro-Velcamp, Theresa, 178
al-Majalla al-ʿArabiyya, 116, 122

al-Majalla al-Tijariyya al-Suriyya al-Amrikiyya/*The Syrian American Commercial Magazine*, 113, 125, 187, 194. *See also* Mukarzil, Sallum
al-Marʾa al-Jadida, 116
al-Nasr, 115
al-Rawda, 56
al-Saʾih, 114–15
al-Samir, 116
al-Wafaʾ, 29, 56, 66–67
Amalgamated Clothing Workers of America, 4, 54, 74
American Federation of Labor, 4, 73–75, 196
American Woolen Company, 1–2, 19, 24–57, 66, 73–75, 98
Amshiti, Selim, 164
Arbeely, Najib, 95, 160–61, 227n138
Arida, Antoun, 191
Arida Brothers Corporation, 22, 95–97, 102–3, 115, 135, 191–93
Arida, George, Joseph, Michel, Richard (Rashid), & Solomon, 191

283

Arida, Kemal, Mikha'il, Nasib, & Rufa'il, 5, 94–97, 99, 230n34
Arlington Mill, 47
Assef, Joseph, 24–25, 44, 76
'Assy Shaheen and Sons, 22, 99, 101, 167, 189–91. *See also* Shaheen, 'Assy, George, & Tawfiq
Aswad, Khalil al-, 113
Ayar, Skender, 163
Ayer Mill, 5, 31, 34, 67
Ayoub Brothers, 175
Azar, Halim, 153
Aziz, Abdo, Abdalla, Aziz & Roger, 28, 32, 66–70

Badran Brothers Company, 115
Baeza, Cecilia, 184
Bardwil, Amin & George (Jurj), 129–31, 153–54, 184. *See also* Bardwil Brothers
Bardwil Brothers, 89, 103, 135, 150, 153–54, 191. *See also* Bardwil, Amin & George (Jurj)
Barnes, Robert, 174
Barnum, Gertrude, 107
Baroudi, Aziz, 164
Barsa, Abdalla & Simon, 5, 96, 230n39. *See also* Abdalla Barsa and Brothers
Barsa, Zahdi Fallaha, 63, 119, 156
Batal, Shehadi, 10
Beirut, 8–9, 11, 13, 22, 90–91, 94, 158, 193
Berger, Victor, 105
Beshara, George, 27–28
Beshara, Maron, 175
Beshara, Salem, 168
Bishara, H. A., 176
Bistany, Adele, 30–31
Bistany, Juliet, 27–28, 31, 60
Bloque Nacionalista de Defensa Pro Patria, 181

Bolis, Mary, 28
Boosahda, Elizabeth, 60
Boston Globe, 23, 37, 40–41, 54
Braun, Marcus, 161–62, 166, 175
Bread and Roses Strike, 2, 19–20, 24–57, 68, 197
Breen, John, 45, 68
Brox (Brux), William, 38
Brox, James, 37–39, 48–49, 53, 213n70
Bureau of Investigation, 131, 160, 166, 169, 171–77, 186

Calef Brothers, 102
Cámara de Comercio Libanesa, 180
Cameron, Ardis, 39, 41
Carita, Rui, 137
Carter, Clark, 42–43, 51, 53, 211n29, 214n76
Casa Marghab, 152–53
Castro, Alvaro de, 150
child labor. *See under* working conditions
China, textile manufacture in, 21, 129, 146, 152–54, 189
Chinese Cultural Revolution, impact of on textile industry, 154
citizenship (American): advantages of for merchants and manufacturers, 126–27, 130–32, 171, 181–82; advantages of for workers, 37, 62, 94, 109, 213n70
Clarence-Smith, William Gervase, 153
Cohn, Fannia M., 105
Collins, Dennis, 45
Committee of Fifteen (1919 Lawrence textile strike), 74
Committee of Ten (Bread and Roses Strike), 37–39, 43–45, 48
Coolidge, Calvin, 75
Correio da Madeira, 142

cottage industry, 64, 82, 92–93, 118, 126, 133–35, 141, 144, 147, 154
counterarchival collections, 59–60
Coury, George, 175

Dalzell, John, 50
Damascus, 62, 88, 91, 94–96, 126, 130, 194
Daniels, Josephus, 183
Denison House, 85–86, 227n137
Dillingham Commission Report (1911), 163
Dow v. United States, 226 F. 145 (4th Cir., 1915), 6, 130
dynamite, 1, 23–26, 43–46, 76, 197, 209n5

Ead, Mary, 30, 33
Eaton, Charles, 113
Ebert, Justus, 39
Eddy Cury and Brothers, 115
Eells, Stillman, 131, 139, 141–43, 146
Ellis Island, 9–10, 28, 87, 89–90, 95, 161–64, 166, 227n138. *See also* labor migration
embroidery. *See* needlework (embroidery and lace)
Emile and Vera Way Marghab, 152
Ettor, Joseph, 25–26, 40, 43–44, 46, 48

Faour Brothers Bank (Daniel, Doumit, & Yusuf Faour), 90
Fares, Anton, 162–63
Farra and Mogabgab Limited, 152
Farra, Gabriel, 152
Farris, Mayme, 186
Fatat al-Sharq, 116
Fatat Boston, 56
Fenton, Edwin, 39
Ferreira, Alfredo Olovo, 148

First Syrian Protestant Church (Brooklyn, NY), 130
First Trinitarian Church (Lowell, MA), 38
Flynn, Elizabeth Gurley, 26, 48, 54
F. M. Jabara and Company, 132, 152, 168. *See also* Jabara, F. M.
Foran Act (1885), 160–61
Fordney, Joseph, 144
Forney-McCumber Tariff, 144
Foss, Eugene, 25, 44, 46
Franca, Armando, 148
Frances, Amin & Eid, 172–73
Freitas Castro and Company, 150

Ganis Brothers, 102
Garment District (New York City), 12, 17, 20, 87, 95, 99, 197
Gates, Carolyn, 191–92
gender norms in garment work, 115–24, 134–35
Ghusn, Farid, 56
Ghusn, Ghusn, 29
Giovannitti, Arturo, 25–26, 39, 46, 48
Goldberg, Samuel, 51
Golden, John, 35
Gomes, Jayme Pompilo, 148
Gomes, Márcia, 132
Gomez, Felipe de Jesus Bello, 179
Goushe, Khalil, 168
Gouveia, Jaoquim de, 148
Great Depression, 19, 100, 113, 178, 183, 191
Gualtieri, Sarah, 60, 134
Guglielmo, Jennifer, 134

H. and J. Homsy, 102
Habeeb, Rosaline Beshara, 27–28
Habib, Fred, 194–95
Habib, Merta, 47, 52–53

Habib, Nabiha, 122
Hadad, Chiary Nicola, 131
Hadad, Michael, 194
Haddad, Abraham, 115
Hajjar, Asʿad, 38
Hajjar, Iskandar Abdalla, 37–39, 48–49, 53–54
Hajjar, Joe (Yusuf), 34, 38
Hajjar, Nimer, 34
Hamati Brothers of Batroun, 90
Hamowy, Elias, 131
Hamrah Brothers Company. *See* Alexander J. Hamrah and Company
Hamrah, Alexander & Peter, 92, 129, 131, 135, 184. *See also* Alexander J. Hamrah and Company
Haney, Nazha, 168
Hardwick, Thomas, 51–52
Hasbun factory (Costa Rica), 184
Hashimoto, Kohei, 158
Haymarket Affair, 25, 45
Haywood, William (Bill), 26, 48–49, 54
Henriques, João Maria P., 133
Hermos, Suheil, 131
Hilu, Amira al-, 121–22
Hilu, Ilyas Marun, 28
Hitti, Philip Khuri, 3
H. Krupp Wholesale, 175
Hollis, W. Stanley, 91
Homs, 92, 94
Homsey, Nicholas, 163–64
Homsy, Albert, 15–16, 82, 226n117
Homsy, Rose Shagoury, 10, 82, 86, 226n117
Houghton, Louise Seymour, 118
Hull, Cordell, 182–83

Immigrant City Archive, 60 *See also* Lawrence History Center
Immigration Act of 1907, 166, 168
Immigration Act of 1921, 178
Immigration Act of 1924, 3, 171, 178, 182
Immigration Act of 1929, 178
importers, Syrian, 15, 21, 88–92, 95–96, 99–100, 102, 127, 130, 143–45 *See also* needlework (embroidery and lace): international trade networks of
indenture, 35, 163
Industrial Worker, 37
Industrial Workers of the World, 1–2, 4, 20, 24–27, 34, 36–46, 48–55, 73, 76, 110, 224n77
International Ladies' Garment Workers' Union, 4, 21, 93, 104–12, 123–24, 194–95
interracial conflict, 4, 31–32, 35–36, 54, 73–74, 181–82. *See also* labor-control practices: leveraging interracial conflict
interracial solidarity, 26–27, 36–37, 39, 51, 55–56, 61, 74, 107–8, 114

Jabara, F. M., 128 *See also* F. M. Jabara and Company
Jabara, Lian, and Mabarak, 103
Jafet factory (Brazil), 184
J. Alvarez, 150
Japan, textile manufacture in, 21, 154, 189, 191–92, 198
Jarjoura, Lutfullah, 67
Jebaily-Lonschein, 194
Jenkins, William, 134, 138, 141, 148–49
Jirash, John, 171, 173
Jones, Gus, 174
Jose de Costa, 151
J. R. Beyda and Sons, 150

Kahlele, Dab, 176–77
Kalil, Najib, 2, 26
Kappaz, Bahieh, 62–63, 119

Karam, 'Afifa, 114, 116
Karem Albrecht, Charlotte, 14, 157
Karsa, William, 125–26, 128–29, 135–37
Kassar Brothers, 102
Kateb, George, 194
Katibah, Habib Ibrahim, 195–96
Kattar, Thomas, 31
Kazen, Philip, 182–83
Kefuri, Alejandro, 176
Khater, Akram, 17, 94, 134
Khoury, Joseph Marad, 29
Khuri, Ibrahim al-, 85
Kiamie, Philip & Najib, 99–101, 112, 231n49
kimonos, Syrian, 4–5, 17, 19–21, 89, 92–111, 119–20, 123, 156–58, 167, 189, 197, 231n55. *See also* white goods
K. Katen and Company, 148
Kneiser, Joseph, 186
Krakauer Zork and Moyo, 176
Kuri, Domingo, 158
Kuri, Filamina, 179–80
Kuri, Jorge, 179
Kuri, Nasib, 162
Kuri Primos, 162
K. W. Saydah and Company, 11, 130, 136, 143, 198. *See also* Saydah, Khalil & Mikha'il

labor-control practices: arrests, 25–26, 40, 46–51, 65, 73, 75–76, 109, 142; curfews, 25–26, 44, 46; debt, 113, 141, 157, 163, 185; deportation threats, 4, 36, 45, 48, 55; ethnic isolation, 104, 106; framing strikers, 44–46; illegal labor contracting, 35; leveraging interracial conflict, 7, 19, 23, 26, 31–32, 35–36, 45, 55–56, 115 (*see also* interracial conflict); police/militia violence, 27, 37, 40,
44, 46, 48–53, 74–75, 109, 111; replacement workers 23, 36, 39–40, 44, 55, 75; retaliation, 106–7, 111
labor migration, 19, 27–29, 35, 63–64, 66, 77, 87, 90, 94, 152. *See also* Ellis Island
lace. *See* needlework (embroidery and lace)
Lama, Pablo, 180
Lane, Thomas, 145
Lawrence History Center, 27, 31, 60, 71
Lian and Mubarak, 150
Liberty Bonds, 80, 110
Lichtenstein, Nelson, 13
Lipson, Samuel, 36, 51–52
Loiselle, Aimee, 152
LoPizzo, Anna, 46
Louis Tweel and Company, 131, 152, 239n24
L. Serruys, 151
Lutfy and Macksoud, 102
Lutfy, Louis (Ilyas) F., 130, 167–68
Lynch, C. F., 47

Maaraowie, Kalil, 28
Macksoud, 89, 135
Macksoud, C. N., 194–95
Madeira, 17–18, 21, 124–55, 156, 168, 198
Madeira Embroidery Club, 138–47
Mahal Amin Merhige, 102. *See also* Merhige, Amin & Nabeha
Mahal Faour, 90
Mahal Kiamie, 99–101. *See also* Kiamie, Philip & Najib
Mahal Mansour Hilu, 90
Mahal (Mikha'il) Arida, 94–95. *See also* Arida Brothers Corporation; Arida, Kemal, Mikha'il, Nasib, & Rufa'il
Mahal Rahim Faris, 90

Mahal Zurayk and Brothers, 90
Maktabat al-Sha'b (the People's Library), 29, 56
Malaxos Freres, 193
Malhoul, Anton, 131
Mallouk companies (various), 11, 103, 138, 143, 146, 150, 153, 198, 242n63. *See also* Mallouk, Elias (Ilyas) & Salim
Mallouk, Elias (Ilyas) & Salim, 124, 127, 129–31, 139–42, 144–45, 153, 184, 242n63. *See also* Mallouk companies (various)
Maloley, Laurice Shagoury, 9–10, 64, 77–78, 85. See also Shagoury, Charles (Khalil), Joseph, Mary, Nora, Rose, & Wadia
Maloof Phonography Company, 112
Marad, Farris, 24–25, 37–39, 44–45, 47, 53–54, 76, 209n5
Marcos, Issa, 164
Margandie, 152
Marghab (Mogabgab), Emile, 132, 152–53
Mattar, S. M., 166
Matuk, Constantino, George, & Jose 179–80, 256n96
Matuk y Hermanos, 179
Mays, Devi, 14f
McCumber, Porter, 144
M. Coito, 150
McMahon, Thomas, 4
McSweeney, Edward, 161
Melhame, Jurj, 90
Menconi, Evelyn Abdalla, 60
merchant capitalism, 12
Merhige, Amin & Nabeha, 92, 115–16. *See also* Mahal Amin Merhige
Mexican Revolution, 173–76
migrant smuggling, 159–77

Miller, Lucius, 93
minimum wage. *See under* working conditions
M. Jardim of Casa Alema, 150–51
Mobayed, Nicholas G., 193
Mogabgab, Anis, 152
Mogabgab (Marghab), Emil, 132, 152–53
Mokarzel-Otash Syrian American Business Directory, 96
Moraway, Kalil, 69
Mouakad, Elias, 5, 89, 102, 230n39
Mukarzil, Sallum, 6, 90–91, 96, 98, 100, 112–13, 125–26, 128, 137, 187–88, 192–93, 195–96. See also *al-Majalla al-Tijariyya al-Suriyya al-Amrikiyya/The Syrian American Commercial Magazine*
Munayyir (Monayer), Khalil, 29, 56, 218n161
Munir, Alsharif, 193

Naff, Alixa, 60, 62, 77, 89, 156, 166, 185–86
Naff, Faris, 168
Najjum, Abdullah, 2, 26
Naser, Katan and Nahass, 102
Nasrallah and Meena, 102
Nassar, Manuel, 176–77
National Recovery Act, 194–96
needlework (embroidery and lace), 4, 21, 78, 81–82; international trade networks of, 88–92, 126–39, 144–55; manufacture of, 13–15, 91–93, 126–29, 133–35, 138, 141, 143–47, 154–55
Newman, Pauline, 107, 232n81
Noemi, Salim Ayub, 177, 179–80

One Big Union, 75

O'Neill, John, 74
O Operário, 139–43
overtime pay. *See under* working conditions

Pacific Mill, 29, 31, 37, 67, 75
Parkway Manufacturing, 79
Pastor, Camila, 180
peddling, 5–7, 15–16, 18, 21, 77–78, 88–95, 100, 113, 156–86, 188, 198
Pen League (*al-Rabita al-Qalamiyya*), 3, 96
Petras, Elizabeth McLean, 93
Philippines, textile manufacture in, 17, 21 153, 189, 198
piecework, 13–15, 17–18, 63–64, 82, 85–86, 93, 119, 130, 133–35, 137, 139–141, 147, 153–55
Pitman, Ernest, 45

Ramey, Anthony & Philip, 11, 28, 30, 70
Ramey, John, 1–3, 19–20, 26, 42, 47–56, 196–97, 201nn2–3. *See also* Bread and Roses Strike
Ramey, Michael, 47, 52–53
Razek, Rana, 160
Reeder, Linda, 134
Regnard, Céline, 9
retaliation. *See under* labor-control practices
Roosevelt, Theodore, 105
Rose and Leaf Club, 154
Rubio, Rebeca, 158
Rufaʾil, Yaʿcub, 117
Ruiz, Feliciano, 182

Saab, E., 65
Saʿad, Habib Pasha, 189
Sabbagh, Alexander, 79
Sabbagh Brothers, 15, 79, 82

Sabbagh, Elias, 82, 85
Sabbagh, Hannah. *See* Shakir, Hannah Sabbagh
Saco-Lowell Shops weaving machines, 193
Safie factory (Guatemala), 184
Safieddine, Hicham, 191
Saliba, Mike, 38
Salim Ayoub kimono factory, 62
Sallom, Assad, 172
Samara, Ameen, 150–51, 245n109. *See also* A. G. Samara and Company
Samar plant (Nicaragua), 184
Samya, Shakara, 44
Sarbo, Antonio, 162
Saydah, Ferris, 141
Saydah Importing Company, 136
Saydah, Khalil & Mikhaʾil, 129–30. *See also* K. W. Saydah and Company
Schikri Hermuda Hermanos, 175
Schlesinger, Benjamin, 110–11
scientific management, 112, 133, 135, 137. *See also* Taylorism
Seikaly, Sherene, 17
Seraphic, Alcibiades, 162–66, 168, 180, 252n45
Shagoury, Charles (Khalil), Joseph, Mary, Nora, Rose, & Wadia, 9–10, 77–78, 82, 86, 226n117. *See also* Maloley, Laurice Shagoury
Shaheen, ʿAssy, George, & Tawfiq, 99, 188–90, 193. *See also* ʿAssy Shaheen and Sons
Shaheen, Joseph, 38
Shakir, Evelyn, 60, 79
Shakir, Hannah Sabbagh, 14–15, 79–83, 118–19
Shakir, Wadiʿ, 56, 85
Shalhoub, Sadie, 195
Shebaby, James (Najib), 71

Shihab plant (Nicaragua), 184
Shohfi Brothers, 102
Simon, Najla Nouhan, 118–19, 236n140
Singer corporation sewing machines, 16, 132
Sirgany and Skaf, 174
Sirgany, Elias, 174
S. Khoury and Company, 102
skilled labor, 4, 30, 114, 132, 152, 194–95. *See also* unskilled labor
Soyer, Daniel, 61
St. Anthony's Church (Lawrence, MA), 2, 29, 48–49, 67, 214n76
St. George's Church (Lawrence, MA), 29, 67
St. Joseph's Church (Lawrence, MA), 29, 67
St. Mary's Church (Lawrence, MA), 67
strike and strike-support practices: absenteeism, 3, 141; bail funding, 65; boycotts, 74; compensation for striking workers, 65, 68, 73–75, 197; curfew breaking, 39, 46; harassment, 74–75; industrial vandalism, 37, 40; marches/parades, 2, 39, 41–43, 46–49, 52, 74; movement to competitor, 32–33; picketing, 23–25, 39–46, 49, 74–75, 105–11, 123, 129, 197; relief kitchens, 39, 41, 105, 197; rioting, 1, 23, 37, 40, 43, 51, 65, 75–76, 182; slowdowns, 32, 147; stoppages, 4, 54–55, 74, 107–8, 110, 114, 124, 144, 147, 193–94, 197; sympathy/general strikes, 4, 20, 48–49, 74, 106–8, 143, 148, 154, 197; throwing projectiles, 1–3, 8, 23, 37, 40, 44, 46, 74–75; violence, 23, 75, 148; walkouts, 26, 32, 37, 41, 73, 98, 105–6, 108, 110, 194; withholding finished goods, 147

strikebreaking. *See* labor-control practices
Suigany and Skaf, 146
Sullivan, John J., 50–53
supply-chain power, 13
Sweetser, E. Leroy, 25, 44, 46–48
Sydenstricker, Edgar, 104
Syria Mount Lebanon Liberation League (New York), 81
Syrian American Chamber of Commerce/*al-Ghurfa al-Tijariyya al-Suriyya al-Amrikiyya fi-Niyu Yurk* (New York, NY), 90, 189
Syrian American Club (Boston, MA), 85
Syrian Burial Society (Boston, MA), 68
Syrian Drum Corps (Lawrence, MA), 2, 42, 46–47
Syrian Ladies' Aid Society (Boston, MA), 60, 77–86, 118, 227nn137–38
Syrian Ladies' Aid Society (Brooklyn, NY), 87
Syrian mutual aid societies, 20, 58–87, 197. *See also* United Syrian Society/*Jama'iyyat al-Ittihad al-Suri* (Lawrence, MA); Young Men of Deir-el-Kamar/*Jama'iyyat Shaban Dayr al-Qamar* (Lawrence, MA); Syrian Ladies' Aid Society (Boston, MA)
Syrian mutual aid society services: bail assistance, 65, 197; burial/funeral assistance and death benefits, 65–68, 73, 86; classes/training, 81, 85; food aid, 20, 69, 81–82, 84, 86; healthcare benefits, 21, 65, 69, 72; heating assistance, 20, 69, 72, 84; housing assistance, 20, 84–85; immigration assistance, 87; legal

cost assistance, 69; meeting space, 81, 86; strike support, 65, 68, 73–75, 85, 197; unemployment insurance, 20, 61, 68, 82–85
Syrian National Club/*Jama'iyyat al-Muntada al-Suri al-'Umumiyya*, 37–38, 48, 56–57, 67, 74–76
Syrian Protestant Church (Lawrence, MA), 29
Syrian shops, 4, 15–17, 21, 89, 93–112, 115, 123–24, 188
Syrian World, 15, 191, 194–95

Tannous, Victoria, 114, 116–22, 235n129
Tanyus Khalil and Sons dry goods shop, 69
Taylorism, 125, 133. See also scientific management
Teebagy, Charles, 77
tenement housing, 2, 25, 27, 29–31, 33, 46, 72, 75, 77
Tombray, Girard, 166
Touma, Yusuf, 81
Tresca, Carlo, 74, 224n77
Triangle Shirtwaist Fire, 104–5
Tripoli, 22, 126, 191–93

União dos Sindicato Operários do Funchal, 140
United Syrian Cemetery (United Lebanese Cemetery), 68
United Syrian Charitable Society (Lawrence, MA), 68, 70
United Syrian Society/*Jama'iyyat al-Ittihad al-Suri* (Lawrence, MA), 30, 45, 56, 60, 66–70, 76, 85
United Textile Workers of America, 4, 34–35, 54, 73–75
unskilled labor, 13, 17, 30, 39, 93, 105, 148, 195. See also skilled labor

U. S. Immigration Commission, 13–14, 22, 24, 28, 30, 35, 62–64, 90, 93, 159–62, 166, 175–76

Van der Linden, Marcel, 12
Vasconselos, John de, 140, 142
Veiga, Nobre de, 142
vertical integration, 99, 113, 126, 133, 177–78
V. Gouves, 150
Vogenitz, Hernan, 146, 150
Vogue, 21, 89

wages. See working conditions
Wallerstein, Emmanuel, 13
Washington Mill, 33, 37
Way, Vera, 152
Wazney, Mahomed, 168
white goods, 4–5, 88–93, 102, 105, 108, 144, 153, 157–61, 169, 185, 198. See also kimonos, Syrian
wildcat strikes, 73
Wolcott, Samuel & W. E., 211n29
Women's Trade Union League, 108
Women's Wear, 129, 131, 153, 157
Wood Mill, 33
Wood, William, 26, 34–37, 43, 46
working conditions: 35/35.5-hour workweek, 195–96; 44-hour workweek, 4, 110–11; 48-hour workweek, 73, 75; 49-hour workweek, 109; 50-hour workweek, 105; 54-hour workweek, 36, 43, 73; 56-hour workweek, 36; 70-hour workweek, 31; bonuses, 141; breaks, 50–51, 114; child labor, 26, 31–32, 50–52, 63, 79, 93, 105, 118; employee-purchased supplies, 105, 109; layoffs, 83–84, 106–7, 115, 124; minimum wage, 89, 105, 114,

working conditions (cont.) 194–96; music for workers, 112; overtime pay, 43, 112; right to organize, 115, 129; sanitation, 19, 26, 105, 109, 115; seasonality/intermittency, 63, 115; sex segregation, 17, 94, 132; training, 114; wage cuts, 36, 73–75, 139–41, 147; wage deductions, 50–51; wage increases, 114; wage theft, 105, 119; water access, 50

World War I, impact of on textile industry, 19, 21, 54, 73, 109–10, 125–27, 129, 132, 144–45, 169–70, 173–74, 178, 187–88

World War II, impact of on textile industry, 153–54

Yarur plant (Chile), 184

Yazbek, Bechara, 180

Yazza, A., 40

Young Men of Deir-el-Kamar/ *Jama'iyyat Shaban Dayr al-Qamar* (Lawrence, MA), 60, 71–76, 84–85

Young Syrian Men's Association, 70

Zahle, 92, 126, 130, 168

WORLDING THE MIDDLE EAST

Emily Gottreich and Daniel Zoughbie, editors

Susan Slyomovics, *Monuments Decolonized: Algeria's French Colonial Heritage*
2024

Arang Keshavarzian, *Making Space for the Gulf: Histories of Regionalism and the Middle East*
2024

Paraska Tolan-Szkilnik, *Maghreb Noir: The Militant-Artists of North Africa and the Struggle for a Pan-African, Postcolonial Future*
2023

Jacob Norris, *The Lives and Deaths of Jubrail Dabdoub: Or, How the Bethlehemites Discovered Amerka*
2023

Nadim Bawalsa, *Transnational Palestine: Migration and the Right of Return before 1948*
2022

Carel Bertram, *A House in the Homeland: Armenian Pilgrimages to Places of Ancestral Memory*
2022

Susan Gilson Miller, *Years of Glory: Nelly Benatar and the Pursuit of Justice in Wartime North Africa*
2021

Amélie Le Renard, *Western Privilege: Work, Intimacy, and Postcolonial Hierarchies in Dubai*
2021

The authorized representative in the EU for product safety and compliance is:
Mare Nostrum Group
B.V Doelen 72
4831 GR Breda
The Netherlands

www.ingramcontent.com/pod-product-compliance
Lightning Source LLC
Chambersburg PA
CBHW021958220426
43663CB00007B/863